FOOD AND FAITH
Second Edition

This book provides a comprehensive theological framework for assessing the significance of eating. Drawing on diverse theological, philosophical, and anthropological insights, it offers fresh ways to evaluate food production and consumption practices as they are being worked out in today's industrial food economy. Unlike books that focus primarily on vegetarianism and hunger-related concerns, this book broadens the scope of consideration to include the sacramental character of eating, the deep significance of hospitality, the meaning of death and sacrifice, the Eucharist as the place of inspiration and orientation, the importance of saying grace, and the possibility of eating in heaven. Throughout, eating is presented as a way of enacting fidelity between persons, between people and fellow creatures, and between people and Earth. *Food and Faith* demonstrates that eating is of profound economic, moral, and spiritual significance.

Revised throughout, this edition includes a new introduction and two new chapters, as well as updated footnotes. The additions add significantly to the core idea of creaturely membership and hospitality through discussion of the microbiome revolution in science, and the daunting challenge of the Anthropocene.

Norman Wirzba is Gilbert T. Rowe Distinguished Professor of Theology at Duke Divinity School, and a senior fellow at Duke's Kenan Institute for Ethics. His first edition of *Food and Faith* was named "Book of the Year" by the Englewood Review of Books, and earned "Honorable Mention" in the 2011 PROSE Award. Wirzba's other books include *From Nature to Creation*, *Way of Love*, *Making Peace with the Land*, *Living the Sabbath*, and *The Paradise of God*, and he is the editor for a book series on the "New Agrarianism."

Food and Faith

A Theology of Eating

Second Edition

NORMAN WIRZBA
Duke University

CAMBRIDGE
UNIVERSITY PRESS

University Printing House, Cambridge CB2 8BS, United Kingdom

One Liberty Plaza, 20th Floor, New York, NY 10006, USA

477 Williamstown Road, Port Melbourne, VIC 3207, Australia

314–321, 3rd Floor, Plot 3, Splendor Forum, Jasola District Centre, New Delhi – 110025, India

79 Anson Road, #06–04/06, Singapore 079906

Cambridge University Press is part of the University of Cambridge.

It furthers the University's mission by disseminating knowledge in the pursuit of education, learning, and research at the highest international levels of excellence.

www.cambridge.org
Information on this title: www.cambridge.org/9781108455961
DOI: 10.1017/9781108631846

First edition © Norman Wirzba 2011
Second edition © Cambridge University Press 2019

First published 2011
Second edition 2019
3rd printing 2020

Printed in the United Kingdom by TJ International Ltd. Padstow Cornwall

A catalogue record for this publication is available from the British Library.

Library of Congress Cataloging-in-Publication Data
NAMES: Wirzba, Norman, author.
TITLE: Food and faith : a theology of eating / Norman Wirzba, Duke University, North Carolina.
DESCRIPTION: Second edition. | Cambridge, United Kingdom ; New York, NY : Cambridge University Press, 2019. | Includes bibliographical references and index.
IDENTIFIERS: LCCN 2018029616| ISBN 9781108470414 (hardback) | ISBN 9781108455961 (paperback)
SUBJECTS: LCSH: Dinners and dining–Religious aspects–Christianity. | Food–Religious aspects–Christianity. | Food habits.
CLASSIFICATION: LCC BR115.N87 W57 2019 | DDC 248.4–dc23
LC record available at https://lccn.loc.gov/2018029616

ISBN 978-1-108-47041-4 Hardback
ISBN 978-1-108-45596-1 Paperback

For Ingrid and Alex Wirzba

Contents

Foreword by Stanley Hauerwas		*page* ix
Preface		xi
Acknowledgments		xix
Introduction: Who Is the You That Eats?		1
1	It's about Fidelity	14
2	Thinking Theologically about Food	40
3	The "Roots" of Eating: Our Life Together in Gardens	75
4	Eating in Exile: Dysfunction in the World of Food	113
5	Life through Death: Sacrificial Eating	156
6	Eucharistic Table Manners: Eating toward Communion	194
7	Saying Grace	236
8	Eating in Heaven? Consummating Communion	269
Epilogue: Faithful Eating in an Anthropocene World		294
Author Index		311
Subject Index		315
Scripture Citation Index		318

Foreword

I must confess, I did not want to know much of what I learned by reading this book. Indeed I found it somewhat painful. In these pages, Norman Wirzba writes about what seems to be our unrelenting desire to degrade God's good creation. But Wirzba is a gentle soul and he has written a beautiful book. That is no small achievement because much of what he has to describe is incessantly ugly. Yet Wirzba has found a way to help us see that by the grace of God we can still learn to live lives of gratitude.

The painfulness I found in reading this book resides in my desire to remain ignorant. I do not want to know how my everyday eating habits make me complicit with cruel treatment of animals. I do not want to know that the way I have learned to eat contributes to the ongoing degradation of the land. I do not want to know how the way my food is produced puts an unjust burden on people who often have no food to eat at all. In truth, I vaguely "knew" about these realities but Wirzba knows how to bring them to my attention in a manner that demands I must acknowledge them. Acknowledgment can be excruciating.

Do not be fooled by the admirable modesty that pervades Wirzba's prose. This is a book of great philosophical and theological depth but its strength has largely to do with Wirzba's "method," which does not call attention to itself. By directing our attention to one of the most common aspects of our lives – that is, eating – Wirzba makes us recognize the fundamental character of our lives.

Put simply, he reminds us that we eat to stay alive but we must kill if we are to eat. So "eating is the daily reminder of creaturely mortality." Again, I may have "known" that before reading *Food and Faith: A Theology of Eating* but Wirzba has now forced me to recognize that the lives we live require the death of creaturely life. For that is what we are – creatures bound together. To understand this forces the recognition that we live through sacrifice.

That Wirzba has forced me to know what I did not want to know I attribute to how he has shown that the ontological commitments that are constituted by our eating require theological display. In the past, when asked by a skeptic, "Why should I be moral?," I have replied, "Do you like to eat?" My response was meant to challenge my interlocutor's question by confronting the assumption that "morality" is clearly to be distinguished from the most basic aspects of our lives. I did not realize, however, until I read Wirzba, that my reply was also one that might make sense in response to the question "Why should I believe in God?"

Too often, attempts to bring a theological perspective to issues involving "the environmental crisis" force "God" to fill in a gap. The "gap" may not be Newton's but the results are often similar to Newton's attempt to rescue some role for God once physics had done its job. Wirzba has avoided that trap by helping us see that our theological convictions are not "explanations" but rather constitutive of the conditions that make life possible. Put concretely, Wirzba helps us see that if we are to talk of God we had better know how to talk about dirt.

Not only must we know how to talk about dirt but we must recognize that we live through sacrifice. The meal we call Eucharist rightly, therefore, becomes the center of Wirzba's book. For it is by partaking of this meal, made possible by Christ's death and resurrection, that we can imagine what it might mean to be reconciled with our mortality. And so reconciled we have some hope of being in communion with the gifts we call creation.

I am confident that anyone reading this remarkably learned book will be grateful for Wirzba's labor. For here Wirzba demonstrates the palpable connection between how we eat and our worship of the Triune God.

Stanley Hauerwas
Gilbert T. Rowe Distinguished Professor of Christian Theology, Emeritus
Duke Divinity School

Preface

Several years ago, on a warm fall evening at Anathoth Community Garden in Cedar Grove, North Carolina, I enjoyed a memorable meal. Roughly 100 people had gathered for a community feast. Though some of the meal was prepared by cooks from Cedar Grove United Methodist Church, the rest was potluck, and so included some of the freshest and best-tasting greens, tortillas, salsa, and chicken I have ever had. As our backdrop, we enjoyed a double rainbow on a massive thundercloud to the east, while the sun slowly made its way down the horizon behind us. Children were running around blowing and catching bubbles. Others danced to the sound of a live bluegrass band. The taste of delectable food, the sounds of laughter and singing, the aroma of fresh flowers and harvest, the hugs of friends and neighbors, and the sensation of a cooling fall night all came together in what I considered a foretaste of heaven.

Why should I or anyone else think that this meal mattered? Is the invocation of heaven not overdrawn? After all, the evening has passed, and the physical sensations are no longer effective in me. No matter how much or how finely I eat, I, along with all the other animal and plant bodies, will still die, and so return to the soil out of which we came and upon which we daily feed. But what if that night and the communion it enacted is indeed a glimpse, however imperfect, of what life ultimately is meant to be?

In this book I develop a theological account of eating, a framework for assessing eating's immediate and ultimate significance. Though it is possible to describe food and eating in countless ways, from a Christian point of view what food is and why eating matters are best understood in terms of God's own Trinitarian life of gift and sacrifice, hospitality and communion, care and celebration. Trinitarian theology asserts that all reality is communion – the giving and receiving of gifts – because it has its source and sustenance in the eternal Triune love described by theologians as *perichoresis*, a making room within oneself for another to be. This means that nothing in creation exists by itself, in terms of itself, or for itself. Creatures are marked from beginning to end by the need to receive the gifts of nurture. Inspired by Jesus Christ, and empowered by the Holy Spirit, we have the opportunity to turn our homes into places of hospitality and ourselves into nurture for others. At its best, eating is a sharing and welcoming movement that makes room for others. Insofar as people learn to live in hospitable ways with each other and within their places, they participate in the eternal, hospitable ways of God that daily create, sustain, and fulfill life.

According to this theological view, we don't really understand food until we perceive, receive, and taste it in terms of its origin and end in God as the one who provides for, communes with, and ultimately reconciles creation. *Food is God's love made nutritious and delicious, given for the good of each other.* The mundane act of eating is thus a daily invitation to move responsibly and gratefully within this given life. It is a summons to commune with the divine Life that is presupposed and made manifest in every bite.

This claim will be difficult to swallow for people who are convinced that food consists of little more than a bundle of nutrients that we simply need to get in the right quantities, variety, and proportion. According to this view, food is primarily a fuel we need to keep our machine-like bodies running at an optimal level. Though some food may taste better than other food, there is little about it that should give us cause for wonder or reverence. Though people in the past may have stopped to say grace before eating a meal, today's educated eater is taught that food is simply a manufactured product that we control.

This is an impoverished description of food. While it is certainly true that we can speak of bread as a collection of material elements (water, salt, yeast, flour), reducing food to this level is like opening a letter and judging it to be nothing more than a page covered with random markings. Rather than reading the marks "I LOVE YOU!" to communicate a life-altering pronouncement inviting a response, all one sees are characters on a page worthy of little more than a passing notice.

Similarly, we can look at a meal and see only a random assortment of nutrients, oblivious to the grace of God made manifest in it. We can forget that food is one of God's basic and abiding means for expressing divine provision and care. To partake of a meal is to participate in a divine communication in which God the eternal Host says something like, "I love you, I want you to be well taken care of, I want to share with you the joys of my life." The Psalmist (104:10–15) puts it this way:

You make springs gush forth in the valleys;
they flow between the hills,
giving drink to every wild animal ...
You cause the grass to grow for the cattle,
and plants for people to use,
to bring forth food from the earth,
and wine to gladden the human heart,
oil to make the face shine,
and bread to strengthen the human heart.[1]

To grow food and eat in a way that is mindful of God is to collaborate with God's own primordial sharing of life in the sharing of food with each other. It is to participate in forms of life and frameworks of meaning that have their root and orientation in God's caring ways with creation.

It takes education, a catechesis within particular communities and traditions, to enable a person to see that the marks on a page are actually words that, if one has the requisite intelligence, sympathy, and imagination, can convey a wide range of meanings. Sometimes these meanings are shallow or of merely temporary interest. But other times they are profound and personally transformative. Knowing the difference is part of what it means to be a good reader. Though one may learn to read, the possibility always exists that one will be indolent, inattentive, or indifferent; the reader sees the words but has not really digested them. How many people have dismissed poetry simply because they did not know how to read the words?

In a similar manner, eaters can consume a wide variety of foods and not really savor any of it as God's love made nurture for us. To eat with theological appreciation presupposes an ability to "read" food as the nutritious manifestation of God's love for the world. It is to be in the world in a posture of reverence for fellow creatures freshly engaged as the work of God's hands. This posture entails a process of spiritual formation in which we allow God the Gardener (Genesis 2:8) to conform us to his image as the one who looks after and provides for creatures. In the daily act of eating, people have the opportunity to appreciate and explore their creaturely condition as beings dependent on each other and upon God. In the work of food's production and consumption, people have the chance to learn where and who they are by becoming tillers and keepers of God's edible garden (Genesis 2:15). Without this ongoing catechesis we run the risk of reducing the gift of food and the grace of eating to a desecration. We risk

---

[1]   All references to scripture are from the New Revised Standard Version of the Bible unless otherwise indicated.

undermining the ecological and cultural conditions necessary for healthy and convivial life together.

In advanced industrial societies, where speed, convenience, and cheap prices have become the most valued characteristics in food consumption, it is hardly surprising that eating has become thoughtless and irresponsible. Though everyone chews, relatively few eat with much understanding of or sympathy for the widespread destruction of the world's agricultural lands and communities, or the misery of billions of factory-produced chickens, sheep, pigs, and cattle. Today's handling of food does not often go much beyond concerns for its appearance, availability, and price. In our global economy food is a commodity much like any other, serving the business need for profit, the consumer desire for cheapness, and the political quest for power. In this context, food ceases to speak as the grace of God. Eating ceases to be the occasion through which we experience life as a membership of belonging, responsibility, and gratitude.

Can a theology of eating be of help? My hope is that the theological account I give in this book will enable us to see and taste food in fresh ways, and that this theological vision will inform the ways we grow and share food. The Psalmist invites us to "taste and see that the Lord is good" (Psalm 34:8). The goodness of creation, its delectability but also God's delight in its flavors cannot really dawn on us so long as we reduce food to a product of our own hands or turn it into a commodity for purposes of power and profit. Food is a gift of God given to all creatures for the purposes of life's nurture, sharing, and celebration. When it is done in the name of God, eating is the earthly realization of God's eternal communion-building love.

HOW TO READ THIS BOOK

In calling this book a theology of eating, two things need to be kept in mind. First, this is *a* theology of eating rather than *the* theology of eating. As an exercise in constructive theology, it has become abundantly clear to me that what I am doing is offering a theological "picture" that represents a particular Christian view. It is not the only picture that can be drawn. Given the depth and mystery that eating is, other Christians, as well as those who represent different faith traditions, will see and taste food differently. I develop theological themes like the garden, sin, sacrifice, Eucharist, hospitality, reconciliation, and communion so that the scope and significance of creaturely membership can be more readily understood. My development of these themes is hardly exhaustive. I invite others to draw them out differently and in ways that widen our appreciation of eating and food.

Second, this is a work of *theology*. It is not an explicit or developed "ethics of eating." This is not to say that ethical issues or practical concerns are absent from this work.[2] Indeed, the welfare of habitats and animals, farmers and food workers, is never far from my mind. What I have not done, however, is provide detailed analyses of the research being done by scientists (in nutrition, chemistry, biology, and ecology), social scientists (in anthropology, sociology, politics, gender studies, history, and economics), and artists and philosophers that are the prerequisites for a formal ethics of eating. As important as these topics are, I do not focus on genetic engineering and the patenting of foods, or on the justice of regional and global trade agreements, though I do hope that what I say in a theological mode sheds some light on these topics.

The topic of vegetarianism, though also much in my mind (and in the minds of a growing number of people), does not receive developed treatment in this book. The main reason for this is that detailed work has been and is being done on this topic by theologians like Stephen Webb, David Grumett, Rachel Muers, and Michael Northcott.[3] For readers interested in pursuing the complexities of this debate, abundant resources are already on hand. This book serves as a contribution to the debate by drawing a wider theological context in which questions about death, sacrifice, self-offering, and gratitude – all topics vitally related to a consideration of vegetarianism – are developed.

I believe a theology of eating to be especially important at this time. Why? Because the market forces now determining much of the world's production, distribution, and consumption of food degrade, sicken, and destroy life. At a time when plant and animal creatures are being reduced to "natural resources" or "units of production," it is crucial that people learn to recover a sense of life's sacred dimension, and thus receive food as a precious gift. In this work, Christians have much to learn from other religious and

---

[2] There is vigorous debate in theology and philosophy on the relation between theory and practice. See the collections *Practicing Theology: Beliefs and Practices in Christian Life*, ed. Miroslav Volf and Dorothy C. Bass (Grand Rapids: William B. Eerdmans, 2002) and *Transforming Philosophy and Religion: Love's Wisdom*, ed. Norman Wirzba and Bruce Ellis Benson (Bloomington: Indiana University Press, 2008) for an indication of the diverse ways in which thinking is transformed by lived practices.

[3] See Stephen Webb's *Good Eating* (Grand Rapids: Brazos Press, 2001) and David Grumett and Rachel Muers' *Theology on the Menu: Asceticism, Meat and Christian Diet* (London: Routledge, 2010) and their coedited work *Eating and Believing: Interdisciplinary Perspectives on Vegetarianism and Theology* (London: T&T Clark, 2008). The last is a particularly impressive collection that encompasses biblical, historical, philosophical, and theological perspectives. For a Jewish consideration, see Richard Schwartz's *Judaism and Vegetarianism* (New York: Lantern Books, 2001).

indigenous traditions. As this book hopes to show, they also have deep sources of insight and inspiration within their own scriptures and theological traditions to share.

For this second edition I have added an Introduction, an opening chapter on fidelity, and an epilogue on faithful eating. I have also expanded on specific themes in various chapters and brought footnotes more up to date. I have written the Introduction because the experience of eating calls for a revised understanding of what we understand human beings to be. Too often, people assume that people exist as separable, independent beings apart from others. We are individuals who then decide to engage others in particular sorts of ways. This is a profound error. When we consider humans as touching and tasting beings, we discover that we have never been alone, and could not ever be singular. Recent research on the human microbiome demonstrates that our bodies are from the beginning, and always, sites of hospitality that, by eating food, nurture countless microorganisms that also nurture us. The paramount question, given this insight, is whether or not in our physiological dependence on others we at the same time practice the kind of fidelity that acknowledges, respects, and honors those we depend on. To eat is to exist in relationships with others that are of the profoundest intimacy. To eat is to know that we are bound to others in a shared and common fate. For our shared fate to be good and beautiful, we must learn to cultivate the forms of fidelity that promote mutual nurture and wellbeing. That is what Chapter 1 is about.

Chapter 2 explores why eating is a moral and theological issue. It examines how our thinking about food has been rendered shallow by the modern narration and reduction of it to a commodity. My focus is on both the decontextualization of food, by which I mean a society's disassociation of food from ecological and productive contexts, and the industrialization of eating, by which I mean the intervention of market and machine logics into the eating act. These developments, I argue, lead to a spiritually impoverished understanding of food that can be corrected once we begin to think of eating as a "spiritual exercise."

Chapter 3 develops the ecological and creaturely context for eating by describing humanity's identity and vocation in a garden. I argue that gardens are indispensable for the flourishing of terrestrial life because gardens and the geo-bio-chemical processes they embody are the places where life's many hungers are met. Eating, both figuratively and literally, has its roots in the soil. Gardens are the practical sites in terms of which people begin to see, smell, hear, touch, and taste the breadth and depth of human membership and responsibility. I describe a gardener's education and how it potentially leads to the development of affections and forms of attention that make possible a spiritually deep appreciation of food. But food is not the only important garden crop. The cultivation of people with special sensitivities is an equally important harvest. I conclude this chapter by showing how human gardening at its best is inspired and shaped by an understanding of God and Christ as the prototypical gardeners who nurture and care for the world.

Chapter 4 describes the malfunction of eating as it is realized and worked out in our natural habitats, our economies, and our bodies. Using the metaphor of exile, I here describe "sinful" eating as "the anxiety of membership," as the refusal to welcome and accept responsibility for the memberships of creation of which we are a part. To eat is to enter intimately into the lives of others. It is to participate in the growth of life but also its death. This chapter describes how eating disorders of varying kinds develop because people are unable or unwilling to accept responsibility for this costly participation that is worked out on ecological, economic, and physiological levels. Here we discuss issues like the degradation of ecosystems and agricultural lands, the injustice and destructiveness of international trade agreements and consumer economics, the ill health of today's marketing and eating practices, and the danger of eating disorders such as anorexia and bulimia.

Chapter 5 considers the very costly nature of creaturely life. For anything to eat, others must die, most often by being eaten themselves. Death is eating's steadfast accomplice. It is not simply the end of life but life's precondition. This chapter examines how this death is to be characterized. I argue that death is best understood not only as the cessation of an individual's biological functioning but as the cessation of membership. I then consider how a sacrificial sensibility can be brought to bear on this topic, arguing that sacrifice is frequently misunderstood to be a violent act done to appease a bloodthirsty God. Turning to the story of Noah, I develop an account of sacrifice that instead highlights the renewal of life through self-offering and service. I further consider how the Eucharist, itself often understood as a sacrifice, can be interpreted to shed light on this particular issue. I end the chapter by showing how a sacrificial sensibility can inform our thinking about vegetarianism and the twin practices of feasting and fasting.

Chapter 6 gives an interpretation of the Christian Eucharist as the key to an understanding of the communion of life. Eucharistic eating heals sinfulness because it restores the memberships that make up every eating community. I develop the view that the Eucharist constitutes a communal way of being that participates in and images God's own Trinitarian life. When we consume Jesus as the "bread of life" (John 6), a transformation of eating occurs, because people are here brought into his life and his way of being in the world. The work of Christ, in other words, is not so much about the salvation of individual souls as about leading people into true, abundant, eternal, resurrection life. Sinful eating degrades and destroys life. Eucharistic eating honors and promotes life. It creates a culture of service, hospitality, and communality that is of paramount importance as we critique today's food economies and work to create a healthier food culture.

Chapter 7 argues that a deep appreciation of eating as a participation in the memberships of life and death should end in gratitude and celebration. In particular, I consider the deep spiritual and practical significance of "saying grace." In my account, I first consider why our eating culture is so permeated by ingratitude, and then develop what gratitude means and how it is best expressed. I argue that saying grace is in fact a profoundly political act because to give thanks for food presupposes that one has committed one's own life to the re-membering or healing of the memberships that have been dis-membered by today's food systems. I conclude by showing that saying grace finds its completion in our offering ourselves and the world to God.

Will there be eating in heaven, particularly if we recall that eating presupposes so much death? Chapter 8 addresses this question by first considering what we mean when we think of heaven. Far from being an escape from this world, and thus a release from membership with each other, heaven is here described as the Spirit's transformation of relationships so that they lead to the wholeness of life. To "be in heaven" is to be in a place in such a way that every relationship is animated only by the power of God's love. If food is God's love made nutritious, and if eating is one of the primary means through which this love is extended through the world, then it makes sense to think that eating (in some transformed way, perhaps) will have a role in heaven as the sharing and enjoyment of God's love. Eating matters in this life and the next because it is a realization – imperfect now but perfect then – of God's eternal communion-building life.

The Epilogue brings us back to the question of fidelity, and argues that in our present, Anthropocene moment, we most need to learn how to be "with" each other and within our places in ways that promote mutual nurture, and that contribute to a comprehensive vision of health. In a world that is being steadily mined and degraded, there is no more urgent task than to learn to come alongside each other in ways that make clear what nurture is needed and what healing is possible. As Christians understand it, this is precisely what the work of the Holy Spirit is about. It is the Holy Spirit that is God's power in the world working to beautify and perfect creaturely life. It is the Holy Spirit, in other words, that equips us to nurture the world that nurtures us.

Acknowledgments

It is an honor to acknowledge the friends and institutions that have both helped make this book possible and helped make it better. Jim Lewis of the Louisville Institute and Dorothy Bass of the Valparaiso Project on the Education and Formation of People in Faith provided generous financial support in the form of grants. Colleagues at the University of Lethbridge, University of Florida, Davidson College, Middlebury College, Loyola College, Yale Divinity School, Canadian Mennonite University, University of Nottingham, Augustana College, Mars Hill College, Furman University, Hope College, Western Theological Seminary, Transylvania University, Loyola Marymount University, and Duke Divinity School offered venues in which ideas could be tested and clarified. Several churches opened their doors to me, providing hospitality and good conversation. Bron Taylor, editor of the *Journal for the Study of Religion, Nature, and Culture*, published material that eventually made its way into Chapter 6. Eric Crahan, formerly of Cambridge University Press, took an early interest in this project and was a most valuable help shepherding the first edition to publication. In preparing the second edition, Beatrice Rehl offered steady encouragement and wise editorial advice. I am grateful for her championing of the book at the Press.

I would also like to offer my thanks to friends who read portions or the whole of this book in draft forms, offering valuable suggestions for improvement: Fred Bahnson, Steven Bouma-Prediger, Brian Brock, Jason Byassee, Ellen Davis, Stanley Hauerwas, Judith Heyhoe, Willis Jenkins, Randy Maddox, Otis and Monica Moss, Sarah Musser, Michael Northcott, Jeremy Troxler, and Matthew Whelan. I am especially grateful to Stanley for his gracious acceptance of my invitation to write a Foreword for this book. Many thanks, too, to Nathan Hershberger in the preparation of the indexes. It is a privilege and a joy to be in the company of so much kindness, wisdom, and good sense. The errors that remain in this book are clearly a reflection of the fact that I have not listened well enough to their good advice.

Writing this book has been a humbling experience. What began as a fairly straightforward endeavor – namely, an attempt to discover what a theological account of eating might look like – has brought me to the realization that my own eating hardly measures up to the reconciling, communion-building desire of God. I am in no position to install myself as the theological food police! I offer this book with the hope that as eaters we might together become more merciful and charitable in the eating that we do.

One of life's greatest gifts is the loving support of a home and family. I have been gifted beyond all comprehension or deserving by my wife Gretchen and my children Emily, Anna, Benjamin, and Luke. My own nurture began with my parents, Ingrid and Alex Wirzba. My mother has cooked some of my most memorable and delicious meals, and my father has been one of the most generous hosts I know. I thank them for their love and example. I dedicate this book to them.

Introduction

Who Is the You That Eats?

> The human body is one vast ecosystem. Actually, it is more like an entire
> planet ... From the perspective of a microbe, I am a durable, living trellis –
> inside and out – on which vast numbers of those microbes cling, climb,
> and grow ... I am their homeland ... I am not who I thought I was. And
> neither are you. We are all a collection of ecosystems for other creatures.[1]

When I tell people that I have a research interest in food, it usually doesn't
take very long before someone says, "You are what you eat." It is a well-
known phrase that means many things. For some, it acts like a health
warning: if you eat junk, it won't take too long before you feel like junk
yourself. Eat wholesome, nutritious food, however, and you will soon feel
yourself to be more alert and alive to the possibilities that are uniquely
yours to realize. For others, the phrase refers to your identity as reflected in
what you value. If you eat organic, local food, that may mean you are the
kind of person for whom environmental concerns are a high priority.
Similarly, there are diverse, delectable ethnic traditions in cooking and
eating. Insofar as you seek out a particular cuisine, you are likely signaling
a desire to identify with the traditions of work and artistry that make the
cuisine possible.

At root, "You are what you eat" communicates your connection to a world
beyond yourself. When we amend it, as Michael Pollan has, and say, "You
are what what you eat eats too," the extent of the connections is magnified,
becoming ever more complicated, because now the diets of all the plant and
animal creatures that fed the chicken that laid the egg that is served up on
your plate, matter too – and, of course, whatever it is that they ate prior

---

[1] David R. Montgomery and Anne Biklé, *The Hidden Half of Nature: The Microbial Roots of
Life and Health* (New York: W. W. Norton & Company, 2016), 126.

that.[2] In other words, to take a bite is never simply to bite into one thing. Every chomp and chew implicates and places you in a world of bewildering diversity and depth. You need others to be yourself. You can't possibly make sense of yourself and your life apart from them. The proof? Stop eating, and before long, you will become hungry *for others*. Resist others entirely, and you will die. Eating is the daily confirmation that you are never alone. That means you need to attend to the creatures that nurture you, and that join you to forests, fields, waterways, barns, gardens, butterflies, bees, chickens, gardeners, farmers, cooks ... the list goes on and on.

But who is the "you" that eats? What sort of being is it that must eat in order "to be"? And how does the action of *eating* others – as compared to *seeing* or *touching* others, for instance – challenge us to think differently about the human person? The mode of sense perception you choose makes a difference.

A quick look at the history of Western thought suggests that eating and tasting have not usually been the preferred sensual point of entry for self-discovery and self-examination. This is a bit surprising, especially if we remember that the Latin word for knowing, *sapere*, also means "to taste." Instead, philosophers and theologians have tended to prefer seeing over tasting as the way to make sense of the world. Metaphors associated with sight are so embedded in our conceptual frameworks – think here of the quest for wisdom as a quest for enlightenment, or spiritual attainment described as a *visio Dei* – that Hannah Arendt is quite right to say that, "from the outset in formal philosophy, thinking has been thought of in terms of *seeing*."[3] It is the mind's "eye" that "sees" another's point of view. Though people may from time to time speak of "ruminating" over a thought, we would think it a bit odd to refer to the mind's "mouth" somehow "tasting" an idea.

To elevate sight as the prototypical philosophical stance, however, has profound, practical implications for the way people understand and position themselves in the world. Seeing is the sense that assumes a safe distance between subject and object. As Hans Jonas put it, "The gain [with sight] is the concept of objectivity, of the thing as it is in itself as distinct from the thing as it affects me, and from this distance arises the whole idea of *theōria*

[2]   Michael Pollan, *In Defense of Food: An Eater's Manifesto* (New York: Penguin Books, 2008), 167.

[3]   Hannah Arendt, *The Life of the Mind* (New York: Harcourt, Brace & Company, 1971), 110. For detailed treatment of how sight and thinking work together in modern philosophers ranging from Descartes to Foucault, see *Modernity and the Hegemony of Vision* (ed. David Michael Levin [Berkeley: University of California Press, 1993]).

and theoretical truth."[4] Sight establishes the independence and the freedom of the viewer, for in seeing another, the one seeing does not need to be directly engaged with the object seen. Objectivity presupposes a knower's personal disengagement, their emotional detachment. Distance, separation, and the freedom not to be affected by another – these are all reasons to elevate sight above a sense like hearing, because to hear another is already to be, at least somewhat, exposed to and at the mercy of the other.

When seeing is taken to be the model for thinking, the practical, perhaps inevitable, result is a conception of persons and others as self-contained entities (or "monads," to use Leibniz's term). Looking at another person, it seems obvious that a person's skin, and the shape and contours it communicates, is the boundary that identifies you as the distinct being that you are. Skin is the hard surface that, like a wall, protects persons from alien intrusion. This thin dermatological membrane is what enables us to differentiate the world outside from the self that is contained within. Skin is like an irregularly shaped envelope that contains the soul, genetic code, or information pattern that enables the story that is you to develop. The true or essential you is on the inside. What you become, and what the rest of us see, is a feature of what gets worked out in the discrete body that contains you.

The idea that you are a self-contained being has profound and far-reaching implications. Consider, for instance, how it underwrites a conception of individual freedom as the imperious ability of persons to move about in the world without restraint, and how it has funded various emancipatory ideals in politics. The goal of a distinctly human life is not only to be autonomous, deriving the laws of behavior (*nomos*) from out of oneself (*autos*). It is to be able to choose for oneself the life one wants, regardless of the place one is in or the beings one is with. Think here of Thomas Hobbes, who (in *Leviathan* I, xiv) took it as a "right of nature," that each man has the liberty "to use his own power as he will himself for the preservation of his own nature." By liberty, Hobbes meant the absence of external impediments that might get in the way of "a man's power to do as he would." For people to become themselves they must be emancipated from external constraints like nature, tradition, or even (if one subscribes to the transhumanist dream) one's physical body. They must think of themselves as individuals, self-standing and alone. Though persons may choose to enter

---

[4] Hans Jonas, "The Nobility of Sight," in *The Phenomenon of Life: Toward a Philosophical Biology* (New York: Harper & Row, 1966), 147. Earlier in the essay Jonas speaks of sight as the sense faculty that is without causal relationship between seer and seen: the object "is apprehended in its self-containment from out of my own self-containment" (146).

into relationships with others, these relationships do not define who they are at their core.

Is a characterization of persons as self-contained beings adequate or honest? What happens if we consider persons not via the sense of sight but instead via the sense of touch?

In one of the earliest philosophical treatments on the phenomenon of touch, Aristotle observed in his text *On the Soul* that touching allows us to discriminate among things in the world (as being hot or cold, hard or soft, for instance). The act of touching, in its very practice, enables people to distinguish the one touching and the thing being touched. But touching is never simply something people do *to* others. To touch another is also to be touched *by* them. Through our skin we feel the presence of the other and are changed by the sensation: the touch provokes a response in us. To be a touching being – Aristotle insisted that we are always touching, even when we are asleep – means that we can never think of ourselves as alone or as apart. As Richard Kearney formulates it, "To be tactile is to be exposed to others across gaps, to negotiate sensitivity *between* other embodied beings, to respond to solicitations, to orient oneself."[5] The phenomenon of touching teaches us that skin is a material witness to a person that, rather than being closed within a container or confined behind a wall, is *open* to the presence of others, *open* to being affected by others. "While we can close our eyes, ears, nostrils and lips, we are always touching and being touched. To live fully is to be constantly exposed to the elements, to being, to life, to others; it is to be forever attentive and attuned, from head to foot, to pain and pleasure, to happiness and grief, to good and ill."[6]

Touching implicates us in a world with others. Rather than being freestanding, or even self-founding, we are who we are only because we live in responsive relation with others. We are not self-contained entities, because to be cut off from the many forms of nurture, influence, help, resistance, and inspiration of others would immediately render us dead. As Tim Ingold describes it, this means that "the skin is not an impermeable boundary but a permeable zone of intermingling and admixture, where traces can reappear as threads and vice versa ... instead of thinking of organisms as entangled in relations, we should regard every living thing as

---

[5] Richard Kearney, "The Wager of Carnal Hermeneutics," *Carnal Hermeneutics*, ed. Richard Kearney and Brian Treanor (New York: Fordham University Press, 2015), 19.
[6] Ibid., 24.

itself an entanglement."[7] Though enabling distinctions between organisms, skin does not, like a wall, keep us separated from others. Being permeable, it is, instead, something like a sieve or mesh through which others pass so that engagements with and nurture from others can occur. Ingold distinguishes organisms *entangled in relationships* from organisms *being their entanglements* because the former suggests an organism that is more or less self-subsisting and then (voluntarily) chooses to enter into relationships. This is a mistake. Life is a meshwork in which an unfathomable number of lines of development interlace and interpenetrate. The idea of self-subsistence is called into question because each organism is *constituted* through its relationships. To "be" is to "be in relationship."

To witness the inescapability of our entanglement with others, we need travel no further than our belly buttons. Here, on the very skin that is sometimes interpreted to separate us from others, we find the unmistakable testimony of each human body's intimate involvement with and need of others. Here we discover that before the "I" can claim to rule or take charge of its own life, it has first been a recipient and beneficiary of the nurture of a mother.

Thinking about belly buttons is difficult, because they reveal the tension between being self-enclosed and, at the same time, dependent on others. The philosopher Jean-Luc Nancy says, "Skin that is intact protects life, holding it together, but in order to do this, it has to tie itself together; it has to tie a knot in the cut umbilical cord."[8] Described this way, a belly button is like cap on the container body, "the signature or seal of propriation" (from the Latin *propriatio*, which means "to make one's own"), that establishes the body as distinct and its own. Belly buttons show that we are formed to be "entirely distinct" because they are caps that seal off the body's originary dependence upon another. But they are also "scars," because they remind us of the cutting of an umbilical cord that joined us to a placenta that joined us to our mothers. Belly buttons remind us that our origin is in others.

In her reflection on the umbilical cord, Anne O'Byrne interprets a belly button to be a sign that we are finite, unfinished, and never pristine beings. "Our coming into the world involves being marked by the wound of birth. We share with all humans and almost all mammals the umbilical scar it leaves – our first scar, the mother of all scars."[9] Like Nancy, O'Byrne

---

[7]　Tim Ingold, *Being Alive: Essays on Movement, Knowledge and Description* (London: Routledge, 2011), 87.

[8]　Jean-Luc Nancy, "Rethinking Corpus," in Kearney and Treanor, *Carnal Hermeneutics*, 77.

[9]　Anne O'Byrne, "Umbilicus: Toward a Hermeneutic of Generational Difference," in Kearney and Treanor, *Carnal Hermeneutics*, 184.

interprets the belly button to be a reminder of a body that is "wholly mine" and "wholly entwined with another" at the same time. But it is a reminder that is also a scar. Why use the language of "scars"?

The straightforward meaning of a scar testifies to the work of repair that follows from an injury or wound. As such, scars signify a rupture having taken place *and* the process that tries to heal the rupture by sealing the body off. Because scars do not quite recover all the qualities of the tissue that was once there (for instance, scar skin tissue is less resistant to ultraviolet radiation and is incapable of growing hair or sweat glands), the healing that happens is a sign of lasting vulnerability and an ongoing challenge to the dreams of autonomy and autarchy that animate so many projects of the self. "If the fold at the center of us is the memory of our beginning in another body, autonomy was never a given but an achievement. We were brought into the world; we did not come of our own accord; it took action by others to sustain us before we were even aware of self or world."[10] We each enter a world that is already alive with earlier generations and earlier couplings that birth us into life. Before we could do anything on our own, we were already being fed by another. Belly buttons are the unmistakable sign that the idea of a self-contained, self-standing person is a deception.

The world perceived through touch is a much messier, much more proximate world than the world perceived through sight. It is not a place populated by discrete, self-standing objects but is rather a dynamic, moving field of entanglements in which self-involvement and intimacy are the rule. The intensity of the intimacy I am talking about becomes especially pronounced when we acknowledge that one of the most primordial forms of touching is the tasty action of eating. When you eat another creature, you do not simply make contact with it. You take it "inside" of yourself, digest it, and incorporate it within. With an intimacy that rivals sexual union, the other's flesh and your flesh "become one flesh." The other does not stand apart or alongside. Instead, when eaten, the other nurtures you, and thus reenergizes, refreshes, and revitalizes you from within. Eating is the daily confirmation that you have never simply been one. To think with the stomach in mind, and to perceive the world and yourself through your mouth, is to know that no creature is ever alone.

This is why some scientists now argue that the idea of an individual organism needs to be replaced with the idea of a "holobiont" (from the Greek for "whole unit of life"). This uncommon locution has been developed to emphasize the

---

[10]   Ibid., 192.

symbiotic character of life, and to reinforce the idea that no organism is ever self-enclosed. Symbiosis is the idea that organisms live by their intimate contact with others. Without this contact, living beings cease to be. Even more importantly, without this contact they could not even come to be in the first place, because the origins of tissues, organs, and organisms are the result of a process called "symbiogenesis," in which life forms emerge out of the diversity of life together, even life *inside* each other. Lynn Margulis puts it this way:

> Living beings defy neat definition. They fight, they feed, they dance, they mate, they die. At the base of the creativity of all large familiar forms of life, symbiosis generates novelty. It brings together different life-forms, always for a reason. Often, hunger unites the predator with the prey or the mouth with the photosynthetic bacterium or algal victim. Symbiogenesis brings together unlike individuals to make large, more complex entities ... These become "new individuals" at larger, more inclusive levels of integration. Symbiosis is not a marginal or rare phenomenon. It is natural and common. We abide in a symbiotic world.[11]

To acknowledge that we live in a symbiotic world is to affirm that *living beings are always already communities of beings*, because each organism *as a holobiont* is "comprised of both host elements and persistent populations of symbionts."[12]

To use a term like holobiont is to acknowledge that an organism is never simply single or one. The moment you try to isolate or individuate yourself, you cease to be. This is where the language of a host *plus* its symbionts can be a bit misleading, if it is taken to mean that the host exists before its entanglement with others. Not so, says Donna Haraway:

> Critters do not precede their relatings ... I use *holobiont* to mean symbiotic assemblages, at whatever scale of space or time, which are more like knots of diverse intra-active relatings in dynamic complex systems, than like the entities of a biology made up of preexisting bounded units (genes, cells, organisms, etc.) in interactions that can only be conceived as competitive or cooperative.[13]

A host does not come first, pre-made, so to speak, and then relate to others, because for a "host" to exist is already for it to be in symbiotic relationship.

---

[11]　Lynn Margulis, *Symbiotic Planet: A New Look at Evolution* (New York: Basic Books, 1998), 9.

[12]　Scott F. Gilbert, Jan Sapp, and Alfred I. Tauber, "A Symbiotic View of Life: We Have Never Been Individuals," *The Quarterly Review of Biology* 87:4 (December 2012), 327–328.

[13]　Donna J. Haraway, *Staying with the Trouble: Making Kin in the Chthulucene* (Durham, NC: Duke University Press, 2016), 60.

Symbiosis constitutes the host, which is to say, somewhat paradoxically, that a host has always already been hosted and nurtured by others.

To appreciate how symbiogenesis works, it helps to attend to the microbial roots of life. The importance of microbes for our thinking about life has only recently come to the fore. When asked for a definition of life, Margulis says *life is bacteria*, because every organism, if not itself a live bacterium, is a descendent of bacteria and their various mergers. "Bacteria initially populated the planet and have never relinquished their hold."[14] All living things depend on the metabolizing work that bacteria perform. Without bacteria, the various processes of growth and decay – photosynthesis, digesting, and decomposition – would not have come to be. In other words, no bacteria, no eating, no life.

Clearly, earlier scientists could not have known in any detail or clarity that a diverse microbial world even exists, let alone that it matters profoundly for our understanding of life. They simply lacked the technology and the instrumentation to perceive what was there all along. But now that we do perceive, we are finding that organisms are composites of many species living together, and that the relationships between them make it difficult to speak with confidence about an organism's precise or essential identity. The integration between bacteria and their hosts is so intimate, and their dependence upon each other for life is so essential, that it is often hard to determine where one species begins and another ends.

Because microbes challenge so many of the assumptions that have guided the biological disciplines – most basically, the taxonomies that differentiate creatures into discrete kinds – we should not be surprised that their study is creating considerable controversy and difficulty. To start, we have barely begun to identify the diversity of microbes inhabiting our bodies, let alone the entire planet, nor do we understand the various things microbes do. But according to Margaret McFall-Ngai, a leading researcher in this area and a member of the National Academy of Sciences, "microbes are the center of the universe ... We now know that they make up the vast diversity of the biosphere, that they live in intimate association with animals, and that animal biology was shaped by interacting with microbes. In my mind, this is the most significant revolution in biology since Darwin."[15]

---

[14]   Lynn Margulis and Dorion Sagan, *What Is Life?* (Berkeley: University of California Press, 1995), 90.

[15]   As quoted by Ed Yong in *I Contain Multitudes: The Microbes within Us and a Grander View of Life* (New York: Ecco, 2016), 20.

The microbial revolution challenges the idea of an individual organism on multiple fronts.[16] *Anatomically*, scientists have long held to the belief that an organism is an integrated whole in which the various parts of an organism represent one consistent life form. This view can no longer be maintained when we observe organisms at multiple species levels not only inhabited by but also dependent upon other species occupying their bodies. As just one example, consider the common cow. Cows could not survive without a rumen that hosts a complex ecosystem of gut symbionts (consisting of cellulose-digesting bacteria and anaerobic fungi, among other microbes) that enable it to digest its plant food. A cow is inconceivable apart from its microbial community. *Developmentally*, it had long been assumed that an organism is the same throughout the various stages of its growth from birth until death. This position can no longer be sustained, because in many cases symbionts play a crucial role helping the host organism complete its life cycle. A newborn infant, for instance, though nurtured in a relatively sterile womb, must have its gut colonized by microbes in order for its intestine to develop properly. As it travels through the vaginal opening, the newborn is transformed from an individual into a community as its body ingests millions of microbes that populate the mother's body.[17] *Physiologically*, we are now seeing that in some organisms the divisions of labor among the various parts of an organic body are "outsourced" to different species. The synthesis of amino acids in the mealy bug, for instance, is now understood to require the shared work of two microbes with its host. Without these "foreign" bacteria, the bug could not be "itself." *Genetically*, it has become clear that the one-gene/one-organism model hardly obtains. Microbial symbionts provide "a secondary hereditary system" that enables the host to survive in changing contexts. The genome, in other words, is not fixed.[18]

---

[16] In the following description, I am summarizing the admirably clear account provided by Gilbert, Sapp, and Tauber in "A Symbiotic View of Life."

[17] Many animal species could not survive without microbes, which is why birth environments are often seeded with microbe capsules or fluids, and why newborns must lick fellow members or consume their feces or some other microbe-rich equivalent. Consider the development of a koala: "When a baby koala is six months old, it weans off its mother's milk and moves on to eucalyptus leaves. But first, it nuzzles mum's backside. She, in response, releases a fluid called pap, which the joey swallows. Pap is full of bacteria that will allow the koala joey to digest tough eucalyptus leaves, and contains up to 40 times more of these microbes than regular faeces. Without this initial meal, all the joey's later ones would be hard to stomach" (Yong, *I Contain Multitudes*, 149–150).

[18] Ingold argues that "Neo-Darwinism is dead." He does not argue against the theory of evolutionary development, nor does he dispute the existence of DNA, RNA, amino acids, chromosome, or proteins. What he resists is the neo-Darwinian interpretation of these realities. "Evolution ... does not lie in the mutation, recombination, replication and

History and environmental factors influence the holobiont at the most fundamental, cellular level, such that the host and symbionts become genetically integrated.[19] *Immunologically*, it had long been assumed that a healthy organism's immune system maintains a wall to keep out pathogen intruders. Viruses, bacteria, and fungi are the enemy, the threatening other that, left alone, will compromise the health of the self. Recent studies have shown, however, that a host's immune system is created, at least in part, by its resident biome. A healthy biome, among other things, distinguishes "friendly" microbes from not, and works to protect the body in ways we are only beginning to understand.[20] And *evolutionarily*, it has become clear that the idea of individual selection must be replaced by group selection, understanding by this "group" not a collection of the same species members but the holobiont, which is a collection of multiple species. There is no individual organism that adapts and survives, because there was no single, self-contained organism to begin with.[21] "Our bodies must be understood as

selection of transmissible traits. It is rather a life process. And at the heart of this process is ontogenesis. The failure to account for the ontogenetic emergence of phenotypic form is the Achilles heel of the entire neo-Darwinian paradigm." "The more we know about the genome, the more improbable it seems that it could serve as an anchor for stability. Indeed it is hard to see how the reproducibility of organic form could be attributed to anything as fluid, as liable to getting tied up in knots, as prone to alteration by retro-transposition, and as susceptible to the transfer of bits and pieces back and forth with the organism's multiple and heterogeneous microbial symbionts, as the genome" (Tim Ingold, "Prospect," in *Biosocial Becomings: Integrating Social and Biological Anthropology*, ed. Tim Ingold and Gisli Palsson [Cambridge: Cambridge University Press, 2013], 1, 6, 11).

[19] This means that a fundamental feature of the neo-Darwinian hypothesis, the idea that the development of an organism is reducible to a (stable, preformed) genetic pattern transcribing or working itself out on a body's development, is fundamentally mistaken. It is but a more recent version of an ancient, Aristotelian mistake that presupposes a body to consist of its matter (*hyle*) plus its form (*morphe*), with the form being responsible for the shape and order of the body. The countless microbes within us destabilize whatever we may have thought about the selfsameness of our genes and our form.

[20] In her meditation on the practice of vaccination, Eula Biss notes that the health of a body is not achieved by a body sealing itself off from pathogen others. The effort to sustain a body in some kind of self-enclosed purity is a mistake. The pursuit of bodily purity, as when parents attempt to shield their children from critters and germs, or when they work to make their home environments as sterile as possible (through the copious use of anti-microbial soaps and toxic cleaning supplies), actually puts the body at risk. Why? Because health is not a property of an individually secured body. "We are protected not so much by our own skin, but by what is beyond it . . . immunity . . . is a common trust as much as it is a private account. Those of us who draw on collective immunity owe our health to our neighbors . . . Immunity is a shared space – a garden we tend together" (*On Immunity: An Inoculation* [Minneapolis: Graywolf Press, 2014], 25, 163).

[21] Ingold argues that attending to life in terms of its biosocial becomings results in a fundamental revision of what we understand evolution to be. It is a revision that "requires us to think of humanity not as a fixed and given condition but as a relational achievement.

holobionts whose anatomical, physiological, immunological, and developmental functions evolved in shared relationships of different species. Thus, the holobiont, with its integrated community of species, becomes a unit of natural selection whose evolutionary mechanisms suggest complexity hitherto largely unexplored."[22]

When scientists began to publish the findings of the Human Microbiome Project (HMP), a project devoted to categorizing and enumerating the microbiological species that live in a healthy human body, they noted that hundreds of trillions of bacteria, and all the genetic diversity and complexity they represent, reside within each one of us (100 trillion in the digestive tract alone). The ratio of microbial to human genes is at least 130 to 1. This means that "individuality" is an emergent and dynamic process, rather than a stable given. Who you are is a feature of a pluralistic ecosystem within and all around you. "This notion of individuals emerging as communities, and within communities, challenges us to reframe how we should behave towards other biological organisms."[23]

Some will find this microbial picture of life unsettling, because multiple cherished assumptions about humanity are called into question by it. At issue are concerns about the extent of human need and dependence but also questions of a self's purity, autonomy, and sovereignty. If people cannot grow or be healthy without a diverse and healthy microbial presence within and upon their bodies, then the ways they think about themselves and their comportment in the world must change. Much more than before, you must think of yourself as *already inhabited* by others and as a *host* that nurtures and is nurtured by others. You are not locked securely behind the wall that is your skin. A more accurate and honest account would reposition you as permeable, inhabited, and vulnerable to the lives of others. This is what the experience of eating teaches us. Attending to the microbial world enables us to taste the depths of our need for others in ways we have never before

---

It requires us to think of evolution not as change along lines of descent but as the developmental unfolding of the entire matrix of relations within which forms of life (human and non-human) emerge and are held in place. And it requires us to think of these forms as neither genetically or culturally configured but as emergent outcomes of the dynamic self-organization of developmental systems. This rethinking ... amounts to a paradigm shift of a consequence for the human sciences of the twenty-first century equal to or greater than that which the Darwinian paradigm had for the sciences of the twentieth" ("Prospect," 20).

[22]   Gilbert, Sapp, and Tauber, "A Symbiotic View of Life," 334.
[23]   Gregory W. Schneider and Russell Winslow, "Parts and Wholes: The Human Microbiome, Ecological Ontology, and the Challenges of Community," *Perspectives in Biology and Medicine* 57:2 (Spring 2014), 208–223, 209.

imagined. Life is always already life together. The art of a human, creaturely life is to know how to move sympathetically, hospitably, and responsibly within this togetherness.[24]

For us to become and be the creatures that we are, we must always become-with and be-with many, many others. You have never been one. You are always many in motion. For good reason, Ingold argues that we need to move away from fixed identities that focus on what we *are*, and instead turn our attention to what we *do* and to what is *done to us*. As this chapter has been describing, *being with* microbes and other creatures means that we are not self-contained or self-directed kinds of things. Symbiotic life, even at the genetic, molecular level, means that we are always in a position of giving and receiving, acting and being acted upon, eating and being eaten, touching and being touched, influencing and being influenced. This is why it would be better to speak of human *becomings* rather than simply human *beings*, especially if we mean by such a being an organism that is single, self-contained, and self-driving. Persons emerge from the womb "not as discrete and pre-formed entities but as trajectories of movement and growth." Who we are, even that we are, is a feature of our ever-changing, dynamic entanglements with others: "human becomings continually forge their ways, and guide the ways of consociates, in the crucible of their common life. In so doing, they weave a kind of tapestry. But like life itself, the tapestry is never complete, never finished. It is always work in progress."[25]

We can now see that the phrase "You are what you eat" needs further amendment beyond "You are what what you eat eats too." We should also say "You are what eats you," and "You are what what is inside you eats,"

---

[24] The practical necessities of microbial health are not restricted to human bodies. As Montgomery and Biklé argue, the analogies between the microbiome in the human gut and the microbiome in the soil run in parallel fashion. Just as we can damage the human gut microbiome through poor diet and the consumption of antibiotics, so too can we destroy soil and plant health by attacking the soil's microbiome with herbicides and pesticides, and by depriving the soil of compost and organic food. "The biology and processes that bind soil, roots, and rhizosphere together mirror those in the mucosal lining of the gut and the associated immune tissue. The gut is the human version of the rhizosphere, the part of our bodies incredibly rich with specially recruited microbes. While cells of the digestive tract interact with gut microbes, root cells cut deals with soil microbes. The human world and the botanical world share a common theme – lots of communication and exchanges with microbes" (*The Hidden Half of Nature*, 244). The practical implications for agriculture that follow from this insight are immense, because now food production must be understood as an exercise in hospitality directed to all eaters, ranging from soil microbes and roots all the way to human eaters and their microbiomes. Montgomery develops the practical implications for agriculture in *Growing a Revolution: Bringing Our Soil Back to Life* (New York: W. W. Norton & Company, Inc., 2017).

[25] Ingold, "Prospect," 8.

if we want a more accurate account of the life story that is you. You never simply eat for yourself. You also eat for the billions upon billions of tiny creatures that, by being hungry, feed you, feed upon you, and are fed by you. You are always already a host to a world outside and inside you, while you are yourself being hosted by others. This means that the places and times of your life are made possible by forms of hospitality, sharing, and symbiogenesis that boggle the mind.

What sort of eating best witnesses to and honors this primordial, unfathomable hospitality? How should we now grow and gather food, or prepare and share it? Who should we invite? How should we give thanks?

1

ℛ

It's about Fidelity

The world's farmers face a Sisyphean, if not Herculean, task: to double grain, meat, and biofuel production on fewer acres with fewer farmers, less water, higher temperatures, and more frequent droughts, floods, and heat waves. And they must do it without destroying the forests, oceans, soils, pollinators, or climate on which all life depends. It is the biggest collective hurdle humanity has ever faced.[1]

More than any other activity, eating *roots* people in the world. Put another way, the activities of gathering fruit, hunting wildlife, growing grains and vegetables, raising livestock, processing and distributing food, and cooking and sharing meals *stitch* us into a vast and dynamic fabric of life that extends from the microscopic to atmospheric levels. Eating is the regular and visceral reminder that we belong in this world, depend on it daily, and could not possibly live without it. Of all the things people do, nothing communicates as clearly as eating the intense intimacy of our need for each other, and our need for a nourishing world. It would follow, then, that our highest priority should be to nurture the world that nurtures us.

It's not happening.

Instead of nourishing the world, the dominant food economies of societies across the globe are mining the soil of its nutrients, destroying its microbial and organic life, depleting and polluting fresh water systems, warming the atmosphere, and driving to extinction thousands of plant and animal species. Close to a billion people still do not have enough to eat, and many millions more do not have the money to purchase whatever food is available. Though an unprecedented number of calories are being produced using

[1] Joel K. Bourne, Jr., *The End of Plenty: The Race to Feed a Crowded World* (New York: W. W. Norton & Company, 2015), 158.

industrial methods, the consumption of these calories is making the planet and many of its (especially poor) people sick. Moreover, the imperial race to commodify and purchase every square inch of arable land and every gallon of fresh water, and the desire to turn every life-form into a unit of production that can be manipulated for purposes of profit or personal comfort, suggests that people have put themselves at war with the earth and its life. It is not a war that people can win. In several respects, and quite literally, the dominant food economy is positioning people to eat themselves out of house and home.

Eating has always been the most practical and intimate way by which people position themselves in the world. This is nonnegotiable. Every bite we take testifies to what we believe an appropriate positioning in the world looks like. What we need to appreciate is that *how* people position themselves in food webs and systems, and the embodied practices through which foods are produced and consumed, vary through time. In these varying positionings people communicate what they believe about food, how they think about their place in the world among others, and what they value about life. Eating commits people to being participants in dramas of life and death with others that are of the profoundest intimacy. But various mind-body dualisms, and the otherworldly spiritualities they underwrite, indicate that people often prefer flight or escape from rather than responsibility and intimacy with the places and fellow creatures that feed them.

Today's widespread desire for cheap and convenient food, for instance, witnesses the belief that people should be able to live in the world without having to exert much thought and effort, or exercise skill and restraint. People expressing this desire are not malicious. They are simply living into their roles as shoppers who stroll among the options and, as (more or less) free sovereigns, pluck whatever items suit their (often media-manufactured) appetites. As a result, the world appears as one vast warehouse or supermarket that people enter from time to time so that they can appropriate what they need, all with the ease of a credit card swipe. It is hard to imagine a more naïve, less committed relation to the world. The experience of shopping for food has become so ubiquitous that we have forgotten how novel this positioning of the human-as-a-shopper and the world-as-a-store really is.

Of course, the purchase of food has a long history, as when people came to local markets to buy the food items they needed. What has changed recently, however, especially in "advanced" economies, is the invention of the grocery store, and then its ascendance as the dominant, even indispensable, site through which people provide for their dietary needs. For many people, eating would become a radically different, if not impossible, affair if grocery stores were suddenly to disappear.

When compared to the countless number of people who made the finding and the growing of food their primary occupation, today's grocery store has made eating an act of unprecedented convenience and ignorance. As Michael Ruhlman has observed, "We had gone from tribes hunting food, gathering it, preserving it, joining in the work of it, protecting it, and then sharing it in larger communities to, thousands of years later, isolated families on suburban streets gathering our food from a single forty-thousand-square-foot store once a week and bringing it back home to eat by ourselves."[2] Because these stores have such a great variety and quantity of foods, much of it attractively packaged, shoppers need to know very little about where their food comes from, how it was grown and produced, and whether it will continue to be there for long. Even if consumers now know to say that food does not literally "come from the store," they don't really know the significance of what they are saying. The proof? Even if given the necessary space, seeds, stock, and supplies, most would starve if asked to grow the food themselves.

My point is not that we should close grocery stores and send people back to the land. It is, rather, to alert us to a new positioning of humanity with respect to the food they eat. Never before have people had to know and care so little to enjoy so much. Never before have people had so much choice about what they will eat. Never before has the provisioning of food been such an undemanding and imperious affair. Going to a grocery store is like going to a magical show: the food just keeps coming out of boxes, much like rabbits and flowers out of a hat. We are not sure how it all happens, but we love that it does. Clearly, it is exhilarating to be in the presence of such a magical and available display, and to know that one can (if one has sufficient funds) take it home. But what if one day we reach in the box and the food isn't there to pull out?

To eat in an Anthropocene world is to eat in a new context in which the geo-bio-ecosystem processes that have given us a more or less stable and dependable agriculture no longer obtain. As the opening quotation from Joel Bourne indicates, growing food for our growing population represents a

---

[2] Michael Ruhlman, *Grocery: The Buying and Selling of Food in America* (New York: Abrams Press, 2017), 15. Ruhlman notes that the ascendance of grocery stores is now coming to an end as online food shopping and delivery to the shopper's door are becoming ever more popular, a development that further exemplifies the shopper's demand for convenience, freedom of choice, and cheapness of price.

challenge unlike any the human race has ever faced. What is at issue is not simply the technical matter of how the food will be grown but, more fundamentally, how people will position themselves as eaters in a much degraded and unpredictable world. As we will see, the dawning of an Anthropocene world reflects the development of a self-understanding in which human control of the world (primarily for purposes of comfort, convenience, and profit) is the highest priority. For civilizations to "advance" and "progress," the people within them need to extricate themselves from the daily, practical demands of the care of places and creatures. They must, as Karl Marx once famously said, be emancipated from "the idiocy of rural life."[3]

This narration of Progress and Emancipation needs to be challenged. To be sure, advanced economies and technologies have yielded many benefits and calories. It would be stupid and ungrateful to deny their goodness and value. But it would also be naïve, even reckless, to ignore the exhausted and degraded ecosystems, the wasted fields, the polluted waters, the abused creatures, the extinction of species, the exploited communities, and all the sick and hungry eaters that have become the hidden and ignored "externalities" of economic success. Do we really want to continue down a path that will eventually require people, at least those who can afford it, to seek a home on another planet because the one we are currently on is becoming uninhabitable? This is not an absurd question. Climate change is already rendering some islands and coastal lands unlivable. As sea levels rise, glaciers melt, and extreme weather hits, tens of millions of people will be without homes and their traditional sources of food and water.

Dreams of complete control, fueled by the desire to live life comfortably and on one's own terms, have shown themselves to be a dangerous and destructive fantasy. What we need, instead, is to learn the sympathies and work of care, work that will not be possible apart from a commitment to cherish the places and the lives that nurture us. For this work, we will need the wisdom of previous peoples who tried, sometimes successfully, sometimes not, to honor the life that feeds their own. By turning briefly to the histories of hunters and gatherers, farmers and engineers, my aim is not to turn back the clock, or to romanticize the histories of native and agrarian communities.[4] It is, rather, to put us in a better position to appreciate the

---

[3] Karl Marx and Frederick Engels, *The Communist Manifesto* (New York: International Publishers, 2014), 8.

[4] The charge of nostalgia inevitably arises the moment criticisms against modern progress are made. Clearly, it is important to avoid idealized, false representations of the past, because

destructive and violent foundation – genocide, slavery, dispossession, eco-cide – upon which so much "progress" has been built.[5] Moving forward requires honesty about the past. If we are to retrieve those insights and practices that will better enable us to be a nurturing, faithful presence to each other and to our places, we also need to know the historical contexts that derided them, and often cast them aside.

WHY FIDELITY?

In this chapter I examine some of the ways people have understood food, and thus also themselves, by describing how they have positioned themselves in their food webs. If eating stitches people in the world with others, how have people understood this stitching, and have they embraced it? Is the

they deprive us of the (often) painful wisdom we need for the present. But it is also foolish to discount the past simply because it is the past, or to assume that little can be learned from it. It is important to note that the term "nostalgia" is of relatively recent (seventeenth century) Swiss-German origin, and referred to the medical condition of homesickness Swiss mercenaries felt being away from their home. The love of one's home can be so intense that to be removed from it is to require hospitalization. For discussion of the complex relations between health and hospitality, and the suffering of leaving a home and the pain of return, see Barbara Cassin's *Nostalgia: When Are We Ever at Home?* (New York: Fordham University Press, 2016). One should ask if much of today's (especially academic) derision of nostalgic sentiments isn't a denial of fidelity to place, and a refusal to accept responsibility for a place's often sordid and violent history. Besides reflecting the rootlessness that characterizes so much professorial life, such derision betrays the wisdom of places revealed in indigenous ways of life, and it denies the importance of rootedness for bodily and spiritual health (recall that indigenous people frequently became ill and died when forcibly removed from their lands).

[5]   The violent foundation of Progress has been invisible to many because the histories of Progress have rarely been written from the perspective of those who faced it. This is why it is so important to listen and attend to the voices of indigenous and traditional peoples, something the conquerors of new lands rarely tried to do. Consider, in this context, the sentiment of Dan, a Lakota elder, who questions the "civilized" character of European settlers: "For us, the earth was alive. To move a stone was to change her. To kill an animal was to take from her. There had to be respect. We saw no respect from these people. They chopped down trees and left animals lay where they were shot. They made loud noises. They seemed like wild people. They were heavy on the land and they were loud … Your people did not know about the land being sacred … The worst thing is that you never listened to us. You came into our land and took it away and didn't even listen to us when we tried to explain" (as presented by Kent Nerburn in *Neither Wolf nor Dog: On Forgotten Roads with an Indian Elder* [Novato, CA: New World Library, 1994], 47, 49–50). A central problem with narrations of Progress is what they leave out. Speaking again of the settlement of North America, why believe this to have been an empty, savage land that was slowly civilized and made prosperous by the heroic exploits of a few brave, white men? This narration ignores the fact that for centuries diverse tribes had been living sustainably, and in ways that fostered care and creativity.

weaving tight or loose? Does it matter if the webs fray or come apart? Put another way, have the varying ways of growing, gathering, and consuming food acknowledged our need of each other, and then honored, perhaps even cherished, the nurture that places and others provide to us?

As I will argue, eating is the daily confirmation that we are always already in relation with others. Even in death, we are never alone.[6] This means that the question is never *if* we will be in relation. It is only ever *how* we will be in relation. To eat is to know that our *being* is always a *becoming with* others in myriad ways. The question of paramount importance, especially in a time when food webs across the world are coming apart, is whether or not people can develop the sympathies and skills that will enable them to be faithful eaters who nurture the world that nurtures them.

To be a faithful eater is to recognize that people cannot eat well for long if they do not make the sources of nurture the focus of their care, appreciation, and celebration. Fidelity to fields, watersheds, crops, livestock, farmers, cooks, friends, and guests is crucial for the maintenance of a healthy and flourishing life. Insofar as fields are damaged, waters polluted, and fellow creatures abused, people are communicating, whether they know it or not, that they don't value them and should not have to accept responsibility for them. The refusal of fidelity – what I will call the desire to divorce – results in life's breakdown because it condones the unraveling of the webs that feed and inspire us. Infidelity is not simply a choice to disown or walk away from this or that relationship. It is, instead, a falsification of our humanity as ones who always need and receive nurture from each other and the places in which we live. It is, ultimately, a denial of the blessings and the requirements of communal life.

Fidelity is fundamental to human experience. Its expression, however, takes many forms. Consider the parent-child relationship. Life for an infant would be impossible apart from a parent who is committed to its protection and care. While yet in the womb, the fetus is intimately bound to its mother through an umbilical cord that feeds and frees the child to develop into the creature that it uniquely is. Following childbirth, parents commit to feeding

---

[6] While alive, each body is host to billions of microorganisms that are vital to digestive processes and to personal health. In death, these digestive processes continue, resulting in the decomposition of bodies turned into food for others. The singularity of the "I" is, therefore, an illusion. It is more truthful to say that every "you" is a zoo. The literature on the importance of microbes within bodies is now very large. For a helpful introduction, see Ed Yong's *I Contain Multitudes: The Microbes within Us and a Grander View of Life* (New York: Ecco, 2016) and David R. Montgomery and Anne Biklé's *The Hidden Half of Nature: The Microbial Roots of Life and Health* (New York: W. W. Norton & Company, 2016).

the child, clothing the child, teaching the child, orienting the child – all with the aim of enabling it to take a responsible role within its society and world. Apart from this parental fidelity, witnessed in diverse acts of love and care, the child could hardly survive, let alone thrive.

Parents, even if they do not choose the particular child that is born, often have the choice about whether or not to have a child. The child, however, does not choose its parents. It didn't choose to be a needy being. It didn't even choose to be in the world. Nonetheless, at a certain point, the child must take up the question of its own fidelity to others. Will it accept responsibility for its parents? Will it commit to the well-being of the world that nurtures it? Will it be a faithful family member, friend, colleague, and citizen? These questions are not a one-off. They remain questions to be answered daily, and unto death. How they are answered will determine the health of the relationships and communities through which it moves.

What is not to be missed or forgotten is that all along life's way, a person grows and develops because of receiving nurture from others. Apart from the care of parents, siblings, extended family, neighbors, friends, teachers, coaches, cooks, farmers (the list goes on and on), and the fidelity such care presupposes, life is severely diminished or comes to an end. Given this vast exhibition of care and fidelity, we can now see why a posture of humility and the exercise of gratitude are such fundamental human traits. Honesty in a human life presupposes that one is attentive to and appreciative of the care one has and continues to receive, while humanity's goodness and beauty are worked out in the fidelity a person shows to its nurturing world.

The question of fidelity arises in the space between the world *as it is* and the world *as we would wish it to be*, or between people *as they present themselves to us* and *people as we would like them to be*. Consider a parent facing a screaming child. The parent will likely prefer that the child not scream, since it interrupts badly needed sleep, and it prevents the parent from accomplishing self-chosen tasks. But the child is clearly in distress. What should the parent do? Obviously, a parent could choose to walk away in frustration, wishing that their child screamed less and was more compliant. To walk away, however, is to forsake one's fidelity to the child. To choose fidelity, meanwhile, is to choose to attend to and accept the child in its distress. It is to work to alleviate its discomfort, all with the goal of enabling the child to flourish to the best of its abilities. A faithful parent does not wish for a different child. Instead, the parent desires to promote the conditions that will facilitate the realization of the potential that is unique to each particular child. Faithful parents work on themselves – by learning to be more attentive, patient, flexible, and skilled – so that they can be better parents. Love is the power that makes such fidelity possible, because love seeks the good of the beloved.

Similar analyses can be made of multiple relationships. Within friendship, why bother with friends who suddenly or slowly become difficult or too needy? Within athletics, why keep a teammate if they are struggling or can't keep up? Within education, why give extra attention to the student who is slowing the rest of the class down? In each case, the temptation is to walk away, wishing that one's friend, teammate, or classmate was different, less of a problem, and more an asset or complement to one's own flourishing. Faithful persons resist this temptation, because they know that the abandonment of others ultimately leads to social, athletic, and scholastic diminishment. They know that such abandonment reflects a forfeiture of love.

For some people, a marriage relationship represents the height of fidelity. In a good marriage, each spouse has the flourishing of the other as their controlling and abiding aim. Fidelity and response-ability to the other's life has become the primary, animating disposition that orients and shapes their own life. Learning to respond in ways that are loving takes time, patience, and a lot of mercy, because love is a hard and exacting discipline that requires of lovers the ability to know the potential and the pain of the ones they love. They need to know when to act, when to listen and learn, when to apologize, and when simply to get out of the way.

The daily temptation is to give up or walk away from the requirements of care. Why? Because spouses are unique persons that do not always live up to, or fall in line with, the expectations (or fantasies) we have for them. People fail and disappoint. This is why the commencement of a marriage is preceded by a vow in which people promise to be faithful to and remain with each other, "to have and to hold from this day forward, for better for worse, for richer for poorer, in sickness and in health, to love and to cherish, until death us do part." In this vow the two become "one flesh," but not in the sense that each person disappears into or is overwhelmed and controlled by the other. Genuine fidelity never results in the abuse of the other. Rather, the love that creates an intimate union is also the love that enables each spouse to be more than they could be alone, because each person carries within their own body the love of the other as an inspiring, nurturing, and empowering force. Marital love is both creative and procreative, issuing new life and the realization of otherwise unrealizable possibilities, because it is the sort of love that is hospitable, making room for others to be, and then nurturing them to realize their potential. In a good marriage, each spouse is more than they could be if left alone.

To be divorced is to signal the breaking of this vow. When divorced, one may still be in relationship with the other through contractual means like payment for child support and mortgage relief. One might continue to have civil and cordial relations for the sake of the family. The dispositions of love and fidelity, however, are no longer present and active. The commitment to care has diminished, if not evaporated, and been replaced by a contractual arrangement in which the parties consent to meet agreed-upon conditions. In contractual relationships, money takes the place of love as the power that holds people together. People come together so that advantage of some sort can be secured. Mutual care and cherishing are thereby replaced by concerns for utility and profitability.

What Does Any of This Have to Do with Eating?

Today's dominant food system, I would argue, demonstrates that the condition of divorce now defines our way of being in the world. We are "in" the world "with" others, but insofar as shopping has become the primary means through which we secure our livelihoods, we also communicate that we don't want to be deeply involved, committed, or held accountable. Eating is a contractual rather than covenantal affair. Having money to buy the food they need, people do not have to develop the sympathy, skill, or virtues that those growing food require. Shopping is easy and carefree. Growing plants and raising animals, however, are difficult, because one must work to care for their needs. Animals often have difficult, noncooperative personalities, while plants grow in their own sweet time, and all of them together are constantly susceptible to disease and death. Learning to care, and finding ways to stay committed in contexts of frustration and impotence, require the sort of love and fidelity that are cultivated in community. It is much easier to walk away, and leave the work to someone else. In multiple respects, industrial modes of eating communicate a breaking of fidelity with the land and its many creatures. They communicate a trust in the kind of magic that will produce ever more food on ever more degraded lands and communities.

Speaking this way, it is important to underscore that people continue to be in relationship with the creatures that feed them. Eating is the daily confirmation of that fact. But the character of these relationships is such that fidelity and love are not their animating heart. Put in slightly different terms, the relationships – and the eating – that join us to others and to places are characterized much more by *contract* than they are by *covenant,* and a contract in which desires for convenience, efficiency, comfort, and affordability dominate. Whereas a covenant relationship presupposes its members to be committed to each other's flourishing, a contractual relationship is fundamentally about securing one's own needs and advantage.[7]

A contractual way of being in the world and with others differs fundamentally from covenantal ways of being that honor the gifted and graced character of life. What needs to be emphasized is that contractual ways of relating to others and to places had to be invented. They are not inevitable, nor have they always been with us, defining who we understand ourselves to be and shaping how we relate to others. Consider the following characterization by Marcel Hénaff:

> We may ask if the whole of the enormous movement of the modern economy – what is now a global production scheme – might not be the last and most radical way to eliminate the gods, to do away with gift-giving and debt. It may be that we produce, exchange, and consume in order to reduce our relationship to the world and to each other to the management of visible and quantifiable goods, to prevent anything from escaping the calculus of prices and control by the marketplace, so that the very concept of the priceless would disappear. Then nothing would remain outside the realm of commerce. Material innocence would finally have been achieved: no more faults, sin, gift-giving, or forgiveness, nothing other than the mistakes in calculations, positive or negative balance sheets, and payments with agreed deadlines.[8]

What Hénaff is describing is a shift in how relationships are conceived and maintained. In premodern traditional and indigenous cultures, the exchange of gifts was not so much about the accumulation of private possessions but rather about the building and maintaining of bonds of reciprocity that keep people attuned to each other and cognizant of the need each has for the other. Giving a gift was not simply about giving back, repaying a debt, or exchanging property. It was, instead, an invitation to establish, continue, and honor a relationship with another who is understood to be a vital member in a shared life. In a contractual world, relationships clearly remain but they

---

[7]   In today's food system, the pursuit of advantage is most clearly communicated in the ownership of "food futures" by some of the biggest financial institutions of the world. Billions of dollars are now being made speculating on the pricing of food staples like wheat. "While millions of children were skipping meals because the price of basic food grains had risen out of reach, the futures traders on Wall Street and in London were making incredible profits" (Bourne, *The End of Plenty*, 140). As financiers speculate, often driving up prices artificially, millions of people starve and are driven to riot. In this context food ceases to register as a source of life and life's connections. It is instead a source of profit.

[8]   Marcel Hénaff, *The Price of Truth: Gift, Money, and Philosophy* (Stanford: Stanford University Press, 2010), 20–21.

have been instrumentalized and made to serve another aim. What they lack is the overall sense of the good of a *shared* life. What they ignore, and thus fail to value, are the virtues of fidelity and love that make a shared life possible.

To live in an industrialized, consumer society means that people can become divorced not only from their spouses but also from their families and communities, and from the geo-eco-bio-zoological sources of life that daily feed them. To speak this way is to presuppose that the fidelity that characterizes a marriage or friendship is a disposition that orients people not only to each other but also to other creatures and the places in which they live. It is likely that urban and suburban readers will find this way of speaking odd. They shouldn't. For centuries, farmers have often characterized the care of fields and animals as "husbandry," and therefore as an art in which the skills of attention, perseverance, fidelity, and affection were constantly being put to work.[9] Hunters and gatherers, meanwhile, frequently spoke of being married to fellow creatures, and fellow creatures to each other.[10]

Being in a divorced condition means that one lives in the world with others such that their care and cherishing isn't the highest priority. This does not mean that all people have suddenly become malicious and unfeeling

[9] Wendell Berry, the foremost agrarian of our time, puts it this way: "a man who is in the traditional sense a *good* farmer is a husbandman and husband, the begetter and conserver of the earth's bounty, but he is also midwife and motherer. He is a nurturer of life. His work is domestic; he is bound to the household" (*The Art of the Commonplace: The Agrarian Essays of Wendell Berry*, ed. Norman Wirzba [Washington, DC: Counterpoint, 2002], 111).

[10] As one example consider Philippe Descola's account of the Achuar people living in upper Amazonia. A hunter from this tribe explains: "all the creatures that we kill in order to eat – are persons just as we are ... We, the 'complete persons,' must respect those that we kill in the forest, for they are, as it were, our relatives by marriage. They live together among their own relatives; nothing they do is by chance; they talk among themselves; they listen to what we say; they intermarry in proper fashion" (*Beyond Nature and Culture*, trans. Janet Lloyd [Chicago: University of Chicago Press, 2013], 4). Of course, not all characterizations of marriage are the same, nor did all indigenous societies use the category of marriage to describe their relation to animals. What the Achuar show, however, is that people can exist in kinship relationships with creatures that extend well beyond a spouse and a human community, relationships that extend to animals (relatives by marriage) and plants (relatives by blood). For an illuminating discussion of the problems of eating animals understood as kin, see Carlos Fausto's, "Feasting on People: Eating Animals and Humans in Amazonia," *Current Anthropology* 48:4 (August 2007), 497–530. Fausto notes that the eating of meat served to create kinship bonds amongst its eaters. Since the animals eaten were also thought to be persons, in eating them one ran the risk of taking on their qualities. Sometimes this was desired, but other times it was not. Cooking the meat, either by boiling or burning, served the important function of turning the meat into a depersonalized object. "Culinary fire makes it possible for carnivorous meals to be noncannibal, allowing kin to produce each other as kin" (513).

brutes. Acts of love and examples of cherishing remain. But the economies in which many people now move, the practical means by which most food is grown, processed, and distributed, and the politics by which they negotiate these various movements, do not have the nurture of others as their central, animating core. They can't because today's dominant, increasingly global food economy is an anonymous food economy in which consumers have little idea of where their food comes from or the conditions in which it is produced. Following Wendell Berry, we can call this an economy of the one-night stand: we meet in the dark, behind a veil of ignorance, expect a good time, pay our money, assume no responsibility, and ask no questions.[11]

A LONG PREPARATION FOR DIVORCE

How did people come to a divorced condition in which they no longer made the nurture of what nurtures them their highest priority? How did attention, fidelity, and respect come to wane?

To be married, people need to be present to each other. They need to position themselves and their bodies in such a way that they can be receptive, attentive, and available to each other. This takes time, humility, and discipline. But it also takes an economic ordering of one's energies and activities so that in the life one shares with one's spouse one also creates a world and a livelihood. The marriage, in other words, forms the spouses into persons attuned to each other, desiring the good of a shared life. For this good to be realized, however, spouses must also desire the good of the wider economic and social world in which the marriage lives and upon which it depends. A good marriage creates a household that, formed as it is by hospitable love, extends outward to welcome and nourish the world around. If this characterization is correct, then it is in the nature of marital love to extend beyond partner spouses to embrace and nurture the communities and creatures that nurture them, because no marriage or household exists in a self-enclosed bubble. It also follows, then, that divorce signals the rupture of this felt connection and the abandonment of this nurturing, hospitable love. People enter onto a path of divorce when the desire to be attentive and available to their spouse wanes.

What we now need to see is how human cultures can be more or less successful at fostering the practical and metaphysical conditions in which

[11] Wendell Berry, "The Whole Horse," in *The Art of the Commonplace*, 236.

fidelity can be more or less realized. My claim, in what follows, is that the long, circuitous movement from hunting and gathering societies to today's urban shopper testifies to the gradual growth of a divorce habitus and mentality. In this history, we can observe within people a gradual loss of interest in and affection for the creatures they are with, and the places through which they move. The desire to exercise *control over* rather than *care for* the nutritional contexts of life takes over.

Humanity's divorce from the world was not a sudden, inexorable, fully accomplished event. It was prepared slowly, and often unmaliciously, as people positioned themselves with each other and in places in ways that deflected their attention elsewhere, and shrank the range of their affections. A quick tour through the history of humanity will show that a desire for divorce need not be fully formed or understood for people to enter onto paths that will eventually bring them to disaffection with, and separation from, the places and the creatures that feed them.

The world of hunters and gatherers, though it is the world that has defined most of human history, is utterly foreign to most people today. Almost no fully intact hunter-gatherer societies remain. They have been pushed out and exterminated (either by disease or violent assault) by people who found their lifeways to be savage and uncivilized. Owing to archaeological evidence and the fieldwork of anthropologists, we now know that the lives of hunters and gatherers were not marked by unremitting and violent struggle against material scarcity but rather by relative affluence, social equality, and personal freedom.[12]

Why, given today's advanced urban economies, bring up hunter-gatherer societies? It is so that we can consider, however briefly, their practical ways of being in the world, their embodied positioning, and what those ways say about the relationships that join people to others and to places. What habits and sympathies must a hunter have in order to be successful in the hunt? To answer this question we will turn to /I!ae, one of the last great hunters of the Kalahari bushmen. Attending to his life, we can see what fidelity to land and creatures looks like, practically speaking. My aim is not to present all hunters as saints, nor is it to claim that every hunter shares /I!ae's

---

[12]   This shift in perspective is often traced to a 1966 conference at the University of Chicago in which anthropologists, Richard Borshay Lee being one of the foremost among these, argued that hunter-gatherer peoples enjoy less disease, a more diverse diet, less conflict, and far more time for leisure and creative pursuits. One of the conference attendees, Marshall Sahlins, was so captivated by what he learned that he wrote what would become a landmark, best-selling book on the topic, *Stone Age Economics* (New York: de Gruyter, 1972).

sensibilities. It is rather to open a window into a way of life that realizes fidelity in a unique and instructive manner.

To hunt in the Kalahari one must know how to read the tracks of animals. Dense scrub on the ground and the absence of hills means hunters rarely enjoy a far-reaching view. They must know how to interpret the tracks that are visible. James Suzman, an anthropologist who spent time with /I!ae, put it this way:

> To be a good tracker requires engaging in a constant physical dialogue with the environment and ultimately an ability to project oneself into the animals that left the tracks. Like poetry, tracks have a grammar, a meter, and a vocabulary ... Tracking required an ability to read between the marks and infer their maker's mood, circumstances, and intentions. To do this required a lifetime of experience and an intimate knowledge of the animals that made the tracks.[13]

As Suzman followed /I!ae, he was surprised to discover how /I!ae's body registered the movements of animals in fingers and hands that seemed to paint the animals he was tracking. What appeared to Suzman to be a fairly barren, even dead place was fully alive and a source of inspiration to /I!ae. The lives of animals had somehow worked their way into his imagination and body, and animated him from within. "Out of a seemingly insignificant set of indistinct prints, scuffs, and twisted grass stems he would conjure detailed descriptions of their movements and motivations. He'd explain where they were going and why, what they were doing, and where they had been. He'd also tell me their gender, their size, and whether they were healthy, hungry, nervous, or agitated."[14] Clearly, /I!ae was present and available to the place and its life in ways that entirely escaped Suzman. The tracking and hunting habits he honed over many years reflect what I would characterize as an intimate, covenantal relationship with creatures and with his place. /I!ae had learned to orient his being and his body in sympathetic alignment with the animals he hunted, an alignment that communicated his respect for them. Without an intimate, affective knowledge – a multisensory attunement – of the animals he hunted, and the places in which they moved, /I!ae knew he

---

[13] James Suzman, *Affluence without Abundance: The Disappearing World of the Bushmen* (New York: Bloomsbury, 2017), 167.

[14] Ibid., 168. Suzman reports that /I!ae "would talk at length about the idiosyncrasies of individual species and would group species together according to habit, diet, color, gender behavior, teeth, treatment of young, fat content – anything that was meaningful" (169).

would starve.[15] /I!ae's hunting ways testify to a shared life in which the bonds joining people, prey, and place are deeply known, respected, and honored.

The hunting culture that informed and sustained /I!ae's life is, for the most part, a relic of the past. For the last several thousand years, the period known as the Holocene, people have experimented with agricultural ways of being in the world. Meteorological conditions, though prone to variations over time and place, were ideal for the development of diverse agricultural societies that depended on the regularity of seasons. And develop they did. Across the globe, people gradually cultivated land, developed irrigation systems, and domesticated plant and animal species, all giving rise to new social and political forms of life.[16] These forms, in turn, put in place economic structures and legal institutions that positioned (some) people to flourish by mining the fertility of the places they inhabited, and by controlling human populations (often slaves) to do agricultural work. Slowly but surely, region by region, land was compelled to submit to an economic or political calculus, rather than to ecological limits and possibilities. To cite one example: to feed the ambitions of imperial Rome, vast tracts of land were converted to grain fields (*latifundia*) worked by slaves. The management of these fields, directed as they were to maximize production, slowly put the soil (along with many slaves) to death. The land now ruined, people had no choice but to move to "virgin" territory.[17]

---

[15] Suzman notes that /I!ae, and hunters like him, aim for an awareness of the animal and its immediate sensory world: "what it sees, what it smells, and what it hears. Moving silently, knees bent and shoulders stooped, bows in hand, they experience the world around them from the perspectives of both the hunter and the hunted" (ibid., 172).

[16] For an up-to-date assessment of the development of agrarian communities and practices (such as the domestication of plants and animals), and their relation to the development of political entities like a state, see James C. Scott's *Against the Grain: A Deep History of the Earliest States* (New Haven: Yale University Press, 2017). Scott argues convincingly that the standard narrative of human "progress" as a gradual, but steady, ascent from the precarity of hunting and gathering to the stability of agricultural societies is misleading. "The domestication of plants and animals made possible a degree of sedentism that did form the basis of the earliest civilizations and states and their cultural achievements. It rested, however, on an extremely slender and fragile genetic foundation: a handful of crops, a few species of livestock, and a radically simplified landscape that had to be constantly defended against a reconquest by excluded nature. At the same time, the domus was never even remotely self-sufficient. It required a constant subsidy, as it were, from that excluded nature: wood for fuel and building, fish, mollusks, woodland grazing, small game, wild vegetables, fruits, and nuts. In a famine, farmers resorted to all the extradomus resources that hunter-gatherers relied on" (112). Agrarian societies were, from the beginning, highly vulnerable to disease and attack.

[17] The story of the destructiveness of ancient agricultural practices is expertly told by David R. Montgomery in *Dirt: The Erosion of Civilizations*, 2nd edition (Berkeley: University of California Press, 2012).

The shift from hunter-gatherer to farming societies represents a profound, if gradual, change in human sensitivities and sympathies. As we have seen, to be a hunter or gatherer one had to have in mind an immense set of knowledge and a wide variety of skills to secure one's own livelihood. Besides being a keen observer of the movements and preferences of birds, animals, and fish, one had to possess precise knowledge of when a diverse array of plants produced their fruit (or risk losing this precious food to an animal competitor). Without this detailed but also wide-ranging and comprehensive understanding, people could not have flourished. Hunting, foraging, and gathering produced in people a deep appreciation of the inextricable inter-twining of human life and the life of the world.[18] To live well, they needed to bring their bodies into a kind of (near-marital) attunement with the bodies among which they moved. They had, in a manner of speaking, to enter into the lives of the plants and animals they depended upon, sense and feel the world from their point of view, so that they could maximize their own nutritional success.

By contrast, agricultural practices, though tentative and small-scale at first, resulted in a considerable narrowing of knowledge, skill, and sympathy. By specializing in the cultivation of one or two grains, and the domestication of a few species of birds and mammals, a far less complex imagination is presupposed and required. To be sure, this agrarian sensibility is still far more extensive and complex than the simplification of mind witnessed in today's typical shopper of food. But the point remains: agricultural practice represents "a contraction of our species' attention to and practical know-ledge of the natural world, a contraction of diet, a contraction of space, and perhaps a contraction, as well, in the breadth of ritual life."[19] Moreover, the varying transitions to agriculture testify to a new human attitude: the sources of life can be classified and ordered so as to enable people to exert greater control over them. "Unwanted plants growing in a plowed field became weeds, and unwanted animals partial to a farmer's grains or preying on his livestock were declared vermin. The conceptual separation farming commu-nities made between the natural/wild and the human/cultural worlds was so widespread that for a long period social anthropologists believed it was a

---

[18] Recent research and archaeological evidence suggests that it would be a mistake to suppose that indigenous people did not manipulate their environments. For an account that describes the various ways native peoples altered their lands, sometimes radically (as in deforestation), see Charles C. Mann's *1491: New Revelations of the Americas before Columbus*, 2nd edition (New York: Vintage, 2011).

[19] Scott, *Against the Grain*, 92.

human universal."[20] To position oneself before another with the aim of being better able to control that other signals the unraveling of a covenant relationship.

The Holocene, and the agrarian societies that it spawned, made possible forms of imagination in which people could characterize themselves as separate, even exempt, from ecological processes. As Cicero put it in *On the Nature of the Gods* (II, 152), human ingenuity and engineering capacity made possible "a second world within the world of nature," a world tailored to suit human desires and ambitions. This "second world," a world we most often associate with the growth of civilizations, the development of ever more sophisticated technologies, and the steady expansion of humanity's footprint upon the earth, rests upon the dubious assumption that cultures can thrive at the expense of the places that nurture them. It rests upon the disastrous notion that economic success can be premised upon ecological degradation. And it results in people who do not think they need to nurture the world that nurtures them. This second world, with all its technological sophistication and economic power, is at war with the world of nature, and is determined to stamp out or override whatever integrity or sanctity places and their creatures may at one time have possessed. It communicates a breaking of the bond between humans and the earth, and a diminishment of the practices of fidelity that nurture the creatures that nurture us.

The construction of a "second world" has led to the dramatic alteration of the natural world upon which it depends. There is, today, hardly a river or wetland on earth that has not been altered, drained, dammed, or rerouted by us. The very chemistry and temperature of our oceans has changed as industrial and agricultural processes have spewed their pollutants into the atmosphere and into stream runoff. Seventy-five percent of the planet's land surface has now been subdued by us, as land has been brought under cultivation, forests felled, mountains blown up and mined, and cities expanded. Human beings and the animals they have domesticated now make up 90 percent of the mammal biomass on earth. One thousand years ago, by contrast, they accounted for only 2 percent. Moreover, the very meaning of domestication has changed to mean the radical manipulation, even invention, of species. So deep and extensive is our alteration of earth that, "It's as if aliens appeared with megamallets and laser chisels and started resculpting every continent to better suit them.

---

[20] Suzman, *Affluence without Abundance*, 213.

We've turned the landscape into another form of architecture; we've made the planet our sandbox."[21]

Earth system scientists now argue that the human presence on earth has become such a controlling and dominating presence that it is no longer accurate to name our epoch the Holocene. We have entered the Anthropocene, the time when human ambition, power, and mastery now influence, even determine, every inch of the planet and all the processes of life, ranging from the cellular level to earth's overall climate. To be sure, natural processes like tectonic plate shifts, photosynthesis, the carbon cycle, and weather are still at work. But to have entered the Anthropocene is to have entered a time in which the effects of natural processes can no longer be understood apart from human activity. If at one time human economies were firmly constrained by natural potential and limits, the situation is now reversed: industrial economies have grown so vast and deep as to determine and direct what used to be thought of as "natural" processes. In the Anthropocene the "second world" becomes a total world that absorbs "nature" within itself, thereby rendering the idea of an "outside" obsolete. The shape of the world, and the character of much of its life, now depends on what (some) humans decide to do. As Bruno Latour has argued, this situation is entirely new in the history of the world. We are not simply in a "crisis" in which, after a while, things will return to some "normal" state. Rather, we inhabit a time of "mutation" in which our relations to the world and its creatures have been fundamentally altered.[22]

There is a fair amount of debate about when the Anthropocene age began. Paul Crutzen, the Nobel Prize-winning chemist widely credited with coining the term, has argued that we should look to the Industrial Revolution, specifically the invention of the steam engine, as the official start date, since this is when the extensive burning of fossil fuels took off (which has led to the accumulation of greenhouse gases in the atmosphere that are slowly warming the planet). Others argue that we should look to the period right after World War II, also characterized as the time of the Great Acceleration, since that is when consumption rates around the globe exploded.[23] Whatever date we choose, it is clear that the Anthropocene represents a new age for

---

[21] Diane Ackerman, *The Human Age: The World Shaped by Us* (New York: W. W. Norton & Company, 2014), 11.

[22] Bruno Latour, *Facing Gaia: Eight Lectures on the New Climatic Regime* (Cambridge: Polity Press, 2017), 8.

[23] For a detailed description of this history, see J. R. McNeill and Peter Engelke, *The Great Acceleration: An Environmental History of the Anthropocene since 1945* (Cambridge, MA: The Belknap Press of Harvard University Press, 2014).

earth, an age in which human histories and geological history have merged into one indivisible movement that the historian Dipesh Chakrabarty has called "geostory."[24] In the Anthropocene, the supposed divisions between nature/culture and ecology/economy that were established in the Holocene have broken down.

The Anthropocene also reflects a new situation for humanity. Who is the human being (*anthropos*) that now defines and determines the world, and how should we think about the ways people have positioned themselves in the world and with others? Can reflection on the ways we procure our food be of help in answering these questions?

AGRICULTURE IN AN ANTHROPOCENE WORLD

In the early years of the twentieth century, while war still raged across much of Europe, another battle was opening up in America over the meaning and value of life. Though not directly aimed at people, or fought on massive, muddy battlefields, it was nonetheless the beginning of a slow and systematic assault against life. The theater of this war was not the battlefields of the Somme or Verdun but rather the farm fields of the Plains and Midwestern states. More precisely, it was a nonmalicious, though nonetheless deadly, campaign directed against the land itself, and therefore also against all the creatures that depend on the land for their life. Though artillery and bullets rarely made an appearance in this battle, barbed wire, heavy machinery, and poisonous chemicals certainly did. Like its mostly European cousin, it was promoted with banners that promised to lead humanity into a glorious and prosperous future.

Agriculture as War? Eating as One's Participation in the Degradation of Life?

The degradation at work within today's food and agricultural systems did not begin suddenly in the twentieth century's second decade. Forms of assault upon land, animals, and people had been at work long before, most notably in agricultural contexts that depended on the brutality of slavery. What was new and of signal importance is that in the early decades of the twentieth century a totalizing mode of production, a modality meant to be universally applied to all the diverse contexts of agriculture, was coming into

---

[24] Dipesh Chakrabarty, "The Climate of History: Four Theses," *Critical Inquiry* 35:2 (Winter 2009), 197–222.

view and was being promoted and applied. This industrial system, communicated in the idioms of rational management and efficient production, was not welcomed by traditional farmers because they understood their way of life, even life itself, to be under attack. For it to be implemented, a great number of educators, growers, suppliers, financiers, politicians, and eaters had to give their support. And to be successful, people had to think about farms, farm animals, farm work, farmworkers, and food in radically different ways, ways that hardly promoted fidelity to the land or its creatures.

The character of this life-degrading system, its philosophical presuppositions, ideals, and objectives, come into clearer view with the birth of what must have been considered a fairly innocuous organization, the American Society of Agricultural Engineers (ASAE). Founded in 1907, the ASAE was established to bring agriculture out of the dark ages of hard manual labor, small-scale production, low yields, and diversified crops and livestock. If one looked at the American agricultural landscape at the turn of the twentieth century, what one saw was a bewildering assortment of farms, each engaging in practices that often differed significantly from each other. If farms were to become more efficient and productive, farms and farmers needed to change. Both needed to be brought under a more rational, standardized regimen of production. And for that to happen, the principles and tools of engineering needed to be applied to agriculture.

The aim of the ASAE was to remake farms into factories that would maximize yield, standardize product, and mechanize labor. E. B. McCormick, one of the early presidents of the ASAE, put it this way in his 1917 presidential address: "The farm in its economic sense is merely an industrial plant. Labor and machinery are employed and capital invested."[25] Raymond Olney, another leader in the field and a President of the ASAE, spoke similarly when in the same year he published in the journal *Power Farming* his essay "The Farm Power House: A Factory Idea":

> No one will object to calling a farm a factory. It is a factory. The soil and seed are the raw materials, and from these are manufactured a variety of finished products, through the agencies of sun, air, moisture, power, and implements. The finished products of the farm factory are cereal, forest, vegetable, and fruit crops, and livestock and livestock products, are they not?[26]

---

[25] E. B. McCormick, "President's Annual Address," in the *Transactions of the ASAE* 11 (1917), as quoted in Deborah Fitzgerald's *Every Farm a Factory: The Industrial Ideal in American Agriculture* (New Haven: Yale University Press, 2003), 89.

[26] Raymond Olney, "The Farm Power House: A Factory Idea," *Power Farming* (November 1917), 7, as quoted in Fitzgerald, *Every Farm a Factory*, 109.

The idea that farmers are husbands of the land and its creatures is entirely absent from this characterization of agriculture.

The sentiments of McCormick and Olney reflect a new cultural sensibility that was emerging in the early decades of the twentieth century, a sensibility that, in terms of its own logic, undermines life's sacred value. It is a sensibility that rests on a fundamental contradiction, because the operational, production logic that requires the *degradation* of life's creatures – by reducing them to machines – cannot also result in their *nurture*.

Efficient production and maximum yield demanded that living creatures be managed *as though they were dead.* Just as the invention of various machines in the eighteenth century, most notably the clock, gave rise to a mechanical understanding of the world, so too the invention of factories in the twentieth century, most notably Henry Ford's automobile plant, resulted in a routinized, standardized, and highly controlled vision of work that was then to be applied to the diverse sectors of society and the economy.[27] Factories had become the model of industrial production systems. As Deborah Fitzgerald describes it, this industrial system was revolutionizing society and was now to be systematically applied to agriculture.

> Timeliness of operations, large-scale production sites, mechanization, standardization of product, specialization, speed of throughput, routinization of the workforce, and a belief that success was based first and foremost upon a notion of "efficiency" – all these principles were drawn directly from the factories and businesses only recently declared successful ... Yet no single innovation created the revolutionary context; rather, each was located within a matrix of technical, social, and ideological relationships that both created and sustained the change. Each innovation depended on other technologies, credit systems, transportation systems, family relationships, tax base, and legislative support, to name a few.[28]

The end result was a transformed society and a profound shift in our understanding of life. A diverse, organic, creaturely world was being remade

---

[27] Frederick Winslow Taylor, trained as a mechanical engineer, gave a clear philosophical account of this factory vision in *The Principles of Scientific Management*, an immensely influential book first published in 1911.

[28] Fitzgerald, *Every Farm a Factory*, 5. "Beginning in the 1920s, farmers and their families had to contend with a new set of opportunities and constraints, most of which grew out of the new industrial production systems. These systems, epitomized by the modern mass production factory and industrial boardroom, linked capital, raw materials, transportation networks, communication systems, and newly trained technical experts. Interconnected and often sprawling, these systems of production and consumption functioned like grids into which fit the more identifiable components of industrialization – the tractors, paved roads, bank credit, migrant labor, and commodity markets" (3).

into a homogenous, mechanical realm in which the most advanced tools of management and manipulation were to be applied. The complexity and mystery of life itself was being reduced to an engineering problem meant to be solved by technical means (not surprisingly, the ASAE would eventually change its name to the American Society of Agricultural and Biological Engineers).[29]

Why does this matter? A world reduced to manipulable, mechanical bits is essentially a lifeless world. Though we might still speak of living beings or living organisms, the moment these beings are understood in terms of their rational management and technical manipulation is also the moment that their integrity or sanctity as living beings is violated.[30] A cow, rather than being a living organism deserving of respect and care, is reduced to a meat and milk production machine to be managed so as to maximize product. Farmworkers, rather than being celebrated as skilled artisans who work in sympathy with diverse forms of plant and animal life, are reduced to unskilled laborers doing menial jobs paid at the lowest compensatory rates possible. They can, and will, eventually be replaced by machines. Meanwhile, plants like wheat or corn are reducible to mechanical stems that can be modified to increase their yield. In his 1928 essay "Mechanization of Agriculture," L. J. Fletcher wrote: "It is entirely practical and possible to make mechanical changes in plants. If a plant presents difficulties in its present form to the use of mechanical power in cultivating or harvesting, it may be changed."[31] And the soil itself? Well, it is just a container or warehouse that

---

[29]   In 2005, and by a strong vote of the membership, the ASAE changed its name to the American Society of Agricultural and Biological Engineers (ASABE). President Jerry L. Wille said, "The profession has evolved and expanded over the last almost 100 years. Our engineering skills deal with the entire food and fiber chain and all agricultural and biological systems. Now our professional Society name will be representative and descriptive of this breadth and depth." Wille was not voicing a new sentiment. Already in 1937 ASAE member C. O. Reed, a professor at Ohio State University, declared that agricultural engineering was distinguished from other kinds of engineering because "it is the engineering of biology" (both quotes from the ASABE's website: www.asabe.org/media/67573/timeline_reverse.pdf). Living systems are reducible to mechanical systems, and so can be manipulated as needed or desired.

[30]   In his book *The Anticipatory Corpse: Medicine, Power, and the Care of the Dying* (Notre Dame: University of Notre Dame Press, 2011) Jeffrey P. Bishop shows how this mechanical metaphysic gradually took hold of the world of medicine, thereby reducing human beings to patients in which the extensions of life and functioning are the primary concern. Quantity rather than quality measures are now made to determine a human life's value.

[31]   L. J. Fletcher, "Mechanization of Agriculture," *Farm Implements News* 49 (September 13, 1928), 22–23, as quoted in Fitzgerald, *Every Farm a Factory*, 104. That Fletcher's article was published in a farm machinery journal is to be expected because from its earliest days the

holds the material elements – most notably nitrogen, potassium, and phosphorous – that fuel plant growth.

Machines do not yield before, respect, or love life. Instead they reduce living creatures to manipulable bits so that they can better serve the dictates of the industrial logic that machines represent. Cows, farmers, plants, soil – all can be remade and used up as necessary so as to produce the goals set by the machine's master. Not surprisingly, when cows, farmers, and fields are treated in this mechanical way they are quickly exhausted, exploited, or simply discarded. The food produced by this system does not have the nurture of life or the health of eaters as its first concern. It can't, because what matters most is the remaking of food's production and consumption into mechanical acts that are determined by concerns for efficiency, standardization, transportability, and profitability. In the shift of agriculture from the art of husbandry to the science of engineering, the violation and degradation of life comes into view.

This brief look at the early years of industrial agriculture helps us appreciate a fundamental characteristic that has come to define humanity's place in the world: the world we live through, the world to which we are necessarily bound, has ceased to register as a living world that evokes in us the dispositions of fidelity, care, and cherishing. It can't, because it is believed to be a separate, dead world composed of multiple bits that can be engineered and ordered at will.

This way of thinking was not confined to agriculture. Urban planning and architecture, as seen, for instance, in the modernist designs of Le Corbusier, followed the same factory, mechanical logic by reimagining a house as "a machine to live in." The best design starts with the assumption that a place is a "blank canvas" upon which engineers then erect buildings to maximize efficiency of movement and space allocation. Le Corbusier's Plan Voisin, his never realized idea for the rebuilding of an area near the center of Paris, assumed that whatever was there before could be bulldozed to oblivion. And the skyscraper apartment complexes he planned to build, all arranged according to the precision of a geometric grid, assumed that people were more or less the same, each a mechanical, standardized bit that simply fits within the overall machine. Not surprisingly, the housing projects inspired by modernist ideals that were eventually constructed to house growing

aims of the ASAE went hand in hand with the spread of farm machinery. Farm implement dealers were key contributors and boosters to the cause of engineering the countryside.

(often poor) urban populations in the most efficient way possible had to be destroyed. They were found to be dehumanizing and demoralizing, an attack on the sanctity and idiosyncrasy of human life.[32]

The industrial logic that has here been briefly described is the practical realization of dispositions long in the making, dispositions that presuppose we can live in a divorced, even warlike, condition with the earth and its creatures. This logic rests on several fundamental assumptions: a dead world, the divisibility of nature and culture, and then nature's own divisibility into an infinite multiplicity of bits or objects. It is a way of thinking that is utterly foreign to hunter-gatherers and traditional farmers. Philippe Descola characterizes this new philosophical orientation well by saying that "nature ceased to be a unifying arrangement of things, however, disparate, and became a domain of objects that were subject to autonomous laws that formed a background against which the arbitrariness of human activities could exert its many-faceted fascination."[33]

Insofar as nature came to be understood as a self-standing, separate realm, a mere stage upon which humans enacted the only dramas that counted, or a massive warehouse from which they could extract whatever they wanted, people could also think of themselves as autonomous and self-contained, moving within the freestanding realm of culture.[34] This new conception of human being-in-the-world, in other words, entailed a new conception of the human at the same time, a conception in which people considered

---

[32] For a discussion of how modernist, rationalist architecture, in some of its expressions, assumes abstracted human beings separated from their places, see Murray A. Rae's *Architecture and Theology: The Art of Place* (Waco: Baylor University Press, 2017), 159–167

[33] Descola, *Beyond Nature and Culture*, xv. The work of Latour, beginning with *We Have Never Been Modern* (Cambridge, MA: Harvard University Press, 1993), and then developed in multiple subsequent books like *The Politics of Nature: How to Bring the Sciences into Democracy* (Cambridge, MA: Harvard University Press, 2004), has argued that the modern belief in the separation of nature and culture is, in practice and in fact, a deception. Cultures have never been separated from nature. What moderns did is characterize the range of "agency" in certain ways so as to exclude from the political process the wide sweep of physical places and most all of its nonhuman creatures. We have only, ever been entangled with others in places. Latour argues it is time for our political processes to wake up to this embodied, lived reality.

[34] Clifford Geertz gave a succinct formulation of this separation when he wrote "The concept of culture I espouse . . . is essentially a semiotic one. Believing, with Max Weber, that man is an animal suspended in webs of significance he has himself spun, I take culture to be those webs" (*The Interpretation of Cultures* [New York: Basic Books, 1973], 5). Following from this influential view, the work of humanity is to apply the meanings and values of a culture constructed in a society's head, and then apply them to a world that is otherwise devoid of meaning and value.

themselves to be emancipated from nature altogether, exempt from its flows and demands, and free to retreat into the worlds of their own making.

In a penetrating analysis of the cultural forces that led to the Anthropocene, the Indian novelist Amitav Ghosh argues that a new conception of human freedom develops in modernity that extricates people from, and renders them oblivious to, the ecological contexts in which they live. Indeed, one could argue that "being independent of Nature was considered one of the defining characteristics of freedom itself. Only those people who had thrown off the shackles of their environment were thought to be endowed with historical agency."[35] As modern writers often described it, those lacking historical agency of this sort, people like hunter-gatherers, farmers, peasants, women, and slaves – precisely those people that are bound through their labor to the land and to the material contexts/constraints of life – failed to be human at all.

This especially modern conception of freedom rests on a deception, a willful turning away from context, even a belligerent blindness. It is a conception that renders a picture of human beings as fundamentally disembodied and dis-earthed, floating apart from earth and never really within it. Latour has seconded Ghosh's observation by noting that, "while we have had social sciences for modernizing and emancipating *humans*, we have not the faintest idea of what sort of social science is needed for *Earthlings* buried in the task of explicitating their newly discovered attachments."[36]

The emancipation Ghosh and Latour describe is not an abstraction. Today's industrial agriculture and food production system reflect this sensibility in food products that are shorn of all indications that they have their roots in the ground. As the development of "food products" like Soylent demonstrate, why not think of eating as a strictly engineered affair in which the chemical nutrients our machinelike bodies need to survive can be consumed with the sip of a beverage? Complete nutrition can be achieved

---

[35] Amitav Ghosh, *The Great Derangement: Climate Change and the Unthinkable* (Chicago: The University of Chicago Press, 2016), 119. Ghosh continues: "freedom came to be seen as a way of 'transcending' the constraints of material life – of exploring new regions of the human mind, spirit, emotion, consciousness, interiority: freedom became a quantity that resided entirely in the minds, bodies, and desires of human beings" (120).

[36] In Bruno Latour's lecture "A Plea for Earthly Sciences," delivered at the British Sociological Association in 2007 (available at www.bruno-latour.fr/sites/default/files/102-BSA-GB_0 .pdf). The term "explicitation," borrowed from the philosopher Peter Sloterdijk, refers to the process whereby people become more aware of the fragility of the material/ecological contexts that make their existence possible. Air, water, land, and all the biophysical processes that were once relegated to the backdrop or stage, now come to the fore and are rendered "explicit" because we sense our own extinction in their demise.

in a bottle. By "taking eating off your plate," Soylent executives assume that people are busy and should not need to bother with food production, preparation, consumption, and cleanup. They should be freed to live lives of their own choosing.[37] This sort of "food" perpetuates the illusion that people live through worlds of their own making. Human ingenuity and technological prowess are making it possible for us to "make to order" whatever food item people desire. In the future, all we will need is a lab, 3D printers, the right software programs, and engineers will design foods we have yet to imagine. Could there be a more imperious and disconnected form of eating?

The divorce between people and land and between people and creatures is complete when food production is an engineering feat and eating a mechanical act. In this development, the eating that people do, rather than rooting and stitching them more deeply into the world, has the effect of making them blind to the land and the creatures upon which they daily depend. Blindness matters, because people cannot love what they don't see. They cannot cherish and protect what they do not believe to be of sacred value.

Fidelity to the world, to other creatures, and to fellow human beings requires that we learn to resist the objectification and commodification of things that define industrial processes and econometric thinking. The food we eat, and the places that grow it, are sacred gifts. They are worthy of our care and celebration. What we now need to see is how a theology of eating helps us appreciate and live into a divinely given world, and there take up the postures of welcome and hospitality that testify to God's primordial, forever nurturing love.

---

[37] It is ironic that a food product designed to free people from all attention to or care for the land also promotes its product as a way of saving the planet: "Food wastes more than just our time. Because all Soylent drinks are made from plants, they require less water and produce less CO_2 than livestock. Our drinks also reduce food waste with a year-long shelf life and don't require refrigeration, unlike fruits and vegetables that get tossed after a few days or weeks in the fridge" (see www.soylent.com).

2

Thinking Theologically about Food

To live, we must daily break the body and shed the blood of Creation. When we do this knowingly, lovingly, skillfully, reverently, it is a sacrament. When we do it ignorantly, greedily, clumsily, destructively, it is a desecration. In such desecration we condemn ourselves to spiritual and moral loneliness, and others to want.[1]

To eat is still something more than to maintain bodily functions. People may not understand what that "something more" is, but they nonetheless desire to celebrate it. They are still hungry and thirsty for sacramental life.[2]

Why did God create a world in which every living creature must eat?

This is a humbling, even terrifying question, particularly for people who are intimately involved in the finding, growing, and harvesting of food. Eating is no idle or trifling activity. It is the means of life itself – but also death. For any creature to live, countless seen and unseen others must die, often by being eaten themselves. Life as we know it *depends* on death, *needs* death, which means that death is not simply the cessation of life but its precondition. Death is eating's steadfast accomplice. It is also each creature's biological end, for no matter how much or how well we eat (for the sake of life's preservation), we cannot erase our mortal condition.[3] Why eat if eating,

---

[1] Wendell Berry, "The Gift of Good Land," in *The Gift of Good Land: Further Essays Cultural and Agricultural* (New York: North Point Press, 1981), 281.

[2] Alexander Schmemann, *For the Life of the World: Sacraments and Orthodoxy* (Crestwood, NY: St. Vladimir's Seminary Press, 1963), 16.

[3] In this book, I assume that eating is originally part of God's good creation. Though eating takes on a different character after the fall, it is not itself an effect or sign of a fallen creation. Did pre-fall eating entail death? The biblical story is not clear about this. Genesis 2–3 suggests that we are not immortal by nature but must constantly receive life as a gift (Adam

even vegetarian eating, implicates us in so much death? Why eat if eating is the daily reminder of our own need and mortality?

We could try to imagine all creatures as self-subsisting, noneating entities that never take a bite, and thus presumably avoid the realities of eating death. But then we would also have to envision a tasteless and lonely world without belonging and fellowship, a world without the varied delights that accompany the procuring, preparing, and sharing of food. Eating joins people to each other, to other creatures and the world, and to God through forms of "natural communion" too complex to fathom.[4] It introduces us to a graced world of hospitality, a creation that from the beginning (and constantly through its soil) absorbs death and makes room for newness of life. Eating involves us in a daily life and death drama in which, beyond all comprehension, some life is sacrificed so that other life can thrive. It establishes a membership that confirms all creatures as profoundly in need of each other and God to provide life's nutrition and vitality.

Food is a holy and humbling mystery. Every time a creature eats, it participates in God's life-giving yet costly ways, ways that simultaneously affirm creation as a delectable gift, and as a divinely ordered membership of interdependent need and suffering and help. Whenever people come to the table they demonstrate with the unmistakable evidence of their stomachs that they are not self-subsisting gods. They are finite and mortal creatures dependent on God's many good gifts: sunlight, photosynthesis, decomposition, soil fertility, water, bees and butterflies, chickens, sheep, cows, gardeners, farmers, cooks, strangers, and friends (the list goes on and on). Eating reminds us that we participate in a grace-saturated world, a blessed creation worthy of attention, care, and celebration. Despite what food marketers may say, there really is no such thing as "cheap" or "convenient" food. Real food, the food that is the source of creaturely health and delight, is precious because it is a fundamental means through which God's nurture and love for the whole creation are expressed.

The biblical wisdom writer Joshua ben Sira understood better than most that the world we share is an awe-inspiring and terror-inducing place. Creation is marvelous and desirable – think of how much of it tastes so

---

and Eve are expelled from the Garden precisely so they would not have access to the tree of life and live forever). I discuss the meanings of death and its relation to food in Chapter 4.

[4] In *Philosophy of Economy: The World as Household* (New Haven: Yale University Press, 2000), Sergei Bulgakov says, "The boundary between living and nonliving is actually removed in food. Food is natural communion – partaking of the flesh of the world. When I take food, I am eating world matter in general, and in so doing, I truly and in reality find the world within me and myself in the world, I become part of it" (103).

good – but it is also fierce and strange, capable of poisoning or killing us despite our best efforts to be careful. Joshua ben Sira observed that creation forms a vast membership in which each creature is made to supplement the needs of others, a membership in which God sends down snow and rain and the life-giving light of the sun. Even so, creation is a dangerous place where hailstones, withering heat, and strange sea monsters threaten human securities and pretensions. God "consumes the mountains and burns up the wilderness" (Sirach 43:21). Who can understand this world and this life? Before the immensity and marvel of creation there is always more to say, even as people acknowledge they "could never say enough" (43:27). Or they are simply reduced to silence, offering a faltering praise, while eating their way into mysteries they are unable to comprehend. In a manner reminiscent of Job, Joshua ben Sira wonders where people will find the resources and the wisdom to be faithful to a world in which life depends on so much they don't understand.

The character and pace of much contemporary life makes it less likely that people will perceive the mystery of food, or receive it as a precious gift and sign of God's sustaining care. Though information about food abounds, many of today's eaters are among the most ignorant the world has ever known. This is because people lack the sensitivity, imagination, and understanding that come from the growing, preserving, and preparing of food. Not having the attention or skill that develops while working in a garden and kitchen, they also miss the necessary knowledge, affection, and insight. Too many people don't really know where food comes from or what is practically required (ecologically but also culturally) for food to be healthy and plentiful over the long term. As a result, they risk perpetuating what Wendell Berry has called one of the great superstitions of our consumer age, namely the superstition that "money brings forth food."[5]

Long ago, Aristotle maintained that for us to know something deeply we must be able to give an account of the "four causes" that come together to make that thing what it is.[6] On this ancient view, to understand what food is requires that we be able to (1) give a detailed account of the material elements and ecological contexts that come together in any food item, and be able to say something about the quality of what is there (material cause); (2) distinguish between differing food items, and be able to say why the

---

[5] Wendell Berry, "In Distrust of Movements," in *Citizenship Papers* (Washington, DC: Shoemaker & Hoard, 2003), 48.

[6] Aristotle describes the "four causes" in *Physics* II, 3 and 7 and again as a feature of wisdom in *Metaphysics* I, 2–3.

distinctions matter (formal cause); (3) appreciate the many geo-bio-chemical processes that contribute to a plant or animal's growth, and the culinary traditions and recipes that enable us to transform raw elements into delicious food (efficient cause); and (4) give an answer for why eating matters, providing an account of the many ecological, physiological, and social purposes of food (final cause).

This Aristotelian account is helpful to have in mind because it shows us how much there is to think about when we think about food. It demonstrates that for us to claim an understanding of food we need as much as possible to be intimately involved in its production and preparation. Failing this practical involvement we will not appreciate the many requirements and costs of food, costs that go well beyond the sticker price. We will not know the health benefits (to us and to fellow creatures) that follow from particular kinds of food production and harvest. Nor will we be able to advocate for a just and sustainable food system, a system in which fields and waters are protected, animals are humanely treated, and workers are safe and paid a living wage. To know food with depth we need to know *what* is there, *how* it came to be there, *what* it is for, and *why* it matters that we have it in particular sorts of ways.

To eat is to be implicated in a vast, complex, interweaving set of life-and-death dramas in which we are only one character among many. No matter how solitary our eating experience may be, every sniff, chomp, and swallow connects us to vast global trade networks, and thus to biophysical and social worlds far beyond ourselves. The moment we chew on anything we participate in regional, geographic histories and in biochemical processes that, for all their diversity and complexity, defy our wildest imaginations and most thorough attempts at comprehension. The minute we contemplate or talk about eating, we show ourselves to be involved in culinary traditions and cultural taboos, as well as moral quandaries and spiritual quests. To amend an ecologist's maxim: we can never only bite into one thing.

Food is about the relationships that join us to the earth, fellow creatures, loved ones and guests, and ultimately God. How we eat testifies to whether we value the creatures we live with and depend upon. To eat is to savor *and* struggle with the mystery of creatureliness. When our eating is mindful, we celebrate the goodness of fields, gardens, forests, and watersheds, and the skill of those who can nurture seed and animal life into delicious food. We acknowledge and honor God as the giver of every good and perfect gift. But we also learn to correct our own arrogance, boredom, and ingratitude. Eating invites people to develop a deeper appreciation for where they are and who they are with so that their eating can be a sacramental rather than a sacrilegious act. A thoughtful, theological relation to food makes possible the discovery that eating is among the most intimate and pleasing ways possible for us to enter into the memberships of creation and find there the God who daily blesses and feeds life.

NAMING AND NARRATING A WORLD OF FOOD

The way we think about food depends on how we name and narrate the world in which we eat. Food does not simply appear, nor is everything food. It is a chosen and named entity that draws its significance from the wider contexts in which it appears. To appreciate the significance of naming, consider the difference between calling a plant a "weed," a "flower," or a "fruit." Any of these names carries with it a set of dispositions and responses that have widely different effects: people *eradicate* weeds, *behold* flowers, and *savor* fruit. How we name and narrate things will greatly affect how we relate to them.

How should we name the world? One very common, though by no means simple, way is to describe it as the realm of "nature."[7] A great number of meanings have been attached to this word because what we think about the natural world depends on the time and culture we are in. For some, nature refers to the world apart from human artifice and culture. As such, it finds its most pristine form in wilderness, a place where people may occasionally visit but are not expected or encouraged to stay.[8] For others, nature is the stage for human action, the place where the natural resources (wood, oil, water, etc.) we need to fuel and feed our lives can be found. In this view, nature resembles something like a massive warehouse or store. Though it exists in

---

[7] In *Keywords: A Vocabulary of Culture and Society* (New York: Oxford University Press, 1976), Raymond Williams observed that nature is "perhaps the most complex word in the language" (219). It encompasses the essential quality of a thing, the inherent force active in things, and the material realm of things themselves. If we focus only on its third aspect we soon discover that the natural world can be described in various, even contradictory, ways, ranging from the relatively benign and life-giving Mother Nature to the cutthroat arena of Tennyson's "nature red in tooth and claw."

[8] It is important to note how "unnatural" the term wilderness is since it has an extensive cultural history. For an excellent brief history of the term in its American context, see William Cronon's essay "The Trouble with Wilderness; Or, Getting Back to the Wrong Nature," in *Uncommon Ground: Rethinking the Human Place in Nature*, ed. William Cronon (New York: W. W. Norton, 1996). Cronon shows how "wilderness" underwrites narratives about nature as the "frontier" and the realm of the "sublime." Wilderness could thus act as a cathedral to inspire worship and as the evil domain that needs to be tamed and subdued. For a more extended and detailed discussion, see Roderick Nash's *Wilderness and the American Mind*, 4th edition (New Haven: Yale University Press, 2001).

its own right, one of its key functions and primary sources of value is its ability to service human needs and desires. For yet others, nature is the cleansing place where the pretensions and distortions of culture can be seen and corrected. According to this view, people go to nature so they can discover what is essential to a good human life.

The science that has been used to describe nature has also varied greatly through time. In his classic study *The Idea of Nature*, R. G. Collingwood observed that Greek natural science understood the world to be permeated by mind or *nous*. The presence of mind, sometimes characterized as divine, accounted for the regularity and order we see. Here the whole world is akin to an organic body with the principles of intelligence internal to itself. Beginning in the sixteenth and seventeenth centuries, however, a distinctly modern view of science emerged that cast the world as a machine. As such, the world is devoid of its own intelligence and value. Though it operates according to natural laws that can be understood and manipulated, the world's intelligibility and reason for being exist wholly outside itself. It has no purpose or point other than the one humans assign to it. Toward the end of the eighteenth century a view of science developed that took as its model for the world not an organic body or a machine but the social processes of historical development. Central to this model is the idea that nature's elements, much like a society's members and institutions, are constantly changing and on the move. Nature is dynamic and unfixed. There is little about it that is "natural" in the sense of being essentially the same through time.[9]

More recently we see that some scientists have called into question the idea of the intelligibility of nature itself. Steven Weinberg, a Nobel Prize-winning physicist, argues that scientific research gives us a "rather chilling" picture because it yields a world that is pointless:

> Not only do we not find any point to life laid out for us in nature, no objective basis for our moral principles, no correspondence between what we think is the moral law and the laws of nature, of the sort imagined by philosophers from Anaximander and Plato to Emerson. We even learn that the emotions that we most treasure, our love for our wives and husbands and children, are made possible by chemical processes in our brains that are what they are as the result of natural selection acting on chance mutations over millions of years.[10]

---

[9] R. G. Collingwood, *The Idea of Nature* (New York: Oxford University Press, 1960).
[10] Steven Weinberg, "Without God," *New York Review of Books* 55:14 (September 25, 2008). www.nybooks.com/articles/archives/2008/sep/25/without-god/.

If the whole universe, and thus also the minds attempting to think about it, are the effect of accidental motion, then the conclusion that the world has meaning or value cannot be trusted. A random world should evoke no admiration. Nor should an accidental mind garner our respect. In Weinberg's view, nothing about the world and its life is sacred. We will have finally become honest about the world and ourselves when we "get out of the habit of worshipping anything."

This brief tour of some of nature's narrations demonstrates that an account of the world's meaning or significance is not provided alongside it. Though we find ourselves in a world, why it matters or what it is for are not similarly given. The meaning and purpose of the world are something people must work out in their interactions with it. As we have just seen, the meanings can differ widely. For some the world is an organism that has integrity that can be violated. For others it is a machine that can be manipulated at will because its value is entirely of an instrumental sort. For yet others, the ideas of meaning and value are themselves fictions and so are not to be taken with much seriousness. Each narration of the world calls forth different kinds of expectations and responsibilities in us: we might show respect, reverence, and restraint, or we might calculate ownership, control, and profit, or we might simply be bored and comfortably numb. Whichever narration we live by will have decisive significance for what we think about food and how we relate to our food-providing world.

A theological account names and narrates the world as "creation."[11] Though not necessarily opposed to scientific narrations as nature, a narration of the world as creation means that our descriptions of the world's members and our telling of the meaning of the world's movements must always be articulated with reference to God as the world's source, sustenance, and end.[12] Understood as creation, the world is not a random accident, nor is it valueless matter waiting for us to give it significance. It is, rather, the concrete expression of God's hospitable love making room for what is not God to be and to flourish. Theologically understood, food is not reducible to material stuff. It is the provision and nurture of God made pleasing and delectable. Food is God's love made nutritious and delicious. Eating is the daily reminder that life comes to us as a gift.

---

[11] I develop the difference between narrations of the world "as nature" versus "as creation" in *From Nature to Creation: A Christian Vision for Understanding and Loving Our World* (Grand Rapids: Baker Academic, 2015).

[12] I have developed aspects of the character of creation in *The Paradise of God: Renewing Religion in an Ecological Age* (New York: Oxford University Press, 2003).

The doctrine of creation is a rich teaching that has wide-ranging implications for how we think of ourselves, the world, and our place (and responsibilities) within it. It touches on how the world began, why the world is at all, why it has the character that it does, and what it might mean for the world to be whole and perfect. Narrated in a Christian way, creation is intimately bound up with the Trinitarian life of the Father, Son, and Holy Spirit.[13]

The event or happening of creation cannot (as deists supposed) be confined to something that occurred only long ago at the beginning. Creation, what we might also call the place and work of divine creativity, is ongoing because the life of God is ongoing. Moreover, the life of creatures is in some sense a participation in the divine life because it is only the animating presence (Spirit or breath) of God to creatures that keeps them from returning to the dust from which they came (Psalm 104:29).

If the world is named as creation, and creation is narrated in a Trinitarian way, then the movement of the world must always be understood and evaluated in terms of the "movement" between the Father, Son, and Holy Spirit.[14] Considering the Trinity, and thereby glimpsing something of the character and significance of the divine relations operative there, we gain the perspective we need to evaluate the mundane relationships that constitute our world today. As Hans Urs von Balthasar put it, if God creates a world, God also communicates God's own Trinitarian love as the basis and goal of created life. "The vitality and freedom of eternal love in the realm of Divine Being constitutes the prototype for what love can be, at its best, in the realm of creaturely existence and development."[15] In speaking this way, Balthasar is drawing on a theological tradition that understands the love operating

---

[13] The idea that creation is a Trinitarian act has a long history in Christian thought. It has its root in scriptural passages (like John's prologue) that refer to Jesus Christ as the Word through whom all things came into being. Irenaeus (in *Against Heresies* 5.28.4) described God as creating with "two hands," the Word and the Spirit. Others, like Basil the Great, referred to Psalm 33:6, which reads: "By the word of the Lord the heavens were made, and all their host by the breath of his mouth." Though Trinitarian creation is presented as a unified act, the presence of Three Persons allows for distinctions to be made. Irenaeus put it this way: the Father plans and commands, the Son performs and creates, while the Spirit nourishes and increases. These distinctions, however, must not be understood in a rigid way lest one imagine three different gods.

[14] It is important to underscore that God's eternal Trinitarian life is always a mystery to us. Whatever Christians claim to understand about God's life is dependent on God's revelation to us in the witness of Israel and the incarnate Son. Jesus Christ is the image or icon of God (Col. 1:15), and so is our "window" into the divine life. Our capacity to see, however, is limited by the power of sin in us.

[15] Hans Urs von Balthasar, *Theo-Drama – Theological Dramatic Theory: Volume V: The Last Act*, trans. Graham Harrison (San Francisco: Ignatius Press, 1998), 79–80.

among the Three Persons to be the same love that creates, sustains, and redeems the world.[16] This means that if we want to know what creaturely life is, what it means and what it is for, we must look to the life of the Triune God.

Miroslav Volf has rightly reminded us that it is a mistake to think that Trinitarian relations can be easily or directly translated into a social program. The world we live in is fallen. Sin has distorted and disfigured the creaturely relationships that were originally whole, good, and beautiful. Too much of our "love" is really an idolatrous desire to possess and control. It is important to note, however, that though sin has done much to de-create the relationships of this world, it does not have the power to block altogether God's presence to the world. God is ever present to the world as its sustaining breath or Spirit, drawing creatures into the fullness of life. God assumed creaturely flesh in the person of Jesus of Nazareth so that our flesh can know and participate in God's own life. We should, therefore, conclude with Volf that while the Trinity does not yield a specific plan of action, it does give the contours of a vision for what relations between creatures ought to be. The witness of the Son, the leading of the Spirit, and the nurture of the church body together make possible a new life individuals could not achieve on their own.

Considering the life of Jesus and the power of the Holy Spirit it becomes evident that the goal of creaturely relationship is achieved in *communion*. Though life under the power of sin can fall into patterns of fragmentation, isolation, and violent destruction, the witness of the Trinity is that life attains its fulfillment in a fellowship of peace and love. The Three Persons of the Trinity do not exist in splendid isolation from each other, as if they were three mini-gods each claiming for themselves their own sphere of power and influence. Rather, the Father, Son, and Spirit exist *with* each other in radical equality and unity. Basil the Great insisted on the use of the word "with"

---

[16]   Balthasar quotes Thomas Aquinas: "Thus God the Father effects creation by his Word, who is the Son, and by his love, who is the Holy Spirit. Thus it is the processions of the Persons that cause the generation of creatures, to the extent that they include attributes of being, namely, of knowing and willing" (ibid., 62); and Bonaventure: "God could not have brought forth the creation on the basis of his will if he had not already brought forth the Son on the basis of his nature" (ibid., 64). Balthasar summarizes their position by saying "All earthly becoming is a reflection of the eternal 'happening' in God, which, we repeat, is per se identical with the eternal Being or essence" (ibid., 67). It is important to describe the Trinitarian movement of love as a "happening" rather than a "becoming" because the divine life, quite unlike our own, is not susceptible to lack or restlessness. The Trinity is the fullness of life, life at peace. But it is not inert because it is the eternal movement of self-offering and receiving communion.

because he believed it testified best to the communion (*koinonia*) among the Persons.[17] In the Trinity there is no subordination or hierarchy. Rather, the Three share life with each other in complete mutuality. Though the Persons are distinct, they always abide in each other. This mutual abiding would eventually be described as *perichoresis*, the one "making room" in itself for the other.

Perichoresis is a radical teaching. It suggests that persons do not first exist as individuals and then at some time enter into relationship with each other (thus making relationship an optional affair). Trinitarian life shows that relationality goes much deeper, *constituting* rather than merely marking reality. Volf indicates that the divine persons "are not simply interdependent and influence one another from outside, but are *personally interior* to one another."[18] In other words, mutual indwelling, the other-in-me and myself-in-another, is at the heart of true reality. True life is lived *through* the gifts of others. As our experience with eating confirms, insofar as a living being attempts to be autarchic (a self-originating and self-sustaining being) it denies all nurture and so precipitates its own death.

Perichoresis speaks to interpenetration without this penetration being a violation. When Jesus says "the Father is in me and I am in the Father" (John 10:38), he does not mean that they dissolve into each other and so cease to be who they are. Rather, they are who they are because of the presence of each other *in* each other. "The relationship between Jesus and the Father is not one of master and subordinate (or slave) but a relationship of perfect friendship or partnership in which the will of one naturally aligns with the other; here obedience follows from perfect fellowship (John 15:15)."[19] This Trinitarian view of reality, this narration of the inspiration and goal of relationships, results in a striking portrait of what it means to be a self: "The self is shaped by making space for the other and by giving space to the other, by being enriched when it inhabits the other and by sharing of its plenitude when it is inhabited by the other, by re-examining itself when the

[17]   My understanding of Basil and the power of the Spirit as the agent of communion is based on Denis Edwards's *Breath of Life: A Theology of the Creator Spirit* (Maryknoll, NY: Orbis Books, 2004), 16–30.
[18]   Miroslav Volf, "'The Trinity Is Our Social Program': The Doctrine of the Trinity and the Shape of Social Engagement," *Modern Theology* 14:3 (July 1998), 409.
[19]   Kathryn Tanner, *Christ the Key* (Cambridge: Cambridge University Press, 2010), 186. Tanner is right to stress the "perfect fellowship" that marks the Father-Son relationship. The language of "alignment," however, can be misleading if it is taken to suggest that at one time there were two independent spheres of life out of alignment that then gradually moved into alignment. Here we encounter one of the central difficulties in thinking the Trinity, namely, the need to maintain the distinctness and the unity of the Three Persons.

other closes his or her doors and challenging the other by knocking at the doors."[20] To be a personal creature is thus to be one who is from the beginning shaped by and called into hospitality and fellowship. Trinitarian creation means that life is founded upon an unending sharing and receiving of each other, a perpetual "making room" within ourselves for others to be. Rather than being a possession, life is a gift – a movement of self-offering and receiving love.

These brief comments on the Trinity reveal that it is a teaching of the utmost existential and practical significance. Far from being an abstract and arcane doctrine, what the Trinity accomplishes is a rethinking of the world and our place within it. *Why does a world exist?* Because it is of the nature of divine love to "make room" for others to be and to flourish. God creates the world as the expression of divine hospitality, and as the place in which people are invited to extend hospitality to others. *What is the character of the world?* The world consists not of individuals but of memberships that in the joining of members to each other make life possible. Membership is not optional. The relationships we live through – most obviously and practically through our eating – constitute, inspire, nurture, and fulfill us. *What is the goal of this world and this life?* To move from membership into the deep communion of love and peace. We live currently in ways that distort and degrade, even refuse, membership, because we see relationships as a burden or threat. But when our life more fully participates in the Triune life we also move into the domain of heaven, which is the perfection of communion.

We can now see that a Trinitarian account of creation transforms our thinking about food. Food is a gift of love. Sharing food with each other we also participate in God's hospitable ways with the world. Eating isn't simply a *reminder* of God's love. It is, instead, our *immersion* within it, and our *participation* in God's self-offering life. To eat in a God-informed way is to *extend* to others and to places God's life-creating, life-honoring ways. This means that God is never distant from us. Rather, God is near to us in the visceral experience of digestion and the maintenance of bodies.

As with all of creation, food does not have to be. The fact that it is, and that it has the potential to occasion great delight, is a sign that God made the world not out of boredom but out of joy. To understand this truth is to want to echo the toast offered by Robert Farrar Capon:

> To a radically, perpetually unnecessary world; to the restoration of aston-
> ishment to the heart and mystery to the mind; to wine, because it is a gift

[20]   Volf, "'The Trinity Is Our Social Program'," 410.

we never expected; to mushroom and artichoke, for they are incredible legacies; to improbable acids and high alcohols, since we would hardly have thought of them ourselves; and to all being, because it is superfluous . . . We are free: nothing is needful, everything is for joy. Let the bookkeepers struggle with their balance sheets; it is the tippler who sees the untipped Hand. God is eccentric; He has *loves*, not reasons. *Salute!*[21]

To receive food as a gift and as a declaration of God's love and joy is to receive food in a theological manner.

A Trinitarian account of creation also transforms the way we eat. While it is certainly true that we eat to live, Trinitarian-inspired eating means that we eat to share and nurture life. In its ultimate, theological bearing, eating is not reducible to the consumption of calories. Instead, it is about extending hospitality and making room for others to find life by sharing in our own. Self-offering, accepting responsibility for another's well-being, turning one's own life into nurture for others – these are the signs of life as empowered by the Spirit. Eating, in other words, is an invitation to enter into communion and be reconciled with each other. To eat with God at the table is to eat with the aim of healing and celebrating the memberships of creation.

A central task of a theology of eating is to help us guard against idolatry, which we can here briefly describe as the effort to magnify and promote human power. The goal of eating is not to worship food or ourselves. Nor is it to offer food production and consumption to the modern idols of control, efficiency, and convenience. As our histories amply show, when eating becomes idolatrous, the result is degraded and destroyed habitats, miserable animals, insecure and abused workers, unjust trade arrangements, and lonely eaters. Our paramount task is to testify against the mutation of food into an exclusive possession or instrument of power. It is to recover the sense that food is a gift to be gratefully received and generously shared.

THE GIFT OF BREAD?

Bread has long been central to the heart and life of Near Eastern and Western cultures. For generations people have associated bread with food, and the availability of bread with good times and food security. In fact, the stories of successful and declining cultures are not complete without an account of the fate of their grain fields. The absence of bread, even the fear

---

[21] Robert Farrar Capon, *The Supper of the Lamb: A Culinary Reflection* (New York: Modern Library, 2002 [1967]), 85–86.

of a bread shortage, was often enough to cause riots or bring armies to a starving halt. After all, who can think of the French peasants storming the Bastille and not also recall their cries for bread, or forget Napoleon's retreating armies afflicted with madness and savagery due to the lack of bread? In the minds of many throughout time, without bread there simply is no life.[22]

Though many of us no longer assume this close metonymic identification between bread and food (that connection has been weakened by the tens of thousands of food products now competing for our attention and our wallets), bread's significance still lingers in our imagination when we refer to money as "bread," or consider wage earners the "breadwinners" of a household. Notwithstanding all our food choices – and the recommendation (!) of the Atkins Diet – bread is still a staple of life, one of the basic ingredients that keep biological and social life on the move. The smell of freshly baked bread is enough to make people want to sit down, get comfortable, and enjoy several slices. The visible, aromatic, and tactile presence of a warm loaf invites sharing and companionship (a "companion" – from the Latin *com*: "with" + *panis*: "bread" – is "one who shares bread"). In addition to providing nourishment, bread communicates home, hospitality, and fellowship, the sharing of our life together. Received at the Eucharistic table as the body of Christ, it is our nurture into God's communal life.

In certain respects, bread is the quintessentially human food, for as Leon Kass has observed, "man becomes human with the eating of bread."[23] Unlike most fruits, vegetables, and meat, the preparation of a loaf of bread presupposes a fairly radical transformation of our natural environments and considerable cognitive and social development. We don't have the stomach to eat grains raw or slightly cooked. To get bread, people must transform grain into flour, change the flour into dough, and then bake the dough at the right temperature for the right time to get something worth eating. Harvesting the grain, in turn, presupposes an agricultural society that has learned a great many skills about cultivation and food storage. To create bread assumes a particular kind of culture that no longer simply gathers its food but works imaginatively and scientifically to transform the gifts of the earth to some shared purpose or end.

[22] For a fascinating, though sometimes problematic, telling of the stories of bread's significance in Western culture, see H. E. Jacob's *Six Thousand Years of Bread: Its Holy and Unholy History* (New York: Lyons Press, 1944).

[23] Leon R. Kass, *The Hungry Soul: Eating and the Perfecting of Our Nature* (Chicago: University of Chicago Press, 1999), 122.

A loaf of bread is the bearer of at least four major narratives or histories: (1) a narrative of natural processes that yield diverse plant growth, yeast spores, salt, sugar, and water; (2) an agricultural narrative about the human domestication of plants, considerable experimentation with grains and heat, and the development of grain economies; (3) a moral/philosophical narrative about the transformation of humanity itself as people grow into the idea that they can control their habitats and relationships with each other in new and potentially hospitable ways; and (4) a theological narrative focused on Jesus as the "bread of life."[24] This means that to consider fully what a loaf *is* requires us to move far beyond a particular slice to include the material, biological, social, and divine sources that feed into every bite.

A "simple" food with this much ecological and cultural depth will, of necessity, presuppose many subplots that add significance to the overall meaning of bread. In our telling of some of them, we should start with the ground, the soil, and the water upon which all bread depends. Without soil, water, and sunshine there can be no bread, because all plant life, grain or not, depends on this life-giving matrix.

It is easy to dismiss soil as nothing more than dirt, and thus forget that organic soil is the indispensable, life-nurturing setting (a placenta of sorts) in terms of which so much of our living is made possible. Good, healthy soil is not dead but teeming with life. Death decays into it and reemerges as new life, all because of the astoundingly complex and mostly invisible work of billions of bacteria and microorganisms. Without their work our world would be overwhelmed by the corpses and stench of death. Soil is a marvel and a mystery that we have not yet even begun to comprehend. It is the hospitable "table" out of which terrestrial life, even the life (weeds!) we may not necessarily choose, literally grows. For good reason, Wendell Berry describes soil in Christ-like terms:

> The most exemplary nature is that of the topsoil. It is very Christ-like in its passivity and beneficence, and in the penetrating energy that issues out of its peaceableness. It increases by experience, by the passage of seasons over it, growth rising out of it and returning to it, not by ambition or aggressiveness. It is enriched by all things that die and enter into it. It keeps the past, not as history or as memory, but as richness, new possibility. Its fertility is always building up out of death into promise. Death is the bridge or the tunnel by which its past enters its future.[25]

---

[24]   The bulk of our discussion on this fourth narrative will occur in Chapter 5.
[25]   Wendell Berry, *The Long-Legged House* (New York: Harcourt, Brace and World, 1969), 204.

For millennia people lived as hunters and gatherers of the fruit of the earth. Though altering their landscapes somewhat, they did not much affect the soil. Then about 10,000 years ago a new form of culture slowly emerged, one dependent on the domestication of animals and plants: agriculture.[26] How this all came to be makes for a fascinating and very complex story but at the heart of this new way of living we find the plow. To grow the grains that would finally make their way into bread, humans had to learn to manipulate the soil.

We are accustomed to thinking of the plow as an unmitigated blessing, the sign of prosperity and peace. We recall the prophets who announce that in better days, swords will be beaten into plowshares (Isaiah 2:4, Joel 3:10, Micah 4:3). But in our alteration of the soil, our literal turning of the earth upside down, we also unleashed tremendous destructive potential. Given enough years of till agricultural practice, people would gradually erode, and thus render relatively lifeless, vast stretches of the world (recall that the "Fertile Crescent" is now mostly a desert landscape). For good reason Wes Jackson points to the plow as a sign of a "global disease," and the invention of the plow as "the most significant and explosive event to appear on the face of the earth, changing the earth even faster than did the origin of life."[27]

From an ecological point of view, the production of grain and the invention of bread are thus hardly benign or morally irrelevant events. To achieve great agricultural success people had to set in motion practices that would over time dramatically alter our planet. To make room for the plow, forests would be felled and wetlands drained. Wild prairie grasses, and the buffalo and wolf populations they supported, would quickly disappear. Indigenous peoples would lose access to their lands and the ways of life they supported.

---

[26] The story of the agricultural revolution in human history is complex and multifaceted: how agriculture developed and why it took particular forms depended on the diverse regions and groups of people in which it emerged. For an excellent survey, see Graeme Barker's *The Agricultural Revolution in Prehistory* (Oxford: Oxford University Press, 2006). People did not simply awake one day committed to the domestication of wheat and the baking of bread. Numerous pressures (climate, topography, vegetation, population) and decisions (about status, security, tradition, experimentation) had to come together to produce this basic food staple. Significant changes in the human imagination and psychology (a shift away from animism, for instance) had to occur. The movement toward agriculture was a diversely applied movement, often slow and gradual, with people combining small-scale cultivation with foraging for centuries before becoming committed farmers. For a recent assessment of the many factors contributing to the development of agriculture, factors like domestication and the rise of state forms of governance, see James C. Scott's *Against the Grain: A Deep History of the Earliest States* (New Haven: Yale University Press, 2018).

[27] Wes Jackson, *New Roots for Agriculture*, New edition (Lincoln: University of Nebraska Press, 1985), 2.

All manner of species of wildlife, plant and animal, would lose their habitats and eventually go extinct. Indeed, the very ideas of wildness and wilderness would emerge and be cast in a new light.[28]

The effects of grain agriculture were never confined to the natural world. Social structures, economic patterns and priorities, and religious imaginations would be profoundly transformed as people moved from hunter-gatherer lives to the more sedentary, structured ways of agricultural life. Indeed, a new understanding of humanity's relationship to the land would gradually emerge as people developed the technological means to control, store, and distribute the grain being harvested on managed fields.[29] How does one think about the sources of food when those sources increasingly come within one's own control and design? Though hunter-gatherers modified and managed their environments in varying degrees, agriculturalists put humanity on a new course.

The course of this development has always been morally and theologically ambiguous. On the one hand, agriculture has clearly made possible the growth of human populations and their increasingly sophisticated cultures. It has enabled, if not always realized, the refinement of skills like animal husbandry, where animals are treated not as economic units but as creatures of integrity deserving respect and care, and made possible sustainable land management practices that increase rather than degrade soil fertility and plant health. On the other hand, it has also contributed to the destruction of the world's plant and animal diversity and the drawdown of its soil and water. It has encouraged cultures that exploit and degrade the gifts of fields, forests, and watersheds.

---

[28]   Stephen Greenblatt, "Towards a Poetics of Culture," in *The New Historicism*, ed. H. Aram Veeser (New York: Routledge, 1989), describes a visit to Yosemite National Park where he comes upon a sign that announces "you are entering a wilderness." This sign is accompanied by a list of rules regarding behavior. Thus "the wilderness then is signaled by an intensification of the rules" and "is at once secured and obliterated by the official gestures that establish its boundaries; the natural is set over against the artificial through means that render such an opposition meaningless" (9). For a treatment of the meaning of wilderness before the modern period see Max Oelschlaegger's *The Idea of Wilderness: From Prehistory to the Age of Ecology* (New Haven: Yale University Press, 1993).

[29]   In *Against the Grain: How Agriculture Has Hijacked Civilization* (New York: North Point Press, 2004), Richard Manning argues that the development of agriculture has been, for the most part, an ecological and social disaster resulting in ruined lands and waters, an expansionist, colonialist mindset, and a poorer diet and declining human health. Agriculture, in Manning's view, turns people away from nature and against each other in a massive fight for control over declining resources. Clearly, agriculture, particularly industrial agriculture, has been susceptible to numerous forms of destruction and degradation. Whether farming always has been or needs to be so is another matter.

This ambiguity is readily observed in the story of American agricultural development. The success of grain presupposed a radical, sometimes brutal, transformation of the natural and cultural landscape (recall the violent removal and decimation of thousands upon thousands of Native Americans, and the farmer's reliance upon slaves in many agricultural sectors).[30] As farmers moved west they brought with them railroads that would then ship the wheat they produced back east to growing cities like St. Louis and Chicago. To grow the wheat, prairie sod had to be overturned, forests cleared, and wetlands drained.[31] To build cities, the flow of resources had to be constant. The physical shape and smell of these cities – as evidenced by stockyards, grain elevators, train stations, and docks – was directly affected by the grain trade. Careers and businesses were made and lost owing to the vicissitudes of the trade in wheat. Gradually, as grain came to be thought of more and more as a tradable commodity, it would cease to carry any strong connection to the natural and farming processes that brought it into being. William Cronon describes it this way: "Elevator receipts, as traded on the floor of 'Change' [the Chicago Exchange], accomplished the transmutation of one of humanity's oldest foods, obscuring its physical identity and displacing it into the symbolic world of capital."[32]

The world of capital would have a dramatic effect on all manner of food products, not simply bread. Rather than signifying the deep, diverse, and multilayered stories of ecological life and agricultural practice, or bearing witness to the gift-quality of life, food items would gradually be reduced to considerations about price and profitability. Control over food products is the primary capitalist priority, and the best way to exercise such control is to extricate food items from their natural and cultural homes. Now rendered abstract and isolated, reduced to elements and nutrients that can be manipulated and recombined into the thousands of "value-added" products we have on store shelves today (look at the ingredients list of most processed food and you will be amazed at how little of it refers to anything we recognize as

---

[30] In *Trace: Memory, History, Race, and the American Landscape* (Berkeley: Counterpoint, 2015), Lauret Savoy draws our attention to how the American landscape bears witness to the violence against peoples and creatures that have lived within it.

[31] A history of how misapplied agricultural techniques and cultural hubris gradually undermined the natural fertility of prairie ecosystems is provided by Donald Worster in *Dust Bowl: The Southern Plains in the 1930s* (New York: Oxford University Press, 1982).

[32] William Cronon, *Nature's Metropolis: Chicago and the Great West* (New York: W. W. Norton, 1991), 120. In "New Threats to Farmers: The Market Hedge," *New York Times*, April 21, 2008, Diana Henriques describes how today's grain farmer works both the fields and the derivatives markets in Chicago to make economic ends meet. It is not enough to invest in soil. One must also invest in market hedges, futures, and options.

food, as living fruit of the soil), food can become a feature of packaging and convenience. The significance, value, and true cost of food, in other words, are either sharply reduced or simplified, so that eventually people forget any connection between the loaf of bread and the lives of soil microbes, plants, and farmers. People can now consume a slice and have no imagination or sympathy for the agricultural community or ecological neighborhood that brought it into being. They can purchase a loaf in a store and have no idea if its existence depended on the destruction of soils and watersheds or the decimation of indigenous cultures and the degradation of today's workers.

We now live in a time when the meaning of bread has for many been severely limited and reduced to what computes in an executive's office or contributes to a biotech engineer's research plan. When grain signifies primarily as a patent and bread registers in terms of store shelf space, we know that we have moved a long way away from the experience of the miraculous gift of life, the mysteries of soil and photosynthesis, the practices and priorities of rural communities, the traditions and recipes and lore of local bakeries, and the hospitality of the home oven. Bread stories that may have been inspired by care, patience, attention, steady work, communal responsibility, sharing, and celebration are now increasingly rewritten as stories of competition, control, efficiency, convenience, and profit, stories that all too often presuppose wasted lands and communities.

This brief description of some of the elements and processes that feed into the production of bread has been important to rehearse because in learning of bread's history we see how bread is also the carrier of diverse and deep meanings. Bread has a life and history that circulates through the lives of many (human and nonhuman) others, contributing to either their life or destruction. How we make bread, how we share and distribute it, are of profound moral and spiritual significance because every loaf presupposes decisions that have been made about *how* to configure the social and ecological relationships that make bread possible. Bread can be eaten in ways that honor the sources and memberships of life. It can also be eaten in ways that do not.

This survey also allows us to ask whether humanity's production and consumption of bread testify to God's reconciling and communal life. As we have traced the histories of bread we have seen that at various moments our primary concern has been to control the elements (soil, water, wheat, workers) that feed into bread. Bread culture, we might say, has not always been hospitable to bread or its eaters. Soil has not been sufficiently nurtured, water has not been protected and preserved, wheat has not been received as a gift, and workers and farmers have not been fairly treated. Rather than being the occasion for sharing and companionship, bread has often been the inspiration for greed, exploitation, and war. When bread is reduced to a commodity, its ability to be a witness and inspiration to communion is compromised.

Bread does not need to register this way. It can be a source of fellowship and an invitation to reconciled life. As we will later see, this is precisely what Jesus as the "bread of life" offers. To eat this bread is to participate in a different way of growing wheat and preparing a loaf, a way that honors soil and water by not degrading them, a way that respects and fairly compensates farmers and farmworkers, a way that freely shares and passes on the gift of seed to others, a way that patiently waits and rejoices in the grace of germination. This communion-building bread is not an illusion or magic. It is being prepared and eaten today by communities of faithful people who receive bread not as a commodity but as God's gift.[33]

THE FATE OF FOOD IN MODERNITY

When we appreciate that a particular food is always bound up with multiple histories, then it becomes clear that as the priorities and practices of cultures and their economies change, so too will the meanings of the food produced by them. Bread will mean something different to a farmer who grows and grinds the wheat and then bakes the bread, than it will to the nonbaking suburbanite who regularly purchases a loaf at the store but has never seen a field. The end result – its look, aroma, and taste – may be very similar. But the meaning will be very different.

Part of the difference in meaning can be explained by how the food is framed or branded. Marketers and advertising executives can, through packaging and stylized media campaigns, give a particular feel or aura to bread. By calling a loaf "artisanal," for instance, they may try to conjure the rustic image of the yeoman who rises early to craft and bake. All ingredients are presumed to be natural or organic, while the production practices are thought to reflect the values of a small agricultural village. Lacking much

---

[33] As one example, consider *Green Sisters: A Spiritual Ecology* (Cambridge, MA: Harvard University Press, 2007), especially chapter 5, in which Sarah McFarland Taylor describes how Catholic "eco-nuns" are modeling different ways to grow, prepare, and share bread. For many of them, the growing of grain and the baking of bread are Eucharistic acts that join us to the land, each other, and to God. Summarizing one sister, Taylor observes, "eating is an act in which earth, water, and sun become human flesh and are transformed. The conversion of food into love and prayer, thought and deed, is ... truly a holy mystery" (175).

direct involvement with bread's production, consumers are increasingly dependent on the stories others tell them about the food they buy. Rather than experiencing firsthand and contributing to the meanings of the foods they eat, shoppers are often reduced to purchasing the meanings they enjoy.

A more significant and determinative factor has to do with the ways in which the meanings of things have been altered by modern changes in practical life. In particular, we need to consider how forces like urbanization, industrialism, and global markets have affected the ways people relate to and understand their world. What people eat and how they grow and eat it have changed significantly in the last centuries and decades. We need to appreciate how these practical changes in economic and cultural life have transformed the meaning of food.

Attending to the history of the Italian community of Bosa, we can observe how a change in the significance and meaning of bread took shape.[34] For as long as anyone could remember, bread was the food staple of the region. Bread was not a commodity but a community project and symbol of life, security, and well-being. Though Bosans may not have always enjoyed each other's company, in the production of bread they discovered they needed and relied on each other. As such, bread deserved communal and ritualized celebration. Bread defined the community's work, starting with the growth and milling of grain but then moving through the baking and sharing of loaves. The eating of bread shaped family and community life because of the extensive social and work relations required to keep it on the table. The labor of husbands and wives, young and old, complemented each other, just as the work of threshing and baking brought the community's men and women together. The meanings of bread in this society went deep and wide.[35]

---

[34]   The following account is based on Carole Counihan's essay, "Bread as World: Food Habits and Social Relations in Modernizing Sardinia," in *Food and Culture: A Reader* (New York: Routledge, 1997), 283–295.

[35]   The way in which the villagers of Bosa combined economic, social, geographic, and religious dimensions into a cohesive symbolic and practical understanding of bread is reflected in other cultures that also depend on a basic food item. Consider the Kalahari Bushmen who depended on the eland antelope as a food staple. This antelope was so important because it was one of the few sizable mammals that could be hunted down on foot. As a valuable source of food, the life of male hunters was concentrated to secure a successful hunt: grass fires were set to attract the eland to the fresh green grass that soon grows thereafter. Women dressed up like the antelope and danced at the ritual of a young woman's first menstruation (acknowledging that a thin or starving woman does not menstruate). Kalahari lore, art, music, and ritual featured the eland because it was understood to be vital to Kalahari survival. Their understanding and appreciation of this antelope was deep. The eland did not simply represent a piece of meat. It was an integral member in

After World War II the food economy in Bosa, and thus also its food culture, shifted dramatically. Owing to changes in government policy (cheap grain imports were allowed, while government pensions and salaries increased), and the capitalization of agriculture (dependence on expensive machinery and petrochemical inputs, and the reduction in the number of small farms), the growth of wheat and other foods in the region all but ceased. Along with other consumer goods, food came to be imported from places relatively far away. Bread could now be purchased more cheaply, conveniently, and anonymously at a store. What disappeared, along with the bread economy, was the tradition and practice of shared work, and with that the sharing of one's bread and giving help to those in need. Rather than being a complex social, geographical, and cultural symbol, bread was reduced to a product. Eating was also transformed as the communal celebrations of bread disappeared. Though Bosans interviewed enjoyed the independence, ease, and convenience of consumer life – there was no longer the need to get up so early, work hard, and have people intimately involved in one's personal business – they also found themselves eating alone more and more. Carole Counihan's conclusion is telling:

> the capitalist mode of production and exchange leads to an atomization of social relations. In subsistence wheat and bread production, men and women depend on each other for assistance and are unable to make a living without mutual exchange of labor and products. Social interdependence declines with the concentration of wheat production on capital-intensive farms and of bread production in a few bakeries operating with wage laborers to make a profit. Bread acquisition takes place through increasingly impersonal money exchange. The continuous giving and receiving of bread and other foods so important to tying people together and ensuring their survival in the past fades away with the demise of subsistence production.[36]

---

the overall life cycle of the Kalahari people. It was understood to be a source of sustenance and an opportunity to exercise the skill and artistry of a people. In a real and practical sense, the Kalahari people could not understand themselves apart from the eland antelope: it had entered into their entire way of being (and not only their stomachs). For a description of the relationship between the Kalahari and the eland, see Elizabeth Marshall Thomas's account in *The Old Way: A Story of the First People* (New York: Picador, 2006), 30–39.

[36] Counihan, "Bread as World," 293. That Counihan is concerned about the demise of "subsistence production" is important because it signifies the ability of genuine need to draw people together (whereas the abundance of excess is often the occasion to push people apart).

It is tempting to romanticize subsistence village life, when we know that all forms of life have their troubles. But what the history of Bosa shows is that the character of social relations, and thus also the meanings of the food itself, are fundamentally altered by industrial economic transformation. In certain respects, the act of eating was radically *simplified* for Bosans. They could now eat bread without the complex knowledge and commitment they previously had as they worked together to grow the grain and share the loaf. They could consume with complete ignorance about where the food is coming from and how it was produced, because in a global economy the food is always presumed to be somewhere ready for sale.

The example of the community of Bosa is important because (1) it represents economic developments that are (and have been) going on all around the world, and (2) it represents a deep severing between people and their food-providing social and ecological contexts. Just as the people of Bosa came to be separated from the land and from each other, they also began to think of themselves in fundamentally new ways: as autonomous and anonymous consumers rather than as members of a region and community held together by shared work and nurture. In this elemental shift the possibility for a meaningful understanding of people as belonging to a life-giving place and membership, involved in the production of food and committed to the maintenance of life, practically disappeared. The desire to be autonomous eaters, freed from the demands of local food production, however, leads to an ironic result: utter dependence on the vicissitudes of foreign markets and international trade agreements.

When food consumers lose the practical connections that bind them to the social and ecological contexts that make their eating possible, the potential for varying kinds of injustice grows dramatically. Because much of our food consumption now places us within global trade networks that are far-flung and mostly invisible to us, and because trade agreements and international loan arrangements require countries to produce commodities for export, the likelihood that what we eat will have been produced in a manner that harms fields, animals, and workers increases considerably. Food consumers end up having little knowledge or say about where their food comes from. Food producers, in turn, will face considerable pressure to grow what they do not want to grow and in a manner they may believe to be harmful.

Sticking to bread as our example, consider how following World War II pressure was applied (by wheat-producing countries) to make bread an international staple by making wheat the predominant form of food aid. In countries like Korea, children needed to be taught how to consume bread, even though Koreans thought of Korea as "the home of rice." More recently, countries in Africa have been under significant pressure to accept genetically modified wheat, despite fears that genetically modified organism (GMO) seed will contaminate African fields and compromise traditional varieties, and thus make African farmers dependent on multinational corporations that hold the patents to the seed and control the fertilizer and herbicide inputs that make the seed grow.[37] What is at issue in examples like this is whether people – especially those living in the Global South and in developing countries – can decide to grow and eat the foods they choose. International trade and aid agreements now dictate the growth and consumption of much of the world's foods. Food sovereignty and democracy, the idea that people have control over and responsibility for the foods they produce and consume, is gradually disappearing from the world.

Two determining features of modern, global eating life need to be noted: the commodification of food and the industrialization of eating practices. By food's commodification I mean that the food many people eat is now purchased at a grocery store that imports its food from far away.[38] How the food arrives at the store and from where; what the companies are that produced the food; what the production practices are; what the conditions of the land, animals, and communities that grew the food are; what the ingredients in the food are – these are all mostly unknown. To receive food as a commodity means that a consumer's understanding and appreciation of the many social and ecological elements feeding into the food are fairly shallow. To be sure, shoppers can inquire into where their food comes from but

---

[37] For the story on how Korea became dependent on wheat imports, see Raj Patel's *Stuffed and Starved: The Hidden Battle for the World Food System* (Brooklyn: Melville House, 2007), 261–262. Patel also discusses the politics behind the push to make African agriculture dependent on biotechnology on pp. 146–153. For a discussion on the complexities of GMO food aid, see Peter Sandøe and Katherine Hauge Madsen's "Agriculture and Food Ethics in the Western World: A Case of Ethical Imperialism?," in *Ethics, Hunger and Globalization: In Search of Appropriate Policies*, ed. Per Pinstrup-Andersen and Peter Sandøe (Dordrecht: Springer, 2007), 201–214. High on the list of fears by African countries is that the acceptance of GMO seed as food aid will compromise their ability to sell traditional, non-GMO varieties to the European market (known for its resistance to GMO crops).

[38] That most people take grocery stores for granted is an indication that their default assumption is that food is a commodity and eaters are primarily consumers. We forget that the full-service grocery store selling meat, fruit, and vegetables, and the many dry goods that fill our pantries is a relatively novel and localized phenomenon. Many people living in developing countries would see its volume and variety as nothing short of a miracle. Though markets and butchers of varying kinds have long existed in villages and cities, the full-service grocery store is less than 100 years old. Previous to this time it could be assumed that most people had a direct hand in the production of some of the food they ate.

companies (and the United States Department of Agriculture) resist, for a variety of reasons, full disclosure. The end result is that people eat with a diminished sense of the depth and breadth of relationships that constitute a food item. Looking at bread, it is harder for people see anything other than the immediate loaf. This narrowing of a food imagination often leads to a narrowing of sympathies and care (for fields and farmers, for instance).

The commodification of food has gone hand in hand with the modern industrialization of food production practices. What I mean is that the business logic that was previously applied to the manufacture of inanimate things is now being applied to food. Paul Roberts has described this transformation in the following way:

> Raw materials such as No. 2 yellow corn or BSCB (boneless, skinless chicken breasts) are now handled like any other commodity: produced wherever costs are lowest, shipped to wherever demand is highest, and managed via the same contracts, futures, and other instruments used for timber, or tin, or iron ore. Food-processing companies employ the same technologies and business models of other high-volume manufacturers. The continuous advances in technology and the ever larger scales of production that drive down costs in cars and home electronics are now also standard in the food business, as is the relentless product innovation one finds in clothing and cosmetics ... To an important degree, the success of the modern food sector has been its ability to make food behave like any other consumer product.[39]

What Roberts is describing is the application of a strictly capitalistic, high-volume, efficiency- and profit-driven logic to food. Food is produced not with the aim of promoting nutrition, freshness, and quality of taste but rather transportability, long shelf life, and uniformity of appearance. The problem with this application is that food, while certainly playing a vital part within any economy, is not reducible to an industrial "product" or an accountant's ledger. Food is an ecological and social reality. It has deep cultural significance.[40] To ignore this fact is to produce harm in eaters (the highly processed, high-fat, sweet, and artificially flavored foods many of us eat are well known to be unhealthy). It is also to harm what we eat.

We can better appreciate this harm when we consider the application of an industrial, utilitarian logic to the production of poultry. The eating of

---

[39] Paul Roberts, *The End of Food* (Boston: Houghton Mifflin, 2008), xiv.

[40] To appreciate the many layers of cultural significance, imagine all that is involved when culture that has developed around the production of rice or corn is now fed by imported wheat.

chicken has soared in the last several decades as people have become increasingly worried about the fat and cholesterol content in other meats. To meet increased demand, poultry producers routinely house tens of thousands of chickens in massive buildings. These chickens, for the most part, never see the light of day. They are not free to peck and roam about outside. Egg layers are often confined to multiply stacked wire cages that scarcely give them room to move. Those on the bottom receive a steady rain of excrement from the chickens above. These are stressful conditions for birds. In some instances they are debeaked so they don't hurt and kill each other. They are fed a steady diet of steroids and antibiotics because without them they would not grow quickly enough or survive until slaughter weight. Those who "care" for these chickens often work in appalling conditions themselves, and so the turnover rate among poultry workers and processors is extremely high. Meanwhile, the owners of these chicken operations have been reduced to serfs on their own land, beholden to the dictates of the large poultry producers.[41]

It is hard to look at these chicken factories and not see the mutation of a living bird into a meat-producing machine. What has happened to chickens is also happening to other animals. Rather than being received as creatures with integrity, and thus deserving of respect and care, cattle, pigs, sheep, goats, turkeys, geese, and chickens are reduced to economic units.[42] In the rush to make a profit – some of the animals have been genetically engineered to grow so fast (in some cases nearly twice their normal rate) that their bodies collapse under the strain – the animal itself is not considered.[43] That it is a gift of God does not enter in.

An industrial logic of production has also been applied to our vegetable and fruit crops. Consider the French fry. To grow an industrial potato, meaning one that is uniform in shape and size (people want French fries that are of the same long, rectangular, tube shape), growers must first "clean"

---

[41]   The story of the industrialization of the chicken is told by Steve Striffler in *Chicken: The Dangerous Transformation of America's Favorite Food* (New Haven: Yale University Press, 2005).

[42]   For an exposition of the brutality of today's meat-producing industry see Jonathan Safran Foer's *Eating Animals* (New York: Little, Brown, 2009).

[43]   In Craig Holdrege and Steve Talbott, "The Cow: Organism or Bioreactor?," in *Beyond Biotechnology: The Barren Promise of Genetic Engineering* (Lexington: University Press of Kentucky, 2008), Craig Holdrege notes that if industrial beef producers simply looked carefully at their cows they would determine that the way they feed them is often a violation of their nature. Cows have rumens, which means they are meant to eat grass. Virtually everything about them, from the structure of their teeth to the four chambers of their stomachs, communicates that they are meant to be on pasture.

the field. They do this by thoroughly killing whatever life is on or in the soil through multiple applications of herbicide. To make a potato grow out of this gray, lifeless dirt, however, requires multiple applications of fertilizer. Potato growers are thus reduced to being managers of poisons so deadly they will not enter their fields for several days after application for fear of major damage to their nervous systems. Where exactly all the poison and fertilizer runoff eventually accumulates or ends is hard to know.[44] But the growing presence of "dead zones" in our oceans and estuaries indicates that what we spray on fields does not simply remain there.

Eating does not need to follow this commodified, industrial way. It can occur in contexts where people take deeper notice of and accept responsibility for what they eat. To appreciate what this sort of eating looks like and what it entails, we should consider the example of Joel Salatin's Polyface Farm.[45] Salatin's chickens do not stay cooped up or crammed in a dark barn. Nor are they force fed and pumped up with antibiotics to keep them from collapsing. The stress and anxiety that is the life of an industrial chicken clearly indicates that this is not how chickens are meant to live. This is why Salatin's chickens live outside, on grass, often following his cattle herd. Chickens are free to forage through the grass and cow pies, looking for bugs and grubs. As they move through the fields they disperse cattle manure and leave behind their own, thereby contributing to the fertility of Salatin's soil. Their eating also helps keep down the bug population, keeping Salatin's cattle much healthier and happier (they don't spend all their time swatting flies). The end results are healthy animals, vibrant soil, and really fantastic eggs.

What makes this farm in Virginia so unique is that Salatin has tried to be intentional about respecting his animals as creatures.[46] They are not "things" or economic units that have been forced to fit a business plan (even though they do clearly factor into such a plan) or maximize meat volume on an industrial assembly/disassembly line. Because they are living beings with integrity of their own, they require Salatin's attention and sympathy. Salatin tries to be attentive to the multiple dramas of life and death on his farm,

---

[44] For a description of potatoes and today's potato industry, see Michael Pollan's *The Botany of Desire: A Plant's-Eye View of the World* (New York: Random House, 2001), chapter 4.

[45] My account of Polyface Farm is based on firsthand observation and conversation with Joel Salatin. Readers can also find a more developed account in Michael Pollan's *The Omnivore's Dilemma: A Natural History of Four Meals* (New York: Penguin Press, 2006).

[46] It should be noted that Salatin has faced some criticism from Frank Reese for not raising heritage varieties of chickens. See the charge by Reese that Salatin's chickens are industrial birds in Foer's *Eating Animals*, 113, and Salatin's brief response in an interview with Gaby Wood printed January 31, 2010, in *The Observer* (www.guardian.co.uk/lifeandstyle/2010/jan/31/food-industry-environment).

dramas about soil and sunlight, worms and microbial life, chickens and rabbits, and pigs and cattle. He has observed that the land and his animals each have particular needs, limits, and potential that are worthy of respect. He understands that as a farmer, his work and energy are implicated in their well-being. What chickens need is not the same as what cattle need.

Salatin's farm is not an industrial production facility. Each creature on it is understood to live within a dynamic, constantly evolving set of relationships. Animals are not uniform products, nor are all pastures the same. They each have their own strengths and weaknesses. A good farmer knows how to relate creatures to each other so that maximum health, fertility, and contentment can be achieved. A farm is a membership in which many creatures live together in symbiotic ways. We can see how this works if we linger in Salatin's barn during the winter months. Unlike cattle in large feedlots that are often compelled to stand knee-deep in liquid manure, Salatin's herd is kept warm and dry on a barn floor that is constantly receiving corn and woodchips (from the farm's woodlot). When the cattle are let out to pasture in the spring, the pigs are invited in to root for the fermented corn. Their digging, besides being a source of food and great joy to the pigs, aerates the barn floor, creating some of the most marvelous compost imaginable. This compost is then spread on fields that are lush and highly fertile (the soil on Salatin's farm when it was first purchased was eroding and devoid of organic content). Unlike some potato fields in Idaho, Salatin's soil is healthy and alive and growing. It has not (using an analogy Wes Jackson once provided) been hammered with pesticides and then put on life support with the aid of fertilizers.

Polyface Farm is noteworthy because Salatin has made it his job to attend to the diverse life-forms under his care, and then learn from their intersections. He has enlarged the scope of his sympathy so that he can be as knowledgeable and precise and careful as possible. His work and his farm are not perfect but they do represent a sustained effort to understand and complement the sources of life that feed us all.[47] When Salatin eats he is *mindful* of the grace and beauty but also the fragility and suffering of all life. Food is not an anonymous, uniform, cheap product but the result – finally the *gift* – of a complex membership in which each member is densely related to others. Salatin's farm is not a food factory. It is an organic, living whole

---

[47] Because Salatin's farm is something of an oasis in a desert of industrial agriculture, individual consumers often drive great distances to purchase his products. This makes for inefficient distribution and contributes to a wasteful burning of fossil fuels. In this case, the problem is not with Polyface Farm itself but with the lack of more farms like it and the lack of local distribution centers to make purchasing more efficient.

that is healthy and sustainable because the success of each member presumes and promotes the well-being of each other member.

What Salatin's highly productive farm demonstrates is that today's industrial food systems are not necessary or inevitable.[48] We can produce food and eat in ways that acknowledge food's deep significance and that nurture and honor the multiple memberships of every food web. When food is commodified and eating industrialized, we run the risk of turning the world into a store or restaurant that exists for purchase and for the sake of personal convenience. We risk transforming the social and ecological sources of life into things that can be exploited to maximize a business plan. As is becoming clear, the costs to personal health, social well-being, and ecological resilience associated with this risk are extremely high.

EATING AS A "SPIRITUAL EXERCISE"

One of the lasting contributions of Eric Schlosser's *Fast Food Nation* is to have shown how a considerable amount of contemporary eating is without mercy or art.[49] Besides the fact that a lot of fast food is bad for personal health, bad for the workers who provide it, bad for the animals raised and slaughtered in its name, and bad for the ecosystems that grow it, the very idea of fast, cheap, convenient food suggests eating is not supposed to be the activity whereby people honor God, appreciate creation, or accept responsibility for their membership within it. Is eating simply a mechanical act to be judged in terms of efficiency and price? To "grab a bite on the go" communicates that people do not believe their eating should occasion the sustained attention or reflection that might lead to greater care of our food networks and more regular celebration of the gifts of life.

Fast eating is but a symptom of the more generalized speed that drives and determines contemporary culture. The frantic pace that often characterizes work and social life makes it much less likely that people will learn the disciplines of attention, conversation, and gratitude that are crucial in a celebratory and responsible life. Failing the art of reflection, people will often

[48] Proponents of industrial agriculture routinely state that only their methods are productive enough to feed the world. Salatin's farm, along with many other diversified, small-scale operations, indicates that this is not the case. The very costly methods of industrial agriculture (expensive fertilizers and pesticides, fossil fuel, equipment, and machinery) and its destructive effects (in soil erosion, water depletion and contamination, species loss) are demonstrating that industrial agriculture is not sustainable.

[49] Eric Schlosser, *Fast Food Nation: The Dark Side of the All-American Meal* (New York: Houghton Mifflin, 2001).

find themselves committed to priorities and engaged in practices that would, if carefully examined, register as unacceptable or wrong. Or they will altogether fail to see and taste where they are, and thus forfeit the opportunity to be alive to the mystery and grace of life.

The temptation to an unreflective life is hardly new. Already in the ancient world Socrates called people to step outside of the conventions and trajectories of popular culture because these lead to the neglect and diminishment of our souls. An unreflective life, in Socrates' view, leads to the accumulation of wants, desires, fears, and illusions that finally end in jealousy, desperation, and war. Socrates called people to a life of philosophy so that they might learn to resist those temptations that lead to a degraded life. He did not ask them to sign on to a body of philosophical teachings or formulas. What he most wanted was for his fellow Athenians to learn to care about what was truly important. He wanted people to be personally transformed by the insights that deep reflection and probing conversation made possible.

Pierre Hadot has described the Socratic style of philosophizing as a "spiritual exercise." Exercises of this sort are not about indoctrination but about developing in people a *way* of life or an *art* for living. The effect of spiritual exercises is to create

> a concrete attitude and determinative life-style, which engages the whole of existence. The philosophical act is not situated merely on the cognitive level, but on that of the self and of being. It is a progress which causes us to *be* more fully, and make us better ... It raises the individual from an inauthentic condition of life, darkened by unconsciousness and harassed by worry, to an authentic state of life, in which he attains self-consciousness, an exact vision of the world, inner peace, and freedom.[50]

The aim of a spiritual exercise is to develop in people the habits that will enable them to live a more ordered, measured, reflective, free, attentive, available, and responsible life. According to the Hellenistic schools of philosophy that developed this technique, too many people live in ways that exhibit fear, worry, alienation, blindness, or hubris. What people needed, therefore, were practical habits that would confront them with how they are currently thinking and living, and strategies to bring their minds and desires into closer alignment with the truth of the world.

It is helpful to characterize eating as a spiritual exercise. The purpose of people who gather around a table to eat is not simply to shovel nutrients into

---

[50] Pierre Hadot, *Philosophy as a Way of Life: Spiritual Exercises from Socrates to Foucault* (Oxford: Blackwell, 1995), 83.

their bodies. Eating together should be an occasion in which people learn to become more attentive and present to the world and each other. Because eating is something we regularly do, it can be the training ground where people learn to articulate their fears and worries but also name the many sources of nurture and help that are evident at the table. With the help of each other we can practice the skills of conversation, reflection, and gratitude that contribute to a more completely human life. Eating with each other we discover the world and learn to evaluate and respond to it. We begin to see that we are part of a community of life that requires us to be responsible members within it. To accomplish these goals, however, will require people to move within a "Slow Food" orbit, and adopt patterns of daily life that are not so frantic and blind.[51]

When eating becomes a spiritual exercise, it isn't simply that people will have occasions to become more attentive to each other and the world. They will also have the opportunity to see, receive, and taste the world with spiritual depth. What I mean is that the careful attention that promotes thoughtful eating, particularly eating that is informed by the Eucharistic table, will also potentially lead eaters into an understanding of food as ultimately rooted in the grace of God. To move into this possibility, however, requires that we look at eating in an unhurried yet fresh way, a way that is open to dimensions of depth that elude us if we are not attentive.

What would it mean to eat with deep appreciation and with a sense of food's theological significance? What we need is a sense of life's fragility and gratuity, a taste for the world's giftedness and grace contained in every bite. Rarely considered in our eating is the truth that food, which is the necessary means for the continuation of our life, is not itself the source of life. To thoughtfully bite into an apple is to realize that even as it nourishes us, the apple has its own nurture beyond itself. Though eating can be among our most pleasurable acts, it is also inherently troubling because we know that we will have to eat again. Eating makes our life possible, but food is not itself the "liveliness" of life. Eating invites us to commune with others, but it also invites us to discover and commune with the source and sustainer of all life.

In describing eating as a spiritual exercise, let me underscore that I am not advocating the "spiritualization" of food. Food does not become more

---

[51] The Slow Food movement began in Italy as a protest against the waste, ill-health, destructiveness, ignorance, and ingratitude of fast-food culture. Slow food is not simply about slowing down our eating. More deeply, it is about developing a comprehensive approach to life that honors eaters, food, food workers, and the fields and animals that give us food. For a lucid overview written by a Slow Food founder, see Carlo Petrini's *Slow Food Nation: Why Our Food Should Be Good, Clean, and Fair* (New York: Rizzoli Ex Libris, 2007).

ethereal and less material as a result of thoughtful eating. Rather, what a theological approach to eating does is enable the perception of food within a context that stretches *through* the many ecological and social relationships of this world *to* the divine creator and sustainer of it. To approach food with a concern for its theological depth is to acknowledge that food is precious because it has its source in God. To catch a glimpse of what might be involved in this theological approach, consider the arresting speech of Father Zossima as given by Fyodor Dostoevsky in *The Brothers Karamazov*:

> God took seeds from other worlds and sowed them on this earth, and made his garden grow, and everything that could come up came up, but what grows lives and is alive only through the feeling of its contact with other mysterious worlds; if that feeling grows weak or is destroyed in you, then what has grown up in you will also die. Then you will become indifferent to life and even grow to hate it. That is what I think.[52]

This way of speaking will strike many as peculiar and odd, even fanciful and ridiculous. What could "other mysterious worlds" possibly mean, and why is it important that people acknowledge that the "seeds" in the gardens of life make contact with a world beyond this one?[53]

Dostoevsky wanted us to understand that it is possible to live in a world and be spiritually dead to it. This is because we can grow to view the world (and our food) as consisting of material entities or varied chemical nutrients that are themselves dead, and thus essentially bereft of all goodness and beauty. The world, in this view, simply is the collection of random and

---

[52] Fyodor Dostoyevsky, *The Brothers Karamazov*, trans. David Magarshack (New York: Penguin Books, 1958), Book 6:3:g, 377.

[53] In his early work, *Philosophy of Economy*, Sergei Bulgakov laments the kind of economic thinking and practice that understands and appropriates the world only as a material fact. There is in this view no appreciation for the world as imbued and fired by Sophia as the divine principle and providence everywhere at work, and no sense of the possibility that economic activity might serve the higher purpose of joining human reasoning and practice with the *logos* that permeates and brings life and order to all things. In tones reminiscent of Father Zossima, Bulgakov says, "Life survives only because its seeds, sown by the Creator, are indestructible" (152). Were they not indestructible the world would collapse into death. "The purpose of economic activity," says Bulgakov, "is to defend and spread the seeds of life, to resurrect nature. This is the action of Sophia on the universe in an effort to restore it to being in Truth" (153). Sophia joins the members of the world into a harmonious whole, even as it joins empirical reality with the realm of God. This joining happens above all in the Eucharist. As Angel F. Méndez Montoya summarizes it, "For Bulgakov, the holy food of the Eucharist is a healing communion. It is anticipated by a natural consumption of the flesh of a world already graced by God, and which incorporates humanity into a life of communion – a 'metaphysical communism' – with the universe: just as the Eucharist activates a deeper human incorporation into communion with God"; Montoya, *Theology of Food: Eating and the Eucharist* (Oxford: Wiley-Blackwell, 2009), 96.

accidental things. This is a world without paradise and spiritual significance. In it, people live under "the tyranny of material things and habits" (370). They do not deeply love, and so are incapable of perceiving "the divine mystery in things" (375). The world is what its surface appearance suggests. There is no transcendence within or beyond it to captivate us. The implication is that we can then freely transform whatever we meet – fields, chickens, agricultural workers, food servers, even whole countries – into a thing or tool that serves a utilitarian or profitable end.

Rowan Williams, along with many others,[54] has described this malaise as the departure of the sacred from the world: "The world without the sacred is not just disenchanted but deprived of some kind of depth – that is, of the sense that what we encounter is already part of a complex of interrelation before it is part of our world of perception." This is a flat and boring world in which things have significance primarily in terms of their ability to satisfy an ego's desires. Things *are* what we *take them to be.* They have no integrity of their own, no sacred core or center. Rather than being icons that open to a greater world of significance and meaning, creatures are reduced to idols that reflect the aspirations, hopes, fears, and designs of people (or, as we said earlier, food is reduced to items that serve an industrial process and satisfy a business plan). In this depthless world it is very difficult to have abiding and significant relationships with others. "We are en route to regarding and treating it [i.e., the world] as related only to the individual will, and thus as, ultimately, only instrumental to that will's purposes."[55] That we relate to others, and how, is a feature of choices that have little grounding and can change from moment to moment.

Dostoevsky feared a world that has been reduced to a utilitarian or economic calculus because in such a world there are no *creatures* but only *things*, things with no abiding significance. This is Steven Weinberg's pointless world in which it makes little sense to cherish food or anything else. Things are not delectable or worthy of our delight. To put it in terms more resonant with our own time, we are all material bodies struggling to survive and adapt in a cold, mostly inhospitable, and unforgiving universe. Whether we survive is a feature of luck or superior cunning. Whatever our fate, however, it is best not to take our struggles or the world with too much

---

54 See, for instance, Philip Sherrard's *The Rape of Man and Nature: An Inquiry into the Origins and Consequences of Modern Science* (Ipswich: Golgonooza Press, 1987), and Seyyed Hossein Nasr's *Religion and the Order of Nature* (New York: Oxford University Press, 1996).

55 Rowan Williams, *Dostoevsky: Language, Faith, and Fiction* (Waco: Baylor University Press, 2008), 229.

seriousness. This is because we live in a world "in which nothing is serious – in which nothing, that is to say, *signifies*, opens unexpected horizons, exhibits depth or suggests a narrative larger than that of [ourselves] as rootless individuals."[56] If nothing is sacred, worship, but also gratitude and responsibility, lose all seriousness and significance. In a world without theological or moral depth, it is impossible to understand violence against others or the world *as* violent, perhaps even blasphemous. This is because there is nothing of significance that can be violated. Equally important, there is nothing of significance that can be worthy of human affection and fidelity. The world – its eaters and its food-producing fields – has ceased to be a gift or blessing because it has been reduced to a brute, mute fact.

Father Zossima's claim that this world is alive through its mysterious connection with other worlds is Dostoevsky's way of pointing to creation's depth. It is his realization that things are never simply "things" exhausted by their surface or material makeup. Their truth and meaning lie beyond or more deeply within them, and registers in us as the realization of their integrity, value, and spiritual significance. Food is not reducible to material stuff because it is the carrier of and witness to life's liveliness. Bruce Foltz describes this as the world presenting a "face" to us: "nature presents a face here, expresses an inner life, only because it is at the same time disclosed as being turned radically and ecstatically toward a distance unto which all the resonance of the life is directed, and from which all life is itself derived."[57] What we see is never simply the seen itself but also that mysterious and unseen (sacred) "reality" that brings what is into being. Our gaze at a creature, in other words, does not stop at the creature's surface but extends beyond it to its dependence upon and source in a creator. The logos through which all things in the world came to be is also the life and light within each thing (John 1:1–5).

To transform eating into a spiritual exercise is to cultivate the practical conditions and habits – attention, conversation, reflection, gratitude, honest accounting – in which food and the world can be perceived to have a face.

---

[56] Ibid., 193.
[57] Bruce V. Foltz, "Nature's Other Side: The Demise of Nature and the Phenomenology of Givenness," in *Rethinking Nature: Essays in Environmental Philosophy*, ed. Bruce V. Foltz and Robert Frodeman (Bloomington: Indiana University Press, 2004), 334. Foltz makes the contrast with a faceless world clear: "An outside alone, pure exteriority, is only a surface. It is a plane, a superficies; it is sheer extension. It cannot present a face, for there is no inside to face out. And because it has no inside, it is not strictly speaking an outside at all. It is unrelenting superficiality, and it is all-inclusive superficiality: not merely surface, but triviality, a surd surface, just there and nothing more" (331).

When we meet and receive the face of creation, personal freedom can be called into question because now we are responsible for what we do, and must give an account as to whether or not we honored the sanctity before us.[58] A collection of valueless, random entities cannot be violated. A gift or blessing can. But for us to see with depth and appreciate the gifted and graced character of the world, we must ourselves be spiritual beings, beings that carry the "seeds" or spiritual sensitivity for a world of meaning beyond the realm of brute, material facts. We must be capable of communion, capable of entering into and seeing the value of a community that is not simply a collectivity. When we fail to recognize spiritual depth in the world, when we fail to be spiritual beings ourselves, it is inevitable that we will grow indifferent to life, perhaps even grow to hate it as a pointless and cruel accident.[59]

Another way to put this is to say that a spiritually trained person has cultivated habits of *prayer* in which a world of others is understood and received in terms of its life in God. The patterns of life are not hurried through. Rather, one's life follows the discipline of a spiritual exercise that slows and focuses one's attention to what is there and important.[60] Practicing attention, people can now receive their world as a place of belonging. They can experience life as wonderful and mysterious but also terrifying and incomprehensible. Practicing the art of a reflective and grateful life, they are more likely to commit to the kinds of activity that do not take them out of the materiality or naturalness of life but turn the ordinariness of life's events into "markers of praise and thankfulness before God, the Life of all life."[61] As people learn to pray, they are transformed so that their perception and reception of the world can be open to its divine presence:

---

[58] It is no accident that Dostoevsky's portrayal of a world with spiritual depth would also cause him to emphasize our responsibility for each other and the need for brotherhood. Our highest calling is to be the servants of each other. This line of thinking that sees transcendent depth in the face of another has been developed more recently in the philosophical work of Emmanuel Levinas. See in particular *Totality and Infinity: An Essay on Exteriority* (Pittsburgh: Duquesne University Press, 1969).

[59] Along with several others, Philip Sherrard has argued, in *Human Image: World Image: The Death and Resurrection of Sacred Cosmology* (Ipswich: Golgonooza Press, 1992), that how we think of ourselves determines how we think of the world around us. "We are treating our planet in an inhuman, god-forsaken manner because we see things in an inhuman, god-forsaken way. And we see things in this way because that is basically how we see ourselves" (2).

[60] For an elaboration of these themes, see my essay "Attention and Responsibility: The Work of Prayer," in *The Phenomenology of Prayer*, ed. Bruce Ellis Benson and Norman Wirzba (New York: Fordham University Press, 2005), 88-100.

[61] Michael Fishbane, *Sacred Attunement: A Jewish Theology* (Chicago: University of Chicago Press, 2008), 119.

There is no mere world or matters of fact for covenant theology; there is always the wonder and duty to the concrete moment at hand, where God's illimitable gift of life is given into our hands – to hear and do what is here and now. Theology does not change nature as such, but rather transforms its reception, through spiritual consciousness. Brute facticity remains, while being simultaneously transfigured.[62]

Food ceases to register as fuel or as a commodity. Eating becomes a sharing in and a sharing of the blessings of God.

When people learn to become prayerful in their eating by practicing the spiritual exercises of attention and reflection in the kitchen and around a table, the opportunity exists that they will begin to realize – through their touching, smelling, tasting, and seeing – how every bite leads them beyond themselves into the worlds of plants and animals, fields and forests, farmers and cooks. Eating demonstrates that we cannot live alone. Growing food reminds us that we do not create life. Food connects us to the memberships of creation and to God. Thoughtful eating reminds us that there is no human fellowship without a table, no table without a kitchen, no kitchen without a garden, no garden without viable ecosystems, no ecosystems without the forces productive of life, and no life without its source in God.

A theological understanding of food challenges us to discern the scope and character of the memberships of life, and then find ways to honor and live appropriately within them. To be a creature is to be a member joined with others in the struggles and joys of a common, always given life. To be a creature is to benefit from the help and nurture of others and, in turn, to be a help and source of nurture in return. As long as we care to live, there is no release from our shared life. Eating is the daily confirmation of that fact.

Insofar as our eating becomes Eucharistic (what this means and entails we will see in Chapter 5), we have the opportunity to turn membership into communion. God calls creatures made in the image of God to be hospitable, to participate in Christ's reconciling ways with the world (Col. 1:20), to eat with justice and mercy, and in doing so to participate in the divine hospitality that first brought creation into being and daily sustains it.

---

[62]   Ibid., 123.

3

〜

The "Roots" of Eating: Our Life Together in Gardens

God's garden, made "in the beginning," does not lie behind us, but ahead of us, in hope, and, in the meantime, all around us as our place of work.[1]

History without gardens would be a wasteland.[2]

What the human being shares with nature, what we demand from nature and entrust to nature, what we long for and reject, this may all become song and poetry, or music and philosophy, or myth and religion; but in the visible world it must sooner or later become a garden, if it desires to make itself visible at all; and the achievement of visibility – as distinct from simple thinkability, and understandability – is its most irresistible drive, as an inherent part, like all the creative drives of the human race, of the one primordial drive to give birth to structure.[3]

It is no accident that scripture locates the first human drama in a garden. The Garden of Eden, literally the "garden of delight," is humanity's original and perpetually originating home, the place of our collective nourishment, inspiration, instruction, and hope. With eyes, tongues, noses, ears, fingers, and toes, it is the place where people first taste and fully sense the grace of God. Here we learn that we are the beneficiaries of a world of gifts, creatures made by and dependent upon God. Amid plants and animals, and in terms of the varying conditions of soil, water, and weather, people discover what it means to be marked by hunger, blessing, mortality, ignorance, and interdependence. Charged to "till and keep" the garden (Genesis 2:15), people are here given their most fundamental identity and vocation. Wherever we

---

[1] Nicholas Lash, *Believing Three Ways in the One God: A Reading of the Apostle's Creed* (Notre Dame: University of Notre Dame Press, 1992), 124.

[2] Robert Pogue Harrison, *Gardens: An Essay on the Human Condition* (Chicago: University of Chicago Press, 2008), x.

[3] Rudolf Borchardt, *The Passionate Gardener* (Kingston, NY: McPherson, 2006), 32.

happen to live, our joy and health but also our skill and understanding must be shaped in some measure by the responsibilities and possibilities of a garden home. Gardens are important because in them we see in an especially clear way the complex array of relationships that join us to soil and water and to creatures and God, relationships that have nurture and feeding at their root.

Gardens are microcosms of the world in which human life and the "natural" forces productive of life meet. Though being places of varying degrees of domestication, gardens are at their most resilient best when they work with the fecund, forever wild grace of life. One does not need to be an expert gardener to appreciate the fact that insofar as we eat, drink, and breathe we are necessarily and beneficially bound to the geophysical and biochemical processes at work in a garden. This is why even nongardeners must be sympathetic and committed to the preservation and nurture of healthy gardens (wherever they are) and good gardening work (whoever does it). The health of our life and the satisfaction of our stomachs depend on the germination and fruit that gardens embody.

To say that gardens are a microcosm of our world is not to say that the whole world is a garden or that gardens are the only places from which people derive their food. The long history of hunter-gatherer societies and fishing communities makes plain that people can be nurtured by land and water in multiple ways. The diverse experiments in farming, ranging from natural systems agriculture to industrial biotech, demonstrate that people can relate to the sources of food in very different ways. I concentrate on gardens in this chapter because they are, as Rudolf Borchardt suggested in one of this chapter's opening epigraph, the places where the human need to give structure to a nurturing world comes most clearly into focus. Gardens matter because they are a primary and especially intimate site for the working out of our "place" in a world that is at once wild and civilized, human and nonhuman. Gardens reveal that we depend on created forces of life over which we have little control, even as they exhibit our desire to give to this life a human shape.[4] To be a gardener is to be involved in one of the most fundamental of human tasks, namely, the effort to understand human creatureliness as our life together with other creatures and God. Put

---

[4] Much of what I say about gardens can also be said about farms. In some respects, farms are extensions of gardening insights and practices worked out over a larger land area. It is notoriously difficult to specify where a garden ends and a farm begins because each can take so many different forms while sharing similar governing principles. I privilege gardens in this chapter because they are an ideal place to evaluate human efforts to modify creation into a home, recognizing that these efforts can undermine creation's vitality and grace.

differently, gardens are a primary and practical site through which a culture takes shape.

It is helpful to recall that in its earlier Middle English usage the word "culture" referred to a piece of land. More specifically, it referred to a *cultivated* piece of land (the Latin *cultura* means "cultivation of soil"), suggesting that the sign of a cultured person was to understand and know how to work with gardening realities like soil and plant and animal life. Gardening work is fundamental because in it we discover how to feed ourselves and others. In it we learn how to care for each other and the earth upon which we necessarily depend. We need to know the gardening insights that make food possible if we are not to fall into practices that degrade or undermine food production. Though it is possible for people to passively inhabit land, they are at their cultured best when they work with it, learn from and modify it, turning a particular plot into a place that satisfies human hunger, desire, and need for art. A culture that is sustainable over the long term will, at a bare minimum, equip its people to appreciate and refine the skills and affections necessary to secure livelihood. Though people may sometimes act as if they can disregard or exceed the limits of land, a truly viable culture is one that has learned to integrate human desires harmoniously with the potential of any given habitat.[5]

This means that gardening is not reducible to a recreational activity, an optional affair, or a leisurely pastime. Nor are gardens primarily scenic and aromatic places of retreat. Gardening work creates in us an indispensable "imaginary" that enables us to think, feel, and act in the world with greater awareness for life's complexity and depth. Gardens are the concentrated and focused places where people discover and learn about life's creativity and interdependence. Insofar as we are good gardeners we will commit to working with God's creativity in ways that strengthen human and nonhuman life together. When we garden poorly or recklessly, we will inevitably lay waste the world.

To be alive – to eat! – is to be the beneficiary of a garden's life-giving ways. Though many of us live in houses that increasingly separate us from land and the realities of plant and animal life, our fundamental and inescapable home is the land that feeds and sustains the house. We live by eating, which means we live through food that invariably has roots extending into garden soil. Whenever we take a bite of food we confirm with the unmistakable

---

[5] Jared Diamond has given a helpful summary of what happens to cultures when they fail to align themselves sympathetically with the land. See *Collapse: How Societies Choose to Fail or Succeed* (New York: Viking, 2005).

evidence of our stomachs that the literal bases of life rest upon the growth and death, and the diversity and fragility, of the countless organisms and processes that dwell together in a garden.

FINDING OUR PLACE IN LIFE

"To be is to be in place."[6] This ancient maxim, first formulated by the Pythagorean philosopher Archytas of Terentum, indicates that place is the a priori condition for anything to be at all. To talk meaningfully about something we must be able to situate it within a place context. To be entirely bereft of a place is impossible, because it is in terms of place that anything at all takes shape and definition. Though we may not fully understand the places we are in, and so at times feel displaced or even lost, we cannot ever be *without* a place and be well. To be alive is to be the beneficiary of the places that literally and figuratively feed us. Refugee existence and the life of exile are such heinous conditions because they sever the life-giving, livelihood-providing connection between people and their lands. They block people's attempts to give themselves to a place, and in this self-giving discover and create a meaningful identity and world.

A place is at once a limit and a condition for the possibility of life. "Limit" should not be understood negatively, because what a limit does is specify the range of relations that are possible: no one eats food in general but always a particular food item, just as no one lives in a house in general but always a particular house. The specific, embodied relations are essential because it is in terms of them that people develop at all. A human life is unimaginable without particular relations to soil, microorganisms, plants, insects, animals, mothers, teachers, and companions. Though we may not always like the people we are with or the food on our plates, we cannot deny them entirely because they are the indispensable *sources* of our life together.

This means that *relation* rather than *substance* is constitutive of a thing's being. Long ago, Aristotle's doctrine on substance maintained that for us to identify something as the unique thing that it is, we must first separate it from all else. This became his famous principle of identity, a principle that still exercises a powerful hold on how we see the world. In this view, things

---

6   Edward S. Casey, *Getting Back into Place: Toward a Renewed Understanding of the Place-World* (Bloomington: Indiana University Press, 1993), 14. My thinking about the meaning and significance of place has been immeasurably enriched by this work and Casey's companion volume, *The Fate of Place: A Philosophical History* (Berkeley: University of California Press, 1997).

exist first as individuals and then subsequently, perhaps optionally, relate to others. Given this presupposition, it would be relatively easy for scientists, social scientists, and humanists to forget that people and other living beings must eat, and that their eating places and defines them.

Gardening life and the biblical story of the Garden of Eden start with a radically different assumption: humanity (*adam*) is what it is, *is* at all, because of its relation to soil (*adamah*) and the life God makes possible through it. Creatures cannot and were never meant to exist in isolation or separation from each other. Kinship and harmony, mutuality and intimacy are to be the rule of healthy life together.[7] This gardening insight should not be surprising to us if we recall Trinitarian, communal life as the basis for the creation of the world. Earthly becoming, however distorted it may be, is a reflection of the eternal, communion-building life of God. It would take the Cappadocian fathers, who were themselves inspired by Trinitarian teaching, to develop a relational ontology: "The human being is *defined* through otherness. It is a being whose identity emerges only in relation to other beings, God, the animals and the rest of creation."[8] Who we are is not a feature of this or that species trait, be it reason or language or ensoulment. We exist and become who we are only as we *respond* to others, *receive* them, and then *give* ourselves in return. The character of a life is always defined *through* our response to the world. "Whatever we do, or do not do for that matter, wherever we are, we are always already called and requested, and our first utterance, like our first glance, is already an answer to the request wherein it emerges."[9] Life happens in responding to the "call" or invitation of the world.

---

[7]   In his commentary on the Yahwist creation story (Genesis 2:4ff), William Brown argues that the movements toward communion and companionship are the overall trajectories of a successful human life with creatures, with others, and with God. Separation and alienation are the marks of a fallen world. See *The Seven Pillars of Creation: The Bible, Science, and the Ecology of Wonder* (New York: Oxford University Press, 2010), 79–91.

[8]   John D. Zizioulas, *Communion and Otherness: Further Studies in Personhood and the Church* (London: T&T Clark, 2006), 39. The Cappadocians argued that the Trinitarian life of God made possible a profoundly new understanding of being and personhood as inherently relational. Beings do not exist in isolation and then enter into relation. They are always already in relation from the start. In *Being as Communion: Studies in Personhood and the Church* (Crestwood, NY: St. Vladimir's Seminary Press, 1985), Zizioulas argued, "Nothing in existence is conceivable in itself as an individual, such as the τόδε τί of Aristotle, since even God exists thanks to an event of communion. In this manner the ancient world heard for the first time that it is communion which makes beings 'be': nothing exists without it, not even God" (17). For another well-developed philosophical account of the importance of relationality in the definition of persons, see Christos Yannaras's *Person and Eros*, trans. Norman Russell (Brookline, MA: Holy Cross Orthodox Press, 2007).

[9]   Jean-Louis Chrétien, *The Call and the Response* (New York: Fordham University Press, 2004), 14–15.

Thinking about embodiment is one of the clearest ways to understand that our being-in-relation is not something we choose. As Maurice Merleau-Ponty put it, "The world is not what I think, but what I live through. I am open to the world."[10] The openness he is talking about happens most basically through our senses: seeing, hearing, touching, smelling, and tasting. Sentience is about discovering a situation or place, and being open to and inspired by it. "My body," says Ed Casey, "continually *takes me into place*. It is at once agent and vehicle, articulator and witness of being-in-place."[11] Bodies are not simply contained by a place. Rather, the elements of a place are continually entering a body that is either receptive or resistant. In an important sense, our bodies do not simply enter the world. Through sensual interaction, whether as food, aroma, sound, caress, or image, the world also enters into us.[12] Growing and eating the unique foods found in specific regions enables us to inhabit the places of our lives with a more detailed understanding and sympathy. Elemental experiences of hunger and pain, but also satisfaction and exhilaration, find their source and direction in the places that call them forth. Insofar as people are displaced or strangers to a place, and thus unable to respond appropriately or appreciatively to the breadth and depth of relations that make up a place, they also diminish the prospect for a healthy and meaningful human life.

One of the defining features of postmodern life is the extent to which people live in what the anthropologist Marc Augé has called "non-places." He writes: "If a place can be defined as relational, historical and concerned with identity, then a space which cannot be defined as relational, or histor-ical, or concerned with identity will be a non-place."[13] Augé has in mind several features of practical life that prevent anything like a deep relationship or receptive openness to others, features like impersonal shopping, constant mobility, and uniform housing. An increasing proportion of our days are spent in transit, in stores and hotels and airports, and in front of electronic

---

[10]   Maurice Merleau-Ponty, *Phenomenology of Perception* (London: Routledge, 1962), xvi–xvii.

[11]   Casey, *Getting Back into Place*, 48.

[12]   "When my body thus responds to the mute solicitation of another being, that being responds in turn, disclosing to my senses some new aspect or dimension that in turn invites further exploration. By this process my sensing body gradually attunes itself to the style of this other presence – to the *way* of this stone, or tree, or table – as the other seems to adjust itself to my own style and sensitivity. In this manner the simplest thing may become a world for me, as, conversely, the thing or being comes to take its place more deeply in *my* world" (David Abram, *The Spell of the Sensuous: Perception and Language in a More-Than-Human World* [New York: Vintage, 1996], 52).

[13]   Marc Augé, *Non-Places: An Introduction to Supermodernity*, 4th edition (London: Verso, 2008), 63.

screens or cash machines. There is little real contact in this world because we are too much on the move. When we do slow down we often meet the impersonal stares or formulaic responses of bureaucrats and clerks, or are compelled to look upon stylized pop-up ads and billboards. Attempts to initiate contact with others frequently reach only a prerecorded, anonymous voice, while the calls that do come our way are often computer generated. The end result of this situation is that our senses become deadened. Our affections wither in the face of so much anonymity. We slowly lose the ability to be alive and responsive to the world. Rather than interacting with a place and making deep, abiding connections, we become more and more passengers always going through, but hardly into, a place. "The passenger through non-places retrieves his identity only at Customs, at the tollbooth, at the check-out counter. Meanwhile, he obeys the same code as others, receives the same messages, responds to the same entreaties. The space of non-place creates neither singular identity nor relations; only solitude and similitude."[14]

When people withhold themselves or are prevented from entering deeply into a place, they become disoriented. Disorientation does not simply happen at the location level when, for instance, a person does not know which room to be in. Disorientation also goes deeper into a fundamental distortion of *who one should be* and *what one should do*. Think for a moment about indigenous cultures that speak of the moral and spiritual dislocation that is the direct result of no longer knowing the places in which life happens.[15] For them a place is never simply a location. A place is

---

[14] Ibid., 83. The German sociologist and philosopher Georg Simmel, writing well before the time of postmodernity, observed that modern urbanization had the effect of deadening the senses that join people to each other and to their places. The speed, stimulation, and anonymity of modern cities, and the reliance on money and other impersonal forms of exchange, created in people what Simmel in 1903 called "the blasé outlook," or what we might describe today as sensory overload. The danger in this development is the attitude of indifference that it fosters in people. Things, people, and places still register, but their value and meaning have been eroded: "They appear to the blasé person in a homogenous, flat and grey colour with no one of them worthy of being preferred to another. This psychic mood is the correct subjective reflection of a complete money economy to the extent that money takes the place of all the manifoldness of things and expresses all qualitative distinctions between them in the distinction of how much. To the extent that money, with its colour-lessness and its indifferent quality, can become a common denominator of all values, it becomes the frightful leveler – it hollows out the core of things, their peculiarities, their specific values and their uniqueness and incomparability in a way which is beyond repair" (Georg Simmel, "The Metropolis and Mental Life," available at www.blackwellpublishing .com/content/bpl_images/content_store/sample_chapter/0631225137/bridge.pdf, 14).

[15] In *Landscapes of the Sacred: Geography and Narrative in American Spirituality* (Baltimore: Johns Hopkins University Press, 2001), Beldon Lane quotes the Navajo writer Pauline

communicated by a name that tells the story of what happened there and what is to be learned from its history. To lose the name of a place is, therefore, to lose the moral and spiritual instruction of how to behave where one is.

Similarly, in traditional agricultural societies where people remain upon the land generation after generation, there is a communal handing down of knowledge that is specific to particular places. One learns, insofar as one consults the communal memory of the region, that certain practices damage or compromise the land, whereas other practices effect healing and fertility. Here too a place is never simply a location. It is a storied space in which human engagement with the land is remembered and important lessons are taught. What emerges in this instruction, whether indigenous or agricultural, is a conception of land as a moral and spiritual topography. Soil, plants, animals are not simply things or commodities. They are, instead, saturated with practical and moral significance.

Intelligence is not an individual capacity confined to a solitary brain. The intelligence people need to move responsibly through this world is formed through mental and bodily interaction with particular places. This is why intelligence must extend to and be drawn from the places we live in and the communities we live with. To fail to know places in detail, and the wisdom that has collectively been learned there, is to lose the possibility of detailed understanding. Failing to understand, human action will grow to be out of step with, and perhaps even destructively contrary to, the processes of life that feed personal life. From an indigenous point of view, the fact that people harm the places in which they live is the clearest indication that they have not drawn their intelligence and understanding from them. In harming their places, they also harm themselves.[16] This is why the removal of indigenous people from their ancestral lands has been such a deep tragedy. It isn't simply that people have lost some land. They have lost their *place*, and thus also their source of sustenance, intelligence, and orientation in life.[17]

Whitesinger, who said, "In our tongue, there is no word for relocation. To move away is to disappear and never be seen again" (260).

[16]   Casey quotes from the Navajo perspective: "To take from the Earth without reciprocating, without having first become a part of the life of the place, is to disrupt a sacred balance and ultimately to grow ill" (*Getting Back into Place*, 35).

[17]   For an excellent development of this theme, see Keith Basso's *Wisdom Sits in Places: Landscape and Language among the Western Apache* (Albuquerque: University of New Mexico Press, 1996). For a theological treatment of these themes, see Willie Jennings's *The Christian Imagination: Theology and the Origins of Race* (New Haven: Yale University Press, 2010). See also Edward Soja's *Postmodern Geographies: The Reassertion of Space in*

In *Braiding Sweetgrass*, the botanist and Potawatomi native Robin Kimmerer describes the loss of an embodied attachment to land as a form of cultural and psychic devastation. In her view, when people are divorced from the land or fail to develop the skill of attending to land (most basically in the growing and harvesting of food), they lose a primary reason to develop sympathy and affection for it. Not loving the land, they also lose out on the experience of knowing the land loves them back in its offerings of food and beauty. She asks, quite rightly, if people can be expected to live well or peaceably or gratefully in a place that is devoid of love. How many of the ills of our society, the aggressive acting out, the numbness and boredom, or the aimless wandering stem from being divorced from the places in which we live, and thus feeling unloved? The need to feel loved is a deep and profound need. Gardens are places where people can discover the love that the land gives to its inhabitants. "Knowing that you love the earth changes you, activates you to defend and protect and celebrate. But when you feel that the earth loves you in return, that feeling transforms the relationship from a one-way street into a sacred bond."[18]

Another way to describe our collective disorientation is to note that many people today do not know how to *dwell* in the places they are in. The evidence is overwhelming, as historians reveal the steady, even systemic, destruction of the many and varied ecosystems that nurture and feed us. Agriculture, rather than being the art that tunes human culture to the needs and potential of soil, plant, and animal, and thus promotes the health of land and people together, has been transformed into an industrial force that erodes, exhausts, and poisons our world.[19] Robert Harrison, in concluding a wide-ranging survey of the place of forests in the Western imagination (and in public policy), observes: "Western civilization has decided to promote institutions of dislocation in every dimension of social and cultural existence."[20] The cultivation of soil *and* humanity that was once the hallmark of a "cultured life" has receded from memory. The vision of persons as gardening creatures tending and keeping a garden world, and in this

---

Critical Social Theory (London: Verso, 1989) for an examination of how historicist tendencies within critical theory are being challenged by an understanding of place.

[18] Robin Wall Kimmerer, *Braiding Sweetgrass: Indigenous Wisdom, Scientific Knowledge, and the Teachings of Plants* (Minneapolis: Milkweed Editions, 2013), 124–125.

[19] For a summary of the effects of industrial agriculture, see *The Fatal Harvest Reader*, ed. Andrew Kimbrell (Washington, DC: Island Press, 2002).

[20] Robert Pogue Harrison, *Forests: The Shadow of Civilization* (Chicago: University of Chicago Press, 1992), 198.

gardening work realizing their identities and vocations, is rarely part of our common practice.

To dwell means to make a home for oneself in a place. Making a home often entails building a house, but what is more fundamental is the attitude and orientation that informs whatever building we may do (since there are forms of building that are clearly not conducive to a nurturing or sustainable home). In a rich essay on the nature of dwelling, Martin Heidegger observed that building is not simply the *means* to dwelling but always already an expression of dwelling itself. Building, no matter what form it takes, is an expression of the character of our responsiveness to others. An architectural or garden design is the concrete statement of whether or not we have been open to the world, attentive to its possibilities, and faithful to the human and nonhuman relationships that feed our being.[21]

Authentic building, says Heidegger, depends on people developing a care-full relationship to the memberships that make up a place. Referring to the German word for building, he notes, "The old word *bauen*, which says that man *is* insofar as he *dwells*, this word *bauen*, however, *also* means at the same time to cherish and protect, to preserve and care for, specifically to till the soil, to cultivate the vine. Such building only takes care – it tends the growth that ripens into fruit of its own accord."[22] Authentic building is not an imposition of the human upon a landscape, nor is dwelling the satisfaction of human desires at the expense of the world. It is rather the thoughtful and kind reception of the web of relationships that constitute the memberships of life. Authentic dwelling is born in the steady fidelity to a place. It results in the "letting-dwell" of the many others that intersect with our own being, which is why Heidegger says, "The essence of building is letting dwell."[23]

---

[21] In *The Nature of Design: Ecology, Culture, and Human Intention* (New York: Oxford University Press, 2004), David Orr argues for an ecologically informed, culturally rich understanding of design that takes it beyond a technical exercise. For another work dealing with place and its importance for architecture and urban design, see Philip Bess's *Till We Have Built Jerusalem: Architecture, Urbanism, and the Sacred* (Wilmington: ISI Books, 2006).

[22] Martin Heidegger, "Building Dwelling Thinking," in *Basic Writings*, rev. edition, ed. David Farrell Krell (San Francisco: Harper, 1993), 349.

[23] Ibid., 361. For the work of dwelling, Heidegger insists that we need the instruction of poets, not because poets give a rosy or profound aura to what we do but because poets, insofar as they are *true* to the world, lead us into a *kind* relationship with each other and with places. Kindness is the measure of a heart that knows how to dwell. See "... Poetically Man Dwells ...," in *Poetry, Language, Thought* (New York: Harper & Row, 1971), 227–229. Whether or not Heidegger realized this kindness in his own life and philosophical work is another matter. I argue in "Love's Reason: From Heideggerian Care to Christian Charity"

A SABBATH ORIENTATION

These preliminary reflections on place, embodiment, and dwelling have been necessary because they show how vulnerable to impropriety our living is. We can be in a place and not know *where* we are or *how* to be there. We can also come to forsake or degrade places because we do not appreciate how vital they in fact are. The issue is not whether we will live in a place, but how. To develop a distinctly theological account of the "how" of proper dwelling I will now turn briefly to biblical teachings on creation since they specifically address how people are to live in the memberships of life. In particular, I will focus on the practice of Sabbath as the climax of creation, and thus as the model for what our life together in a place should look like.

The doctrine of creation is often presented as being primarily about the origin of the world. From a scriptural point of view, while talk of origins is important, even more important is the larger concern of the character of the world. When examining ancient cosmogonies it becomes clear that a scientific account of the mechanics of origination was not foremost in their minds. People wanted to say something about the world as they currently found it, how the world deeply *is*, and thus also something about how humanity should live. Knowing how the world is depends in some measure on how we think the world is founded. So, for instance, we find Mesopotamian creation stories that describe the world as beginning in violence, proceeding through struggle, and ending in death. Subscribing to a story like this would mean that people are committed to seeing the world and their life within it in terms of violent struggle. Creation stories thus paint a moral or spiritual topography, a metaphysical map that gives adherents the bearings they need to get through life.

The Christian story of creation, deeply founded upon a Jewish story, tells of a world founded and ending in peace rather than violence. God creates through the redemptive word and work that rescues creatures from threat and destruction, and that orients them toward abundant and fruitful life. "God creates by word rather than sword."[24] Attending to this creation story, people learn to know what life is, how it should be received as a gift from God, and then lived as an expression of worship. Here people discover the

---

(in *Postmodern Philosophy and Christian Thought*, ed. Merold Westphal [Bloomington: Indiana University Press, 1999]) that in certain respects he did not.

[24]   Brown, *The Seven Pillars of Creation*, 44. Brown goes on to say that "God works *with* the elements of creation, not over and against them, much less without them, elements enlisted by God as 'empowering environments.' Creation is a cooperative venture exercised not without a degree of freedom" (45).

character and meaning of the places they are in, as well as receive direction on how to live in these places.

Reading Genesis 1 it is tempting to conclude that human beings are the climax of creation, the most important creatures among all that God has created, and the ones for whom all other creatures exist. God's command, "Be fruitful and multiply, and fill the earth and subdue it; and have dominion over the fish of the sea and over the birds of the air and over every living thing that moves upon the earth" (Genesis 1:28), is readily interpreted to mean that people can do with creation almost anything they want. Though there might be occasional reference to the idea that people are stewards of God's creation, and so must exercise restraint in their subduing and taking, the general idea is that creation exists to make human dwelling as comfortable and convenient as possible.[25] In this view, to be placed in creation is to use it to one's own benefit.

This interpretation of the story is highly problematic. To see how this is so we must start again at the beginning. During the six days of creation God speaks the world into existence and order. Light is separated from darkness, as is the sky from the waters. Dry land is made to appear, along with countless species of plant and animal life. It is a glorious scene that God routinely pronounces good. Here the love of God becomes concretely manifest as the hospitality that makes room for others to flourish and be themselves. For the very first time the divine life finds expression in creatures that can be seen, touched, heard, smelled, and tasted. What is to be done in the face of all this goodness and beauty? God inaugurates the first time of *Shabbat.*

The climax of God's creative work is not the creation of humanity (or the satisfaction of human desires exclusively defined) but the experience of Sabbath.[26] Sabbath is not an optional reprieve in the midst of an otherwise frantic or obsessive life. It is the goal of all existence because in the Sabbath, creation becomes what it fully ought to be. It is an invitation to paradise understood as genuine delight. In Sabbath experience, the deep meaning of creation is revealed as the freedom of each creature to realize its God-given potential, and in that freedom to offer its worship back to God. Because God

[25]   In *The Paradise of God*, chapter 4, I give an extended critique of the stewardship model, placing it within a broader account of creation's moral and spiritual topography.

[26]   I have developed the meaning and practical implications of Sabbath life in *Living the Sabbath: Discovering the Rhythms of Rest and Delight* (Grand Rapids: Brazos Press, 2006). In *God in Creation: A New Theology of Creation and the Spirit of God* (Minneapolis: Fortress Press, 1993), Jürgen Moltmann says, "The goal and completion of every Jewish and every Christian doctrine of creation must be the doctrine of the Sabbath" (276).

finds rest and delight in the creation freshly made, so too can creatures find their own rest and delight. Abraham Joshua Heschel expressed this well when he wrote, "The Sabbath ... is more than an armistice, more than an interlude; it is a profound conscious harmony of man and the world, a sympathy for all things and a participation in the spirit that unites what is below and what is above."[27]

Scripture tells us that God blessed and hallowed the seventh day "because on it God rested from all the work that he had done in creation" (Genesis 2:3). God's rest has nothing to do with fatigue, as if God could become tired of creative work. Rather, it has to do with the intense joy and peace, the supreme delight and contentment that followed from God's life-giving work. When people think of Sabbath they tend to think in terms of exhaustion: rest is a break, the time to escape from the harried pace of life. For God, however, rest is best understood as God's complete entrance into life and as God's availability to and joy in the beauty and goodness that is there. Directly contrary to human restlessness, the constant, frantic searching and striving for a different place or a better community, *God rests because there is no other place God would rather be.* God rests because the place where God is, is the place of God's love and concern and work, and there simply is no other place worth going to. Sabbath is not a reprieve from life but an ending of the restlessness that prevents deep engagement with it. By observing the Sabbath, people come to understand how destructive their restlessness really is.

This Sabbath view gives a strikingly different picture of what our orientation into a place should be. Theologically understood, to be properly in a place is to be fully present and receptive to its gifts. A Sabbath orientation teaches people to be attentive and faithful to the goodness and grace that are the concrete expressions of God's love. Sabbath teaches us to *savor* the places we are in as God's delight made delectable. When faced with God's care and creation's goodness and beauty, the spontaneous response should be exuberant joy. People should be overcome with the desire to celebrate and worship. Though it is proper to consume creation for the purposes of life, human use must therefore always be oriented to the larger concern that the whole creation experiences the delight that marked God's first *Shabbat.*

Sabbath observance is true to the extent that it participates in God's own delight in the beauty, goodness, and delectability of creation. God sets the

---

[27] Abraham Joshua Heschel, *The Sabbath: Its Meaning for Modern Man* (New York: Farrar, Straus and Giroux, 1951), 31–32.

pattern for what appropriate Sabbath practice looks like.[28] Sabbath dwelling
becomes possible as people give up the restless search for a more lucrative
world and more agreeable friends, and instead embrace the places and
communities that have been given as the concrete manifestations of God's
love. Sabbath eating becomes possible as people give up the restless search
for ever more exotic foods or ever more fantastic eating experiences, and
instead commit to simple meals lovingly prepared that honor the seasons
and places where one is. It is through this embrace that people experience
what it really means to be at rest, and what it means to dwell.

Reflecting on the significance of the Sabbath as the crown and climax of
creation, Karl Barth observed that humanity's participation in God's *Shabbat*
transforms people to the core. True rest is only possible when we realize that
we do not create ourselves and the world but instead live by the grace of
God's goodness:

> The command to celebrate the Sabbath, and therefore to cease and abstain
> from all our own knowledge, work and volition, even from all our arbitrary
> surrenders and inactivity, from all arbitrary quiescence and resting – this
> command claims from man that which on the basis of his self-
> understanding he can understand only as a sacrifice of his human nature
> and existence, and against which he can really only rebel as life rebels
> against death . . . It demands that he know himself only in his faith in God,
> that he will and work and express himself only in this imposed and not
> selected renunciation, and that on the basis of this renunciation he actually
> dare in it all to be a new creature, a new man.[29]

Barth speaks here of the "sacrifice" of human nature because people are
inclined, often out of deep insecurity and fear, to secure and possess the
world for themselves. People prefer to refuse the grace of God, thinking they
can design a better or more suitable or more profitable world on their own.[30]

---

[28] Nicholas Lash has made the valuable observation that to express belief in God does not
amount to the expression of an opinion. To confess belief is to make a promise and commit
one's life in a certain sort of way: "learning to 'believe in' God is learning to see all things in
the way God sees them: as worth infinite expenditure of understanding, interest, and care"
(*Believing Three Ways in the One God*, 22). Belief in God as the Creator does not, therefore,
take people out of the world but engages us more deeply with it. Sabbath practice is the first
clue to what this engagement looks like. The ministry of God in Jesus Christ shows that
delight in the world must go hand in hand with the commitment to address and alleviate its
suffering and pain. Made in the image of God, people are charged to cherish the world as
God does.

[29] Karl Barth, *Church Dogmatics*, III.4 (Edinburgh: T&T Clark, 1960), 57–58.

[30] In the summer of 1946, while lecturing amid the rubble of what was once the University of
Bonn, Karl Barth said, "The greatest hindrance to faith is again and again just the pride and

In Barth's view, people need to be remade so they can enter more deeply and dwell more responsibly and faithfully in the world. People need their sensory faculties and their daily practices to be transformed so they can live in the memberships of creation with understanding and delight. They need to be remade so they can receive the world as a gift.

It is important to underscore that scripture places humanity's education for transformation in a garden. Unlike a store or a mine, gardens are places that call for particular kinds of work and dwelling: "The LORD God took the man and put him in the garden of Eden to till it and keep it" (Genesis 2:15). Human life in its paradisiacal state is not governed by luxurious ease – a state in which we simply pluck fruit without effort or understanding – but by the attention and practical discipline that enables us to know deeply where we are and who we are with. Human need and desire are thus shaped by the potential and limit of a particular place. To eat, Adam must garden rather than simply shop. Food is not simply a "resource" to be mined or a commodity to be purchased. Adam's work, and the insight that comes from gardening disciplines, enables him to eat with a deep appreciation for what he is eating. It is this appreciation that enables him to experience the Garden of Eden as paradise, as a "garden of delights." It is by *tasting* the gifts of God, by fully sensing with his hands, feet, eyes, ears, nose, and tongue that Adam learns what it means to live rightly in the garden.[31] It is by immersing himself in the garden that he comes to know *and* love where he is. His commitment to the garden and his resolve to learn from and repair his mistakes makes it possible for him to live properly and fittingly where he is. Without the carefull and attentive work that draws Adam deeply into the life flowing through the garden, he would not know his world as delectable and as the source of health and joy. Work, understanding, care, and joy are thus inextricably linked through embodied need. Gustatory satisfaction, in turn, introduces Adam to the love of God.[32]

anxiety of our human hearts. We would rather not live by grace. Something within us energetically rebels against it. We do not wish to receive grace; at best we prefer to give ourselves grace" (*Dogmatics in Outline* [New York: Harper & Row, 1959], 20). We should wonder if the political violence of bending the world to human will and desire is not being repeated in an analogous way in the effort to genetically reengineer the world.

[31] We should recall that the Latin term for discernment and understanding, *sapientia*, is etymologically linked to *sapere*, which means "to taste." Tasting gives us the immediacy of contact that generates intimate, detailed knowledge.

[32] Commenting on Thomas Aquinas's observation that God's love is shaped by friendship and delight, Lash writes that "God 'delights' creation into life." To respond to this love is therefore to commit to finding all things delectable. It is to learn to see and receive all creatures in the light of God (*Believing Three Ways in the One God*, 74–75).

The love of God that Adam discovers is not abstract but embodied, discovered in the intimacy of savoring food. Nor is it without pain for, as we will see, life in a garden, particularly fallen and sinful life, is not struggle-free. Just as a garden home and gardening work were essential for Adam to learn where he was and how to live, so too are gardens indispensable for us as we try to live and eat our way into the memberships of creation.

A GARDENER'S EDUCATION

It is tempting to be sentimental about gardens and to enter into them with fairly romantic notions about the fecundity and beauty of life. This is where my own gardening education began. The first time I tried to grow straw-berries I made a disheartening discovery. Just as the berries were almost ripe, turning a sweet, deep red, I noticed that the ants and slugs in my neighbor-hood were coming to the same conclusion. They moved into my strawberry patch, made themselves at home, and began to eat. Determined to be rid of these invasive pests, I went to the local garden center and surveyed its rows of pest-management options. After choosing one product from among the multiple bottles on display, I returned home and set to work. Fortunately, I read the warning label first. It said, in effect, "Do not let pets or young children near the sprayed area for several days. Burn any clothing that comes into direct contact with this product." I was going to put this poison on my strawberries and then after several days eat them!

I should have been prepared for this. Raised on a farm, I knew that farmers regularly use highly toxic herbicides and pesticides (they have to wear protective clothing and masks to prevent direct contact and inhalation) to control weeds and bugs. My strawberry experience, however, was differ-ent. On the farm I was growing crops for livestock or for unknown, faceless people who lived far away, and so I did not feel quite so strongly about food safety or quality – the sad excuse of every anonymous economy, and the working presupposition of today's industrial agriculture. But I was going to serve the strawberries to my family and eat them myself. The "pest-manage-ment" option I had chosen suddenly looked very different in this personal context. It was not a management device at all but rather a death-wielding poison. In my bewilderment and frustration I simply watched as the ants and slugs enjoyed some very fine berries.

This experience compelled me to rethink the whole idea of gardening. I had thought, quite naively, that I would grow my fruit and vegetables in a picturesque plot, the plants rising steadily and beautifully to attention in my neatly formed rows, and that when harvest time came I would simply pluck the fruit and enjoy. In my accounting system there was no room for rock-hard clay, weeds, pests, uncooperative weather, hungry rabbits and birds, neighborly dogs, or stray soccer balls. I envisioned myself as the gardener in complete control of the garden, and my garden as a place where I could get the commodities I wanted without too much effort, study, or patience. Without realizing it, I had come to think of my garden as a store where, in the words of Sears, I could painlessly and conveniently enjoy "The good life, at a great price, guaranteed." The reality of gardening, however, put me directly in touch with my own ignorance and sloth, and with my too willing disposition to resort to violence.

Gardening is never simply about gardens. It is work that reveals the character of humanity, and is a demonstration of who we take ourselves and creation to be. It is the most direct and practical site where we can learn the art and discipline of being creatures. Here we concretely and practically see how we relate to the natural world, to other creatures, and ultimately to the Creator. We discover whether we are prepared to honor these relations with our work and celebration, or despise and abuse them. When and how we garden gives expression to how we think we fit into the world. Through the many ways we produce and consume food, we bear witness to our ability or failure to receive creation gratefully and humbly as a gift from God.

Too few people today have gardening as their avocation, let alone their most fundamental vocation. We are relieved to be free of the sweaty burden and commitment to a place that facilitates the growth of wheat and the production of bread. Thinking ourselves to exist in a postagricultural world, the majority of people are now incapable of imagining themselves *as* gardeners, let alone gardeners of the sort that honor God and celebrate creation as the expression of God's love and hospitality. We have forgotten that God is the first gardener, the one who *planted* Eden (Genesis 2:8), and that we are called through our gardening (among other things) to be God's abiding "image" on earth.

God the gardener is a striking image (one we will return to at the end of this chapter). It helps us understand that the divine creative activity is fundamentally about "making room" for others to be and to flourish.[33] Gardening work is a form of hospitality in which the focus is on the welcome

---

[33] I have developed this point in *The Paradise of God*. For a more detailed exegetical treatment of these issues, see Terence E. Fretheim's *God and World in the Old Testament: A Relational Theology of Creation* (Nashville: Abingdon Press, 2005), particularly chapter 2. Though describing several images of God as creator, Fretheim does not describe God's creativity in gardening terms despite the witness of Genesis 2:8.

and well-being of others. God's character is revealed in Genesis as the love that enables the life of another to be itself. Gardening work is thus potentially a powerful demonstration and extension of God's own work, for what gardeners do is nurture the conditions in which life can take root and grow. Gardeners are at their best when they approximate the detailed and patient sympathy for creatures under their care that God shows all the time for the creation as a whole. The crucial difference, of course, is that God makes the gardens grow. As gardeners the best that people can do is support the growth that comes from beyond their power and comprehension. Created in the image of God, humanity's highest calling is to testify to the hospitality that God first demonstrated in planting the world.

Gardening is hard, humbling work. It requires attention and patience and a tremendous amount of detailed knowledge about soil and plant and animal life, not to mention weather and the peculiarities of different growing zones and topographies. It presupposes that the schedules of the day and season are not entirely our own as we respond to the changing needs, limits, and possibilities of each garden. It would be a bad idea, for instance, to take a vacation when the raspberries are coming ripe, or to put off making salsa to the cooler days of October when the tomatoes and peppers have already rotted into the ground. The times and terms of watering and weeding are set by the plants, not by us. Gardening work, in short, reveals that we are bound by and to the memberships of creation. For a garden sustainably to service our needs we must first serve and preserve it (Genesis 2:15).

To garden effectively is to bring human living into fairly close, appreciative, and sympathetic alignment with the life going on in the garden. It requires us to know a particular plot of land and understand its potential, and then work harmoniously with it (what works well in one soil, region, and climate may not work well in another). To garden is to unseat oneself as the center of primary importance and to instead turn one's life into various forms of service that will strengthen and maintain the many memberships that make up the garden. It is to give up the much-trumpeted goal of modern and postmodern life – individual autonomy – and instead live the life of care and responsible interdependence. This is what the biblical command to "till and keep" the garden means. When we garden well, devoting ourselves to the strengthening of the memberships of creation, personal ego and ambition gradually recede from the lines of sight so that the blessings and glory of God can shine through what we see. When we serve a garden well by learning to calibrate our schedules and desires to complement gardening realities, life has the chance to thrive and to smell and taste really good.

A chance, however, is not a guarantee. One of the hardest lessons of gardening is that success is always under threat of disease and death. Though gardeners might do everything they know to be correct – proper soil preparation, sufficient moisture, appropriate plant maintenance and protection – there is always the possibility that calamity will intervene. Good gardeners are precisely those who do not run from the calamity. Michael Pollan puts it this way:

> All the accomplished gardeners I know are surprisingly comfortable with failure. They may not be happy about it, but instead of reacting with anger or frustration, they seem fairly intrigued by the peony that, after years of being taken for granted, suddenly fails to bloom. They understand that, in the garden at least, failure speaks louder than success. By that I don't mean the gardener encounters *more* failure than success (though in some years he will), only that his failures have more to say to him – about his soil, the weather, the predilections of local pests, the character of his land. The gardener learns nothing when his carrots thrive, unless that success is won against a background of prior disappointment. Outright success is dumb, disaster frequently eloquent. At least to the gardener who learns how to listen.[34]

Could it be that our declining interest in gardening is rooted in our fear of failure and our impatience with loss? Very little in our culture encourages us to learn the eloquence that comes from disaster. Few among us know how to face our own fragility, vulnerability, and ignorance. We shun the humus, the rich organic layer of soil, much like we shun the humility that comes from a life devoted to the land and its creatures. More than we care to admit, we resist the truth that we live more by gifts and mystery than by the cunning and might of our presumed power.

Humility is not about self-debasement or self-loathing.[35] It is rather the realization that for our living we depend on many others, even the sacrifices of others. As we begin to take stock of the great number and variety of gifts that feed into our being, we also see how inappropriate and dishonest it is to think we could live alone or on terms set by and for us. Need and interdependence define the human condition.[36] That we live at all is always already

---

[34]   Michael Pollan, *Second Nature: A Gardener's Education* (New York: Delta, 1991), 143–144.
[35]   I have developed the theme of creaturely humility in "The Touch of Humility: An Invitation to Creatureliness," in *Modern Theology* 24:2 (April 2009), 225–244.
[36]   One of the citizens of Bosa referred to in the previous chapter gave clear expression to the flight from interdependence when she said, "In the old days, when we used to break bread at home, we had to call on neighbors, and this was a form of dependence. Now that today we buy bread already made, this dependence has ended and we are free in our homes"

the sign that we have received, whether appreciatively or not, gift upon gift. Being an authentic creature presupposes that we know how to receive these gifts with humility and gratitude.

Gardening work can be characterized as a form of catechesis that helps us come to terms with our own need and impotence. In his wide-ranging exploration of the meaning of gardening throughout the ages, Robert Pogue Harrison observes that "care is constantly being thrown back upon the limitations of its powers of action, is constantly reminded of its own inefficacy and essential passivity when it comes to phenomena like weather, blight, parasites, and rodents." Gardening does not proceed in mechanical, predictable fashion, where we can be sure that a particular input will net the desired output. Gardens are places of struggle, surprise, and deep mystery, places where we are often reduced to silence and awe. The presence of poisonous plants and predatory animals testifies to the fact that gardeners must be forever vigilant and careful, knowing the world does not exist to satisfy personal desires. Though we may want this or that outcome, in the end we must learn to receive humbly what the garden provides. "The fall from Eden was as much a fall into the humility of impotence as it was into shame."[37]

But there is more. We have not only to contend with our own arrogance and gardening failure and unpredictability. We also have to face the fact that every garden *by necessity* presupposes a massive amount of plant and animal death. Though our culture encourages the denial of death, gardens are constant reminders of the fact that whatever lives, lives only for a short while, and that for anything to live at all, others must die (most often by being eaten). The sight and aroma of death are simply unavoidable. Seed germinates into new life, then grows (hopefully) to maturity and fruitfulness, only to die back into the ground. Soil, we could say, is the ever-open receptacle for death. Deep in the bowels of the earth countless bacteria, microorganisms, fungi, and insects are engaged in a feeding frenzy that absorbs life into death and death back into the conditions for life. Facing this ground, immersing one's hands in it, as every gardener does, is often too much of a reminder that we come from the ground and one day will be welcomed by the ground in death: "you are dust, and to dust you shall

(Counihan, "Bread as World," 289). This woman went on to say she was glad not to have people in her house who saw (and thus could report to others) her affairs. What must not be overlooked, however, is that the freedom to be in one's own house can quickly turn into the freedom to be lonely, isolated, and at the mercy of a commodity economy.

37 Robert Pogue Harrison, *Gardens: An Essay on the Human Condition* (Chicago: University of Chicago Press, 2008), 28.

return" (Genesis 3:19). It is a reminder that can turn into fear but also revenge: "because the earth is the place where our death is at home, we have an urge to take revenge on it ... A great deal of the destructiveness in our dealings with nature arises, it seems, from a stubborn refusal to come to terms with our finitude, to accept our fundamental limitations."[38]

A GARDENER'S POINT OF VIEW

Gardeners and nongardeners live in two different worlds. Or, more exactly, they occupy a shared world in very different ways. This is because gardeners *see* differently. Though they share eyes with everyone else, the disciplines of gardening life promote distinct forms of vision that give gardeners special sensitivities and a more detailed understanding of their place. How they see is a feature of the kind of life they live, the patterns of their days, and the nature of the engagements they have with fellow creatures. Gardening, in other words, trains our five sensory faculties and our desires so that we can engage and appreciate life's fragility and vitality with greater sensitivity and understanding. Gardeners occupy a unique imaginary.

The training of a gardener begins with a recalibration in the pacing of one's life. The timing of a gardener's life is set by the garden, not the gardener. "Garden time," as opposed to the frantic speed that characterizes much of our living, is a much slower time that is attuned to seasons, daily weather, biological cycles, and the bodily rhythms of exertion and fatigue. It is framed by a Sabbath sensibility that is committed to being with others in terms of their schedules so that the love and grace of God can be seen in them. Gardening work simply cannot be rushed or hurried. When a seed germinates and when a plant produces its flowering fruit are determined by growth schedules that have little regard for our impatient desires. The Chinese Confucian philosopher Mencius captured the need to correct our impatience in the following story:

> You don't want to be like the man from Sung. There was a man from Sung who was worried about the slow growth of his crops and so he went and yanked on them to accelerate their growth. Empty-headed, he returned home and announced to his people: "I am so tired today. I have been out

---

[38] Robert P. Harrison. "Toward a Philosophy of Nature," in *Uncommon Ground: Rethinking the Human Place in Nature*, ed. William Cronon (New York: W. W. Norton, 1995), 436. Harrison has developed this theme in *The Dominion of the Dead* (Chicago: University of Chicago Press, 2003).

stretching the crops." His son ran out to look, but the crops had already withered.[39]

The need to slow down is not for the sake of slowness itself. Rather, what gardeners are after is the sort of timing and pacing that will enable them to see in a detailed way all that needs to be seen. People need to slow down so they can better fit into the memberships of life. We can't attend to the needs of others if we don't know them. Nor can we know others if we don't first slow down and patiently live with them. In our haste we will overlook or underestimate the many processes of life that feed into our own. Failing to see and appreciate even a fraction of what is going on in our place, we will, besides being destructive, also forfeit a powerful inspiration for our collective work, joy, and satisfaction.

A fundamental obstacle to proper and honest seeing is the detached and abstract view of human agency we have. In her famous essay "Against Dryness," Iris Murdoch observed that trends in modern philosophical and literary life encouraged a view of persons as naked, solitary wills who then take the world by force. People think of themselves as "isolated free choosers, monarchs of all [they] survey" (a parallel formulation would be to say that we think of ourselves as isolated free consumers, shoppers of all we survey). There is little appreciation here for the fact that people live in terms of deep cultural traditions and complex backgrounds of lived experience, backgrounds that include bodily attachments to other bodies. What we need, said Murdoch, are the skills and vocabulary of attention.[40]

Attentiveness is crucial because it enables a reconfiguration of self-identity as deeply immersed in a specific place and time. Failing careful attention it is virtually inevitable that we will experience ourselves as lost in this world and without a deep sense of belonging. Living in "non-places," we don't perceive how fellow creatures literally and figuratively feed into our living. Too often, people prefer to live the myths of individual self-description rather than the shared narratives and practices of our living together. Rowan Williams describes this situation succinctly: "The skills have been lost of being present for and in an other, and what remains is mistrust and violence."[41]

---

[39] Quoted by Michael Steinberg in *The Fiction of a Thinkable World: Body, Meaning, and the Culture of Capitalism* (New York: Monthly Review Press, 2005), 129.

[40] Iris Murdoch, "Against Dryness," in *Existentialists and Mystics: Writings in Philosophy and Literature*, ed. Peter Conradi (New York: Penguin Books, 1998), 290–293.

[41] Rowan Williams, *Lost Icons: Reflections on Cultural Bereavement* (Edinburgh: T&T Clark, 2000), 175.

When we become more attentive, a most important result becomes possible: we begin to see the world as it more nearly is rather than as we wish it to be. To be attentive is to know that we are always already in a world that touches, feeds, and responds to us in bewildering varieties of ways. It is to see how frequently and how easily we get in the way of others because we are so intent on imposing our way. At root, the skill of attentiveness manifests a willingness to love the world. The discipline of attention works to remove destructive ambition and ego so that what lies before us can speak for itself. It testifies to the desire to work *with* rather than *against* others.[42] In its deepest and most concentrated forms, attention becomes a form of prayer, a practice in which the truth and integrity of the world and the grace of God can shine.[43]

One of the more common forms of inattention is widely reflected in our refusal to learn from and let natural processes and relationships run their course. Industrial food production mandates that gardeners and farmers shortcut natural protective measures through the often indiscriminate use of pesticides, or they accelerate growth rates through the heavy use of fossil-fuel-derived fertilizers. To make life as easy and profitable as possible we grow foods in monoculture, making them highly vulnerable to pest and disease infestation, and we substitute machine technologies and power for the hard-won wisdom that comes from working patiently and in sympathetic relationship with plants, animals, and habitats. What we fail to realize is that we cannot continuously short-circuit creation's energy flows and memberships without also compromising the health of the whole. The life

---

[42] Describing the shift that happens when a farmer learns to live in a farm rather than against it, Berry observes: "When one buys the farm and moves there to live, something different begins. Thoughts begin to be translated into acts. Truth begins to intrude with its matter-of-fact. One's work may be defined by one's visions, but it is defined in part too by its problems, which the work leads to and reveals. And daily life, work, and problems gradually alter the visions. It invariably turns out, I think, that one's first vision of one's place was to some extent an imposition on it. But if one's sight is clear and if one stays on and works well, one's love gradually responds to the place as it really is, and one's visions gradually image possibilities that are really in it. Vision, possibility, work, and life – all have changed by mutual correction ... One works to better purpose then and makes fewer mistakes, because at last one sees where one is. Two human possibilities of the highest order thus come within reach: what one wants can become the same as what one has, and one's knowledge can cause respect for what one knows" ("People, Land, and Community," in *The Art of the Commonplace: The Agrarian Essays of Wendell Berry*, ed. Norman Wirzba [Washington, DC: Counterpoint, 2002], 187).

[43] In *Gravity and Grace* (London: Routledge, 1963), Simone Weil says, "Absolutely unmixed attention is prayer" (106). I have developed this insight in "Attention and Responsibility: The Work of Prayer," in *The Phenomenology of Prayer*, ed. Bruce Ellis Benson and Norman Wirzba (New York: Fordham University Press, 2005), 88–100.

processes of birth, growth, and death are indescribably complex. Our task is not to subvert or degrade them but to learn as much as we can so that we will do as little damage as possible. This is why patience and restraint are preeminent gardening virtues.

Expert gardeners know how to pay attention to what is going on in the garden. They know when particular plants are waterlogged or suffering from lack of water. They know when a crop is close to harvest and so take the appropriate protective measures. They know when a fruit tree is particularly susceptible to pest infestation and when it needs pruning. And they know that each plant has different needs at different times. This sort of vigilance and understanding takes time – lots of it – all governed by a gardener's sympathies and absorption. Karel Čapek, the great Czech author, said, "The gardener wants eleven hundred years to test, learn to know, and appreciate fully all that is his."[44] One lifetime is not enough because there is too much to observe. Good care is learned communally through trial and error, and is the result of patient observation and detailed sympathy.

Garden time enables sensitivity for life's complexity and depth. When looking at a garden one does not only see the plants but also the history of geo-bio-chemical processes that make plant life possible. Gardeners appreciate the fragility and vitality of life, making it more likely that each bite taken will be savored as a taste of grace, as a memory of life's struggle and success, and as the hope for what life is yet possible. A gardener discovers that so much of life is unseen, going on in the dark ground even in winter. Čapek observed that October is really the first spring month because the roots of healthy life are always embedded in the ground, and so presuppose good soil preparation. Though vegetation has ceased to grow upward in autumn, life grows downward. "We say that Nature rests, yet she is working like mad. She has only shut up shop and pulled the shutters down; but behind them she is unpacking new goods, and the shelves are becoming so full that they bend under the load. This is the real spring; what is not done now will not be done in April."[45]

Because so much of the real work of the garden happens underground and is the effect of processes that we can aid but not control, one of the most important lessons a gardener must learn is to serve the soil. The first priority in good gardening is to grow healthy and rich soil (through the application of compost and manure) because without it there can be no healthy plants or animals. This service begins by not taking from the soil more than what one

---

[44]   Karel Čapek, *The Gardener's Year* (New York: Modern Library, 2002), 116.
[45]   Ibid., 107.

gives back. Sir Albert Howard, one of the twentieth century's greatest agrarians, referred to this work as the Law of Return, the practice in which gardeners and farmers continuously restore organic matter to the soil.[46] In our time we have become robber barons of the soil, treating it as an inexhaustible bank that has no limits on withdrawals.[47] Through various gardening and farming practices the soil is leached and depleted of nutrients, while its complex structure is destroyed. We alternately kill the soil and its microorganismic life with toxic pesticides, and then revive and feed it with fossil-fuel-derived fertilizers. We forget that soil is a complex matrix in which life and death join in an unfathomably complex dance so that more life can grow.[48] True gardeners honor this dance among microbes and bugs, bacteria and fungus, because this is where it all starts and returns. This is why Čapek insisted that a real gardener cultivates soil more than plants. "He lives buried in the ground. He builds his monument in a heap of compost. If he came into the Garden of Eden he would sniff excitedly and say: 'Good Lord, what humus!'"[49] For people to eat well, and continue to do so, they must make it a top priority to feed the soil that feeds them.

Perception is a complex art that requires discipline and skill as well as a community and tradition to help us interpret what we perceive. It isn't only that we lack attention and focus.[50] We don't know what to look for. We lack the skill-forming apprenticeships that would enable us to perceive the significance of what lies before us. Sensing significance and meaning does

---

[46] See Howard's two great works, *The Soil and Health: A Study of Organic Agriculture* (Lexington: University Press of Kentucky, 2006 [originally 1947]) and *An Agricultural Testament* (New York: Oxford University Press, 1943).

[47] For a clear account of this history, see David Montgomery's *Dirt: The Erosion of Civilizations* (Berkeley: University of California Press, 2007).

[48] In *The Hidden Half of Nature*, David R. Montgomery and Anne Bilké describe how scientists are rediscovering the complex life of microorganisms in the soil and in the human body. Soil health and human health depend on the nurture of soil and animal body biomes. In *Growing a Revolution*, David R. Montgomery shows how agriculture can contribute to soil health and fertility on a large scale.

[49] Čapek, *The Gardener's Year*, 23.

[50] Though I emphasize attention here, this is not to discount the importance of the casual glance as an important means for taking in the world. Edward Casey is clearly correct when he notes: "Glancing is its own form of looking. At the same time, it contributes to other kinds of visual perception, which depend on it for its exploratory spirit, its sudden sallies into the outer fringes of the known world, as well as its adept insights into what lies close-up, right under our ethical and epistemic noses. The truth is that, inessential as glancing might seem to be, we could not do without it. Glancing is interwoven into perception at every point, indeed it is indissociable from it. The most studied gaze is riddled with glances, which perforate it at every turn, letting in the fresh air of a continually adventuresome looking" (*The World at a Glance* [Bloomington: Indiana University Press, 2007], xii).

not simply or automatically happen. This is because genuine perception involves us in traditions and practices of naming and evaluation, and in forms of language and behavior that inspire and order our living. The key to successful gardening is that the gardener be available to learn what the garden has to teach. Equally important, the gardener must learn from fellow gardeners who have labored before or labor alongside. Shared perception and work, combined with traditions of cuisine and eating together, form the context in terms of which perception can become precise and meaningful. Communities of gardeners and traditions of gardening, in other words, enable us to perceive with precision but also with purpose. Failing this *formed attention* we will invariably do more harm than good.

Harrison has argued that humanity is at a real crossroads where we must decide whether we will serve life or continue to submit to consumer dreams that are devoid of responsibility, work, and genuine delight. We live today the paradox that in our attempts to re-create Eden we have instead assaulted creation:

> Precisely because our frenzy is fundamentally aimless while remaining driven, we set ourselves goals whose main purpose is to keep the frenzy going until it consummates itself in sloth. If at present we are seeking to render the totality of the earth's resources endlessly available, endlessly usable, endlessly disposable, it is because endless consumption is the proximate goal of a production without end.[51]

What we fail to appreciate is that our consumer frenzy trains us to be the world's most ignorant, destructive, and superficial eaters. Insofar as consumers perceive food as a commodity rather than with depth and significance, the miraculous gift of life is reduced to the ho-hum of the credit card swipe. What gardening teaches, however, is that human happiness is never simply about what we consume. It is, rather, inextricably tied to the service we offer to the garden, the sort of service that builds humus and nurtures plants, and in so doing cultivates life for us to share and enjoy together. The joy of a human life grows as people join their desires and work to the ever-fresh processes of life at work in a garden. It is the intimacy of our engagement to a place that will teach us to see how much there is to cherish in this world.

The intimacy of our engagement will also help nurture a new appreciation for our place in the world as members of a larger whole all sustained by God. As members we depend on the membership of the whole to feed and sustain

---

[51] Harrison, *Gardens*, 165.

us. When the awareness of membership grows, it will also become clear that people are not the sources of life and value. Value is a feature of the fecundity of relationships that make up the memberships that nurture us. One of our greatest temptations is to think that we live alone. This temptation can then lead to either despair (the feeling that we do not belong or matter) or arrogance (the presumption that only we matter). Gardening work addresses both of these dangers by bringing us face to face, mouth to fruit, hand to soil, and nostril to flower with the larger realities of plants and animals that literally feed us. Working in a garden, we know with our hands and our stomachs, and not merely with our heads, that we belong to a membership called creation.

The bodily understanding that creation is a *membership* is of the highest significance. For a variety of reasons we have come to believe that the attribute we call "life" is a feature of an isolatable organism. This is a mistaken belief that has put us (and creation) into a lot of trouble. The problem is that when we focus on individual organisms we forget about the memberships and the grace that circulate throughout creation and bind us together. Organisms depend on an animating, life-giving context for their every move:

> We have been taught that we are separate living *things*, surrounded by other living *things*, but not so. The realities of the world are ecological systems of which organisms are components and without which no creatures of any kind could exist. The biggest ecological system, the planet or Ecosphere, is composed of regional and local landscape and waterscape ecosystems of which life is one property. Living on the land, under the sky, we people are inside the prairie landscapes, inside the continental ecosystem, inside the Ecosphere. The health of each and all is our health.[52]

The ecologist Stan Rowe's insistence that we live *inside* an ecosystem rather than apart from or above it changes the view we have of ourselves entirely. We do not exist outside ecosystems which we can then choose to enter at freely chosen times. We are always already inside the ecosystem, just as the ecosystem is always already inside us in the form of microbes, food, water, and air. Rowe is reflecting the view from the garden which teaches that we have no life outside the garden because our eating always places us within it and it within us. The conceptual lines we draw that separate people from

---

[52] Stan Rowe, *Home Place: Essays on Ecology*, rev. edition (Edmonton, Alberta: NeWest Press, 2002), 23–24. If Rowe were a theologian he would want to add a yet greater and more encompassing life-giving context, namely, the creative, sustaining life of God.

other creatures, while very important in certain respects, are continually being crossed and blurred by the daily facts of our eating, drinking, and breathing. Besides being arrogant, it is simply false to believe that we stand apart from creation and can then choose to do with it as we want. Because we eat, we are always firmly *within* creation just as creatures are always already *within* us, and so must learn to live responsibly there, cognizant and appreciative of the many members of creation that sustain us.

It is for this reason that Rowe advocates that we drop the word "environment" and replace it with "home place." A home place more clearly communicates that the memberships of life do not merely *surround* us (as the word environment indicates) but inspire and interpenetrate with our being on numerous levels. Creation is our home, the abiding place of nurture and sustenance, but also responsibility and celebration. As our sustaining home, it more readily calls forth our affection and care. Unlike a roadside motel, a place we merely use for a while for our benefit, homes are places we cannot do without because they are the places where the roots of our living go deep. Homes evoke affection in a way that motels do not.

We can see now that gardening makes possible two phenomenological conversions, two transformations in perception and action. First, it enables us to see the world with depth, a world beyond the realm of objects and commodities, a world that invites our praise of God. Second, it enables us to engage the world as a membership that is more than a collection of parts. In this integrated and interdependent world we share life and death with others. As members capable of a moral and spiritual life we also play the special role of nurturer and celebrant and witness. Put another way, though everything that lives eats, we are the ones privileged to garden, feast, and be hospitable. We are the ones who can give voice to gratitude and develop eating practices reflective of faith, hope, and love.

A gardener's education begins with the realization that we are never exempt from the needs and requirements of care. It is formed through sustained attention to and responsibility for the places that give us life. It ends with the praise that affirms the grace of our life together. Gardening is an essential education from which no one is exempt.[53] What is at stake is the realization that our life literally grows out of the ground and is a gift

---

[53] There are curricular implications to this claim. School programs, along with whatever else they teach, should incorporate gardening insights so that students remember and appreciate where they come from, what they depend upon, and what responsibilities they need to keep in mind. We already teach considerable amounts of science without assuming that each student will become a scientist. In a similar manner, we should involve students in a gardening education even if they do not go on to become master gardeners. Gardening

deserving of nurture and celebration. Insofar as we eat and drink, insofar as we seek structure and order and beauty, we must tune our living to the potential of each place.

GODLY GARDENING

Besides being a practical, life-nurturing task, gardening is also always a spiritual activity. In it we attempt to make room for what is beautiful, delectable, and even holy. Every act of gardening thus presupposes and embodies a way of relating to creation and to God, a way that invariably invokes moral and theological decisions. Though membership in a garden is a given, *how* we will take our place in the membership is not. Our aim, theologically understood, must be to develop into Godly gardeners, gardeners who work harmoniously among the processes of life and death, and in their work testify to the life-creating presence of God in the world. This means that besides vegetables, flowers, and fruit, gardeners are themselves undergoing a spiritual cultivation into something beautiful and sympathetic and healthy. A caring, faithful, and worshipping humanity is one of the garden's most important crops.[54]

As with vegetable crops, we cannot assume that the cultivation of humanity will easily or always produce the desired fruit. Gardeners are not automatically rendered virtuous simply by being in a garden and performing gardening work. Gardeners can be petty, impatient, and destructive like anyone else. They can be arrogant and presumptuous, and so bear witness to themselves rather than the grace of God. This insight is well captured in an Israelite tradition that elevated wilderness life over life in the garden. Deuteronomy records God's provision of a new land "flowing with milk and honey." This land is not like the land of Egypt

> where you sow your seed and irrigate by foot like a vegetable garden. But the land that you are crossing over to occupy is a land of hills and valleys, watered by rain from the sky, a land that the LORD your God looks after.

insights and sympathies need to be in all our minds and hearts no matter where we live or what we do.

[54] The growth of community gardens across the country is a testimony to the potential of gardens to build memberships and reconcile relationships between people and between people and the land. For a description of how Cedar Grove United Methodist Church in Cedar Grove, North Carolina, has made a community garden an extension of the ministry of the church and a witness to the healing and feeding life of God, see Fred Bahnson's "A Garden Becomes a Protest: The Field at Anathoth," in *Orion Magazine* (July/August 2007), www.orionmagazine.org/index.php/articles/article/312/.

The eyes of the LORD your God are always on it, from the beginning of the year to the end of the year. (Deuteronomy 11:10–12)

Besides giving us a striking portrayal of God as the ultimate gardener and farmer (God "looks after" the land continuously), this passage warns us of the temptation to take life into our own hands and presume that we can control it. As the history of Egypt shows, when people take control of the forces of life, their power invariably becomes oppressive and violent (the greatness of Egypt was not founded upon kindness and mercy). The Israelites are to be different.

They are to bear witness to the power and glory of God, a power that is evident in rain that waters the land that produces grain, grass, wine, and oil (11:14–15). As a people, they are to remember that God feeds them (recall the stories of manna and quail in the wilderness), and that whatever work they do in food production is always dependent on God's primordial and sustaining work. Deuteronomy is not suggesting that the Israelites are to do nothing with regard to food – they will grow grain and raise livestock – but that the work they do ought always to allow God to be seen and honored. Life and the prospect of gardening success is never our achievement. It is a gift and grace of God.[55]

To speak about the spiritual cultivation of people means that we need gardening exercises like weeding and fertilizing to be applied to us. It is not only plants that need specific kinds of nurture to become healthy and strong. So too do people. Weeds that crowd out desirable life in a garden can also take root in our hearts, crowding out virtues and desires that testify to the glory of God. Traits like envy, arrogance, and impatience need to be yanked out of us so that the love of God and creation can take root. We need to learn first that we are creatures dependent upon God and each other, and then act accordingly. In large part, this is what the work of the church is: to graft (Romans 11:17–24) its members to the life of God in Christ so that together they can become a healthy and whole membership that reflects and extends to others God's healing, feeding, and reconciling life.

For Christians the shape and character of real life are embodied in the person of Jesus Christ. One way to think of his presence among creatures is to say that he came to cultivate the gardens of this earth and our lives. The history of sinfulness reveals that our gardens have become overrun by weeds and bad fruit and our gardening practices have become unjust and vain.

---

[55] My thanks to my colleague Stephen Chapman who alerted me to this passage in Deuteronomy and helped me understand its importance for this chapter.

Though the gospels refer to Jesus as the shepherd who takes care of his flock, it is also helpful to think of Jesus as the gardener who came to clean up his garden and lead it into abundant and fruitful life. We have no direct proof that Jesus was a gardener in a professional sense.[56] What is clear, however, is that he, like most people in the world's history, had an intimate understanding of gardening realities. How else are we to account for the numerous horticultural images that are often the medium of his message and kingdom? Jesus advises his followers to put their trust in God rather than themselves, learn from the lilies of the field, and gratefully receive the gifts of God (Matthew 6:25–33).

It makes sense to think of Jesus as a gardener particularly when we recall that God is the first gardener. "And the Lord God planted a garden in Eden, in the east; and there he put the man whom he had formed. Out of the ground the Lord God made to grow every tree that is pleasant to the sight and good for food" (Genesis 2:8–9). God does not merely create the world and then let it go. Rather, God attends to the world by tending it like a gardener, holding its soil and breathing life into it.

> You visit the earth and water it,
>   you greatly enrich it;
> the river of God is full of water;
>   you provide the people with grain,
>   for so you have prepared it.
> You water its furrows abundantly,
>   settling its ridges,
> softening it with showers,
>   and blessing its growth.
> You crown the year with your bounty;
>   your wagon tracks overflow with richness.   (Psalm 65:9–11)

God is continually in his garden creation, watering and feeding it but also weeding and pruning it. God delights in the fruitfulness of its life, just as God

---

[56] I would argue it is no accident that in John's gospel the site of Jesus' resurrection is a garden, and that in 20:15 Mary takes the risen Lord for a gardener (perhaps we are to understand the Garden of Gethsemane as the place of "new creation" much like the Garden of Eden was the place of the first creation). According to the gospels, we know that gardens were places Jesus frequented often with his disciples (18:2), and that the Garden of Gethsemane was an important place of spiritual discernment (Matthew 26:36 and Mark 14:32). Much of Jesus' ministry dovetails precisely with the sorts of work gardeners do (feeding, healing, attending, caring, etc.). Indeed, the "fruit of the Spirit" referred to by Paul (in Galatians 5:22–23) – love, joy, peace, patience, kindness, generosity, faithfulness, gentleness, and self-control – take on a more exacting and practical meaning when understood in a gardening light.

expresses profound sorrow over its disease or death. God is continuously watchful and alert to the dangers that can disrupt the garden's life. God is faithful even when the garden does not produce fruit as planned.

It is an important teaching of scripture that God is intensely present to creation all the time as the source and sustenance of its ongoing life. To take one example, Psalm 104 speaks of God as the one who makes springs gush forth and the grass grow. God waters the mountains and trees and gives drink to every wild animal. Being the ultimate gardener, God brings forth food from the earth. The whole spectrum of creation's vitality and diversity is characterized here as the fruit of God's continuous, careful work. God is the breath that moves through every life's breath. Were God to withhold this divine, creating breath, all things would die and return to the dust of the ground. God's abiding presence, in other words, continuously creates, sustains, and renews "the face of the ground." Though God clearly delights in creation's wildness (Job 38–39), it is also clear that in many respects God's relationship to creation is like the relationship gardeners have with their gardens. By participating in the gardening work God does, people are put in a position to sense and appreciate God's life-building ways. It is much less likely that we will know God as the source of life if we have little or no sensitivity for the curiosity, patience, care, attentiveness, affection, steadfastness, delight, and sorrow that are the signs of God's own gardening life.[57]

The human task is to live a life reflective of God's intentions in the world. This is what it means to be made in the image of God. "Man is a microcosm in whose flesh resonates and reverberates the pulse of the whole creation, in whose mind creation comes to consciousness, and through whose imagination and will God wants to heal and reconcile everything that sin has wounded and put in disharmony."[58] Put differently, in the creative gardening work

---

[57]   This point is particularly important in an era when many people believe that talk about God has become abstract and merely formulaic. What motivates all this speaking about God? Is it anything more than the private anxieties of a bewildered or bored ego? Are the gods people regularly worship and prop up with intense emotional or dramatic effort anything more than idols or the objects of wish-fulfillment? Gardening is not a proof of God's existence, nor is it faith's guarantee. What a gardening life does, however, is draw us closer to the source, action, and mystery of creation. Thomas Merton was aware of how greater intimacy with creation leads to a sense of the presence of God when he wrote: "We are living in a world that is absolutely transparent, and God is shining through it all the time. This is not just a fable or a nice story, it is true . . . God manifests Himself everywhere, in everything – in people and in things and in nature and in events . . . You cannot be without God. It's impossible, it's just simply impossible" ("A Life Free from Care," in *Thomas Merton: Essential Writings*, ed. C. M. Bochen [Maryknoll, NY: Orbis Books, 2000], 70).

[58]   Vigen Guroian, *Inheriting Paradise: Meditations on Gardening* (Grand Rapids: William B. Eerdmans, 1999), 7.

we do we have the opportunity to mirror and extend God's own creating and sustaining nature in the world.

How does God garden? Scripture gives us an idea because it frequently casts God as the one who gardens his nation Israel. Consider the prophet Isaiah, who writes:

> On that day:
> A pleasant vineyard, sing about it!
> I, the LORD, am its keeper;
> every moment I water it.
> I guard it night and day
> so that no one can harm it;
> I have no wrath.
> If it gives me thorns and briars,
> I will march to battle against it.
> I will burn it up.
> Or else let it cling to me for protection,
> let it make peace with me,
> let it make peace with me.
> In days to come Jacob shall take root,
> Israel shall blossom and put forth shoots,
> and fill the whole world with fruit.   (Isaiah 27:2–6)

In this passage Isaiah is building on an earlier song in chapter 5 referring to a vineyard that fails to produce good grapes. That vineyard is destroyed and made desolate. It is deprived of rain, and only thistles and thorns grow. In Isaiah's mind, the house of Israel is a garden called to produce beautiful plantings of justice and mercy. The Israelite garden, however, produces instead the injustice of the wealthy who consolidate resources into the hands of a few, the arrogance of a people who take no notice of the world as God's gift, and the deception of those who call evil good and good evil.

> For the vineyard of the LORD of hosts
> is the house of Israel,
> and the people of Judah
> are his pleasant planting;
> he expected justice,
> but saw bloodshed;
> righteousness,
> but heard a cry!   (Isaiah 5:7)

The Israelite garden has become infested with life-choking weeds, while Israelite gardening has departed from the gardening practices of God that yield delightful and healthy fruit. The Israelites cannot produce good fruit because their soil is bad and their inspiration for work is of the wrong kind.

In chapter 27 the scene has changed. God has taken over as the gardener, with dramatically different results: drought is replaced with abundant water; God battles against and defeats the thorns and thistles (now understood as the enemies of Israel); and the garden is itself a place of peace. God's wrath is no more, and the land of Jacob ceases to be a wasteland. As a nation it flowers into beauty and life-giving fruit.[59] With God as the gardener, a proper kind of vigilance and care has been restored so that the forces of perversion and destruction can be observed and weeded out. God guards the garden night and day so that the life within it cannot be harmed. In tones reminiscent of the Garden of Eden, God is present to and active within the garden so that creation as a whole can manifest again the joy and delight that marked God's first *Shabbat*. "In days to come Jacob shall take root, Israel shall blossom and put forth shoots, and fill the whole world with fruit" (27:6).

In this passage, and others like it, Israel is referred to as a garden or vine that has been planted by God.[60] That the garden will be productive of good fruit is determined by how well Israel patterns its gardening after the desires of God. Poor gardening, gardening that does not attend to the needs of the garden's members or that exploits some members to the benefit of others, will inevitably bring about the garden's collapse. For the Israelites the collapse was hardly metaphorical: it was witnessed in abandoned orphans and widows, an unjust and exploitative economy, ravaged and desolate landscapes, and finally in exile. The desolation of the land was the clearest sign of a desolate faith.[61] The recovery of the nation and the renewal of its faith, in turn, would have to be worked out in terms of the care of the land. As the prophet Jeremiah described it, hope for the nation is to be found in a garden at Anathoth that will serve as a witness to God's protection, provision, and care. This will be a garden of hope because it will be founded on the gardening principles established by God: steadfast love, detailed fidelity,

---

[59]   For helpful commentary on both of these passages, see Brevard S. Childs's *Isaiah* (Louisville: Westminster John Knox Press, 2001).

[60]   Psalm 80:8–9 is another instance: "You brought a vine out of Egypt; / you drove out the nations and planted it. / You cleared the ground for it; / it took deep root and filled the land." Cf. also Hosea 14:4–7.

[61]   Ellen F. Davis has given us an excellent account of Israelite faith as it is worked out in agricultural and gardening contexts. Davis makes clear that Israelite religion was far more attuned to the requirements of the land than is often supposed, and that this attunement was intimately bound up with how it understood God. See *Scripture, Culture, and Agriculture: An Agrarian Reading of the Bible* (Cambridge: Cambridge University Press, 2009).

and attentive care. God says to the people: "I will rejoice in doing good to them, and I will plant them in this land in faithfulness, with all my heart and all my soul" (Jeremiah 32:41).

In John's gospel these Godly gardening motifs come together in a new way when Jesus says, "I am the true vine, and my Father is the vinegrower" (John 15:1). Here Jesus takes upon himself terms formerly applied to Israel, though in taking them on he also modifies them. For instance, in John, the vine is identified as the source of life (Hebrew texts refer to God as the source). If people are to live a fruitful and beautiful life, they must be grafted directly onto Christ as the true vine. The effect of this transformation is to make the union between God and God's people all the more intimate. We are to abide in Christ as Christ abides in us (we will return to this important theme in Chapter 5) with the same intensity of attachment that is characteristic of a branch connected to a vine (15:4). Apart from the vine, the branch literally has no life, could not even have begun to have life. But as grafted, the branch knows true life because it is continually fed and nurtured by life's divine source.

This is arresting imagery because it communicates not only how dependent we are on God but also how important it is that we synchronize and tune our living to the true life that God reveals to us in Christ. Human life is to grow out of Christ, who is the vine, so that we can then be the agents of God's continuing care in the world. We cannot mirror God's nature if we are not inspired and fed – not gardened – by God.

John's language of the vine needs to be contrasted with those passages that refer to Jesus as the bread of life (6:35) and as the source of living water (4:14). Drinking this water and eating this bread, people experience what true life is. Bread and water, however, have to enter in from outside. A vine is not really "outside" its branch. Branch and vine are seamlessly connected such that it is hard to pinpoint exactly where one ends and the other begins. In this account we can see how the meaning of persons as *imago Dei* is deepened and strengthened since one cannot really see a branch without also taking note of the vine. The branch, by being what it is, reflects automatically the nurture and goal of the vine. If people are branches grafted onto the vine of Christ, drawing their inspiration and sustenance from him, their lives will (naturally or inevitably) witness to the life of Christ. Raymond Brown has argued that this shift is important, indicating that John is moving his disciples to see that it is not enough to believe in Jesus, perhaps from some distance or in an abstract or formulaic way. To be a true follower, one must love Jesus, since love is the best language we know to express the intensity of intimacy that characterizes true life.[62] Love is the most fundamental force that holds a membership together. Abiding in Jesus is what will enable people to welcome rather than resist Christ's cultivation and pruning. Love will enable people to let go of personal ambition so that others can be humbly received and served as the gifts of God that they are.

In this farewell discourse John is inviting people to become intimate followers of Christ rather than ignorant servants performing tasks by rote or out of fear. True followers are beloved friends of Jesus who know from the inside what the intention and the life of the Father is all about. If they are grafted onto Jesus – most basically by continuing Christ's ministries of feeding, healing, forgiving, and reconciling – then they will be continuing in the world God's own life-building ways that have been in place since the first day of creation. They will garden creation like God does. Jesus is the vine that makes possible every fruit-bearing branch. If Christ was not in us, had not chosen us, as John says in 15:16, then we would not even be. Insofar as people draw their inspiration and nurture from him, creation's gardens will grow and flourish.

The plain fact, however, is that people can choose not to be "in" or gardened by Christ. We can, in futile fashion, try to be a branch that grows all of its own, and thereby refuse the memberships of creation and community. We can deny that we always draw our life from a garden and so must serve and accept responsibility for it. The results are plain: not only will we not produce any fruit but we will be capable of nothing. Destruction and desolation will follow in our wake. "Whoever does not abide in me is thrown away like a branch and withers; such branches are gathered, thrown into the fire, and burned" (15:6).

This theological account of our life in Christ is important because it enables us to think deeply about the significance and goals of life. As we know from the various histories of creation's degradation and destruction (and as our next chapter will show), not all gardening practices reflect or honor the ministries of Christ. Whether out of fear, anxiety, or arrogance, we tend to exhaust and waste life. In the face of all this destruction, the need to learn what true or real or complete life looks like – what the gospel calls "abundant life" or "resurrection life" – has become all the more urgent. We need to undergo the sort of spiritual cultivation that will equip us to become the sorts of gardeners that will heal, sustain, and celebrate God's good creation.

---

[62]   Raymond E. Brown, *The Gospel According to John (xiii–xxi)* (Garden City, NY: Doubleday, 1970), 672.

If Christ is the true vine, then all life owes its existence to him and is the effect of his love.[63] What we know from the gospel accounts is that this love is deeply sacrificial. It is love that is pure because it has been cleansed of all vestiges of envy, fear, hatred, manipulation, desperation, and arrogance. To be a follower of Jesus is to participate in this love and be united to it.

> The union which is thus achieved is not cheap. In speaking of the purifying of the vine, the parable evokes the dying of Jesus, and in so doing inevitably implies the dying of those who abide in Jesus. The two deaths, of Jesus and of the disciples, are inseparable. Thus the first blossoming, the breakthrough into the realm of divine love, is preceded by a form of death.[64]

We should recall that John's gospel uses an image familiar to every gardener to describe the kind of death that is a prelude to more abundant life: "Very truly, I tell you, unless a grain of wheat falls into the earth and dies, it remains just a single grain; but if it dies, it bears much fruit" (12:24). Without the giving of one's life, the life of the garden will come to a halt (we will return to this theme in Chapter 4).

The language of sacrifice and self-giving should not come as a surprise to those who wish to participate in God's gardening ways. This is because Christ is the embodiment of God's nature as the one who gives without end. Christ reveals the "eternal kenosis" that is active in the divine Trinitarian life, and so demonstrates that "God desires to give and realize his love in what is other."[65] God's original creation of the Garden of Eden was and continues to be an act in which God "makes room" for what is not God to be and to flourish. Rowan Williams observes that it is when we practice the self-denial and self-dispossession that mirror God's life that we are also enabled to receive each other and the world as divine gifts rather than personal possessions.

---

[63] John's gospel begins with an account of Jesus as the eternal Word that brings all things into being and gives them life. The life Jesus gives is true, abundant, eternal, resurrection life and so is to be contrasted with the sort of "life" that is violent or abusive or exploitative. Jesus is also the "light" (John 1:4–5) that enables us to see the difference between different kinds of life.

[64] Thomas L. Brodie, *The Gospel According to John: A Literary and Theological Commentary* (New York: Oxford University Press, 1993), 481–482.

[65] Rowan Williams, "Creation, Creativity and Creatureliness: The Wisdom of Finite Existence." This speech, originally delivered in Oxford, is available at www.archbishopofcanterbury.org/997?q=creation+creatureliness. The reference to "eternal kenosis" is from Sergius Bulgakov's *The Lamb of God* (Grand Rapids: William B. Eerdmans, 2008), 99.

From a practical point of view, the love here talked about makes itself manifest in a garden when the gardener learns to get out of the way. Gardening is not about drawing attention to the gardener. Contrary to the trajectories of so many of today's work strategies, Godly gardening is not an exercise in self-glorification. In it there is rather a kind of self-forgetfulness that sets in. Čapek captures this self-forgetting in the following:

> I will now tell you how to recognize a real gardener. "You must come to see me," he says; "I will show you my garden." Then, when you go just to please him, you find him with his rump sticking up somewhere among the perennials. "I will come in a moment," he shouts to you over his shoulder. "Just wait till I have planted this rose." "Please don't worry," you say kindly to him. After a while he must have planted it; for he gets up, makes your hand dirty, and beaming with hospitality he says: "Come and have a look; it's a small garden, but – Wait a moment," and he bends over a bed to weed some tiny grass. "Come along. I will show you Dianthus musalae; it will open your eyes. Great Scott, I forgot to loosen it here!" he says, and begins to poke in the soil. A quarter of an hour later he straightens up again. "Ah," he says, "I wanted to show you that bell flower, Campanula Wilsonae. That is the best campanula which – Wait a moment, I must tie up this delphinium …"[66]

The true gardener, inspired by God, demonstrates the kind of curiosity, delight, and devotion in which no detail is too small not to be attended to, and no life so insignificant as not to warrant celebration. Like God, gardeners find their Sabbath rest in the garden, are committed to its well-being, and know there is no other place they would rather be and no work they would rather perform. When we garden well, creatures are nurtured and fed, the world is received as a blessing, and God is glorified.

---

[66] Čapek, The Gardener's Year, 7–8.

4

∾

Eating in Exile: Dysfunction in the World of Food

The willingness to abuse other bodies is the willingness to abuse one's own. To damage the earth is to damage your children. To despise the ground is to despise its fruit: to despise the fruit is to despise its eaters. The wholeness of health is broken by despite.[1]

We no longer live in a world of single threats to the food economy . . . we may well be on a course for a perfect storm of sequential or even simultaneous food-related calamities that fundamentally change our ability to maintain food security.[2]

The anorexic body seems to say: I do not need. It says: Power over the self. And our culture, in such a startlingly brief period of time, has come to take literally the idea that power over the body has a ripple effect: power over the body, over the life, over the people around you, power over a world gone berserk.[3]

Today's global, industrial food culture is a culture in exile because it exhibits the marks of injustice, estrangement, and bewilderment. What should we eat, *really*? Why do many *still* not have enough to eat when sufficient food is being produced to feed everyone? Why is so much "food" so unhealthy? How long will our soil be able to grow food? Why are there now nearly 500 "dead zones" in our oceans and deltas? Will the spinach, the quintessential symbol of healthy food, make us ill or even kill us? These questions reveal that food's production and consumption, rather than being wholesome

---

[1] Wendell Berry, *The Unsettling of America: Culture and Agriculture* (San Francisco: Sierra Club Books, 1977), 106.

[2] Paul Roberts, *The End of Food* (Boston: Houghton Mifflin, 2008), 301.

[3] Marya Hornbacher, *Wasted: A Memoir of Anorexia and Bulimia* (New York: Harper-Flamingo, 1998), 85.

means of connecting with the world and each other, have in many instances become sites of contention, ill-health, and destruction.

To be in exile does not simply mean that we are in the wrong place – a problem of location and logistics. It also means that the ways and manners of our being anywhere do not exhibit a harmonious fit – a problem of moral and spiritual discernment. As I will use the term here, to be in exile marks an inability to live peaceably, sustainably, and joyfully in one's place. Not knowing or loving *where* we are and *who* we are with, we don't know *how* to live in ways that foster mutual flourishing and delight. More specifically, we don't know how *through our eating* to live sympathetically in the memberships that make creation a life-giving home. As a result, we now face a situation in which industrial, global patterns of food production and eating are undermining creation's overall health. To be in exile is to find oneself in a world that is increasingly inhospitable or unlivable.

Those who live in developed countries have not had to think much about food. Walking into a supermarket reveals an abundance of attractive and relatively inexpensive food. Rarely does one find an empty shelf of anything. In large part, this abundance is attributable to the Green Revolution associated with the work of Norman Borlaug. This revolution in agriculture nearly doubled corn, wheat, and rice yields between the 1950s and 1990s. To achieve this record output, farmers used newly developed seed varieties in combination with increased irrigation and the application of fertilizers and pesticides.[4] Small farms growing a variety of foods using manual labor were replaced with large farms growing one crop using heavy machinery. All in all, the Green Revolution was hailed as a production and efficiency success story. Borlaug received the Nobel Peace Prize in 1970.

All is not well with this revolution. The problem is not simply that the world's human population is continuing to rise (prompting some food analysts to say we need to double yields again). A deeper problem is that this revolution is not really "green" or sustainable. For instance, the Green Revolution should also be called the "brown" revolution because it is saturated with the use of fossil fuels to provide fertilizers and pesticides and to run the equipment to irrigate, cultivate, harvest, transport, and process whatever commodities are grown. We should not pretend that our burning of oil and gas does not have atmospheric consequences. We also

---

[4]   Vaclav Smil has described how the world's growing population would not have been possible without the invention of synthetic fertilizers (particularly nitrogen). See *Enriching the Earth: Fritz Haber, Carl Bosch, and the Transformation of World Food* (Cambridge, MA: MIT Press, 2000).

need to register that steadily increased yields have now plateaued or are declining, suggesting that wheat, corn, and rice varieties have likely reached or are near reaching their maximum productivity. When we add ecological indicators to the mix, factors like climate change, soil erosion and toxification, water depletion and pollution, and disease drift, the hope for dramatically increased yields in the future looks unrealistic.[5] Though some point to biotechnology and the genetic development of super-productive seed varieties as agriculture's best hope, the vast majority of genetically modified seed grown today is not to increase yield but to withstand herbicide use.[6] It is unrealistic, if not fanciful, to put our hope in "super-seeds" grown on an exhausted, degraded, and poisoned planet.

Reflecting on the costs and limits of industrial agriculture reveals the naivety of the hope many people have that food will always be available and cheap. It is not a solution to expect farmers, many of them already poor, to become dependent on patented seeds and expensive fossil-fuel-derived inputs.[7] It is not a solution to increase yields at the cost of an overall *decrease* in soil fertility, freshwater availability, and species diversity.[8] It is not a

---

[5] Punjab, India, once considered by many the symbol of Green Revolution success, is now poised (because of water depletion and soil degradation) to become a dustbowl, an agricultural catastrophe. Indian farmers use three times as much fertilizer as they did thirty years ago to achieve the same yields, while insects have grown resistant to pesticides. Cancer rates among farmers, along with farmer debt and suicide, have grown dramatically. For more on this story see the series of news reports carried by National Public Radio at www.npr.org/templates/story/story.php?storyID=102893816. Scientists now suggest that the Green Revolution needs to undergo its own "greening" to bring it into alignment with ecological principles. See David Tilman's "The Greening of the Green Revolution," *Nature*, 396 (November 19, 1998), 211–212. See also Joel K. Bourne's assessment of the legacy of the Green Revolution in India in *The End of Plenty: The Race to Feed a Crowded World* (New York: W. W. Norton & Company, Inc., 2015), 77–97.

[6] The International Assessment of Agricultural Knowledge, Science and Technology for Development (IAASTD), after considerable wrangling over the promise and drawbacks of genetically modified seed (Monsanto and Syngenta pulled out of discussions), concluded that the use of these technologies can have significant adverse health effects for environments and people. Biotechnology has not made more food available for the world's billion poor. Moreover, the use of seed patents puts small-scale farmers who cannot pay licensing fees in jeopardy. For the Executive Summary of the IAASTD report, see www.agassessment.org/docs/SR_Exec_Sum_280508_English.htm.

[7] See chapter 2 of Raj Patel's *Stuffed and Starved: The Hidden Battle for the World Food System* (Brooklyn: Melville House, 2007) for a journalistic account of how farmers around the world are committing suicide, often by using the pesticides they would spray on their fields, because they are mired in the debt accumulated to pay for agricultural inputs like seed, fertilizers, and herbicides.

[8] For detailed accounting of the destruction of ecosystems and the loss of biodiversity, see the reports of the Millennium Ecosystem Assessment, www.millenniumassessment.org/en/index.aspx.

solution to champion farming systems and economies that funnel wealth to an ever smaller number of people and corporations, and thereby produce what has sometimes been called the "Greed Revolution."[9] It is not a solution to erode food democracy around the world and further consolidate the world's food supply in the hands of a very small number of very large companies,[10] or to establish international trade agreements that siphon resources from the Global South to northern countries, thereby leaving the world's poor impoverished and unable to feed themselves.[11] While it is certainly true that modern society has relieved many people of the need to think about food's production and availability, the upshot of this ignorance is that we have condoned and supported food systems that are degrading to land, animals, and people alike. To be cut off from a practical understanding of how food is grown and what is needed (ecologically but also culturally) to keep good food in plentiful supply is to put ourselves in a position of exile, a position in which our eating and food production practices precipitate alienation, ill-health, and injustice.

Our food confusion is not confined to the production side. Consider the multiple, often contradictory dieting fads that regularly sweep the nation. Dire warnings about red meat are followed by a popular, mostly meat diet. Bread, a several millennia-old staple, is proclaimed the dieter's enemy. Meanwhile, governments, though proclaiming the health benefits of a fruit and vegetable diet, give massive subsidies to the very food sectors that fill our stores and schools with high-fructose corn-syrup-laden sodas and candy. It is no wonder that people don't know what or how to eat. Michael Pollan has described this situation as the American paradox of food: "a notably unhealthy people obsessed by the idea of eating healthily."[12] Degraded land, sick bodies, and mass confusion indicate that we are ill at ease in the worlds of food.

---

[9] Bourne, *The End of Plenty*, 73–74.

[10] The concept of "food democracy" is described in *The Paradox of Plenty: Hunger in a Bountiful World*, ed. Douglas H. Boucher (Oakland, CA: Food First Books, 1999) and by the Institute for Food and Development Policy. For a recent tabulation of how food consolidation is taking place in the various food sectors of our economy, see the report by Mary Hendrickson and Bill Heffernan at www.nfu.org/wp-content/2007-heffernanreport.pdf.

[11] For a discussion of how Third World activists (including Martin Khor, Walden Bello, Vandana Shiva, Dot Keet, Sara Larrain, and Oronto Douglas) are viewing the policies and effects of global trade agreements and international monetary policy, see *Views from the South: The Effects of Globalization and the WTO on Third World Countries*, ed. Sarah Anderson (Mitford, CT: Food First Books and International Forum on Globalization, 2000).

[12] Michael Pollan, *The Omnivore's Dilemma: A Natural History of Four Meals* (New York: Penguin Press, 2006), 3.

Because we are among the world's most ignorant and confused eaters, it is difficult for us to identify, let alone understand, our exilic condition as a problem. Marketing professionals have worked very hard to convince us that unhealthy food is normal (there is simply too much money to be made from people who are vaguely unhappy and functionally ill). Not knowing where food comes from or the biophysical and socioeconomic conditions under which it is produced makes it difficult to advocate a more just, healthy, and sustainable food system. When food is reduced to a commodity and we to consumers, it is inevitable that our primary concern will be that food be inexpensive, convenient, and in plentiful supply. The ease of exilic eating and the facility with which the unjust and destructive dimensions of our food economies can be hidden and ignored make it likely that we will learn to prefer the state of exile, forgetting, perhaps even forsaking, our food-providing home.

When describing today's exilic condition it is important to underscore that being in exile isn't simply a matter of personal choice. In her important study *Weighing In*, Julie Guthman has rightly criticized leaders of the food movement who suggest that if people eat local and eat organic then personal health and the health of farmland and ecosystems will naturally follow. This recommendation fails because it does not attend to the political systems and the economic structures that doom (especially poor) bodies to unhealthy food. It does not attend to how government policies, most notably through the USA Farm Bill, virtually guarantee the growth of commodities (rather than food) and the closure of small farms. If we are to correct our exilic condition, we have to address the systems and structures that produce, distribute, and recommend particular foods and particular kinds of eating. We need to correct economic injustice, and appreciate that perhaps the best means to healthy food, healthy bodies, and healthy lands will be to eliminate poverty and income inequality.[13]

EXILES FROM THE GARDEN

It is important to note that the first human transgression is an eating transgression. Adam and Eve were exiled from the Garden of Eden

---

[13] Julie Guthman, *Weighing In: Obesity, Food Justice, and the Limits of Capitalism* (Berkeley: University of California Press, 2001). Guthman argues that our food system is part of a political economy that produces inequality and ill-health. Educating individuals to eat differently, as important as that is, is not enough. The "political economy of bulimia" must be addressed head-on by people working to change the laws and policies that perpetuate the system.

because they ate from the tree of the knowledge of good and evil, the fruit of the one tree that God expressly forbade them to eat. How are we to understand this refusal to eat and live appropriately in the garden? Why do people rebel against the limits, demands, and joy that gardens embody?

The knowledge of good and evil represents one of the oldest and most pervasive forms people have for marking and understanding boundaries. To transgress a boundary is to do evil. To observe a boundary is to do what is right. To have no bounds is to be a god. Because we are God's creatures we are clearly finite and in need of the help of others, which means that we live within and in terms of memberships of nurture, memberships that make life possible but also entail certain responsibilities on our part to serve and protect the garden (Genesis 2:15). We know this because we have to eat, demonstrating in each bite that we depend on others for our sustenance and life. As creatures that eat, we have to live in terms of what a nourishing garden allows and requires of us. Eating introduces us to a fundamental law: to eat well, people must nurture the land that nurtures them.

The temptation to eat from the tree of the knowledge of good and evil, and the potential it brings that we will consume *and thus erase* the very idea of boundaries altogether, proves too great. Adam and Eve eat the forbidden fruit, believing that in their eating they will become like gods who know no bounds and are accountable to no one. In their act, we find a symbolic expression of the dreams that have guided and continue to inspire much of our histories: that we can live in a garden home without responsibility for it; that we can exceed the carrying capacity of ecosystems and habitats by ceaseless taking; that we can eat without discipline and much cost or effort; and that we can overcome impotence and forestall death by living in a techno-virtual paradise. What we fail to realize is that dreams of this sort keep us in a state of perpetual exile.

Every time we deny the memberships of need and nurture that define us as creatures, and refuse the responsibilities that accompany our member- ship, we reach again, much like Adam and Eve did, for the alluring fruit of the forbidden tree. This tree remains lodged in our dreams as the possibility that one day we will cease to be creatures and instead live the life of a god. What we don't understand is that as long as we try to live like gods we banish ourselves from the garden. We don't need God to drive us out. We go willingly in a desperate search for a limitless, carefree life we cannot have, while the land of nurture and delight beneath our feet suffers the neglect and destruction of our anxious ways. Though we may be successful for a while, it is impossible to refuse the care of creation and expect it to be a long-term, life-giving home.

If we are to enjoy the abundant, delectable life God makes possible, we must first become disciples or apprentices of God the gardener.[14] Perhaps this is why the prophet Jeremiah, speaking to people who knew intimately the pain and place of exile, admonished them to plant gardens and seek the welfare of the city as a sign of hope (Jeremiah 29:5–7). Insofar as people practice the attention and discipline of good work, work that honors the Creator and affirms the need and nurture of creation's memberships, they share in the life-giving ways of God. The crucial point, however, is that human hope for a good life and a healthy home depends on the affirmation of creatureliness and the embrace of the memberships of life. The path out of exile is a path inspired and directed by God's own care-full, life-creating work in the world.

Eating, along with the work and sharing that all eating presupposes, is the most fundamental means we know for understanding and appreciating the range and depth of creation's memberships. When we are involved in food production, and when we eat with intelligence and sympathy, we learn about our place in the world. We discover that creation is an indescribably complex, vast, and deep food web, and that others intersect with us at multiple points as sources of inspiration and nurture. We begin to see and taste how some patterns of life are inappropriate because they compromise, exhaust, or destroy this food web. We determine that some skills and practices further life and so are to be commended. Recall that it is as Adam tends God's garden that he learns about what it means to enjoy life as a creature. He experiences through his stomach what it is to belong and be at home where he is.

Adam failed in his responsibility to care for his fellow creatures, and in his failure we are all introduced to the place of exile. We "fall" into patterns of relating to each other that invariably harm and diminish creation's good. Dietrich Bonhoeffer described our situation clearly in the following way: "The Fall ... is revolt ... it is the creature's becoming Creator, it is the destruction of creatureliness. It is defection, it is the fall from being held in creatureliness ... it is not simply a moral lapse but the destruction of creation by the creature."[15] Another way to put this is to say that in a fallen state people suffer the *anxiety of membership*. We know that we belong to

---

14   Nicholas Lash describes this life as discipleship, as life that allows God's love to order and shape all our loves. "Discipleship is a matter of learning to display, in the school that we call Christianity, that courtesy to creatures in which reverence for the Creator finds expression" ("Creation, Courtesy and Contemplation," in *The Beginning and the End of "Religion"* [Cambridge: Cambridge University Press, 1996], 173).

15   Dietrich Bonhoeffer, *Creation and Fall* (New York: Macmillan, 1959), 76.

others, that they need us just as we need them, and that we need to work to take care of each other, but we can't bear the responsibility or the gift. We take flight before the prospects and the obligations of interdependent need. We prefer to think we can stand on our own, not realizing that in denying need and responsibility we also forfeit the joy of belonging. Denying memberships, we become profoundly lost.

The truth, of course, is that none of us can stand alone. To try is invariably to flail about and fall. It is also to die by starvation. Each of us is "held in creatureliness" through the multiple food webs that constitute and circulate through every living organism. Eating is the daily confirmation that we need others and are vulnerable to them. When we eat well, we honor and accept responsibility for the gifts of God given to each other for the furtherance of life. We move more deeply and more sympathetically into the memberships of creation. But when we eat in exile we eat alone and with considerable violence, without deep connection or affection, experiencing food and each other as mere objects and threats or as the means to our power, control, and convenience.

Scripture characterizes this crisis in eating and responsibility as sin. Sin is a disoriented life and a misdirected desire. According to traditional accounts, the first sin is pride, the naïve and arrogant disposition in which sinners think more of themselves than they ought. Adam and Eve did not want to dwell among creatures all joined together by their interdependent need but instead wanted to have life on their own terms. This is why shortly after eating the forbidden fruit Adam and Eve felt shame. Shame is the realization that our freedom has gone wrong. It is the painful knowledge that a decision cannot be justified before another because it violates God and another's freedom to be. When we are ashamed of ourselves we understand that our desire has broken faith with the memberships that constitute and enrich our life.

Bonhoeffer observed that Adam and Eve's shame is both a recognition that they are limited creatures and that they have transgressed their limits. Having transgressed, they are no longer able to appreciate limit – what we have been calling mutual interdependence and the knowledge that we are constituted and sustained through our relationships with others – as the grace of God that holds all together in creaturely unity. Limit of any kind is now perceived as the wrath, hatred, and envy of God. They cannot engage each other in love because now others appear as a threat. The memberships of creation are broken and death takes on a character previously unknown. Understood this way, we can appreciate Adam and Eve's desire to cover their nakedness: "Nakedness is the essence of unity and of understanding, of being for the other, of objectivity, of the recognition of the other in his right, in his limiting me and in his creatureliness ... Nakedness is innocence."[16] Though Adam and Eve tried, in some sense, to become as God, they quickly came to know their effort to have been a disaster. Their only recourse was to hide.

Interpreting the garden story as we have, we can now see that sin is a form of rebellion against our creaturely condition and calling. When we turn away from the creation that God has made, preferring instead the worlds of our own making, and when we refuse the humble life of service and care, preferring instead a life of convenience and self-glorification, we at the same time separate ourselves from the world and the God of life at work in it. We twist and distort God's life-giving power so that it serves the very narrow register of our own fear, ambition, and vanity. In this alienating gesture we deprive ourselves and other creatures of their ability to be and to flourish. Slowly we turn the whole world, even our own bodies, into a place of exile.

Another way to put this is to say that sin is a refusal of relationship and a refusal of responsibility for the well-being of others. Consider Lash's formulation: "All things exist as expressions of God's knowledge and love; as finite refractions of the absolute relation – eternal utterance, inexhaustible donation – that God is. Sin is refusal of relation, self-enclosure in a futile search for safety."[17] Of course, our search is not only for safety. Sometimes we are simply lazy or angry or arrogant or bored or afraid. The knowledge that we will die, that we live by the dying of others, and that we must care for the dying can be a terrifying realization. It gives rise to all kinds of self-deception and flattery but also arrogance and our lashing out at others. Herbert McCabe has put this point succinctly:

> The root of all sin is fear: the very deep fear that we are nothing; the compulsion, therefore, to make something of ourselves, to construct a self-flattering image of ourselves we can worship, to believe in ourselves – our fantasy selves. I think all sins are failures in being realistic; even the simple everyday sins of the flesh, that seem to move from mere childish greed for pleasure, have their deepest origin in anxiety about whether we really matter, the anxiety that makes us desperate for self-reassurance.[18]

---

[16] Ibid., 78–79. In his later work Bonhoeffer states, "Shame can be overcome only where the original unity is restored" (Bonhoeffer, *Works: Vol. 6, Ethics* [Minneapolis: Fortress Press, 2005], 306).

[17] Lash, *Believing Three Ways in the One God*, 101. As Lash goes on to explain, sin is a refusal of God's love as it is made concrete in the life-building and life-sustaining ways of creation. To refuse this love is also to refuse life. This is why it can be said that "sin snuffs out the breath of God, extinguishes the Spirit" (115).

[18] Herbert McCabe, *God, Christ and Us*, ed. Brian Davies (London: Continuum, 2003), 17–18.

For many people, the creaturely world of finitude, impotence, and vulnerability but also membership and gift is too hard to bear. And so we feel compelled to construct and flee to the more controlled, convenient, and comfortable worlds of our own making, worlds in which life can be experienced on our own terms.

Our dwelling, however, does not need to be fearful and destructive. We do not have to live the exilic patterns of dislocation and disaffection that, as we will now see, are reflected in ecological, economic, and physiological ways. God calls humanity to a life of membership informed by mercy and care, fidelity and love. Our dwelling in creation is to be inspired by the God who dwelt among us, and in that dwelling showed us the ways of forgiveness and peace and joy. We need to recall here the divine love and delight that first brought creation into being: "God 'delights' creation into life. To hear God's Word of life, to take God's utterance to heart, is to find all things 'delectable,' to delight each other in the light of God."[19]

ECOLOGICAL EXILE

It is difficult for us to appreciate the fact that we have entered a fundamentally new period in the earth's history. People prefer to believe, and have been trained to think, that because natural processes have been going on for millennia, they will continue in the same way for millennia to come. Nature's ways are sure, its gifts unlimited, and its capacity to absorb human assault without end. Nothing people do could possibly threaten the vast resources and capacities of the earth, or so we naively, and sometimes desperately, hope. Life will hold together and continue as it always has.

This "hope" is both ignorant and dangerous. It is ignorant because it is maintained in the face of considerable evidence showing the world's ecosystems to be in crisis, and in some cases on the verge of collapse. It is dangerous because our blindness prevents us from making the political, economic, and personal changes that can halt, and in some cases potentially reverse, the destruction.

An ecosystem is most basically a food system, a place in terms of which nutrient energy flows through one creature after another. When an ecosystem suffers or collapses, so too does the food chain it embodies. How distressing, then, to discover that vast regions of the earth are dying or are in serious distress, and that our food-producing habitats are being exhausted

[19]   Lash, *Believing Three Ways in the One God*, 74–75.

and degraded at an alarming rate (often in the wake of our food production techniques). All around us the memberships of creation are coming apart. Species are going extinct 1,000 times faster than the normal rate, with the result that as many as half of the earth's species will be severely diminished or completely disappear in the next 100 years.[20] Much of the degradation is the direct result of a global economy that has grown so dramatically that it boggles the mind. James Gustave Speth tells us that it took all of human history to build the $7 trillion economy of 1950. Today, economic activity grows by that same amount every decade.[21]

Economies cannot grow at rates like this without exacting a heavy toll on our lands and waters. J. R. McNeill, a leading environmental historian, has documented this toll in terms of more specific indicators: from 1800 to 1990, energy use saw a 75-fold increase, with coal production accounting for a 500-fold increase; human population grew from a billion in 1820 to over seven billion today (and remember that the overall appetite of today's citizen is far greater than it was nearly 200 years ago); world gross domestic product (GDP) increased more than a hundred-fold from 1500 to 1990; global freshwater use jumped from 110 cubic kilometers in 1700 to 5,190 in the year 2000, a nearly fifty-fold increase; and soil degradation, either through mining or agriculture, has effectively compromised two billion hectares, an area roughly the size of the United States and Canada combined. Much of the growth in consumption was centered in Europe and North America, but since World War II the economies of countries around the world, especially India and in Asia, have exploded.[22]

The scope and scale of today's ecological degradation is one of the clearest signs that the memberships of creation are broken. It is becoming harder and harder for many species of life to find their places a life-giving, stomach-satisfying home. To be sure, much of the economic and agricultural development of the last 200 years has made it possible for millions of people to crawl out from under the constant threat of starvation and its accompanying social and personal, psychic and bodily effects. A growing global economy, and the international food system that grew within it – a system built on vast trading routes, new food preservation and storage techniques, new plant

---

[20] For more on how today's extinction patterns and rates differ from previous extinction events, see Elizabeth Kolbert's *The Sixth Extinction: An Unnatural History* (New York: Henry Holt and Company, 2014).

[21] James Gustave Speth, *The Bridge at the Edge of the World: Capitalism, the Environment, and Crossing from Crisis to Sustainability* (New Haven: Yale University Press, 2008), x.

[22] J. R. McNeill, *Something New under the Sun: An Environmental History of the Twentieth-Century World* (New Haven: Yale University Press, 2000), particularly chapter 1.

varieties, massive amounts of fertilizer and pesticide, machine invention, and "free" trade – has made possible many more food calories than people have ever seen before. But the ecological costs of our vast production are monumentally high, so high that our temporary productive "success" threatens to undermine future possibilities.[23]

When we consider several key environmental indicators, it becomes apparent that the human anxiety of membership has developed in ways that Adam could never have anticipated.[24] To appreciate this we will examine, in summary form, the state of our earth's atmosphere, forests, soil, water, fisheries, and genetic diversity. Our main concern will be to see how ecological degradation in these areas affects food sustainability and security.

The Atmosphere

The importance of the atmosphere becomes apparent the moment we hold our breath. Air circulates through our bodies, making possible the burning of food energy and thus the movement of our life. When we breathe, we share in the life of all living creatures that surround us with their own breath. The concentrations of elements within our atmosphere are precisely tuned so that life can flourish: mostly nitrogen (78 percent), then oxygen (21 percent), a very small amount of argon, and then much smaller amounts of carbon dioxide (0.035 percent), neon, helium, methane, hydrogen, and ozone (and a few others). It is of the utmost importance that the balances be maintained. One of the simplest ways to kill life is to deprive it of its breath, or alter the composition (however slightly) of what an organism breathes.

When something like an environmental consciousness emerged in the 1960s, the atmosphere was often in the forefront. The concern at the time was pollution and air quality. More recently, however, the dominant concern has been the unprecedented release of carbon dioxide into the atmosphere. As people have burned carbon, either in the form of trees or fossil fuels like coal, oil, and natural gas, they have dramatically altered the atmosphere's

---

[23] Paul Roberts's *The End of Food* is a superb exposition on the interrelationship between eating, agriculture, and the world economy. It informs this chapter throughout. Bourne's recent *The End of Plenty* does an excellent job documenting the challenges and opportunities that farmers face in a degraded world.

[24] A great number of scientific and environmental organizations are documenting the earth's degradation. The following account depends most often on the findings of the Union of Concerned Scientists, the Worldwatch Institute, the UN's Millennium Ecosystem Assessment, and the Institute for Agriculture and Trade Policy. A succinct, up-to-date summary can be found in Speth's *The Bridge at the Edge of the World*, chapter 1.

CO_2 concentrations.[25] This development is so significant because CO_2 is a heat-trapping gas. As heat radiates from the earth, CO_2 molecules reflect it back, causing the earth's overall surface temperature to increase. As the earth warms, and as climate patterns change as a result of the warming (more violent storms, unpredictable rains), food systems are disrupted. Vegetation dies either through drought, too much heat, or flooding. Fish species decline as oceans warm, currents are disrupted, and coral reefs bleach and die. Animals suffer from heat and from the spread of disease-carrying insects that flourish under warmer conditions. Agricultural productivity drops as plants are stressed by even slight increases in temperature (it is estimated that for every 1 °C increase in temperature, wheat, rice, and corn harvests will decrease by 10 percent).[26]

It is impossible to predict exactly all the adverse effects that will follow in the wake of climate change.[27] We can't fully anticipate the sorts of social, political, economic, agricultural, and technological modifications that will become necessary as societies respond to region-specific change. What we do know, however, is that plant and animal species already under stress from human encroachment and habitat loss will suffer even more. Unpredictable weather cycles will jeopardize the plants that have adapted to relatively stable climate conditions and temperate zones. Glaciers and mountain snowpacks will melt, decreasing freshwater supplies and stalling irrigation agriculture. Rising ocean levels will erode or completely inundate coastal zones and islands, creating millions of refugees among the people who have settled near ocean developments. All this will happen in the context of a still-growing human population that will need more, not less, food. Never before has humanity faced the prospect of such ominous ecological change or collapse.

Forests

It is hard to imagine that forests once covered most of the land on which we currently live (well over half of North America, most of Europe, Brazil, Asia,

---

[25] For a clear treatment on how humans have changed the earth's climate see William F. Ruddiman's *Plows, Plagues, and Petroleum: How Humans Took Control of the Climate* (Princeton: Princeton University Press, 2005). The literature on climate change and global warming is now immense. For an up-to-date assessment, see Joseph Romm's *Climate Change: What Everyone Needs to Know* (Oxford; Oxford University Press, 2015).

[26] See Lester R. Brown's *Outgrowing the Earth: The Food Security Challenge in an Age of Falling Water Tables and Rising Temperatures* (New York: W. W. Norton, 2004).

[27] The most thorough and up-to-date treatment of these matters is in the reports of the Intergovernmental Panel on Climate Change, particularly the Working Group II Report, "Impacts, Adaptation and Vulnerability." It can be accessed at www.ipcc.ch/-ipccreports/ar4-wg2.htm.

and Indonesia). Forests play an indispensable role in the maintenance and preservation of life. They are home to countless species of plants and animals.[28] Here the diverse forms of food and fiber many creatures need are generated. Trees are like the lungs of the planet, breathing in carbon dioxide (and sequestering carbon) and emitting the oxygen we all need.

Over the last several centuries, but even more dramatically in the last decades, people have been felling forests to make room for agriculture, mines, and roads, and to feed our need for wood, paper, and fiber. Deforestation rates in the tropics have been as high as one acre lost per second. Roughly one-third of the world's forests are now gone. This is a tragedy of monumental proportions because of the numerous "ecosystem services" that forests provide: soil stabilization, water retention and flow stabilization, climate modulation, disease buffering, and biodiversity protection.[29] As the forests disappear, land is exposed to the forces of erosion, while less of the sun's heat energy is absorbed and stored in plant growth (coal can be understood as the sun's energy stored in plants and then used thousands of years later). The latter point is especially important because vegetation manages and reflects sunlight to promote evapotranspiration, cloud cover, and subsequently rainfall. Deforestation thus contributes to decreased rainfall, which leads to less vegetation, which eventually leads to the growth of deserts.

Deforestation is not simply about the loss of a few trees. It is about the massive disruption of food and energy flows. It is about the loss of habitat and the extinction of countless species, many of which we have never met, let alone appreciated. It is about the alteration of the world's climate systems. Forests play such a vital role in the health of global ecosystems that we simply cannot expect a viable human future without them.

Soil

Soil has been under assault for roughly ten thousand years, since the agricultural revolution in human societies began. In our thoughtless alteration of the ground, our literal turning of the soil-holding roots upside down, we have unleashed tremendous destructive potential. Given enough

---

[28]   The classic book on forests as a source of food is J. Russell Smith's *Tree Crops: A Permanent Agriculture* (New York: The Devin-Adair Company, 1950).

[29]   Ecosystem services refer to the conditions and processes at work in a habitat that enable the feeding and flourishing of life, especially human life. See the essay by Norman Myers, "The World's Forests and Their Ecosystem Services," in *Nature's Services: Societal Dependence on Natural Ecosystems*, ed. Gretchen C. Dailey (Washington, DC: Island Press, 1997), 215–235.

years of till agricultural practice, people would gradually erode, and thus render relatively lifeless, vast stretches of the world. The United Nations estimates that an area roughly the size of China suffers from varying degrees of desertification (land that otherwise would account for one-fifth of the world's food production), while each year an area the size of Nebraska becomes too degraded for crop production or is lost to urban sprawl.

The problem is not simply soil erosion. Soil quality is equally important. Industrial agricultural techniques compromise vital soil structure, rendering it incapable of sustained plant growth. For instance, excessive irrigation waterlogs the soil, which then brings mineral elements in the water to the surface. As the water evaporates, soils become saline and thus essentially lifeless. In addition, the use of heavy machinery, a staple of modern industrial agribusiness, compacts the soil so that water cannot be absorbed (further exacerbating erosion), roots cannot grow, and microorganisms fail to flourish. Within a short time span, soil fertility and crop yields decline significantly.

The preferred method to increase soil fertility has been to apply heavy amounts of fossil-fuel-based fertilizers, especially nitrogen. But as soil scientists study the effects of steady streams of fertilizer application, it is becoming apparent that dirt is not simply a lifeless, chemical receptacle for nitrogen, potassium, and phosphorous.[30] Good soil, the kind of soil that enables healthy, vigorous plant growth, depends on a complex mix of organic matter and microbial life. In the soil's rich humus, nutrients cycle through each other. Dead organic bodies are transformed into the basis for yet more life. The soil physicist Daniel Hillel characterizes it this way:

> [Soil is] a rich mix of mineral particles, organic matter, gases, and nutrients which, when infused with vital water, constitutes a fertile substrate for the initiation and maintenance of life. The soil is thus a self-regulating biological factory, utilizing its own materials, water, and energy from the sun ... The soil also acts as our earth's primary cleansing and recycling medium, in effect as a "living filter," wherein pathogens and toxins that might otherwise foul our environment are rendered harmless and transmuted into nutrients.[31]

---

[30] New research is suggesting that the use of synthetic nitrogen reduces the quantity and quality of a soil's organic matter. See www.grist.org/article/2010-02-23-new-research-syn thetic-nitrogen-destroys-soil-carbon-undermines-/. See also David R. Montgomery's work on soil health and agriculture in *Growing A Revolution: Bringing Our Soil Back to Life* (New York: W. W. Norton & Company, Inc., 2017).

[31] Daniel Hillel, *Out of the Earth: Civilization and the Life of Soil* (London: Aurum Press, 1991), 23–24.

Today's industrial agricultural techniques short-circuit these soil processes, making it much more difficult to maintain crop yields. In the
meantime, however, as ever more fertilizer is applied in hopes of improving
productivity, vast amounts of nitrogen-rich fertilizer run off or leach into
our groundwater and streams, killing aquatic life and making the water unfit
to drink. Eventually the nitrogen-fortified water accumulates in coastal
regions, creating massive "dead zones." These dead zones suffocate aquatic
life or lower oxygen levels so much that the reproductive capacities of fish
are severely impaired.

Our culture has not trained us to see how vital the human connection
with soil is. But if we remember that food is absolutely essential, and that all
terrestrial nourishment comes from the carcasses and plant debris that are
continually being reconstituted in the soil, then we can begin to appreciate
that our coming from and returning to the soil is not simply a metaphor.
Every time we take a bite we incorporate soil: "death turns into life, grows
up, feeds life and dies again, returning to the workshop underground to be
restored to life."[32]

Water and Fisheries

Nearly 75 percent of the earth's surface is covered in water. When babies are
born, 75 percent of their body weight is water. The flow of water is everywhere in our world, even the places that on the surface seem dry to us.
Waterways are the planet's circulatory system. Rain falls, enters the soil,
evaporates, or is absorbed by plants that are eaten by animals. The absorption and evaporation of water forms a vast hydrological cycle that circulates
through all living tissues like a system of arteries, veins, and capillaries:
"water circulates endlessly from the heavens to the oceans and land, held
briefly within all living things before continuing the cycle. You might see the
whole enterprise of life as just a vehicle for the transformation of water."[33]

Though water is everywhere on earth, only the tiniest percentage of it is
fresh water that is available for human use. Over 97 percent of the world's
water is in oceans too salty for us to consume. Another 2 percent is locked in
glaciers and icecaps, leaving less than 1 percent of the water for terrestrial
(and freshwater aquatic) life to share. Even so, the water that people need is
not equally distributed. Regions of Africa and Asia, though having large

---

[32]   David Suzuki, *The Sacred Balance: Discovering Our Place in Nature* (Vancouver: Greystone
Books, 1997), 80.
[33]   Ibid., 62.

growing populations, have too little, while Canada, with its relatively small population, has nearly 20 percent of the earth's fresh water by volume. Wherever the water is, however, it is being depleted, diverted, squandered, or polluted.

Nearly 70 percent of freshwater withdrawal is for agricultural purposes, which means that "Agriculture is a thirsty business."[34] As the need for increased food production continues, ever greater amounts of water will be necessary. The water is simply not there. Glaciers are receding, underground aquifers are being depleted at unsustainable rates, and many of the world's major rivers (the Colorado, Nile, Ganges, and Yellow rivers) periodically run dry before they reach their ocean destinations. Nearly 60 percent of the world's major rivers are now dammed or fragmented in some significant way, often for power generation or to create reservoirs for agriculture and recreation. Because so many of our waterways have been diverted or dammed, the immense forests, fields, and watersheds/wetlands that depend on water flow are compromised. These water stresses invariably work themselves out on the political stage. It is projected that by the year 2025, 65 percent of the world's people will be living in water-stressed countries. All this will occur in a context where the worldwide demand for water will double by the year 2050. Besides being a recipe for ecological and agricultural catastrophe (the Green Revolution is heavily dependent on irrigation), water shortages will lead to violent conflict and forced migrations as people grow thirsty, hungry, and desperate.[35]

It is not only freshwater systems we need to worry about. Ocean fisheries are also in serious distress. Many fishing grounds (estimated by some at 75 percent) have been fished to exhaustion. If current trends continue, scientists predict that by the year 2050 all commercial ocean fisheries will collapse. As Speth points out, however, our marine problems are not confined to overfishing. Coastal pollution, the destruction of mangroves, and the bleaching of coral reefs (due to global warming) are all taking a major destructive toll. For many people, fish are the major source of food and aquaculture a primary means of life. If people hope to continue to eat fish for long, various forms of sustainable aquaculture will need to develop quickly to meet the need.[36]

---

[34] Bourne, *The End of Plenty*, 205.

[35] Speth, *The Bridge at the Edge of the World*, 32–33. Speth's treatment has been very informative throughout this section. See also Fred Pearce's *When the Rivers Run Dry: Water – The Defining Crisis of the Twenty-First Century* (Boston: Beacon Press, 2007), and Peter H. Gleick's *The World's Water 2006–2007: The Biennial Report on Freshwater Resources* (Washington, DC: Island Press, 2006).

[36] Bourne describes some of these efforts in *The End of Plenty*, 165–181.

Genetic Diversity and Integrity

An examination of the plant variety in today's typical diet reveals a dramatic shrinking of the gene pool. According to the FAO, humans can eat roughly 30,000 plant species. Ten thousand or so have been eaten at some time. Though 150 kinds of plants are eaten in diets around the world today, only four – corn, wheat, rice, and soy – provide the bulk (60 percent) of our plant calories and protein.[37] Even within species there are often hundreds of varieties of corn or potato or apple, but we actively grow and trade only the tiniest percentage. For instance, Andean farmers have bred over 3,000 varieties of potatoes. They come in all shapes and colors, having a distinct flavor and aroma. In the United States, it is estimated that over 7,000 varieties of apples have been grown at one time or another (6,000 of these are now completely gone). This diversity is not reflected on our fields or in our large grocery stores. Seventy-five percent of genetic diversity in our agricultural crops has been lost in the last century. Why?[38]

The food gains of industrial agriculture have been premised on the homogenization of plant and animal species. This has happened in two major ways. First, farmers have been taught that to become as efficient as possible they must grow crops in monoculture.[39] This means that large fields are planted with one crop. Other farmers do the same, using the same crop varieties. The reasoning behind this practice is simple: it is much easier and more cost-effective to harvest one plant when using a large machine to do the work (a combine cannot simultaneously harvest peas, wheat, and corn because the crops are each harvested so differently and at different times). Of course, if the farmer is not dependent on large machine power, then it is possible to grow a variety of crops in the same area (picking what is ripe and leaving the rest for later, and using the manual dexterity of workers to adjust

---

[37] www.fao.org/docrep/004/v1430e/V1430E04.htm/July 12, 2018

[38] For a vigorous critique of global, industrial agriculture and its threat to genetic and cultural diversity, see Vandana Shiva's *Stolen Harvest: The Hijacking of the Global Food Supply* (Cambridge, MA: South End Press, 2000).

[39] There is vigorous debate on whether or not monoculture agriculture is in fact more efficient at producing food. A great number of variables need to be factored in, including the sustainability of industrial, chemical practices, and the fact that much industrial agriculture produces commodities for livestock or for industrial purposes (corn, for instance, has multiple uses). Intensive forms of agriculture that grow multiple crops in close succession and proximity with each other can sustainably produce much more food. See the work of Masanobu Fukuoka, *The One-Straw Revolution* (New York: New York Review Books, 1978) and Joel Salatin, *The Sheer Ecstasy of Being a Lunatic Farmer* (Swoope, VA: Polyface, 2010) as vivid examples of farmers who grow food at rates that exceed industrial counterparts and on a smaller carbon/land footprint.

to differing plant qualities). Second, the sale of seeds has been taken over by a very small number of companies that only make available certain varieties (most often those varieties that have been engineered to work in tandem with the same company's pesticide products). The age-old practice of farmers retaining and then trading their seed with others is gone. As agriculture has been transformed into big-scale agribusiness, the genetic pool from which seed stock is derived has shrunk dramatically.[40]

A similar process is at work with respect to livestock. Americans eat roughly 400 million turkeys each year. Though many breeds of turkeys exist, 99 percent of those eaten will come from a single breed. The Broad-Breasted White is the turkey of choice because it is laden with white meat. It has also been bred to survive the rigors of large confinement operations (left on their own they would get so heavy they could not walk, forage, or mate).[41] What can be said of turkeys also applies to cattle, pigs, chickens, sheep, and goats. Though many breeds have existed throughout the ages, only a fraction of them are raised today. Breeds are chosen because they can survive industrial production techniques.

As eaters, we should be concerned because monoculture farming, besides reflecting a centralized and controlled food economy, is highly vulnerable to disease and pest infestation. Healthy ecosystems contain a diverse mix of species: different plants benefit from each other's proximity. For instance, a nitrogen-fixing legume feeds cereal crops that cannot fix nitrogen on their own. Other species, in turn, are valuable because they possess traits that discourage pests. Moreover, growing polycultures means that the farmer or gardener is much less likely to suffer complete crop collapse: if one or two crops fail, others, because of their specific adaptive qualities, will survive. Species diversity is thus at the heart of food security. This is why a number of the world's leading food advocates drafted a "Manifesto on the Future of Seed": "Diversity is our highest form of security. Diversification has been the most successful and widespread strategy of agricultural innovation and survival over the past 10,000 years. It increases the array of options and the chances of adapting successfully to changing environmental conditions

---

[40] The story of the industrialization and commercial integration of agriculture is masterfully told by Pollan in *The Omnivore's Dilemma*. For an assessment of the long-term viability of industrial agricultural techniques, see Fred Kirschenmann's essay "The Current State of Agriculture: Does It Have a Future?" in *The Essential Agrarian Reader: The Future of Culture, Community, and the Land*, ed. Norman Wirzba (Lexington: University Press of Kentucky, 2003), 101–120.

[41] For a brief analysis of the turkey industry, see Barbara Kingsolver's *Animal, Vegetable, Miracle: A Year of Food Life* (New York: HarperCollins, 2007), chapters 6 and 19.

and human needs."[42] When the world is sown in only one or two crops, we are only one pest or disease away from total food disaster.

A second major factor in the homogenization of today's food supply has to do with the genetic modification of species. Biotechnology has become one of the fastest growing areas in science and industry because what is at stake is not only the development of new species but also their control (through patents, Monsanto controls 90 percent of all commercial genetically modified plant traits). When a company owns the patent to a seed's genetic code it is illegal for farmers to save and share seed.[43] All seed, as well as the fertilizers and herbicides needed to grow them, must now be purchased. Given this reality, we should not be surprised that major food companies are reaping windfall profits while farmers' earnings decrease steadily.

It would be foolish to be opposed to all genetic modification, since farmers have used cross-breeding for centuries to improve herds and plant varieties. Farmers have traditionally selected specimens from their crops and herds because they showed traits that made them stronger and more productive, more nutritious and tasty, or simply more beautiful. What makes today's genetic modification so ominous is that, among other problems, it threatens to unleash "genetic pollutants" into our natural habitats and so upset finely tuned balances that keep food chains resilient through time. Genetic engineers often fail to appreciate the diverse, complex environments in terms of which species develop and adapt.[44] Ecosystems develop over millions of years. Their stability and resilience is a feature of unfathomably complex interactions. When we release new genetic material, especially material that would not have developed on its own (a number of our genetic designs cross species barriers), we often have no idea what the adverse effects might be. While it may be more profitable to grow super-salmon, we simply do not know all the ways in which these salmon will threaten the balances and the stability of other aquatic populations.

Another major problem with some forms of genetic engineering is the escalation of herbicide use. For instance, many of today's genetically modified plants are designed to withstand the application of herbicides

[42]   *Manifestos on the Future of Food and Seed*, ed. Vandana Shiva (Cambridge, MA: South End Press, 2007), 91.
[43]   Ellen Davis has argued that the patenting of seed is a direct affront to the free provision of a generous God. See *Scripture, Culture, and Agriculture: An Agrarian Reading of the Bible* (New York: Cambridge University Press, 2009), 42–65.
[44]   For an insightful discussion of these matters, see Craig Holdrege and Steve Talbott's *Beyond Biotechnology: The Barren Promise of Genetic Engineering* (Lexington: University Press of Kentucky, 2008).

(nutrition and food quality are not often the main drivers of biotech research and development). Monsanto's "Round-Up-Ready" seeds are a prime example. The Round-Up herbicide kills everything but the soy or corn designed to survive its application. The danger with these genetically modified plants is that they often cross-pollinate with other, often wild, plants, producing herbicide-resistant pests that will then require a more lethal poison to contain them. Or the genetically modified traits "drift" into fields of farmers who are trying to grow traditional varieties. Farmers thus find themselves in an escalating (and expensive) toxins race while the fields, streams, and animals suffer the effects.

The consolidation of the food sector into the hands of a few giant corporations, besides being a major ecological concern, is also clearly a global threat to food democracy and food security. Should our global food system depend on the small variety of plants and animals they promote? Should seeds, the genetic codes of food, be patented and owned and controlled by anyone? What is to be said to the poor farmers around the world who cannot afford the expense of biotechnological invention?

This brief survey of ecological degradation suffices to show that people by *providing for themselves* often work against the very memberships that sustain them. In our often thoughtless and aggressive hoarding of the gifts of God we demonstrate again and again the anxiety of membership. We act as though we can thrive while the habitats and organisms that feed us can languish and die. In a fit of ecological amnesia, we have forsaken our natural neighborhoods and abdicated our responsibility to care for them. Having forfeited the opportunity to share in God's delight in a world wonderfully and beautifully made, we now find ourselves eating through a sick and poisoned world. This state of affairs did not just happen. It has been a planned and well-funded development reflected in political priorities, social institutions, and economic patterns that facilitate and reinforce the conditions of exile.

ECONOMIC EXILE

Economy, understood in the very broadest sense, refers to the laws or rules (*nomos*) by which people structure their activity and their places to make a home (*oikos*). Ecology refers to the orders and patterns (*logos*) that are at work within a habitat (*oikos*), enabling it to be a living and functioning whole. The etymology of these two terms indicates that it is essential for a human economy to constantly have in view the potential and the limits implied in any created place. Economies do not exist in the abstract. They depend on particular watersheds, forests, fields, and the creatures that live in them. Put simply, there can be no food economy if there are no fields providing grain, no cows producing milk, and no workers transforming milk into cheese. There can be no sustainable economy if economic "success" presupposes the degradation of the *oikos* upon which cows and people depend.

As was the case with our thinking about the created world, it is important to emphasize how the context for economic activity has changed dramatically. If in the past our main concern was that we did not have enough labor, technology, and investment capital to exploit land and natural resources, the situation today is that we do not have enough resources to feed the appetites of a growing workforce and ballooning financial institutions. This means that the question of how a human economy fits within an ecological context has assumed profound importance. When we remember that creation forms a vast membership that envelops, infuses, and gives life to every part, and that this membership is governed by rules and powers that we have barely begun to appreciate, let alone understand, then it is imperative that we structure our economies with considerable caution, restraint, and humility, because the long-term success of our ambitions depends upon our practices being in alignment with creation. Alignment is crucial because the sources of life do not find their origin in us but in the God-given creation that constitutes and sustains us. People merely borrow or modify whatever good is first there. Wendell Berry has made this point clearly: "the human economy, if it is to be a good economy, must fit harmoniously within and must correspond to the Great Economy; in certain important ways, it must be an analogue of the Great Economy."[45]

In a variety of ways, today's global, free-market economy guarantees that we will disregard, diminish, and destroy the larger economy of creation, and so deprive ourselves of the experience of home. It does this by (1) encouraging patterns of life that keep us from seeing and correctly interpreting where we are, and by (2) forming groups of people who, because of their habits and dispositions, find it very difficult to live in any place with sympathy, affection, responsibility, and joy. Paradoxically, the economic disciplines and practices that are supposed to help us live long and well within our homes are now largely responsible for ensuring that we will live perpetually in a state of exile.

---

[45] Wendell Berry, "Two Economies," in *The Art of the Commonplace*, 223.

First, how does our economy prevent us from seeing and appreciating where we are? In many respects, the success of today's consumer economy depends on the inattentiveness of its consumers. Very few people appreciate the extent to which their shopping decisions contribute to the degradation of the world's ecosystems. Fewer still understand how this ecological degradation has the potential to catastrophically jeopardize long-term food safety and sustainability. Current rates of soil erosion, water contamination and depletion, deforestation, and species and habitat loss – all in the context of a rapidly warming and volatile climate – make it much less likely that we will be able to grow the food we need. In spite of this reality, economists and the political leaders who champion their versions of order continue to pronounce the need for a "growth economy," apparently oblivious to the fact that an acceleration of the current economic machine can only hasten our collective ruin.[46] Speaking of American farm and food policy that encourages overproduction (and therefore the destruction of our land base), Paul Roberts says our economic strategy is "very much like outfitting your teenage son's car with a turbocharger and then replacing the brake with a bigger insurance policy."[47]

How the mania behind the mantra for growth became so strong makes for a very long and complex story about what people think "progress" means and entails. But if we turn to the origins of modern economic theory, and then more specifically to today's food economy, we can begin to see more clearly how our collective blindness develops.

In a sustainable food economy, growers make sure they do not exhaust or degrade the land, water, livestock, and workers upon which their livelihood rests, for to violate these ecological and social boundaries is to put their well-being in jeopardy. To take these precautions, however, farmers or gardeners must have intimate knowledge of the land in terms of which they live. Without detailed and patient attention they cannot assess the effects of their labor. They can't really see when and where abuse is happening or take the steps to correct it. To order their economic lives well they have to know

---

[46] In remarks presented at the Hudson Institute, Herman Daly referred to the inability of leading economists to understand basic ecological realities. He quotes Nobel laureate Thomas Schelling, who said, "In the developed world, hardly any component of the national income is affected by climate. Agriculture is practically the only sector of the economy affected by climate, and it contributes only a small percentage – three percent in the United States – of national income. If agricultural productivity were drastically reduced by climate change, the cost of living would rise by one or two percent, and at a time when per capita income would likely have doubled." See www.hudson.org/files/documents/BradleyCenter/Transcript_2008_06_30_Rural_Philanthropy.pdf.

[47] Roberts, *The End of Food*, 121.

where they are and what their place allows. They have to regulate their work and priorities in terms of the larger ecology at work around them.

The modernization of the food economy has worked steadily to undermine our care for places. This is because a growth economy's overriding concern is to increase production while keeping costs as low as possible. Sustainability, which we can here define as the *dynamic economic activity that conserves the potential and respects the limits of a place and community*, was simply dismissed by classical economists as an obstacle to progress.[48] In their view, scarcity could only be overcome by growth. As Herman Daly has shown, the crucial shift in modern economic theory that had to happen was for people to take their eyes off the natural resources and labor that feed the economic machine, and instead focus on maximum exchange and efficiency. This shift made possible the externalization (and forgetting) of ecological and social costs like degraded habitats and ruined communities.[49] Put broadly, modern economic practice would encourage us to ignore or deny that our economic decisions as producers and consumers always occur *within and in terms of* a place, and that economies, no matter how large or small, are always a subset of the larger economy of a created, source-providing world.[50]

If the goal is steady growth, and maximum productivity and efficiency are the means, then it is only a matter of time before the carrying capacity of a place has to be overridden. Consider again small farmers. As long as they are committed to keeping the land and livestock healthy and productive, limits will be respected. The farmers will know that a pasture can feed only ten cows, and that to try to feed fifteen or twenty will gradually deplete and destroy the pasture. To make up for the degraded pasture the farmers might put their fields on steroids through the application of fossil-fuel-derived fertilizers, or simply walk away and begin on a fresh piece of land that has

---

[48]   In *The Wealth of Nature: Environmental History and the Ecological Imagination* (New York: Oxford University Press, 1993) Donald Worster has observed that Adam Smith developed his position "in total disregard of the economy of nature" (214).

[49]   Herman E. Daly, *Beyond Growth: The Economics of Sustainable Development* (Boston: Beacon Press, 1996), writes: "The whole idea of sustainable development is that the economic subsystem must not grow beyond the scale at which it can be permanently sustained or supported by the containing ecosystem" (28).

[50]   It is important to remember that for centuries prior to the invention of the modern idea of growth there was, in addition to the larger natural context, a moral context that shaped and restrained economic patterns and priorities. Appetite was to be constrained by concerns for justice and moderation. The idea that appetites could be unlimited was widely condemned as sin. For a still helpful discussion of the transformation in moral sensibility that had to occur to make room for the growth economy, see R. H. Tawney's *Religion and the Rise of Capitalism* (New Brunswick: Transaction, 1998), first published in 1926.

not yet been exhausted or degraded. In either case, the result is the same: the integrity of a place, its potential and possibility, has been denied for the sake of increased production. What few economists seem to realize is that these practices of artificial life support and relocation cannot go on indefinitely. We have run out of fresh places to move to, while the places we are in are suffering from toxic overload.

The theory of "comparative advantage" took the growth economy to an international stage. According to this theory, first formulated by the nineteenth-century economist David Ricardo, economic growth is maximized when nations specialize their productive activity and then trade for the rest (Adam Smith had argued that specialization leads to efficiency). If Brazil can produce beef cheaper than Italy, then Italians should stop beef production and instead concentrate their energy and resources on commodities they can produce more efficiently. Similarly, Brazil should stop its production of commodities that are being produced more efficiently somewhere else. Owing to the spread of maximum efficiency, the volume of productivity will increase while the costs (to consumers) of that productivity will go down.

The spread of global efficiency has often gone hand in hand with monoculture crop production and massive government planning and intervention. But as James C. Scott has shown, this simplified yet highly controlled economic structure turns out to be far less productive because it does not allow for local adaptation, complexity, diversity, and ingenuity. Modern industrial agriculture is the handmaid of both communism and large-scale capitalism. It depends on violence and destruction. Speaking of the Soviet effort to increase farm production through efficiency techniques, Scott observes:

> What must strike even a casual student of collectivization, however, is how it largely failed in *each* of its high modernist aims, despite huge investments in machinery, infrastructure, and agronomic research. Its successes, paradoxically, were in the domain of traditional statecraft. The state managed to get its hands on enough grain to push rapid industrialization, even while contending with staggering inefficiencies, stagnant yields, and ecological devastation. The state also managed, at great human cost, to eliminate the social basis of organized, public opposition from the rural population. On the other hand, the state's capacity for realizing its vision of large, productive, efficient, scientifically advanced farms growing high quality products for market was virtually nil.[51]

---

[51]   James C. Scott, *Seeing Like a State: How Certain Schemes to Improve the Human Condition Have Failed* (New Haven: Yale University Press, 1998), 217.

It is hard not to see the recent efforts of the World Trade Organization (WTO), when combined with the centralizing, consolidating thrust of multi-national corporations, as leading us to the exact same result as that witnessed by Soviet collectivization: "large-scale capitalism is just as much an agency of homogenization, uniformity, grids, and heroic simplification as the state is, with the difference being that, for capitalists, simplification must pay."[52]

In the abstract, it looks like the theory of comparative advantage leads to a win-win situation, particularly when it comes to food systems. It does lead to more and cheaper food. The problems with this approach, however, emerge as we begin to pay attention to the particular places and communities that are affected by growth policies of this sort. Consider, as an example, the production of coffee. According to the growth models espoused by the World Bank, only those countries that can grow coffee the most efficiently should grow it. Since there is a large market for coffee, several countries will vie to get the largest contracts. The large contracts will go to the producers with the lowest price. Achieving the lowest price, however, will dictate that environmental safeguards and worker safety and compensation be at the barest minimum. If a new competitor enters the market with a yet cheaper product (a product often made cheaper by government price supports or foreign investments), longstanding producers must look to produce another commodity more cheaply.

The people of Peru and Colombia, for instance, discovered that the theory of comparative advantage can work directly against their well-being. Because Vietnam could sell coffee more cheaply on international markets,[53] Peruvians and Colombians resorted to growing coca for the production of cocaine, thereby creating serious social problems. One might argue that they should simply find another commodity to sell. But economies, especially economies that take ecological realities and social traditions seriously, cannot switch overnight. It takes years to develop fields or orchards or factories. In the meantime, opportunity has often passed a people or nation by. This misfortune can easily be justified on economic terms. Economist Brink Lindsey argues that "creative destruction lies at the very heart of the market process; it is not a market failure."[54] Put another way, people should

---

[52]   Ibid., 8.
[53]   Vietnam's success in coffee production did not occur in a vacuum. Foreign investment and government policy played an important role. For the story, see Roberts, *The End of Food*, 157–160.
[54]   Quoted in Stephen A. Marglin's *The Dismal Science: How Thinking Like an Economist Undermines Community* (Cambridge, MA: Harvard University Press, 2008), 233. Marglin also quotes a leaked memorandum from Lawrence Summers, one-time chief economist at

expect that communities and places will be destroyed for the sake of the growth idea. Exile is at the heart of economic normalcy.

As the reach of food markets and trade agreements has expanded to include most countries in the world, the potential for destruction has increased dramatically. The danger is not with trade itself, since food has been crossing borders for centuries.[55] More significant is the prospect of global food production being tied to the profit-driven interests of multinational corporations.[56] When this happens, land, water, minerals, energy, genetic diversity, as well as the many forms of social capital, are consolidated and then managed by a small number of elites. Because poor people cannot afford to enter the global economy, they are easily abandoned and forgotten, or they are made the objects of charity and relief efforts.

The politics and economics of world hunger are enormously complex.[57] What is becoming clear, however, is that market globalization simply must be matched by responsible governance that safeguards human rights. The United Nation's (UN) Food and Agriculture Organization (FAO) has stated that freedom from hunger and the right to adequate food is a basic human right that belongs to everyone. The FAO's panel advises that "the international community, through its institutions and organizations, must recognize its duties to offset the negative consequences of globalization on a very un-level playing field, and to advance conditions that generate equal opportunity for all."[58] Many of these negative consequences are directly tied

the World Bank and president of Harvard University, demonstrating that the logics of economic efficiency and growth will require the destruction of places: "A given amount of health-impairing pollution should be done in the country with the lowest cost, which will be the country with the lowest wages. I think the economic logic behind dumping a load of toxic waste in the lowest-wage country is impeccable and we should face up to that" (37). Economic logic of this sort indicates that no place is safe unless it has the financial resources to prevent exploitation.

[55] See the essays gathered in *Food and Globalization: Consumption, Markets and Politics in the Modern World*, ed. Alexander Nützenadel and Frank Trentmann (Oxford: Berg, 2008). At times food trade has been linked to imperial power, but at other times it has been linked to the movements of migrant populations that settle around the world. In other words, the tension between preserving local food economies and opening food markets to the world is very old.

[56] For a useful summary on the geopolitics and political economics of global food production, see Peter Atkins and Ian Bowler's *Food in Society: Economy, Culture, Geography* (London: Arnold, 2001).

[57] See here the classic treatment by Francis Moore Lappé in *World Hunger: Twelve Myths*, rev. edition (New York: Grove, 1998), as well as Tony Weis's *The Global Food Economy: The Battle for the Future of Farming* (London: Zed Books, 2007) and Thomas J. Bassett and Alex Winter-Nelson's *The Atlas of World Hunger* (Chicago: University of Chicago Press, 2010).

[58] Quoted by Mary Robinson in "Social Justice, Ethics, and Hunger: What Are the Key Messages?," in *Ethics, Hunger and Globalization: In Search of Appropriate Policies*, ed. Per Pinstrup-Andersen and Peter Sandøe (Dordrecht: Springer, 2007), xii. See also William

to economic policies like trade liberalization, privatization, the deregulation of national industries, and the opening of markets to foreign companies. Critics of "free" market ideology point out that the freedoms are all stacked in favor of the wealthy, making global trade a new form of colonialism, when what is needed is the kind of freedom that enables people to feed and provide for themselves. According to advocates of food sovereignty, communities can only be healthy and whole (it is important to underscore how much illness is directly correlated with nutritional defects) when respect for the environment, cultural diversity, and mutual dependence are affirmed. Global hunger cannot be adequately addressed so long as trade and production are tied only to market mechanisms that greatly privilege the powerful and the wealthy.

So far we have seen how the production side of economic life – the relentless drive for growth – creates a condition in which the integrity of places and communities ceases to register. Having little or no significance, other than as fodder for the growing economic machine, they effectively disappear from moral view. On the consumption side, however, the situation is no better. Today's global food economy, with its lengthy distribution networks traversing continents and oceans, makes it difficult for eaters to know the places and communities that produce and prepare food. Having so little knowledge or direct contact with food's contexts – the fields and waters, livestock crates and pens, the factories and distribution centers, worker communities and restaurants – it is next to impossible for us to act in ways that would promote the good of any place or community.

Many people today eat food they have never seen in the ground or water. This is because as modern forms of storage (especially refrigeration) and transport developed in the late nineteenth and early twentieth centuries they could purchase food produced far away. The supply lines that stock our stores have steadily gotten longer, particularly as Ricardo's theory of comparative advantage took hold internationally. Because salad can be grown efficiently in California, California growers have made this one of the state's specialties. The result, however, is that a resident on the east coast of the United States must have salad fixings shipped a great distance. Besides being

D. Schanbacher's *The Politics of Food: The Global Conflict between Food Security and Food Sovereignty* (Santa Barbara: Praeger, 2010), where the case is made that a country's peoples, rather than foreign or international lending agencies (like the World Trade Organization) and corporations, should have control over the production of food, and *Stuffed and Starved*, where Raj Patel gives numerous stories of how world hunger connects with economic policies.

hugely wasteful of energy[59] – applying the logic of economic efficiency, we would be much smarter if we simply drank oil! – residents of Boston no longer know or care about what it takes to produce a head of lettuce. They have no idea if the land was laced with toxic chemicals, if it was near lagoons of animal waste that are the by-products of large feedlot and animal confinement operations (and so susceptible to E. coli contamination), if its production is wasting or depleting water resources, or if the farm laborers were treated fairly and paid a just wage. The eating of lettuce in Boston thus takes place within a fog of ignorance and blindness. The places and communities that provide the salad have disappeared.

What can be said about lettuce can also be said about most food products today. Ours is, as Wendell Berry once put it, an anonymous economy of the "one-night stand": "'I had a good time,' says the industrial lover, 'but don't ask me my last name.' Just so, the industrial eater says to the svelte industrial hog, 'We'll be together at breakfast. I don't want to see you before then, and I won't care to remember you afterwards.'"[60] We don't want to know the social, ecological, or health costs associated with our ignorant consumption because if we knew them we would need to give up the idea of "cheap" food "on demand." Meanwhile, as the previous section showed, the real costs to places and communities around the world are mounting.

Having seen how current economic practices make it very difficult for us to know and thus care for any place, we now need to consider how consumer habits and priorities, along with the policies and structures that recommend them, undermine the possibility of living into a given place with understanding, affection, and care. Harvard economist Stephen Marglin has described how the mainstream teaching and practice of economics today presupposes a world consisting of self-interested, calculating individuals who use markets to satisfy self-chosen goals. Economists do not consider how extreme forms of individualism undermine the development of communal relationships,

---

59   Brian Halweil gives this summary: "The transcontinental head of lettuce, grown in the Salinas Valley of California and shipped nearly 5,000 kilometers to Washington, DC, requires about 36 times as much fossil fuel energy in transport as it provides in food energy when it arrives. By the time this lettuce gets to London (and California lettuce does get shipped to the United Kingdom), the ratio of energy consumed to calories provided jumps to 127" (*Eat Here: Reclaiming Homegrown Pleasures in a Global Supermarket* [New York: W. W. Norton, 2004], 37). The inefficiency of energy use is not restricted to transport. Michael Pollan observes: "From the standpoint of industrial efficiency, it's too bad we can't simply drink the petroleum directly, because there's a lot less energy in a bushel of corn (measured in calories) than there is in the half gallon or so of oil required to produce it" (*The Omnivore's Dilemma*, 46).

60   Wendell Berry, "The Whole Horse," in *The Art of the Commonplace*, 236.

nor do they have the tools for integrating community concerns into their accounting. "By promoting market relationships, economics undermines reciprocity, altruism, and mutual obligation, and therewith the necessity of community."[61] Even though experience tells us that community and place really matter, those practices and priorities that would facilitate their nurture and growth are systematically ignored and excluded. Moreover, in promoting an economic program that emphasizes individualism and consumer acquisition, economists are creating (distorting) a world in their own image. Economists don't just describe a world for us. As their ubiquitous presence in political discussions shows, their pronouncements shape public policy and opinion.

Marglin's point is that the economic systems we have today, especially their emphasis on "free" markets, did not just happen. People had to learn to think differently about human behavior and the aims of a good human life. As the incursion of free-market ideology moves across the globe, we can see that this is a painful, sometimes violent, learning, coming often as a shock to native people who prize more communal values.[62] In fact, the vices of the great moral and spiritual traditions – pride, greed, prodigality – first had to be transformed into economic virtues for Adam Smith's ideas about production, acquisition, and work to take hold. Today's economies, in other words, are planned. They depend on founding myths or assumptions that need to be seriously questioned if we are to make significant changes in the way we live.

Of these founding assumptions, one of the most important would have to be self-interest as the major driving force of economic life. Smith famously said that we should not count on the benevolence of the butcher to provide us our meat. Instead, we should look to the butcher's interest in making money as the chief reason for their work. One could ask: have not butchers always sought to make money? It depends on what one means by "making money."

Making money is not the same as providing for one's living. In the latter case, the context of consideration is larger because it is the *living* that matters most, and the variables that factor into good living can extend fairly wide: a good living can include having enough rest, having time with family and friends, securing the needs of the community, honoring God in one's work,

[61] Marglin, *The Dismal Science*, 27.
[62] See Walden Bello's *The Food Wars* (London: Verso, 2009), and *People-First Economics: Making a Clean Start for Jobs, Justice, and Climate*, ed. David Ransom (Oxford: New International Publications, 2009).

protecting a field, and so on. When one is concerned first about making a good living, one acknowledges that larger (social and ecological) factors in life matter greatly and to a considerable extent shape and define what personal success looks like. In other words, one learns to see that it is silly to claim personal success if one's family, community, or home place are in ruins. This is because success is primarily a well-functioning community and a thriving habitat. A well-cared-for community leads to a healthy member-ship. It presupposes a regard for others.

For self-interest to take hold in the economic imagination, a radically different view of the person had to emerge, a view that defined success in terms of the individual's private profit rather than a community's or place's health. This new view on self-interest was slow in the making, requiring several changes in manners and customs to develop alongside it. Marglin identifies the following: "The transition from war to peace, the discovery of growth, the growing familiarity of individualism, the emergence of conse-quentialism, the mutation of passions into interests, and the idea that demand was unproblematic – all these developments created a climate in which self-interest became not only legitimate but praiseworthy."[63] People needed to measure personal worth in terms of private wealth. Once this mindset was firmly in place, then making as much money as possible could become the overriding goal, even if it meant that one's efforts would undermine the nurture of communities and the health of habitats.

It is a short step from the legitimation of self-interest to the enshrinement of competition and destruction as the normal, even necessary, courses of economic life. Again, one could ask if competition is not a great good since it promotes economic efficiency and development. To address this issue we need to widen the scope of consideration. In the abstract, competition is clearly good because competitors will stretch their potential and squeeze every resource to get ahead. Their getting ahead makes it possible for us to benefit from their success. Problems emerge, however, when the competitive drive diminishes the communal and ecological contexts in terms of which our common life together is possible.

To appreciate this concern we need to return to the idea of the economy of creation, or what Berry calls the Great Economy, as the ultimate context for understanding and evaluation:

> We cannot *afford* maximum profit or power with minimum responsibility because, in the Great Economy, the loser's losses finally afflict the winner.

---

[63]   Marglin, *The Dismal Science*, 114.

Now the ideal must be "the maximum of well-being with the minimum of consumption," which both defines and requires neighborly love. Competition cannot be the ruling principle, for the Great Economy is not a "side" that we can join nor are there "sides" within it. Thus, it is not the "sum of its parts" but a *membership* of parts inextricably joined to each other, indebted to each other, receiving significance and worth from each other and from the whole.[64]

The problem with making competition an economic ideal is that it finally leads us into a state of war against each other and against our home. Virtues like kindness and neighborliness, virtues that are indispensable in community life, have no room in a world where competition is king. Moreover, when people espouse competition as an economic ideal they fail to appreciate the necessity of membership. Winners of a competition are mistaken if they think they can stand alone, separated from the pack, because it is our creatureliness, our being held in multiple chains of nurture (food, education, support, friendship) that is always fundamental. The logic of competition, when taken to the extreme of the winner who is dependent upon and beholden to no one, results in individuals who must finally starve and die.

Put another way, when competition reigns it becomes virtually impossible for people to practice Sabbath. Recall that Sabbath observance is about learning to rest in God's generous goodness and receive the world as a gift. As Barth said, it requires the sacrifice of sinful desire. Competition, however, resists reliance on anyone because the basic assumption of competitors is that they must secure success for themselves. Competition encourages us to think of our work as a project in self-salvation, a project in which we control the world in hopes of securing a satisfying end. What this vision denies is that human work, whatever form it takes, rests fundamentally in God's prior creative and sustaining work. When we move into a Sabbath frame of mind we are freed from the anxiety of being successful. Brian Brock has captured this transformation well when he writes:

Separating our work sharply from responsibility for its success allows Christians to praise God who alone can make it fruitful. This renders work a discipline of responsibly preparing for *God's* sustenance, combating the illusion that it is our work which is actually sustaining us. Maintaining this gap between work and its success simultaneously frees us from falling into

---

[64]   Berry, "Two Economies," 233.

work as an arena in which we must fight for survival, and provides a new appreciation of the rich ability of creation to sustain life.[65]

Consumers most experience the anxiety of membership as the anxiety of ownership. If in previous times people secured their identity primarily by the care of a field, their participation in a guild, or their work in a community, transformations in modern life (most notably the breakdown of social structures and communal networks) made it necessary for people to express themselves in other ways. One of the most popular was through consumption practices. Through one's purchases one could now acquire an identity. It did not matter which social class one belonged to. Consumer products became the vocabulary that framed thinking about success and progress. The historian Gary Cross describes this transformation as it was taking hold in late nineteenth- and early twentieth-century American life in the following: "Americans experienced a loss of communal culture with its personal but fixed roles and witnessed the birth of a mass society in which relations were more impersonal and ephemeral but also more individualistic and even expressive. Products gave Americans ways of identifying themselves in groups when the old associations of family and neighborhood no longer worked."[66]

In a consumeristic culture one of the overriding worries, even obsessions, is whether or not as individuals we have enough. People learn to crave the success and notoriety of being the one who stands out and rises above the pack, yearning to have the newest product, possess more than our neighbor, and lack for no consumer thing.[67] It can turn into an intensely lonely quest because to be at one's competitive best one must eschew sharing and neighborliness. It is also a frustrating quest because as a consumer one is

---

[65]   Brian Brock, *Christian Ethics in a Technological Age* (Grand Rapids: William B. Eerdmans, 2010), 296–297.

[66]   Gary Cross, *An All-Consuming Century: Why Commercialism Won in Modern America* (New York: Columbia University Press, 2000), 38.

[67]   Cross is right to point out that the consumerist transformation of American culture was a social event. Shopping became a means to identify with others who were also on the journey toward fulfillment of the American Dream. Consumerism helped overcome ethnic and ideological differences. In this respect, it acted like a great social equalizer. Social equality, however, does not amount to social memberships in which the good of one's life is understood to depend on the good of the membership of which one is a part. There is a major distinction to be made between a collection of individuals, an association of relatively like-minded people, and a genuine community in which people work for the good of the whole as the first priority. On this score, Cross admits that few Americans have the psychological and social resources for the long-lasting commitments that constitute community (239). My point is that today's economic practices deliberately undermine the acquisition of these resources.

at the mercy of products that are designed to make us quickly tired of them (the improved version has already come along). The paradoxical result is that we are committed to a life of consumer fulfillment that keeps us perpetually unfulfilled. Meanwhile, the ecological and communal sources that feed our cravings are increasingly exhausted and degraded.

The consumer desire to have more is an inherently frustrating and insidious desire. Because it so often rests on comparisons with what others have, one inevitably comes up short since someone else will always have more or better. It is essential to remember that many in today's developed economies enjoy a range and quantity of consumer products that would have been unimaginable to the cultural elites in previous generations, and still we are not satisfied. The problem, in many instances, is not with what we don't have but in being unsatisfied with what we do have.

We need to appreciate that today's consumer economy trains us to be discontented and ungrateful. Rather than being consumers who discover and learn to embrace their memberships with each other (by seeing and then appreciating how these memberships feed and nurture us), today's shoppers find themselves growing further apart, suspicious of each other as competitors who may have more or better than we have. In this context it becomes very difficult for any of us to live deeply, or with affection and responsibility, in the places where we are. The habits of our economic lives point us in the opposite direction: the direction of exile.

BODIES IN EXILE

The division and destruction we are working out on the land and in our economies must finally be worked out in our bodies too. The damage cannot be neatly confined to an external sphere. We should recall here Berry's fundamental maxim: "you cannot damage what you are dependent upon without damaging yourself."[68] To compromise and destroy food systems is *necessarily* also to compromise or destroy the life of all human and nonhuman eaters. We do not appreciate this because we have turned food into a commodity and our bodies into something like a self-standing machine. We seem unable to understand that we are biological beings, and that our bodies are alive because of eating relationships with other bodies of creation.[69]

---

[68]   Berry, *The Unsettling of America*, 116.

[69]   We should not be surprised that modern philosophical and scientific traditions that reduced nature to a lifeless, telos-free machine, would also reduce the human body to a

The damage we are doing to ourselves is not only done by accident or as the unanticipated side effect of damage done elsewhere. The destructive logics of division, competition, and inordinate ambition that drive our economic life can also be seen at work in the ways we treat our bodies. Seeing them much like a commodity, people have come to understand their bodies as sites for improved performance or aesthetic enhancement, while marketers see every body as a site to maximize profitability. Large sums of money are spent to enlarge breasts, lengthen penises, shorten digestive tracts, suck fat, and redesign body parts.[70] While some of these procedures may not be life-threatening, some, like the voluntary amputation of limbs,[71] clearly are. Together they indicate that many people are not at home in their bodies. They find them unsatisfying or inherently objectionable.

What we are witnessing today is the industrialization and politicization of human bodies in unique ways.[72] Rather than being practical and intimate places where the biological and social gifts of nurture are perpetually received and given again, bodies have become the objects of competing, often contradictory, designs. What nutritionists tell us about eating (eat less, eat better) is often in direct violation of what our food industry promotes (eat more, especially cheap, unhealthy calories). Our own experience that bodies come in all shapes and sizes is daily negated by media images that idolize the thin, sleek physique. If the bodies we are given do not suit the

mechanism in which the primary medical concern becomes the prolonging of "life" at whatever cost. Jeffrey P. Bishop argues that, "Medicine's metaphysical stance, then, is a metaphysics of material and efficient causation, concerned with the empirical realm of matter, effects, and the rational working out of their causes for the purposes of finding ways to control the material of bodies ... For Western medicine, and perhaps for scientific and technological thinking, the important problem ... is how to manipulate the body or psyche in order to get the effects we desire. Bodies have no purpose or meaning in themselves, except insofar as we direct those bodies according to our desires" (*The Anticipatory Corpse: Medicine, Power, and the Care of the Dying* [Notre Dame, IN: University of Notre Dame Press, 2011], 20–21). When the body's manipulation is worked out in a capitalist framework, with its relentless need to grow markets, then it becomes inevitable that bodies will be the targets of unending solicitation and assault.

[70]   See Lauren Slater's "Dr. Daedalus: A Radical Plastic Surgeon Wants to Give You Wings," in *Harper's* (July 2001), www.harpers.org/archive/2001/07/0072395. Slater raises questions about normalcy and what is permitted in the realm of plastic surgery. The surgeon interviewed notes that while it is okay for him to *remove* an extra thumb, he's not allowed to *add* one!

[71]   Carl Elliott, "A New Way to Be Mad," in *The Atlantic Monthly* (December 2000), www.theatlantic.com/magazine/archive/2000/12/a-new-way-to-be-mad/4671/.

[72]   For an introduction to the wide range of analyses that have been brought to bear on human bodies, what they are, how they signify, what they mean, and how these meanings are contested, see Alan Petersen's *The Body in Question: A Socio-Cultural Approach* (London: Routledge, 2007).

latest fashion, we are encouraged (through surgical technique, genetic therapy, extreme dieting or exercise) to sculpt or design new ones. The competition, disorder, and destruction we witness in our lands and economies are clearly being worked out in our bodies and in our eating. People are often made to feel so insecure about their bodies that eating disorders have become an expected, even normal, path in the development of large sectors of our populations.

The industrial logic that governs our world today is a natural outgrowth of the refusal of membership. It is a logic that expresses itself in several key ways. One of its most significant forms is the idea that we are each self-standing, self-legislating beings in control of our own fate. Our lives, and thus also our bodies, are ours to do with as we please. The main purpose of governments is to give us the space, freedom, and protection to carry out the plans we choose. The main objectives of science and economy are to bring more and more of the world within our control. Successful education is judged by the student's ability to consume more. Within this logic there is little room for a deep consideration of what it means to live responsibly and gratefully within a community, or to make of any place a welcoming home.

What makes this picture of persons so striking is its inability to characterize life in terms of membership and interdependent need. There is little appreciation for the fact that we live through our bodies, and that each individual body is necessarily dependent on a bewildering diversity of other bodies for its nurture and life.[73] Bodies are not things or commodities that we have or possess. In the most fundamental sense, *every body is a place of gift*. It is a vulnerable and potentially nurturing site in terms of which we come to know and experience life as the perpetual exchange of gift upon gift. This realization inevitably leads to the conclusion that bodies are therefore also places of responsibility. How have we received what we have been given, and what have we done with these gifts of nurture? Through our bodies we learn that who we are is a feature of where we are and what we receive. Through our bodies we discover that what we become is a feature of what we have given in return. Bodies are the physical and intimate places where we learn that life is a membership rather than a solitary quest.

The anxiety of membership, what we have described as the fear of interdependent need and responsibility, compels us to see bodies (in some extreme cases even our own bodies) as alien and as a threat. We worry that

---

[73] For a thoughtful theological reflection on the place of bodies in spiritual development see Stephanie Paulsell's *Honoring the Body: Meditations on a Christian Practice* (San Francisco: Jossey-Bass, 2002).

the fragility of life will be the occasion for someone else to take advantage of us. Recoiling before our own vulnerability and need, we come to view others with suspicion. We become filled with the desire to control every body that we can. Modern food systems, but also the patterns of our eating, demonstrate that the best way to exercise control is to transform what is first and foremost a gift into an object or commodity.

It is no accident that an industrial food system works very hard to "obscure the histories of the foods it produces by processing them to such an extent that they appear as products of culture rather than nature."[74] When food is a product of culture, it is then a product of our own hands. Liberated from nature, it is not susceptible to biological realities, needs, or vulnerabilities. Food that may have begun in the ground must lose all traces of soil, sunlight, and fragile plant and animal life so that it can be redesigned, engineered, improved, packaged, stored, and delivered in whatever ways the food producer sees fit. While being hugely profitable to food companies, the commodification of food has led to the paradoxical result that consumers now need protection from the food industry if they are to be healthy. How has this come about?

Healthy bodies grow up in relation to other bodies. Scientifically speaking, what this means is that a human body develops in relation with other natural bodies, most basically through what it eats. When we eat well, consuming a diet of whole food that reflects a healthy food chain of well-nourished plants and animals, we stand the best chance of being whole and healthy too.[75] An industrial food system, however, disrupts the continuity between eaters and what they eat, severely damaging both in the process.[76] By unnecessarily

---

[74] Pollan, *The Omnivore's Dilemma*, 115.

[75] The position developed here owes much to Michael Pollan's *In Defense of Food*. Pollan shows how disastrous it has been to think of eating as a machine's ingestion of a few isolatable nutrients. Foods and bodies are complex in themselves and in their relations to one another. This is why the best strategy – because it is the one that acknowledges the complexity of food and the limits to what we can know – is to eat whole foods, foods that honor the depth of memberships that feed into every bite. Every link in a food chain, even the ones we do not currently know or appreciate, is vitally important. "Food consists not just in piles of chemicals; it also comprises a set of social and ecological relationships, reaching back to the land and outward to other people" (144). The surest sign of the degradation of food is that it has been "improved" by a food executive!

[76] It is important to underscore that the disruption also applies to animals and plants. Industrial agriculture, with its heavy reliance on chemical fertilizers and pesticides, produces plants that are less vital and nutrient-complex, whereas the regimens of confinement and feeding produce animals that are often sick and near death. For a detailed description of the ill effects for plants and animals resulting from our industrial food system, see *The Omnivore's Dilemma* (especially chapters 4 and 9), and Andrew Kimbrell's *The Fatal Harvest Reader* (Washington, DC: Island Press, 2002).

processing foods, or by designing food products from synthetic compounds, food providers have found multiple ways to give us food that is, as Roberts says (with some understatement), "ill-suited to our physiology":

> Our scientifically bred produce grows so quickly that it contains measurably fewer micronutrients. Our processed foods are often packed with large quantities of salt, fat, and sweeteners, not to mention hundreds of chemical additives, some of which, such as the preservative sodium benzoate and yellow food coloring, are definitively linked to medical problems, such as hyperactivity. And where the wild animals our ancestors gnawed on were naturally lean, our grain-fed livestock is specially bred not only to put on lots of fat, but to partition that fat *inside* the muscle.[77]

Without doubt, our industrial food systems, though giving us less whole (unprocessed) food, are giving us more calories than ever before. The problem is that these calories, while relatively inexpensive, are making us obese and sick. The plentitude of calories, though a boon to the economy – Roberts quotes Tomas Philipson, a University of Chicago economist: "the obesity problem is really a side effect of things that are good for the economy" – has in fact become a major worldwide health concern.[78]

The National Institutes of Health reports that approximately two-thirds of Americans are either overweight or obese. Even if we grant that this is a contested statistic, recognizing that the measurement of obesity has political, medical, and financial ramifications (the healing and dieting industries are multibillion dollar ventures),[79] we cannot overlook the fact that industrial patterns of eating pose a serious health threat to the individuals involved. Eating a high-fat, high-sodium, and highly sweetened and processed diet contributes to (among other conditions) cardiovascular problems and early onset diabetes. American eating leads to an estimated 100,000 diet-related deaths each year. If in the past it was primarily the rich who were fat, we now face a situation in which a disproportionate percentage of obesity and diet-related disease is found among the poor. The economics of food production means that the cheapest food is also the most fattening and unhealthy. Efficiency and profitability require larger grocery stores, those that have

---

[77] Roberts, *The End of Food*, 83. See also David Kessler's *The End of Overeating: Taking Control of the Insatiable American Appetite* (New York: Rodale Books, 2009).

[78] Roberts, *The End of Food*, 95.

[79] See J. Eric Oliver's *Fat Politics: The Real Story behind America's Obesity Epidemic* (New York: Oxford University Press, 2006), and Nortin M. Hadler's *Worried Sick: A Prescription for Health in an Overtreated America* (Chapel Hill: University of North Carolina Press, 2008).

more nutritious and higher quality food in them, to move into the suburbs where the poor cannot easily reach them. The economic divide between rich and poor is not confined to bank statements. It is being worked out in their bodies in the forms of good versus poor nutrition.[80]

As healthcare professionals have warned us about an "obesity epidemic," they have often assumed that obesity is: a relatively new problem, a feature of eating too many calories, a public health threat, a drain on medical expenditures, an effect of not enough exercise, a problem that afflicts especially poor people and minorities, and the effect of low education and poor food choices. Depending on how much one listens to this diagnosis, one will readily come to believe that being obese is a moral failure, and that to be good is to be thin. The solution? Make more money, live in a better neighborhood (with better food options), get a membership at an athletic club, and show more personal discipline.

As Guthman has shown, this framing of the "obesity epidemic" fails to attend to the structures and systems that make and keep people poor, and that keep them working long hours, often in stressful conditions. It fails to attend to the environmental racism that privileges white and more affluent communities so that they have food choices people of color do not. It fails to consider the industrial forms of agriculture and food production that lace our foods with preservatives, artificial flavors, trans fats, and other chemicals (like endocrine disruptors that disturb hormone function) that have not been scrutinized for their health effects. And it fails to address the neoliberalist philosophy that elevates private wealth at the expense of the public goods and services (like education, health care, and environmental protection).[81]

---

[80] Mark Winne has described this situation well in *Closing the Food Gap: Resetting the Table in the Land of Plenty* (Boston: Beacon Press, 2008). It should also be noted that the classism and racism evident in our food system is also being worked out more broadly in terms of neighborhoods and communities. Besides having minimal to no access to nutritious food, the poor often live in the places of the worst ecological degradation. For a discussion of what has come to be called ecological racism, see *The Quest for Environmental Justice: Human Rights and the Politics of Pollution*, ed. Robert D. Bullard (San Francisco: Sierra Club Books, 2005).

[81] "Neoliberal policies have helped produce many of the food qualities, built environments, and chemical exposures associated with obesogenesis. At the same time, these policies have made available for investment and marketing many (but by no means all possible) solutions to problems they have generated [for example, as when a company responsible for the production and marketing of high-fat foods makes available low-fat alternatives and dietary supplements]. Thus, the body has become a site for a spatial fix for capitalism's inherent growth problems" (Guthman, *Weighing In*, 164). If a body can only consume so much food, the solution is to design "foods" and pharmaceuticals that reduce food absorption, and

That the eating of food has become in our time one of the major causes of anxiety, guilt, and disease ought to compel us to rethink what it means to be a healthy body. Why do so many people, young and old, feel badly about their bodies? There is no simple answer to this question. Market forces, personal/family histories, gender stereotypes, class location, genetic predispositions, emotional upheaval, low self-esteem, racial profiling, public shaming, athleticism, a perfectionist disposition – these are just some of the factors that contribute to our malaise. Industrial eating patterns – quick eating, much of it on the go – means that people are losing the ability to listen to and trust their bodies. Meanwhile, the various projections of what an ideal body should be mean that people can become unaccepting of the fact that body weights and shapes change naturally through time. Feeling bad about one's own body, feeling unloved and unaffirmed, makes it all the more likely that one will develop unhealthy eating habits as a response.

Can we experience health when the bodies we depend upon – soils, waterways, tomatoes, bees, chickens – are made sick by industrial processes? We could only think that we can be healthy while the memberships around us are sick if we believe that we are self-standing beings in control of our own fate. In holding this assumption we are mistaken. Whatever life we enjoy is the daily result of our receiving from each other the gifts of nurture and sustenance. Every time we eat we bear witness to our being benefited by the memberships of which we are a part. The prospect of our continuing health is thus made dependent on the strength of the relationships that bind us to each other. This is why Berry is correct in insisting that there can be no health without wholeness or conviviality

> Only by restoring the broken connections can we be healed. Connection *is* health. And what our society does its best to disguise from us is how ordinary, how commonly attainable, health is. We lose our health – and create profitable diseases and dependences – by failing to see the direct connections between living and eating, eating and working, working and loving. In gardening, for instance, one works with the body to feed the body. The work, if it is knowledgeable, makes for excellent food. And it makes one hungry. The work thus makes eating both nourishing and joyful,

thereby expand the need for more food products. "Ingesting nutritionally vacuous – or deleterious foods – that exist to solve the problems of profitability for the food industry puts the ecological burden on the body, as does inhaling fouled air or drinking fouled water … bodies became a site for commodifiable cures to the conditions and illnesses created through these foods and exposures" (181). Obesity, in other words, and other food-related illnesses, are, in the minds of some people, highly desirable because they are also highly profitable.

not consumptive, and keeps the eater from getting fat and weak. This is health, wholeness, a source of delight. And such a solution, unlike the typical industrial solution, does not cause new problems.[82]

An exilic eating condition takes its most extreme form when eaters become divided from and then turn against their own bodies. Marya Hornbacher, in her remarkable memoir detailing the suffering of bulimia and anorexia, describes the growing suspicion and then hatred she came to feel toward her own body: "the body – my body – was dangerous. The body was dark and possibly dank, and maybe dirty. And silent, the body was silent, not to be spoken of. I did not trust it. It seemed treacherous. I watched it with a wary eye."[83] In her mind, her body was deeply flawed (too fat, improperly proportioned, not having the right lines or curve). But not only her body: the world outside, with its many bodies, was also seen as a threat.[84]

Food is the carrier of multiple meanings. What we eat, when, how much, and who with are all potent witnesses to what cultures and their people hold dear. In periods of history when hunger and scarcity are endemic, food registers very differently than in times of food abundance. So, for instance, in today's urban cultures of the West, "food has become a pervasive symbol of affluence and the contemporary ethic of pleasure-seeking."[85] Every occasion, it seems, is an occasion to eat. At the same time, however, the social contexts for eating and the traditions of instruction that enfolded eating habits within an overall picture of a good life have been eroding as people eat on their own more and more. Food has become a marker of one's personal style or fashion. Given the tremendous variety of food products, and the fact that international cuisines are now well represented in many settings, it is relatively easy for people to develop an individual identity around particular kinds of foods.

What is equally clear, however, is that the meaning of eating is also a market-manufactured reality. The abundance and variety of food, besides symbolizing prosperity, also mirrors the ambitions of food companies and marketers that clearly want us to eat more, even eat excessively (their economic livelihood depends on increased consumption). When the message to eat more is combined with the equally powerful current social

---

[82] Berry, *The Unsettling of America*, 138.   [83] Hornbacher, *Wasted*, 14.

[84] It is dangerous to attempt a short, definitive account of the conditions and meanings of bulimia and anorexia because these are such complex disorders laden with physiological, psychiatric, personal, family, social, economic, gender, ethnic, and cultural dimensions. There is no single cause for these eating disorders.

[85] Richard A. Gordon, *Eating Disorders: Anatomy of a Social Epidemic*, 2nd edition (Oxford: Blackwell, 2000), 186.

message that fatness means stupidity, laziness, or lack of willpower,[86] it is easy to see how eaters are put in an impossible position. On the one hand they are encouraged to eat too much, while on the other hand they are told (by dieting gurus, a weight-reduction industry but also religious leaders) that thinness means self-control, refinement, intelligence, genuine faith, and what Richard Gordon called "the civilized containment of appetites." How is this contradictory set of messages to be handled?[87]

In our culture, thinness has clearly won out as the overriding symbol of success and beauty. Thinness is linked to moral virtue and integrity. It is even viewed as the achievement of a higher spiritual state.[88] The achievement of thinness is thus widely seen as a triumph in personal power and self-control. Fat people are chastised because they "let themselves go" and have not exercised enough self-control. The overarching taboo, suggests Hornbacher, is not so much food or flesh but the loss of self-control.[89] Eating and then purging become means to exercise control over oneself, containing the body, and bringing oneself into self-possession. "The convenience in having

---

[86] For a multifaceted look at how fatness registers in societies through time, see *Bodies Out of Bounds: Fatness and Transgression*, ed. Jana Evans Braziel and Kathleen LeBesco (Berkeley: University of California Press, 2001). Its destructive register today can be seen in Michelle Mary Lelwica's observation: "The widespread belief that thinner is better is both cause and consequence of the dominant culture's war on fat in general, and the oppression of fat women in particular. Given the verbal abuse, scapegoating, social stigma, job discrimination, and internalized self-hatred that many fat women face on a daily basis, it is not astonishing that some women will do absolutely anything to be thin" (*Starving for Salvation: The Spiritual Dimensions of Eating Problems among American Girls and Women* [New York: Oxford University Press, 1999], 57).

[87] The fact that Western women have borne the greater brunt of this contradiction requires more careful, extended consideration than we can give here. Naomi Wolf's popular *The Beauty Myth: How Images of Female Beauty Are Used against Women* (New York: Morrow), first published in 1991, provoked a great amount of discussion and writing. A more scholarly treatment can be found in Susan Bordo's *Unbearable Weight: Feminism, Western Culture, and the Body* (Berkeley: University of California Press, 1993). What is clear from these and other studies is that obsessions about body image and size are intimately bound up with gender.

[88] See Part 2 of Simona Giordano's *Understanding Eating Disorders: Conceptual and Ethical Issues in the Treatment of Anorexia and Bulimia Nervosa* (Oxford: Clarendon Press, 2005), 91–131. The adulation of thinness is here linked with a historically pervasive dualism of soul and body. Dieting is thus a form of religious asceticism elevating the soul at the expense of the body. In "The Fat Jesus: Feminist Explorations of Fleshy Christologies" (in *Feminist Theology* 19:1 [2010], 20–35), Lisa Isherwood develops a sustained critique of the Christian dieting industry and the shaming of bodies that are at work within them. She argues that God's affirmation of embodiment in Jesus, along with Jesus' embrace of fleshiness in the touching, healing, and feeding of bodies, especially the bodies of people at the margins of society, is a call to churches to stop body shaming of all kinds.

[89] "Our most hallowed virtue in modern society is self-control, personal 'power'" (Hornbacher, *Wasted*, 53).

an eating disorder is that you believe, by definition, that your eating disorder cannot *get* out of control, because it *is* control. It is, you believe, your only means of control, so how could it possibly control you?"[90] "By controlling the amount of food that goes into and out of you, you imagine that you are controlling the extent to which other people can access your brain, your heart."[91] Control of the body and of food intake reaches its most tragic extreme in anorexia, when the person commits not to eat at all. Viewing oneself to be utterly without need and in complete control, the body is literally cut off from all nurture and meaning, bereft of all membership with other bodies. It is left alone to starve and die. It is a "thing" rather than a creature loved and nourished by God.

Hornbacher came to realize that the power of the bulimic and the anorectic person is an illusory power. The body and the natural realm of which it is a part cannot be conquered because the power finally to take one's own life does not amount to a conquest. It is a victory comprised entirely of loss. Nonetheless, the power a person thinks he or she has exerts an attractive, almost magical pull. One comes to think one can erase material, natural limits and take flight from bodies altogether and enter into a supernatural realm. Such flights, however, are a flight from life itself. A healthier life, Hornbacher came to realize, requires us to embrace life and resist the impulse of death.

> The leap of faith is this: You have to believe, or at least pretend you believe until you *really* believe it, that you are strong enough to take life face on. Eating disorders, on any level, are a crutch. They are also an addiction and an illness, but there is no question at all that they are quite simply a way of avoiding the banal, daily, itchy pain of life.[92]

The various forms of exile this chapter has described – ecological, economic, and physiological – share the belief that we can thrive alone and at the expense of others. They deny the fact that we eat, and so depend on each other for our health and well-being. Because of this denial we forfeit the hope of communion.

[90] Ibid., 66.   [91] Ibid., 68.   [92] Ibid., 280–281.

Life through Death: Sacrificial Eating

"Biological" or physical death is not the *whole* death, not even its ultimate essence . . . in [the] Christian vision, death is above all a *spiritual reality*, of which one can partake while being alive, from which one can be free while lying in the grave. Death here is man's *separation from life*, and this means from God Who is the Giver of life, Who Himself is Life.[1]

Death is not an eventuality that with luck, waits for another day. It is today's cup from which God now insists you drink. If you think that somehow you can choose today not to carry the deaths of your past life and former loves, you are wrong. There is no choice about that: if you rise at all, it will be from those. And it will be from those as perpetually present to you – as carried by you and offered by you to all the others who alone can give you life. The only choice you have is between accepting those deaths or pretending to a life that doesn't exist.[2]

Very truly, I tell you, unless a grain of wheat falls into the earth and dies, it remains just a single grain; but if it dies, it bears much fruit. (John 12:24)

The Eucharist, as a communion of love in and through Christ's sacrifice, involves learning cruciformity as members of Christ's sacrificial Body. As such, the Eucharist fulfills Israel's mode of sacrificial worship, in which sacrifice and communion are inextricably integrated.[3]

Eating is the daily reminder of creaturely mortality. We eat to live, knowing that without food we will starve and die. But to eat we must also kill,

---

[1]   Alexander Schmemann, *Of Water and the Spirit: A Liturgical Study of Baptism* (Crestwood, NY: St. Vladimir's Seminary Press, 1974), 62–63.

[2]   Robert Farrar Capon, *Food for Thought: Resurrecting the Art of Eating* (New York: Harcourt, Brace, Jovanovich, 1978), 156.

[3]   Matthew Levering, *Sacrifice and Community: Jewish Offering and Christian Eucharist* (Oxford: Blackwell, 2005), 27–28.

realizing that without the deaths of others – microbes, insects, plants, animals – we can have no food. "The whole of nature," says William Ralph Inge, "is a conjugation of the verb to eat, in the active and passive."[4] This means that our earthly life's movement is (among other things) an eating movement *through* death that also *ends* in death. No matter how much or how well we eat, our biological life, as well as the lives of others, will come to a mortal end.

The inevitability and ubiquity of death in no way guarantee that we will know how to face it. Just as the recognition of creaturely interdependence and need can prompt us to refuse the responsibilities of life together – a condition we described in the last chapter as the anxiety of membership – so too can the knowledge of our death result in strategies of distortion, denial, or destruction. The sinful, self-glorifying drive that attempts to secure life at the expense of others also leads to the attempt to secure life as a private possession to be protected and extended at all costs.

For us to live (and eat) well, we need to know what death *is*. As I will argue in this chapter, we can only know death properly when it is placed in Trinitarian perspective. In the temporal and mortal flesh of Jesus Christ, God's communion life is revealed as the life that offers itself completely. Jesus transforms the meaning of life (more on this in the next chapter) *and* death by placing both within the eternal self-offering that God is. Hans Urs von Balthasar (quoting Ferdinand Ulrich) says that the Father's primal begetting of the Son is a complete giving of all that the Father is.

> This total self-giving, to which the Son and the Spirit respond by an equal self-giving, is a kind of "death," a first, radical "kenosis," as one might say. It is a kind of "super-death" that is a component of all love and that forms the basis in creation for all instances of "the good death," from self-forgetfulness in favor of the beloved right up to that highest love by which a man "gives his life for his friends." "Life is only genuinely alive insofar as it . . . grows beyond itself, lets go of itself. It is rich only insofar as it can be poor, insofar as it loves . . . Death will not allow itself to be pushed to the very end of life; it belongs right at the center, not in mere knowledge, but in action. Death characterizes our breakthrough into a life that is ever greater. It is through this positive death that we amass life."[5]

According to this Trinitarian view it is a mistake to view all death as evil. Good death is a kenotic passage through which life moves. We believe this

---

4   William Ralph Inge, "Confessio Fidei," in *Outspoken Essays* (Second Series) (London: Longmans, Green, 1926), 56.
5   Balthasar, *Theo-Drama: Theological Dramatic Theory: Volume V*, 84.

because death's meaning is revealed in the light of the self-giving Christ who is the true life of the world.

To speak theologically about death we need to distinguish it from the "expiring" that is the mark of biological death. To expire is to have one's life end or run out, as when bodily organs fail owing to exhaustion, disease, or destruction. Understood biologically, death is the cessation of an individual's biochemical function. It is the termination of the ego and the obliteration of the dream of a self-standing, self-fortifying life. Viewed theologically, how-ever, death is a self-offering movement in which individuals give themselves to others for the furtherance of their lives. This characterization of death presupposes a fundamentally different understanding of life. Rather than viewing life as a possession, the person inspired by Christ understands that life is a gift to be received and given again. The seed that yields the fruit of life must first die into the ground (John 12:24). All attempts to secure life from within or to withhold oneself from the offering that is the move-ment of life will amount to life's loss. This is why John continues by saying, "Those who love their life will lose it" (12:25). For a life to be full, it must be given away.[6]

To live well, which means to learn to receive gratefully the gifts of others, requires that we also learn to die well by turning our living into a gift for others. Why? Because it is the most fitting acknowledgment of the gifts of life sacrificially given, and our most faithful way of participating in God's own self-offering life as revealed in Christ. Creation is an altar on which creatures are offered to each other as the expression of the Creator's self-giving care and provision for life. To be made in the image of this Triune creator is to be invited to share in the shaping of the world as an offering of love. The passage from death to genuine life is a loving movement of self-offering in which people lay down their lives for others in gestures of nurture and help (I John 3:14–16).

The movement of self-offering is not easily made. People readily resist turning themselves – their resources, energy, even their bodies – into a gift to others because they fear being rejected or abused. What if the life offered is

---

[6]   When Christian disciples live under the pattern of Christ's passion and redemptive death, their own death ceases to be of importance. This is because death ceases to be a conclusion or a definitive passing away and instead becomes a beginning and a promise grounded in God's Trinitarian and resurrecting love. Quoting Adrienne von Speyr, von Balthasar writes: "Since the whole world is involved in the Son's Trinitarian movement, in the Spirit, to the Father, 'death in its entirety belongs to the past.' For it is only 'he who does not love' who 'remains in death' (I Jn 3:14); 'so he never shared in life. Love, by contrast, is the constant transformation from death into life'" (ibid., 141).

deemed worthless and so is unnoticed or wasted for no good end? This very real fear tempts us to become unsympathetic, separate from others, and refuse membership. It is a fear that leads to alienation and the perception of others as a threat to the legitimacy of a self-standing ego. It is important to see that in this context biological death takes on an entirely new character. Now death is characterized as an evil because it is the obliteration of the autarchic and autonomous self that has been the focus of all one's energy. Death is the enemy because it makes a mockery of our vanity. It shows the futility of the idea that the purpose of our life is self-enlargement and self-glorification.[7]

When scripture declares death to be a punishment and the effect of sin, it has in mind the alienated and alienating life just described. Paul proclaims that "the wages of sin is death" (Rom. 6:23) and that "the last enemy to be destroyed is death" (1 Cor. 15:26) not because he wants dying understood as self-offering to come to an end. Quite the opposite. Paul pleads with fellow followers of Christ that they present their bodies "as a living sacrifice, holy and acceptable to God" (Rom. 12:1). Death becomes an enemy that needs to be defeated because sinful self-regard has turned life into something it was never meant to be. Our fear of death, in turn, contributes to our inability to make the gestures of self-giving love. Rather than being a movement of fellowship and mutual care, sin has twisted life into an oppressive reality in which bodily death can only appear as the permanence of isolation and as the confirmation that hatred and suspicion and envy are stronger than love. Sin trains people to resist a life of self-offering just as it teaches them to fear physiological death as the extinction of the ego.

Alexander Schmemann called this sort of death, the death that signifies as the refusal to join in membership with God's life in creation, the Original Sin. Though continuing to exist in a physiological way, "Man died because he *desired* life for himself and in himself, because, in other terms, he *loved* himself and his life more than God, because he preferred something else to God."[8]

---

[7] The development of medical technologies that prolong life at whatever cost is a clear example of how death has become the great enemy of our time. Stanley Hauerwas observes, "We live in a death-denying world that seems determined to develop technologies that will enable us to get out of life alive. Yet the more we strive to be free of death the more our lives are shaped by the death-determined means we create to try to free ourselves of death. Even more paradoxical, the means we use to free ourselves from death only serve to increase our isolation from one another" (*A Cross-Shattered Church: Reclaiming the Theological Heart of Preaching* [Grand Rapids: Brazos Press, 2009], 87).

[8] Schmemann, *Of Water and Spirit*, 64. In his short book *O Death, Where Is Thy Sting?* (Crestwood, NY: St. Vladimir's Seminary Press, 2003), Schmemann developed this point

The sin talked about here is not any one particular act but a disposition and an entire way of being, a way of living that is not attuned to life with and for others but a life of self-enclosure and self-magnification. It is a way of being that represents a fundamental violation of what it means to be a creature in relation with others altogether dependent upon God.[9] To sin is to refuse to receive the world as a gift. It is to reject love as the means through which the gifts of food and life are perpetually transformed into offerings that nurture creation and bring glory to God.

In Paul's mind, the resurrection of Jesus accomplishes a decisive victory over death (1 Cor. 15:54). What is put away and shown to be false is the fear that self-offering leads to no good. What is defeated is the matrix of sin that isolates individuals and destroys the fellowship of life together. In the resurrection of Christ we see that love is stronger than hate and peace more powerful than violence. As Stanley Hauerwas puts it, in Jesus' death and resurrection we witness the possibility for "a communion that overwhelms the loneliness our sin creates."[10] Self-offering is not a waste, nor does it lead to eternal oblivion. The giving of oneself, instead, leads to life as it really ought to be: "those who hate their life in this world" – that is, those who realize individual life is not a possession or an idol to be guarded or worshipped at all costs, those who categorically reject the isolating project of self-glorification but instead willingly give themselves over for the good of others – "will keep it for eternal life" (John 12:25). Resurrection life follows a cruciform, self-offering path.

---

with respect to Genesis 3. In the garden Adam and Eve were not to eat from the one tree. It was not given as a gift to them, and so did not carry God's blessing. "This means that if man ate this fruit, he did not eat in order to have life with God, as a means of transforming it into life, but rather as a goal in itself, and thus, having consumed it, man subjected himself to food ... The very fall of man consists in the fact that he desired life for himself and in himself, and not for God and in God. God made this very world a means of communion with himself, but man desired the world purely for himself alone. Instead of returning God's love with love for him, man fell in love with the world, as a goal in itself. But herein lies the whole problem, that the world cannot be an end in and of itself, just as food has no purpose unless it is transformed into life. So too, the world having ceased to be transparent to God, has become an endless commotion, a senseless cycle of time in which everything is constantly in flux, constantly vanishing, and, in the final analysis, dying" (73–74).

9   "In essence, my body is my relationship to the world, to others; it is my life as communion and as mutual relationship. Without exception, everything in the body, in the human organism, is created for this relationship, for this communion, for this coming out of oneself. It is not an accident, of course, that love, the highest form of communion, finds its incarnation in the body; the body is that which sees, hears, feels, and thereby leads me out of the isolation of my *I* " (ibid., 42).

10 Hauerwas, *A Cross-Shattered Church*, 87.

By linking death to sin, scripture enables us to see that death is never simply a biological phenomenon. Death is as much about the *character* of life as its end. This is significant because it underscores that life is to be judged by its quality and not only its quantity. When viewed from this perspective, illness, persecution, hunger, or despair can be characterized as forms of death, as dimensions *in* life that undermine or distort it. Death is a source of anxiety not only because it brings about the termination of an individual's life but because it denies communal well-being.[11] It stops short the friendship and the fellowship of life we rightly enjoy. When biological death happens in old age and in the company of a flourishing family, as it does to Abraham (Gen. 25:8), it is not something to be despised or resented. Living to a ripe old age is like maturing into a stalk of grain that has produced ears of seed for the feeding of the world (Job 5:26). In other words, death is evil insofar as it is a force that degrades life. It is not evil if it follows a fulfilled life, a life enriched by the kenotic, self-offering love that is the mark of God's own life.

Echoes of this way of thinking are also to be found in the Christian scriptures. Jesus engages in acts of feeding and healing because hunger and sickness, being glimpses of premature mortality, are understood to undermine life's quality. In Jesus' kingdom the sick are cured, lepers are cleansed, demons are cast out, and the dead are raised (Matt. 10:8), showing that Jesus is the champion of communion and life. Biological death is not an unqualified evil. Nor is it the last word in the story of life (we will return to this theme in Chapter 7). As John's gospel suggests,[12] the real issue is not biological death but the death that distorts or denies the abundant life that

---

[11]   Kevin Madigan and Jon Levenson argue that Jewish and Christian scriptures challenge us to think of death and resurrection in more communal and less individualistic terms. To be in Sheol as the "place" of the dead is not simply to die and be in a grave. It is to live an endangered form of existence of weakness and defeat, and to experience loneliness and abandonment. "Those who entered it were thought to be cut off from the land of the living, from the intimacy of kith and kin, and from the life-giving participation in the worship of the LORD, whom (as many a psalm tells us) the dead do not praise" (*Resurrection: The Power of God for Christians and Jews* [New Haven: Yale University Press, 2008], 65).

[12]   In John there is no Garden of Gethsemane/Mount of Olives scene of anguish because Jesus willingly lays down his life so that it might be taken up again (10:17–18). Jesus' death is cast as the unleashing of a new paradigm of existence in which the giving of oneself in love makes for true life. Lloyd R. Bailey observes: "Biological death is not a fundamental problem and is seldom mentioned. Nor is it even symptomatic of the deathwardness of an entire world, which must be transformed. Rather, it is a metaphor for a quality of existence which the followers of Jesus are able to transcend. They do not participate in a death-oriented existence, even though they biologically expire" (*Biblical Perspectives on Death* [Philadelphia: Fortress Press, 1979], 94).

Jesus as the "bread of life" makes possible. The prospect we should fear most is the "life" that knows no love, the isolating sin that prevents us from offering ourselves to the world. Jesus says to Mary, the sister of Lazarus, "I am the resurrection and the life. Those who believe in me, *even though they die*, will live, and everyone who lives and believes in me will *never die* " (John 11:25–26, emphasis added). Biological death matters (Jesus did weep over Lazarus's death) but what matters even more is the isolation that undermines a full and healthy life together.

The significance of death is not exhausted in the cessation of an organism's life. Death's deeper and more tragic meaning is made manifest in the separation of an organism from the God of life who is everywhere at work in creation as its sustaining and nurturing life. Death is an enemy of life insofar as it degrades and despises the gifts of nurture and help. Death is overcome and the fullness of life is achieved when persons participate in Christ's self-offering life. When people discover that "eternal life" is not about securing the unending existence of their individual being, they are freed to make their living into a gift for others.

RETHINKING SACRIFICE

Sacrificial practice represents one of humanity's oldest and most culturally widespread means for negotiating death. Numerous theories have been advanced to explain why diverse cultures engaged in this practice and what the sacrifices offered could have meant.[13] Our aim in this section must therefore be limited to an exploration of how sacrifice, particularly as it took shape in Israelite and Christian faith traditions, can speak to an understanding of life through death. Our task is to determine whether a sensibility attuned to the dynamics of sacrifice has the potential to turn people into more responsible, caring, and grateful eaters. My aim is not to suggest that we erect altars so that animals can again be burned. Nor is it to deny that the language of sacrifice has been abused and used as a tool to dominate and exploit groups of people (as when women have been asked to "sacrifice" themselves for their husbands or families, or when citizens have been asked to "sacrifice" themselves for an unjust war). It is, rather, to develop a logic or grammar of sacrifice that can be of practical use as we face the reality that

---

[13] Classic readings from several of the leading modern interpretations of sacrifice have been gathered by Jeffrey Carter in *Understanding Religious Sacrifice: A Reader* (New York: Continuum, 2003).

eating is a matter of life and death. Genuine sacrifice, I will argue, presupposes and results in the care of life, rather than its exploitation and abuse.[14]

Little in today's cultural context prepares us to view sacrifice with sympathy or appreciation. Though we may applaud Noah for his rescue of the animals, we look with horror at the altar he built to offer to God a burnt offering from among "every clean animal" and "every clean bird." We wonder how the man who endured derision building the ark, and then devoted such energy to the saving of life, could also kill it. We worry about the claim that God could receive the smoke of the burnt flesh as a "pleasing odor" (Gen. 8:20–21).

One influential way to think about Noah's sacrifice is to see it as a corollary of human violence.[15] On this view people are by nature aggressive. The energy and intensity used to hunt and kill animals must be socially approved and safely redirected into ritual action so that it is not unleashed against fellow humans. Commenting on Noah's sacrifice, and recalling the violence of the generations leading up to God's decision to "blot out from the earth" (Gen. 6:7) people and animal life, Stephen Webb argues that sacrifice is "a way of venting tension and anxiety – a cathartic release of violence onto an innocent victim, the animal." God allowed, but did not desire, sacrifice "in order to insure that the world would not fall into the same violence that had led to God's destructive anger. The killing of animals is thus an outlet for aggression."[16]

This way of speaking presupposes that the sanctioned, contained violence in a sacrifice is somehow a divine concession. Human beings are violent at

---

[14]   As I develop my account of sacrifice I will make imaginative use of Noah's sacrifice. I do not claim that this story *proves* my account or reproduces something like *the* Jewish understanding of sacrifice, an impossible task given the diverse locations and times in which Jewish sacrifice was operative. Developing this story allows me to give narrative context and flow to points about sacrifice I wish to make.

[15]   In *Homo Necans: The Anthropology of Ancient Greek Sacrificial Ritual and Myth* (Berkeley: University of California Press, 1983), Walter Burkert developed a theory of sacrifice around the theme of human violence. See also the discussion edited by Robert Hamerton-Kelly, *Violent Origins: Walter Burkert, René Girard, and Jonathan Z. Smith on Ritual Killing and Cultural Formation* (Stanford: Stanford University Press, 1987).

[16]   Stephen H. Webb, *Good Eating* (Grand Rapids: Brazos Press, 2001), 99. In his earlier *On God and Dogs: A Christian Theology of Compassion for Animals* (New York: Oxford University Press, 1998), Webb gives a more nuanced treatment, noting that it is difficult to know the origins and purposes of animal sacrifice in Hebrew scripture. Though likely not a legitimation of meat eating, the sacrificial system put a constraint on meat eating. Sacrifice is the expression of "a humble and grateful reverence for life, implicitly recognizing that the taking of life can occur only if the life of the animal rests ultimately in God's, not human, hands" (135). The ritual of sacrifice, in other words, "served to place slaughter in a context that mitigated the wanton taking of life" (138).

the core. Better to let them have this violent outlet, rather than to let it be bottled up and then explode in uncontrolled and potentially catastrophic ways. But does the idea of a divine concession make sense? Does the fact that lying and thievery are such ready temptations entail that God, in specific (especially difficult) circumstances, will grant an exemption allowing us to lie or steal?

An interpretation of sacrifice as contained or divinely sanctioned violence is problematic. Its focus, as we will see, is too much on the killing and not enough on the personal and social preparation leading up to it. As an interpretation, it also fails to take into account Jonathan Z. Smith's observation that "animal sacrifice appears to be, universally, the ritual killing of a domesticated animal by agrarian or pastoralist societies."[17] The position of domesticated animals in agrarian societies makes it unlikely that the human relationship with them would be governed by violence. From an economic standpoint, it would be self-defeating and stupid to treat violently the animals that play such a vital role in the livelihood of an agrarian household. A goat or sheep, for example, though clearly not a pet, was nonetheless an important member of a household economy. As such it should be treated with respect and care rather than contempt.

A better understanding of the sacrifice of animals can perhaps be found by recognizing that in a subsistence agricultural economy, like that of the early Israelites, the care of animals would have been informed by an understanding of God as the Good Shepherd who cares for his flock. To offer to God what was so precious and integral to the economic well-being of the family – a strong, healthy animal, or the best, first-fruits of the field – meant that sacrifice could hardly be taken lightly. In giving up a choice portion of one's sustenance, one gave significantly of oneself. In the death of a healthy and strong animal there was also a death of sorts in the one making the sacrifice.[18] The offering of the animal was at the same time a self-offering because in presenting the animal one also offered the hours of personal care that nurtured the animal to a full life. One offered one's future life because for a farmer or pastoralist one's future was inextricably tied to the health and breeding potential of the herd.

---

[17] Jonathan Z. Smith, "The Domestication of Sacrifice," in Carter, *Understanding Religious Sacrifice*, 332 (all italics in the original).

[18] E. E. Evans-Pritchard observes that among Vedic, Hebrew, and Muslim rites, what one consecrates and sacrifices is not simply the victim but "always oneself, and this is sometimes symbolically represented, by laying of hands on victims" ("The Meaning of Sacrifice among the Nuer," in Carter, *Understanding Religious Sacrifice*, 201).

We should also note that interpretations of Noah's sacrifice as a violent act make little narrative sense. To appreciate this we need to rethink the flood story. On one popular telling, the significance of the ark is that it saves a remnant of human and animal populations. God wipes out evil so that creation can have a fresh start. This interpretation does not consider what happens inside the ark as carrying great significance. What matters is that some animals and humans survive so they can restock the world.

According to a rabbinic tradition, however, it was precisely the months inside the ark that mattered most because it was there, in the work of feeding and caring for the animals, that Noah revealed what it means to be a righteous one. On this view, the ark was not primarily an escape vessel but a school for the learning of compassion. Here Noah refined the sympathies and dedication that are crucial for the development of a caring, hospitable relationship with the world. By giving up self-interest, Noah learned how to transform himself and his work into a gift for the good of others. This gift was not cheap, particularly if we side with rabbis who claimed that during the twelve months in the ark Noah was so busy attending to the needs of the animals that he did not even stop to sleep.[19] The triumph of Noah's life is that, like God, he recognized the needs of others and then attended to them. What Noah learned is that the whole world is God's ark because it is the place where God shows himself to be a hospitable host.

Without Noah's hospitality on the ark the animals would not have survived. As Jewish midrashic traditions developed this story, the parallels between Noah's care of the animals and God's care for all creation became pronounced: "The knowing of need is the highest measure of that curious, tender concern that characterizes God and God-like man."[20] Noah was a righteous person because like God he was able to provide for the creatures entrusted to his care. He knew the animals by their need and potential, and not only by their names.

On this telling of the story, it does not make sense to say Noah's sacrifice was a venting of tension or an outlet for aggression. Noah did not need such an outlet because he cared deeply about the animals. The altar, in other words, was not a place of violence but a place of self-offering. After the flood, human culture is given a fresh start, a start that, significantly, begins with a sacrificial act. What is done at the altar is done not only for the past (perhaps

---

[19] Jack P. Lewis, *A Study of the Interpretation of Noah and the Flood in Jewish and Christian Literature* (Leiden: Brill, 1978), 145.

[20] Avivah Gottlieb Zornberg, *The Beginning of Desire: Reflections on Genesis* (New York: Doubleday, 1995), 61.

as an expiatory act for prior sin) but also for the sake of a future that is to be shaped by sacrifice and by the sense that an authentic human culture can successfully grow only when it is founded on the principle of self-offering love.

When we turn to the Hebrew scriptures we find that sacrifice was fundamentally about entering into and nurturing a relationship with God. Sacrifice was the practical means to communicate with God, solicit divine aid, and repair a relationship that was not right. The Jewish scholar Jacob Milgrom writes:

> In essence, the system of sacrifice provided a metaphor, a method, for the Israelites to reach God, responding to the deep psychological, emotional, and religious needs of the people. Indeed, this is the meaning of the Hebrew word for "sacrifice"; it comes from a verb meaning "to bring near." Thus a sacrifice is that kind of an offering that enables us to approach God.[21]

In the sacrificial act the ancient Israelites took from their means of livelihood (domestic animals or the harvest of the fields) and offered it as a gift to God. Bringing these gifts into the presence of God, both the giver and the gift were rendered sacred (the Latin roots for the English word "sacrifice" come from *sacrum* and *facere* and mean "to make sacred"). As an offering these gifts could now become a means of communion between God and humanity.

Sacrifice is a form of communication that involves a double offering: a giving of the gift *and* a giving of oneself. In this communication we indicate a willingness to be spoken to and molded into a different kind of person as a result of the offering. In offering a lamb, the shepherd showed the willingness to calibrate their life according to the ways of God the Good Shepherd.[22] Similarly, in offering fruit and vegetables, we show ourselves willing to become gardeners like God, who exercises detailed care and provision in the garden of creation. Sacrifice addresses guilt because it is a witness to our commitment to heal relationships that have been degraded and broken by

---

[21] Jacob Milgrom, *Leviticus: A Book of Ritual and Ethics* (Minneapolis: Fortress Press, 2004), 17.

[22] Jonathan Klawans has argued that because Jewish sacrifice presupposed the analogy "as God is to Israel, so is Israel to its flocks and herds," sacrifice acted as an imperative to improve the care of the animals. "The sacrificial animal must be birthed, protected, fed, and guided – all things that Israel wished for themselves from their God. The meaning of sacrifice, therefore, derives not primarily from what the animals offered Israel, but rather from what Israel provided its domesticated animals, which parallels the care that they wished their God to provide for them" ("Sacrifice in Ancient Israel: Pure Bodies, Domesticated Animals, and the Divine Shepherd," in *A Communion of Subjects: Animals in Religion, Science, and Ethics*, ed. Paul Waldau and Kimberly Patton [New York: Columbia University Press, 2006], 74).

sin. It speaks to the need to reform our lives so that honest and life-giving communion can be restored.

Why is offering, especially the offering of a living being, of such importance when establishing communion? To answer this question we need to recall the basic creaturely experience of interdependent need. For people to live they must eat, which means they must consume the lives of others. This is a humbling and terrifying predicament to be in because it compels us to acknowledge that we cannot survive on our own but depend on the lives and the deaths of others. No matter how resourceful we are, we are not the sources of our own or any other life.[23] How should we receive and become worthy of the countless lives that are given as a means for our own sustenance and good? When we ponder this question, we discover an overwhelming disproportion between the extent and cost of gifts received and the human ability to adequately express gratitude for them. We sense a fundamental inability to comprehend our own experience as maintained and continually intersected by the living and dying of countless others.[24]

In a genuine sacrifice, there are two "offerings." In the "giving up" of the animal or the fruit, one communicates a willingness to trust in God to provide for what one needs. The world does not exist to be made into a private possession to be hoarded and kept for oneself. In the development of this dispossessive attitude and posture, the second offering comes into view: the "giving over" of oneself to the care of another. When one recognizes that others are gifts from God, one also recognizes that the best response is to cherish and celebrate the gifts given. The development of a sacrificial sensibility isn't, therefore, simply of pious significance. It is economic, because it results in a life in which sharing is the practical, logical outcome.

Faced with what is perhaps an inescapable incomprehension, it makes sense that people would offer in response food, the basic, nonnegotiable

---

[23] This realization may help us understand why Noah was instructed not to consume the blood of animal flesh (Gen. 9:4). To eat or drink the blood, understood by the biblical writer to be the medium of life, is to presume to take and possess (and thereby also control) life itself, and thus no longer to receive it as a gift.

[24] The philosopher Jean-Louis Chrétien helps us see that this lack of comprehension goes to the heart of humanity. To be in a relation with another, particularly a nurturing relation, requires us to acknowledge "the excess of a human being over himself, an excess of what one is and can be over what one can think and comprehend" ("Retrospection," in *The Unforgettable and the Unhoped For*, trans. Jeffrey Bloechl [New York: Fordham University Press, 2002], 119). Our falling short, however, is neither a "contingent deficit nor a regrettable imperfection." "It is the very event of a wound by which our existence is altered and opened, and becomes itself the site of the manifestation of what it responds [and relates] to" (122). I would add that the event of a wound is also, in certain respects, an event of blessing.

means of personal and social livelihood, and not merely words.[25] Food, besides being fuel, speaks or signifies as the gift and the means of life. To offer food to another, especially the precious and costly food of animal flesh, is to acknowledge that life is not to be taken for granted or hoarded as a possession to be used however one wills. Though people may work for their food by being directly involved in the growth and harvesting of what they eat, and thus have a legitimate claim on its consumption, it is inappropriate to think that the sources of life have thereby been earned. As a gift, food is something that we must learn to receive and share in such a way as to be always cognizant of its givenness.

To offer food to another expresses a profound insight into the gifted and interdependent character of the human condition. In this offering people acknowledge that as creatures they are beneficiaries of an incomprehensible and costly generosity and hospitality. The clearest sign of this acknowledgment is that people themselves become generous and hospitable with others, offering from themselves and their livelihood what they have already received. To invite others to one's table and share food with them is to communicate that life is not a possession to be jealously guarded. To share food is fundamentally to share life. It is to participate in the nurture and the strengthening of the memberships of creation. "True giving is participating, participating in the life and work of the donee, participating in one's universe as a sympathizing member. No one can participate without giving first. Giving is essential for a meaningful existence ... All communication begins with giving, offering."[26]

It makes narrative and theological sense, therefore, to think that when Noah emerged from the ark and built an altar to God he gave expression to the new sacrificial sensibility and devotion he had learned while being on the ark, a sensibility that would form the basis for an authentic creation-honoring, God-glorifying culture. By offering the animals to God, Noah gave a graphic and costly demonstration of the view that all life is precious, belongs to God, and has its proper end and meaning in God. By giving

[25]   Guy G. Strousma in *The End of Sacrifice: Religious Transformation in Late Antiquity*, trans. Susan Emanuel (Chicago: University of Chicago Press, 2009) paraphrases Sallustius, the fourth-century friend of the Emperor Julian and author of *Concerning the Gods and the Universe*, a late treatise defending the practice of sacrifice, to say: "Blood sacrifices represent our own lives, which we are symbolically offering. And prayers detached from sacrifice are worth nothing, because they are nothing but words, whereas if pronounced during sacrifices, they become animated words, *empsychoi logoi*" (62).

[26]   Jan van Baal, "Offering, Sacrifice and Gift," in Carter, *Understanding Religious Sacrifice*, 290–291.

himself to the nurture and care of the animals, Noah showed that he had received the gift of life in an appropriate fashion. Offering a sacrifice to God, Noah showed himself to be willing to offer himself to others as well. Thomas Aquinas understood this when he suggested that "man in offering sacrifices avowed that God was the first principle of the world's creation and the last end to whom all must be related."[27] Building the altar was a natural extension of the service Noah rendered in the ark, service that affirmed the animals as the gifts of God and as existing for God's good delight. Sacrifice, in other words, reoriented Noah's life by directing it to God's caring, sharing, and sustaining purposes. It gave a profound new meaning to creation as the expression of God's own generous and costly giving.

The biblical record demonstrates how easy it is to distort and pervert what sacrifice is about. Sacrifice is readily turned into a tool that degrades creatures and oppresses people when self-assertion is confused with self-offering. This is why the prophets railed against those who used sacrifice to improve their own standing. They directed their attention to the incongruity of people who promote or demand sacrifice *without offering themselves* at the same time. Hosea proclaimed that what God wants is not a burnt offering but steadfast love (6:6), while Isaiah argued that a multitude of sacrifices is useless if offered by evildoers who forsake the oppressed, the widows, and the orphans (1:10–17).

One can argue that prophetic denunciation of sacrifice spoke to what had become a cheapening of sacrifice, a turning of sacrifice into a merely pious show: people came to the temple and simply purchased an animal to sacrifice, and so did not bring with them an animal that reflected the love they had given to it. The proof that sacrificial practices had become a sham is that there was so much injustice in the land. Conversely, the proof that sacrifice is genuine is that the people making the sacrifice are also offering themselves to each other, and in that self-offering eradicating injustice. Sacrifice offered in a context of sin and injustice is a lie because sin is not the path toward communion with God and creation. Sin is the refusal of self-offering. It is the desire to have life for oneself rather than from and for God.[28]

[27] Quoted in Eugene Masure's *The Christian Sacrifice* (New York: P. J. Kenedy, 1943), 56. For an excellent development of this theme, see Willis Jenkins's *Ecologies of Grace: Environmental Ethics and Christian Theology* (New York: Oxford University Press, 2008), 115–152.

[28] Eugene Masure has suggested (*The Christian Sacrifice*, 34) that death is "the only possible route to God's ownership" of a living being. As long as the animal is alive it can still be claimed as a possession in some way. That periodic and ritual death was required is an

The destruction of the Jerusalem temple in AD 70 was a traumatic event because it put an end to the sacrifice that served as the path of communion with God.[29] Rabbinic Judaism regarded the temple as the place where God and humanity met, the place where sin was acknowledged and addressed so that life together could be restored and put on a righteous path. In the wake of the temple's absence, how would humanity and God commune with each other? The trauma and a solution to it are recorded in the following account from *Fathers According to the Rabbi Nathan*, IV.V.2:

> One time after the destruction of the Temple, Rabban Yohanan ben Zakkai was going forth from Jerusalem with R. Joshua following after him. He saw the house of the sanctuary lying in ruins. R. Joshua said, "Woe is us for this place that lies in ruins, the place in which the sins of Israel used to come to atonement." He said to him, "My son, do not be distressed. We have another mode of atonement, which is like atonement through sacrifice, and what is that? It is deeds of loving kindness." "For so it is said, 'For I desire mercy and not sacrifice, and the knowledge of God rather than burnt offerings'" (Hos. 6:6).[30]

Though the temple altar as the place where people offered the gifts of life and livelihood would come to an end, the need to offer oneself in a sacrificial manner would not. Acts of mercy and charity, as well as practices of prayer and study, even the witness of martyrdom, would gradually be understood as taking the place of the altar. This is because the logic of sacrificial self-giving is at the heart of a culture informed by the example of God's own self-offering love.

indication of how difficult it is for people to give up claims to possession. Masure also argues that because the animal was offered to God it would not be understood to be annihilated or destroyed but instead magnified and exalted for being accepted by God. Since the offering (being accepted by God) is not itself deprived but the offerer clearly is (the claim to possession is gone), Masure concludes: "In most ancient and elementary religions, therefore, what was really immolated was, in men's minds, not the victim but the offerer" (37).

[29] For an account of the significance of sacrificial practice in the ancient Mediterranean world and the trauma its ending produced, see Maria-Zoe Petropoulou's *Animal Sacrifice in Ancient Greek Religion, Judaism, and Christianity, 100 BC–AD 200* (Oxford: Oxford University Press, 2008).

[30] Quoted by Jacob Neusner in "Sacrifice and Temple in Rabbinic Judaism," in *The Encyclopedia of Judaism*, 2nd edition, ed. J. Neusner, A. J. Avery-Peck, and W. S. Green (Leiden: Brill, 2005), 2370.

EUCHARISTIC SACRIFICE

As early Christian communities worked to come to terms with the meaning and significance of Jesus Christ, they found the language and the grammar of sacrifice unavoidable. John's gospel (1:29) and Paul's letters (1 Cor. 5:7, Rom. 3:25) described Jesus as the sacrificial lamb who takes away the sin of the world. According to Paul, it is in the sacrifice of Jesus that the righteousness of God was definitively disclosed.

Though the Acts of the Apostles records that the early followers of Christ "spent much time together in the temple" (Acts 2:46; cf. Luke 24:53), it is also clear that Christians did not make animal sacrifice central to their life together.[31] Their rejection of sacrifice, however, did not stem from a blanket condemnation of the altar or a rejection of the logic of self-offering (Jesus, like the prophets before him, may have been critical of temple abuses but he did not reject the temple as such). Rather, it came from the realization that in the life, death, and resurrection of Christ, sacrifice had been cast in a new light and put on a different path. As the letter to the Hebrews put it, Christ inaugurated a new covenant between God and humanity that was founded upon his life and blood.[32] Christ is not reducible to being a victim. He is the high priest who offered himself so that the isolating, degrading, and death-wielding ways of the world could be overcome. Jesus "has appeared once for all at the end of the age to remove sin by the sacrifice of himself" (9:26). Christians no longer need to go daily to the temple and offer sacrifices

---

[31] Petropoulou writes: "It is indeed surprising that, although early Christians came from among pagan polytheists and Jewish monotheists, both of whom practiced animal sacrifice, Christianity should emerge as a religion in which animal sacrifice did not constitute the central act of the cultic syllabus" (*Animal Sacrifice in Ancient Greek Religion, Judaism, and Christianity*, 209). There is evidence, however, that some Christians, perhaps out of lingering fidelity to pagan observances, did practice animal sacrifice (hence the need for second-century apologists to write against continuing sacrificial practices, 246–248). See also chapter 7 of David Grumett and Rachel Muers's *Theology on the Menu: Asceticism, Meat and Christian Diet* (London: Routledge, 2010) for a survey of Christian practices of sacrifice.

[32] Hebrews states that "without the shedding of blood there is no forgiveness of sins" (9:22). In a series of works, Margaret Barker has argued that the reference to Jesus' blood recalls the role of blood in temple sacrifice. Like the Jewish high priests, Christ offers blood as the source of life that cleanses sin and heals wounds. Blood renews creation because it transforms alienation and destruction into life-giving communion. Referring to Leviticus 17:11, Barker says "the blood in atonement rituals was said to be life not death and it was the life which atoned" (*On Earth as It Is in Heaven: Temple Symbolism in the New Testament* [Edinburgh: T&T Clark, 1995], 44). When Christians later drank wine as a symbol of Christ's blood they testified to the new covenant and life made possible through his self-offering death. For further development of this theme see Margaret Barker's *The Great High Priest: The Temple Roots of Christian Liturgy* (London: T&T Clark, 2003).

because Christ has made of himself the definitive offering that forever heals the breach and opens the lines of communication between God and the world. Christ's self-offering marks the "end" or completion of sacrifice because he gives the unsurpassable expression to how self-offering leads to true life. In his daily life we see what "giving up" and "giving over" look like and require. He turns all of us into altars for the receiving and giving again of the gifts of God. He turns our bodies and our entire being into gifts to be given to others. Christ is the "pioneer and the perfecter of our faith" (12:2), the one who establishes *through himself* communion with God. As we will more fully see in the next chapter, to drink his blood is to participate in the communion with God and creation his life makes possible.

David Bentley Hart captures this point well when he says that Christian sacrifice is best understood in terms of the "drawing nigh" that the Hebrew term *qurban* suggests. Christ's sacrifice is

> a miraculous reconciliation between God, who is the wellspring of all life, and his people, who are dead in sin. Sacrifice, in this sense, means a marvelous reparation of a shattered covenant, and an act wherein is accomplished again and again, that divine indwelling, within the body of his people, that is God's purpose in shaping for himself a people to bear his glory.[33]

Christ's blood, like the blood sprinkled in the Jewish temple, is not a substance of terror reflecting violence and death but the medium of reconciliation, healing division and renewing life by putting it on a divinely inspired, self-offering path. Christ is a continuation of the temple because it is in him that heaven (the place of God's life) and earth (the place of creaturely life) meet. By participating (through baptism and Eucharist) in his sacrificial life, Christ's followers taste the fruit of heaven.

When Christians declared Jesus to be the final and complete sacrifice who atones for sin (see Rom. 3:25, Heb. 2:17, and I John 2:2), they were not simply making a statement about the man from Nazareth. They were saying something about the character of God. More specifically, they were saying that a sacrificial logic of self-offering has been at the heart of the divine life from all eternity. Jesus' death, as Avery Dulles observed, "cannot be dismissed as an incidental and unintended consequence of his

---

[33] David Bentley Hart, "'Thine Own of Thine Own': Eucharistic Sacrifice in Orthodox Tradition," in *Rediscovering the Eucharist: Ecumenical Conversations*, ed. Roch A. Kereszty (New York: Paulist Press, 2003), 143. For further discussion on the continuity between Temple practice and the Eucharist, see Jonathan Klawans's "Interpreting the Last Supper: Sacrifice, Spiritualization, and Anti-Sacrifice," in *New Testament Studies* 48 (2002): 1–17.

mission."[34] Christ is no mere scapegoat, nor is his death reducible to lessons people should learn about their implacable thirst for violence. Jesus' death speaks to God's way of being with the world, and thus also to creation's inner meaning. On the cross Jesus encountered the alienating and violent death of this world and transformed it into the self-offering death that leads to resurrection life.

Ian Bradley has rightly argued that contemporary suspicions about sacrifice prevent us from seeing the self-limitation and self-surrender that emanate from the very being of God. Legitimate worries that sacrifice can lead to degradation and exploitation often block the realization that those who wish to follow Jesus must similarly commit themselves to constant and costly self-giving. "The God who is revealed in Christ is continually sacrificing himself, as much in the activity of creation as in the work of redemption through his Son. He is the author of life through sacrifice."[35] In this view, the sacrificial logic of self-offering that is made evident on the cross was already at work at the foundation of the world. If God's creation of the world is understood as the expression and concrete manifestation of divine intra-Trinitarian love, and love entails a willingness to give oneself wholeheartedly to another (even to the extent of laying down one's life for another [I John 3:14–16] or "emptying oneself" in service to another [Phil. 2:6–8]), then it is appropriate to see in the work of creation God's willingness to pour himself out so that creaturely life can exist.[36] Divine death, understood as the self-offering that reaches a climax in the cross, is the origin and the condition for the possibility of true, resurrection life. The goodness and beauty of the world but also its costly and sometimes terrifying grace are revealed through God's constant self-giving.[37] This means that Jesus laying down his

---

34 Avery Dulles, "The Eucharist as Sacrifice," in Kereszty, *Rediscovering the Eucharist*, 175.

35 Ian C. Bradley, *The Power of Sacrifice* (London: Darton, Longman and Todd, 1995), 11. Bradley continues: "the Cross is not just an emblem of suffering and shame, although it is that assuredly: it is the instrument of creation as much as redemption, the tree of life which renews all and the sacrificial pillar which supports the entire cosmos" (85).

36 For a wide-ranging set of essays that explore and develop creation as the work of God's self-emptying love, see *The Work of Love: Creation as Kenosis*, ed. John Polkinghorne (Grand Rapids: William B. Eerdmans, 2001).

37 "For Christian thought the true order of sacrifice is that which corresponds to the motion of the divine *perichoresis*, the Father's giving of the Son, the Son's execution of all that the Father is and wills, the Spirit's eternal offering back up of the gift in endless variety, each person receiving from and giving to each other in infinite love" (David Bentley Hart, *The Beauty of the Infinite: The Aesthetics of Christian Truth* [Grand Rapids: William B. Eerdmans, 2003], 353). Hart is right to emphasize that sacrifice is not a moment or movement within economies of violence or exchange. Christ's sacrifice, building on the Jewish understanding of God, "underwrites not the stabilizing regime of prudential

life for others, a cruciform movement that is the climax of divine love, is the practical, embodied expression of the eternal love that creates and sustains the whole of the world.

The movement of sacrifice that characterizes God's life also characterizes created life. Creation is an immense altar upon which the incomprehensible, self-offering love of God is daily made manifest. Here, in the living and dying of creatures, in the seed that dies into the ground, we discover that sacrificial offering is a condition for the possibility of the membership of life we call creation. Creation, understood as God's offering of creatures to each other as food and nurture, reflects a sacrificial power in which life continually moves through death to new life. This power, however, is deeply paradoxical, "binding and bringing together what is broken and fragmented through a process which itself involves surrender and suffering ... Sacrifice is the supreme *opus Dei*, the working out of God's power to make holy and to make whole."[38] Because there is no life without sacrificial love, and no love without surrender, the destiny of all creatures is that they offer themselves or are offered up as the temporal expression of God's eternal love.[39]

It is important to underscore that for this offering of creatures to be a genuine sacrifice, it must give glory to God. History reveals that there are numerous ways in which creatures and groups of people can be exploited and abused out of vanity and fear or from the need to secure an advantage for another (recall how women, races, and indigenous peoples have been forced to "sacrifice" their freedoms and dreams so that the ambitions of men or colonial powers can be achieved). People along with other creatures can be degraded by being reduced to pawns in a complex game of retribution or appeasement, just as they can be debased as economic units in a business plan. None of this activity reflects genuine sacrifice because self-glorification or the glories of a nation or corporation have eclipsed the glory of God. It would be more accurate to describe exploitation for what it really is, an

---

violence, but the destabilizing extravagance of giving and giving again, of declaring love and delight in the exchange of signs of peace, outside of every calculation of debt or power" (350). In this giving "creation is seized up into the sheer invincible pertinacity of that love, which reaches down to gather us into its triune motion" (358).

[38]   Bradley, *The Power of Sacrifice*, 35.

[39]   It is extremely difficult to come to terms with God's offering of creatures to each other, particularly when it is acknowledged that the vast majority of these offerings are not freely or self-consciously made by the creature. One is tempted to see in such offering a violation of the creature. But if the creature does not have the freedom to make the offering, does it make sense to say its freedom has been violated? The issue of whether or not some nonhuman creatures have the capacity for freedom, and thus the ability to make a sacrifice, cannot be taken up here.

anti-sacrifice, because here God's life-giving power has been turned against life. Sacrifice has been twisted into idolatry.

One way to characterize Christian life is to see it as the school in which people learn to make an appropriate sacrifice. As the path of deep and true communion, sacrifice is both the way *of* and the way *to* God. When Christians considered the death and resurrection of Jesus Christ, they saw in him the pattern for their own sacrificial living. Frances Young has argued that these early Christians used the language of sacrifice not only to describe Christ's atoning work but also to express the faithful life and worship that must be a participation in his work if it is to have any effect. In other words, Christ's sacrifice was not understood so much in juridical or substitutionary terms but as a representative act in which Christians are called to partake. "By identification with Christ through faith, mankind is restored to perfect worship of God and complete self-offering to God in a life of proper obedience. This is why there is such a close relation between the atoning death of Christ and the imitation of him which Christians called their sacrifice ... They in Christ, and Christ in them, offer the sacrifice."[40]

The apostle Paul planted this way of thinking when he claimed that to be baptized is to be baptized into Jesus' death: "we have been buried with him by baptism into death, so that, just as Christ was raised from the dead by the glory of the Father, so we too might walk in newness of life" (Rom. 6:4). What Paul is after here is a description of the transformation of persons so that former patterns of living, patterns that can be described as sinful because they are focused on self-satisfaction or self-glorification, are put away for good.[41] Freed from the bondage of sin, baptized believers can now live a true and complete life with Christ. The old self is "crucified" so that a new self can be born, a self that no longer participates in or is held captive by the kind of death that alienates or destroys. Because Christ through his resurrection has defeated the death associated with sinfulness, Paul admonishes his followers to be "dead to sin and alive to God in Christ Jesus" (Rom. 6:11).

---

[40] Frances M. Young, *The Use of Sacrificial Ideas in Greek Christian Writers from the New Testament to John Chrysostom* (Cambridge, MA: Philadelphia Patristic Foundation, 1979), 299.

[41] Jerome Murphy-O'Connor argues that in Paul's letters the self-offering death of Jesus functions like a lens that helps Christians pattern their own living on him. "For Paul the self-giving which animated the whole existence of Jesus came to its highest expression in his death (cf. Gal. 2:20), and provided the most radical demonstration of the way God desired his creatures to live. 'He died for all, that those who live might live no longer for themselves' (2 Cor. 5:15)" (*Keys to First Corinthians: Revisiting the Major Issues* [Oxford: Oxford University Press, 2009], 211).

This sacrificial manner of speaking and practice came together for Christians in the consecration of the Eucharistic meal. In Paul's instruction to his followers about how to celebrate the Lord's Supper, he concludes by saying, "For as often as you eat this bread and drink the cup, you proclaim the Lord's death until he comes" (1 Cor. 11:26). At the Lord's Supper, Christians do not merely recall Christ's sacrificial death but participate in it in such a way that their living is a proclamation of the resurrection life he made possible on the cross. "In the sacrifice-sacrament of the Eucharist, we learn charity by offering with Christ his own saving sacrifice. The sacrament of the Eucharist is a 'school' of charity; it builds the Church by enabling us to enact Christ's sacrifice with him."[42] Christ's self-offering, in other words, sets the pattern for what all appropriate self-offering looks like. Christ's sacrifice establishes a new covenant sealed with his own blood, a covenant that makes full and complete communion possible.[43]

Scholars describing Christian sacrifice frequently characterize it as a "spiritualization" of Jewish practice because animals are no longer offered on an altar. Young, for instance, says "The Christian spiritualization of sacrifice was radical. In general it meant that only prayer, charity, a life of Christian virtue, and self-offering in martyrdom were reckoned to be suitable sacrifice for the one true God who was in need of nothing but the loyalty and devotion of his creatures."[44] To speak this way can be misleading, especially if we recall that a sacrifice is an offering from one's livelihood and life. To practice mercy and charity, as early Christians were called to do, was thus to engage in practices that had to be material in their manifestation.

We see one dimension of this sacrificial sensibility when we turn to the *Didache*, an early, nonscriptural Christian text. Referring to the sort of hospitality that is to govern a Christian household when a charismatist or prophet arrives, the *Didache* instructs:

> You are therefore to take the first products of your winepress, your threshing-floor, your oxen and your sheep, and give them as firstfruits to the charismatists, for nowadays it is they who are your "High Priests." If there is no charismatist among you, give them to the poor. And when you make a batch of loaves, take the first of them and give it away, as the commandment directs. Similarly when you broach a jar of wine or oil, take

---

[42] Levering, *Sacrifice and Community*, 199.

[43] Mark's gospel records Jesus to have said about the cup, "This is my blood of the covenant, which is poured out for many" (Mark 14:24), suggesting that like the sacrificial blood carried out by the temple priest, his blood is an offering that renews creation. See again the reference to the work of Margaret Barker in n. 32.

[44] Young, *The Use of Sacrificial Ideas in Greek Christian Writers*, 98.

the first portion to give to the charismatists. So, too, with your money, and your clothing, and all your possessions; take a tithe of them in whatever way you think best, and make a gift of it, as the commandment bids you.[45]

The language and the reference to high priests makes it clear that the gifts of charity are here understood as a continuation of sacrificial offerings. What is different is that there is no altar. Though sacrifice as practiced in a temple had come to an end, this did not mean that the offering of gifts of livelihood – bread, wine, meat, clothing, oil, and money – came to an end as well. In the sharing of food with each other, the sacrificial altar is transformed into a table and the kitchen table into an altar.

Sacrifice becomes distinctly Christian when it is offered *through* Christ. Summarizing the position of the second-century apologist Irenaeus, Rowan Williams observes: "We do not work our salvation in offering the Eucharistic oblation; we witness to the share we have been given in the glorified life of Christ, manifest in the rest of our lives as charity, humility, and pity. And the purity of our offering depends upon our commitment to the Christ through whom it is offered."[46] This means that Christians sacrifice truly when they cease to strategize to appease or bribe God. Their offerings become genuine when they are no longer made out of fear or anxiety, or with the hope of consolidating position and glory in the world. Instead, Christian sacrifice is about learning how to make one's life into a gift that creates communion.

At the Eucharistic table, in the sharing of bread and wine and in the participation in the life and death of Jesus, Christians see, smell, touch, and taste that life and love are possible because of the giving of life for each other. "If, then, life is given us, we understand that it is by means of death. And if we in turn are to give life, death must likewise intervene."[47] Cruciform self-giving is here proclaimed as the foundation and life of the world.

CONSIDERING EATING MEAT

It is tempting to think that a vegan (not relying on animal products in any form) or vegetarian (consuming animal products but not the animals themselves) diet can avoid the concerns raised about sacrifice and the life-and-death character of life. This is an illusion. As every gardener knows, a strictly

---

[45] *Didache*, 13, in *Early Christian Writings: The Apostolic Fathers*, ed. Andrew Louth, trans. Maxwell Staniforth (Harmondsworth: Penguin Books, 1968), 234.

[46] Rowan Williams, *Eucharistic Sacrifice: The Roots of a Metaphor* (Bramcote: Grove Books, 1982), 11.

[47] Ghislain Lafont, *Eucharist: The Meal and the Word* (New York: Paulist Press, 2008), 95–96.

vegetable diet cannot avoid the death of a great number of creatures ranging from microorganisms in the soil to rodents and other small animals above the ground, all of which are constantly feeding on each other. Clearly, not all deaths are the same. How does one compare the death of a microbe with the death of a cow? Considering vegetarianism, however, enables us to think more deeply about the nature of eating as an act that leads us into the life and death of creation. It invites us to think carefully about how human eaters are best to approach and consume the gifts of plant and animal life.

Though the term "vegetarianism" is fairly recent, having arisen in the 1840s, the idea that people should refrain from the eating of meat is ancient. It is an idea that has a long and diverse history.[48] In the minds of some, an all-vegetable diet bore witness to a prehistoric idyll of peace in which no animal killed another for food. Others rejected a meat diet because, like Pythagoras, they believed in the transmigration of souls from human into animal bodies. Still others refused meat because of its symbolic associations with religious sacrifice or a particular class of eaters and their manners.[49] The killing of animals for food might, as Porphyry believed, have the unwelcome effect of creating a brutish, violent, and unrestrained humanity. In eating or not eating animal flesh it is never simply the animal's life that is at stake. Of equal, and sometimes greater, importance is the training and refinement of persons into a morally and spiritually sensitive humanity.

Vegetarian arguments tend to come in three general forms: not eating meat contributes to better personal health, prevents cruelty to animals, and saves the earth. First, vegetarians sometimes point to the "China Study," a collaborative twenty-year study between Cornell University, Oxford University, and the Chinese Academy of Preventive Medicine, which concluded that people who eat a heavy animal-based diet suffered greater incidents of chronic disease (heart disease, diabetes, obesity, cancer) while those who ate a plant-based diet were healthier and tended to avoid chronic conditions. Second, vegetarian advocates point to the consumption of over eight billion animals in the United States alone, many of which are raised in crammed confinement, pumped with steroids and antibiotics, and then slaughtered in inhumane fashion.[50] And third, vegetarians point to the fact

---

[48] For two recent histories see Colin Spencer's *Vegetarianism: A History*, rev. edition (London: Grub Street, 2000) and Tristram Stuart's *The Bloodless Revolution: A Cultural History of Vegetarianism from 1600 to Modern Times* (London: HarperPress, 2006).

[49] For historical treatment on the many reasons Christians have given to abstain from meat, see Grumett and Muers's *Theology on the Menu*.

[50] Jonathan Safran Foer describes the degrading and inhumane aspects of today's meat production practices in *Eating Animals*.

that an animal-based diet requires that precious soil, water, plant, and fossil fuel resources first be converted into animal feed before they can become food for us, thus making very inefficient use of those resources.

Many of these arguments are compelling and need our attention and support. The meat-heavy American diet is unhealthy, does indeed depend on the abuse of animals, and is wasteful of natural resources.[51] The health of humans, animals, fields, and waterways would be better served if people ate less meat, particularly the sort of meat raised and slaughtered according to industrial models of production. Does it follow, however, that all consumption of meat is wrong? Are there theological considerations that can be brought to bear upon this very complex and important issue?[52]

As Christians have looked for guidance about the eating of meat they have frequently turned to biblical passages like Genesis 1:29 where God gives to animals and people "every plant yielding seed that is upon the face of all the

[51] In *The Third Plate: Field Notes on the Future of Food* (New York: The Penguin Press, 2014) Dan Barber travels the world to explore a new meal imagination, one that is not so heavily meat dependent, and that attends to the health of ecosystems, plants, and animals. It is unfortunate that some of his recommendations are out of reach for people with low incomes.

[52] It is impossible in this brief section to do justice to the many detailed questions surrounding the eating of meat. For starters, what "meat" means is hardly a universal or uncontested matter (is fish a meat?). Moreover, relationships between people and the animals they eat vary greatly according to time, place, and tradition. For the most recent and sophisticated analysis of these and other issues, see the collection of essays edited by David Grummet and Rachel Muers in *Eating and Believing: Interdisciplinary Perspectives on Vegetarianism and Theology* (London: T&T Clark, 2008). Similarly, there are a great many cultural and historical factors to consider with respect to how people understand and relate to animals. In his classic essay "Why Look at Animals?" John Berger argued that modern capitalism inaugurated a decisive shift in the treatment of animals, a shift that was dependent on several practical developments: urbanization, the commodification of meat, the development of zoos, and the growth of an animal "pet" culture (in *About Looking* [New York: Vintage, 1992]). Meanwhile, Stephen Budiansky has rightly argued in *Covenant with the Wild: Why Animals Chose Domestication* (New Haven: Yale University Press, 1999) that some of the efforts of animal rights activists, though well-intentioned, actually do more harm than good. In part this is because urbanites are susceptible to romantic idealizations of nature as a place of harmony. Having little sustained or practical relationship with a diversity of animals in their contexts, they do not know how to appreciate animals other than as pets. Webb has gone so far as to suggest that pets are "the paradigmatic animal" and that through our domestication of animals we can bring "the wild back into an ordered relationship." Clearly, and as the history of agriculture shows, the domestication of some animals is a noble calling. But to claim that tamed animals are "the original form of all animals" (Webb, *Good Eating*, 80–81) amounts to anthropomorphism gone too far. It may lead to an inability to see animals as genuinely *other*. For a diverse collection of views on the theological meaning of animals and animality, see *Creaturely Theology: God, Humans and Other Animals*, ed. Celia Deane-Drummond and David Clough (London: SCM Press, 2009).

earth, and every tree with seed in its fruit; you shall have them for food."
Here, in God's original paradise, all creatures ate a vegetarian diet. Later
prophets, such as Isaiah and Hosea, suggest that a vegetarian diet will also
mark God's future peaceable kingdom: "The wolf shall live with the lamb,
the leopard shall lie down with the kid . . . The cow and the bear shall graze,
their young shall lie down together; and the lion shall eat straw like the ox"
(Isa. 11:6–7). These two passages act like bookends, indicating that vegetarianism is God's intention from beginning to end. The fact that people in the
Bible eat meat is a reflection of God's "concession" to human sinfulness and
creation's fallen state, a concession made to Noah after the flood when God
said, "Every moving thing that lives shall be food for you; and just as I gave
you the green plants, I give you everything" (Gen. 9:3).[53]

Because the culture of scripture is agrarian, we should not be surprised
that stories about farmers and shepherds abound, and that people, clearly
with God's blessing, raised animals for food. Hebrew religion and cultic
practice would have made no sense without an agricultural context since it
was domesticated animals and the fruit of the field that were at the heart of
its sacrificial rites. When we turn to the Christian scriptures there is little
indication that Jesus was vegetarian or that he, while protesting abuses,
opposed the tradition of temple sacrifices.[54] If Jesus believed a vegetarian
diet to be the ideal, should we not expect clearer evidence that he taught and
practiced it, especially when we consider the radical character of Christ's
teaching in other areas? Moreover, passages such as Peter's vision declaring
all animals clean and fit to be killed and eaten (Acts 10:9–16), and Paul's

---

[53]   In *Good Eating*, Webb argues that this concession does not amount to a reversal of God's
abiding intention that no creatures eat meat. "God's change of heart about meat-eating is
clearly portrayed as a concession to human sinfulness and to the hardness of our heart. The
divine ideal has not changed; God's claims on us are eternal" (72). The claim of a divine
concession, I would argue, makes little sense. Does God make a concession to lying or
cheating when, in particular cases, obeying the commandment proves difficult? God does
not adjust what God desires because of hardness of heart. Instead, God chooses to adjust
the heart so that it is animated by love.

[54]   See the two essays by Richard Bauckham, "Jesus and the Animals I: What Did He Teach?"
and "Jesus and the Animals II: What Did He Practice?," in *Animals on the Agenda:
Questions about Animals for Theology and Ethics*, ed. Andrew Linzey and Dorothy Yamamoto (Urbana: University of Illinois Press, 1998), as well as the essay by David G. Horrell,
"Biblical Vegetarianism? A Critical and Constructive Assessment," in Grummet and
Muers, *Eating and Believing*. Horrell concludes that the Bible does not provide clear and
conclusive evidence to support an argument for vegetarianism. "What the Bible can
contribute, however, is broader facets of a worldview which inspires and sustains a
commitment to discipline bodily practices out of a christologically shaped regard for the
other, to foster the flourishing and praise of the whole creation, and to anticipate in practice
the eschatological renewal of all creation" (53).

admonition to the church in Rome that members not judge each other on the basis of whether they eat a meat or vegetable diet (Rom. 14), suggest that the eating of meat was not banned by the early Christian community.[55]

Given these two opposing views on meat consumption in the Bible, it may be helpful to turn to earlier observations about sacrifice and its logic of self-offering. My intent is not to "solve" the issue here but to see whether the theological picture I am drawing in this book can illuminate the issues for us in helpful ways. Recall that sacrifice as previously described is not something people do to God to gain benefits or secure favors. Rather, sacrifice is God's self-offering way of being with the world, a way that people are invited to participate in so that the fullness of life together can be achieved. Creation itself, understood as the physical manifestation of God's self-giving love, is the altar upon which this unfathomable grace is daily worked out. Creatures eat, grow, heal, and die as the expression of this sacrificial movement. When Genesis (1 and 9) describes God as *giving* plants and animals to every living creature for food, this giving is a reflection of the self-offering that characterizes God's creative and sustaining life from the beginning. Two important observations (with several practical implications) follow from this point.

First, a refusal to eat meat *may* reflect a refusal to come to terms with the life and death that characterize creation. It *may* signal an inability to appreciate appropriate death as a movement into and constitutive of life. Robert Farrar Capon has put the matter bluntly:

> [L]ife itself is resurrection, or else it isn't life ... death is not an inexplicable accident that happens to life; it is the very engine by which life runs. It is by the deaths of chickens, chicory, and chickpeas that you have lived until today. And even the life you now have is a perpetual dying ... For to live is always to be rising from the dead. To reject death is to reject the only possible soil out of which life can come.[56]

[55] Paul was, however, worried about eating meat that had first been sacrificed to idols, fearing that such eating would suggest loss of allegiance to God and perhaps prompt a member weak in the faith to fall (1 Cor. 8). It is important to appreciate how the purchase and the eating of meat, a relatively rare event in the ancient Mediterranean world, were tied to animal sacrifice. For early Christians to refuse meat was often a case of refusing to be identified with pagan or Jewish sacrificial practices. See Andrew McGowan's *Ascetic Eucharists: Food and Drink in Early Christian Ritual Meals* (Oxford: Clarendon Press, 1999) for detailed treatment of this topic. For a summary exposition of meat consumption in the ancient world, see John M. Wilkins and Shaun Hill's *Food in the Ancient World* (Oxford: Blackwell, 2006) and Nathan MacDonald's *What Did the Ancient Israelites Eat? Diet in Biblical Times* (Grand Rapids: William B. Eerdmans, 2008).

[56] Capon, *Food for Thought*, 154–155. Capon specifies the point with respect to bread, describing it as the great sacrament of life: "Unless the seed has died there would have been no wheat; unless the wheat had been ground, no flour; without the destruction of

The seed that must die into the ground so that it can produce much fruit is not reducible to a biological or ecological principle. It is also a theological principle transforming material existence into the abundant resurrection life that Christians are called to lead. This does not mean that eaters are to take lightly or rejoice in the death of creatures given by God as food. All sentimental and romantic notions of faith and life are brought to ruin at the cross.[57] But it does suggest we must – through care-full and compassionate living – learn to accept and honor the gift of the death of others as God's means of provision and salvation for the world.[58] As David Clough has recently argued, Christian theological arguments for and against vegetarianism can be made. This does not mean, however, that Christians can eat meat indiscriminately: "if we are to make use of animals for food, we should ensure that such use respects their relationship to us as fellow creatures of God … and seek to promote their flourishing when we can, and obstruct it only when we must."[59]

Accepting the gift of life, particularly since it also means receiving the deaths of others, is an extraordinarily difficult thing to do. How can we make ourselves worthy of ending and eating another's life? People much prefer to think that they can eat life cheaply and without having to acknowledge the suffering and death that accompanies every diet. This preference, of course, is made much easier by the fact that fewer eaters than ever before are now involved in the growing of vegetable and animal food. When food appears as

---

carbohydrates by the yeast, no rising; without the murder of the yeast by fire, no finished bread; and without the finishing off of the bread by you and me, no accomplished us at all. But the crucial point is that without this whole tissue of deaths at every moment, there simply would be nothing" (156).

[57] Jewish philosopher Michael Wyschogrod makes a similar argument about the temple. Temple sacrifice compelled people to confront honestly the reality of death and then sanctify it with God's presence. Faith is made unworthy when it brackets or hides death. See the discussion by Levering in *Sacrifice and Community*, 42–43.

[58] As Stanley Hauerwas and John Berkman have said, it is an illusion to think that we can understand the stories of our lives apart from sacrifice. Though we need to exercise caution here by not turning the language of sacrifice into a tool for the exploitation of others, "the good news for the other animals is that Christians do not need to ask the other animals to be part of a sacrifice that has no purpose in God's kingdom" (in "The Chief End of All Flesh," *Theology Today* 49:2 [July 1992]: 208). Responsible eating will endeavor to keep in mind and honor the living and the dying that are God's chosen means for creation's growth and good.

[59] David L. Clough. "Consuming Animal Creatures: The Christian Ethics of Eating Animals," in *Studies in Christian Ethics* 30:1 (2017), 30–44 (the quotes appear on 31 and 37). When rigorously pursued, this recommendation is radical because it requires a fundamentally different agriculture, one that commits farmers to animal husbandry and consumers to the purchase of humanely raised animals. The practical result would be a drastic reduction in the amount of meat consumed.

a refined and attractively packaged commodity shorn of all connection with the world of life and death, with the fish of the sea, the birds of the air, and the animals of the earth, then it is likely that people will come to believe that their diets really can be satisfied without the sacrifices of countless living beings. Food, when understood in a theological way, however, is not a "product." The food we consume is God's creation, a vast and unfathomably deep community of creatures that is sustained by God's sacrificial love. Every time we eat, we are called to recognize the profound mystery that God created a world that, from the beginning (even in something like a pre-fallen state), lives through the eating of its members.

Vegetarians might well point out that a plant-based diet significantly reduces the amount of death necessary for the feeding of creation. This is clearly a valid point, making it appropriate that faithful eaters not cause unnecessary or cruel death simply to satisfy a meat-heavy (and food industry promoted) preference. But what is the value of a plant's life? It is surprising to see that many vegetarians, while arguing against the abuse of animals, rarely extend their argument to the abuse of plants and fields. This is surprising, especially as we are learning that the lives of plants are far more complex than people have often believed.[60] They are clearly sentient beings, even if they do not have a central nervous system. Philosophers that have recently made bio-power a central concern, have tended to be silent about the lives of plants. Jeffrey Nealon argues their silence stems from a perceived threat to human sovereignty if plants are taken seriously. If plants are admitted into the moral community, then our positioning in the world becomes impossibly problematic. "What festivals of atonement, what sacred games shall we have to invent, if the salad bar can no longer function as the ethical refuge from the rest of the menu at the steakhouse?"[61] By assuming that eating plants is morally unproblematic, vegetarians may actually be contributing to the debasing of plant life.

When faced with our embodied entanglements in the lives and deaths of countless seen and unseen others, the temptation is to seek to take flight from the messiness and the pain of life together. This desire to

---

[60] The literature on the lives of plants is now growing to be large. For a good sample, see Daniel Chamovitz's *What a Plant Knows* (New York: Farrar, Straus and Giroux, 2013), Robin Wall Kimmerer's *Braiding Sweetgrass*, David George Haskell's *The Forest Unseen: A Year's Watch in Nature* (New York: Penguin Books, 2013), and, for a more philosophical approach, Michael Marder's *Plant-Thinking: A Philosophy of Vegetal Life* (New York: Columbia University Press, 2013).

[61] Jeffrey T. Nealon, *Plant Theory: Biopower & Vegetal Life* (Stanford: Stanford University Press, 2016), 27.

take flight, I would argue, is akin to the Gnostic tendency to deny the incarnation, in all its embodied and fleshly character, and the cross of Jesus Christ. It amounts to a refusal to accept creation on God's terms, terms that bear witness to a sacrificial logic of life through death to new life. To reject God's gift of another's life and death in the name of a world free of death or suffering would require the erasure of all life, not simply physiological life but also the life of self-offering love.

Second, as creatures made in the image of a self-giving God, humanity's most fundamental task is to participate in God's self-offering life dedicated to the nurture and well-being of all creatures raised and eaten. In this view, the paradigm of eaters as mostly unknowing and uncaring consumers is a dangerous one because it suggests that people can eat without concern for the health of the soil, the plants, and the animals they depend upon. But when people understand creation as the concrete manifestation of God's sacrificial love then it is imperative that food production and consumption recognize and honor the costly grace of life. Practically speaking, what this means is that domestic animals, and fields and forests, must be treated with kindness and with a view to their health and flourishing. Insofar as one can, one should make the effort to purchase meat and plant foods that were raised, grown, harvested, slaughtered, and prepared in ways that respect the integrity of the creatures and the places in which they lived. Culturally speaking, it entails our learning to elevate and support agrarian arts and animal husbandry as among humanity's most noble vocations. The best way for urbanites and suburbanites to do this is to support good farming with their votes (regarding agricultural and food policies) and their purchasing power.

In some respects, it is appropriate to think of Hebrew sacrificial rites as the spiritual but also practical context in which people were taught to care for the gifts of animal and vegetable food. Here it is important to recall that the gifts had to reflect excellent and loving care. To prepare to offer a sacrifice meant that one also had to prepare to be a good shepherd and a good farmer or gardener, one who exercised the same patience, attention, and provision that God the Good Shepherd (and God the Gardener) provided. The animal's blood, shed at the altar, rather than being a sign of pollution, could thus be viewed as an expression of the shepherd's desire to live in the divine love that heals, restores, and nurtures to new life.[62] In other

---

[62] My interpretation of sacrificial blood disagrees with Michael Northcott when he argues that "the shedding of blood in Hebrew culture was perceived as polluting and dangerous" (*A Moral Climate: The Ethics of Global Warming* [Maryknoll, NY: Orbis Books, 2007], 238).

words, sacrifice sanctified meat eating because it also sanctified the farmers and shepherds who brought the offering to the priest who would then kill and offer the gift in a manner that demonstrated care and compassion.

The implication of this sacrificial understanding is that a great deal of industrial agriculture, livestock production, and slaughter practices must stop. It isn't simply that too many animals are raised and killed in conditions that are inhumane and degrading to their natures. It is that an industrial logic that prizes economic efficiency and monetary profitability is made to be the measure and goal of all agricultural practice. Under this logic, waters are polluted, soil is poisoned and eroded, and plant life (along with the animals and people that feed on it) is weakened and compromised. It is not enough to refrain from the eating of meat if the rest of one's food is produced and consumed in ways that exhaust, degrade, or destroy creation's life.

If we make appropriate changes in industrial agriculture and food production, many large confinement animal feeding operations, along with the vast fields of monoculture crop production that often feed them, will disappear. Fields will return to mixed use and pasture purposes (particularly those fields susceptible to erosion). With a decrease in use of synthetic fertilizers we will need to increase the number of animals on the land. Animal herbivores play a vital role in improving and maintaining soil fertility, and in converting sun energy and plant fiber into usable food for people. Though the number of animals raised for agricultural and food purposes will decrease significantly when compared to today's numbers, they will continue to play a valuable, even indispensable, role in the promotion of agricultural and ecological health.[63] We do not know of a healthy

---

In a context of impurity and violence blood could be understood this way but within the walls of the temple, the place where heaven and earth meet, blood signified the divinely breathed "life" that heals and purifies what has been broken and defiled. If blood was the medium of pollution and danger it could not very well also be the means for the atonement of sin. Margaret Barker notes that it was the priest who absorbed the pollution of the nation, not the blood (*The Great High Priest*, 49). Jesus established a new everlasting covenant because his blood was not merely the blood of goats and bulls, all fellow creatures, but the blood of the living, creating God (Heb. 9:11–15).

[63] In *Animal, Vegetable, Miracle*, Barbara Kingsolver gives a clear description of the many unforeseen problems that would arise if all domestic animals were suddenly "freed": animals used to human care would simply starve or be hunted down by predators; dairy cows would die from the pain of ruptured udders; many of the world's poor living on marginal lands would be deprived of the very animals that secure their already fragile economies and diets (220–226). For further treatment of the beneficial role herbivores play in a healthy agriculture, see Simon Fairlie's *Meat: A Benign Extravagance* (East Meon, Hampshire, UK: Permanent Publications, 2010).

ecosystem that is devoid of all animal life. Insofar as a good farm is a healthy
ecosystem, it is naive to expect an agriculture without animals.

The sacrificial logic I have been describing, and the self-offering care that
is its practical correlate, suggest that animals can be eaten in ways that
respect their integrity and well-being and that honor God. But for this
condition to be met it is crucial that these animals be accorded the attention
and care that reflects God's own self-giving care for creation. True animal
husbandry – patterned after God the Good Shepherd – the sort that grows
out of a caring bond between person and animal, can be a suitable context
for the faithful eating of meat.[64] Husbandry takes the killing of animals out
of the realm of violence (understood here as the power that works against
the purposes of God) and immerses it in the sacrificial logic that commits us
to their care and well-being.

FEASTING AND FASTING

The logic and the practice of sacrifice leads to both feasting and fasting as
two complementary and mutually correcting rhythms of a self-offering life.
If sacrifice is about healing the alienation and violence that destroy membership and about establishing the communion that leads to abundant life,
then feasting, understood as the celebration of the good of others and of our
membership in a common life, and fasting, understood as the restraining of
personal desires that otherwise would seek to possess and consume the
world, must be two of its correlative practices. People should feast so they
do not forget the grace and the blessing of the world. People should fast so
they do not degrade or hoard the good gifts of God. In short, we feast to
glorify God and we fast so we do not glorify ourselves. The proper practice of
both presupposes a sacrificial sensibility.

To see how this is so we can begin by asking the question: What is to
prevent feasting from turning into a lavish and unhealthy exercise in self-
glorification, an exercise in which the gifts of the world are aggressively and
perhaps violently appropriated to suit a vain end? It is worth recalling that
Jewish sacrifices often ended with a festive meal in which thanksgiving to
God was expressed, and that the Eucharistic meal was a time of rejoicing.
God was present at these meals not because God was being fed. Rather, God
was present as people fed on food acknowledged to be a gift of God.
Communion with others and with God was established as people sought

---

[64] Christopher Southgate makes a similar point in his essay "Protological and Eschatological
       Vegetarianism," in Grummet and Muers, *Eating and Believing*.

to align their own acts of self-offering with God's. As Matthew Levering (reflecting on Jewish commentary) notes,

> the feast would have no meaning outside the context of the sacrificially governed relationship, because the feast is the realization or crowning of the sacrificial movement. Cut off from the context of sacrifice, from the sacramental spectrum that moves from expiation to thanksgiving, the feast would ... indicate selfish cleaving to the world, a solipsistic and sinful satisfaction grounded upon human pride.[65]

When feasting loses its inspiration in a sacrificial sensibility it may become hollow and destructive, or an exercise in vanity. The host, rather than witnessing to the gifts of food and life shared together, may put personal ambition or success on display. To demonstrate the magnitude of success it then becomes necessary to emphasize lavish consumption, particularly in a consumerist culture where conspicuous (and wasteful) consumption is the mark of achievement. What is consumed, however, does not register as the grace of God but as a sign of the host's power and wealth. At a party like this, it is less likely that either life or those in attendance will be honored or celebrated as blessings of God.

What a party like this lacks is the Sabbath sense that the food and drink people enjoy together is the expression of God's self-offering love made delicious. Recall that God's first *Shabbat* was the occasion for complete rest and delight in a world of creatures wonderfully and beautifully made. In a Sabbath world there should be no exploitation or hoarding, no sense that where people are or who they are with are not good enough, and no fear that people are being manipulated to calm someone else's insecurity or inflate their vanity. Instead there should be the joy of knowing that the world is sustained and loved into being by the God who is continually pouring and emptying himself out for creation's good. There is gratitude and affirmation, a genuine cherishing of the gifts of God. The realization of Sabbath, in other words, is also the realization of a genuine feast.

In his book *In Tune with the World*, Josef Pieper argued that a utilitarian, pragmatic, calculating, profit-obsessed culture cannot experience genuine festivity. Though there may be pomp and circumstance, there can be no genuine feasting because the love and concord with one another that make conviviality possible are missing. At a genuine feast hosts give themselves to their guests, give of their time, talent, and livelihood. They make everyone present feel genuinely welcomed and affirmed. Here the focus is not on the

---

[65] Levering, *Sacrifice and Community*, 65.

host but on the divine giver who graces all in attendance with the sources of life. As John Chrysostom put it, "Where love rejoices, there is festivity."[66] When people feast together they gratefully acknowledge their place in the memberships of creation and the generosity of the Creator. "The happiness of being created, the existential goodness of things, the participation in the life of God, the overcoming of death – all these occasions of the great traditional festivals are pure gift."[67]

Feasting is not the opposite of fasting. Gluttony is. This observation will puzzle those who think that feasting is primarily about consumption. If it is, then not to eat – to fast – would be its opposite. But feasting, though it involves consumption, is not primarily about intake. It is about self-offering and the generous honoring and sharing of gifts that have been gratefully received and cherished. Though it has many dimensions, gluttony reflects an inordinate and inappropriate desire for food, a desire that is focused on self-satisfaction rather than sharing and communal celebration. Gluttony is the opposite of fasting because it knows nothing of self-offering. For gluttons, the comforts of the stomach have become an end in themselves. For gluttons, the belly has become a god. Their end, says Paul, is destruction (Philippians 3:19)

Gluttony is well-known as one of the seven deadly sins (the others being extravagance, greed, sloth, wrath, envy, and pride). Taken together these sins make it virtually impossible that a person will turn their life into a gift to be offered to others. The sins are each dispositions that keep the focus on an individual self and its anxieties or glory. For a glutton, the primary concern is that food or drink be immediately available and in copious and fine supply. Thomas Aquinas, while clarifying the many entry points into the sin, says gluttons want to eat too soon, too expensively, too much, too eagerly, too daintily, and too fervently.[68] What has happened is that food has become an obsession, even an idol that eclipses the more important matter of life itself. For the sake of self-satisfaction, the needs of others and the responsibilities of maintaining life's memberships are kept from view. In direct violation of Jesus' command not to worry about dress or food (Matt. 6:25), gluttons are fundamentally anxious about and distrustful of God's considerate provision for every creature's need. For them, food has been reduced to an object that can then be hoarded and abused. It has ceased to register as a gift to be gratefully received and shared.

---

[66]   Quoted by Josef Pieper in *In Tune with the World: A Theory of Festivity* (South Bend, IN: St. Augustine's Press, 1999), 23.
[67]   Ibid., 62.   [68]   Thomas Aquinas, *Summa Theologiae* II.II.cxlviii.

The sin of gluttony is not confined to individual persons. It is possible for a whole culture to become gluttonous in its aspirations and manners, and in so doing deprive many of the world's peoples of the food and nurture they need. The desire to have fresh fruits and vegetables all year long, regardless of their taste and nutritional value, or the ecological toll long-distance transport takes, can readily be understood as a desire to eat without patience. The desire to eat too eagerly is often manifest in the fact that many people eat fast-food on the run or eat highly processed convenience foods that are ready to eat in three minutes or less. The aggressive marketing and consumption of foods that are high in fat and sodium, along with the very large serving sizes offered at restaurants, suggest that too many of us are eating too much. Meanwhile, the cravings of people to eat exotic, specialty, or sumptuous foods from around the world (many of which would only be served on special occasions because they are expensive and costly to prepare), and the inability to be satisfied with a simpler fare of locally grown and seasonally available foods, may be an indication that people seek to eat too exquisitely. Altogether, these trends lead to a gluttonous culture and a world in which there are now as many dying, undernourished people as there are dying, overnourished ones.

There are many reasons why people obsess over or are anxious about food. Some of our problems clearly spring from advertising campaigns and media messaging that keep food constantly in view and within easy and cheap reach. Others spring from deep-seated and long-established patterns that associate eating with personal and social development (or maldevelopment), which means that people may eat in inordinate ways because they lack love and trust, feel neglected or abused, or seek validation and comfort.[69] Because patterns of eating are so closely and so early (as in the breastfeeding relationship) tied to patterns of loving, we should not be surprised that a culture that is confused about love should also be confused about how to relate to food. To make matters worse, there is a growing trend to vilify those who appear to be gluttons (mistakenly equating gluttony with being overweight), accusing them of taking up too much space or consuming too many of the world's resources. The inability to understand the spiritual roots of gluttony (as the inability to sacrifice) or to appreciate a culture's role in fostering this anxious condition, makes it all the more difficult for individuals to find the help and direction they need.

---

[69] For a brief discussion of the many personal and social dimensions and effects of gluttony, see Francine Prose's *Gluttony: The Seven Deadly Sins* (New York: Oxford University Press, 2003).

One of the more powerful indicators suggesting (and contributing to) the misshapen character of our food desires can be observed in the disappearance of fasting as a regular and important part of personal and social life. Fasts take many different forms. Some fasts are for the whole day (even multiple days) or only part of the day. Some fasts apply to particular kinds of food (meat, delicacies, dessert), while others apply to all food and drink. The reasons for undergoing a fast are equally diverse. When we look to scripture we learn that people fast in response to mourning, anguish, punishment, or military defeat. Fasting is often associated with times of prayer, discernment, or preparation for a journey or battle. It can serve as the sign of repentance and sorrow, or as an act of compassion for those in need, or as a commemoration of an important event or personal figure. Sometimes fasting takes individual form; at other times, social or communal forms. Given these many occasions, uses, and methods it would be a mistake to reduce fasting to one purpose only.

As leaders in the early church reflected on the importance of fasting they often came to describe it as a spiritual exercise, a practice devoted to the clarification and development of spiritual sensitivities.[70] St. Basil the Great, for instance, in his sermon "About Fasting," cataloged many reasons that fasting should be a regular part of the Christian's life. He observed that fasting enters deep in the soul where sin can be sought out and addressed; reverses the inordinate desire and greed Adam showed when he ate from the tree God had specifically commanded he not eat;[71] promotes discipline and waiting; forms people with "a gentle ego, a calm gait, and a thoughtful face. There is no intemperate, arrogant laughter, but rather fitting speech, and purity of heart"; leads to a healthier life and to a heightening of appreciation for the food we eat; contributes to self-control; prevents the practice of usury; and reverses eating that leads to insolence.[72]

What these many reasons share is the realization that eating is not simply about taking in fuel nor is fasting reducible to stopping the intake. Feasting and fasting are two of the primary ways we enact relationships. How we eat,

---

[70] David Grumett and Rachel Muers's *Theology on the Menu* does an excellent job showing the many forms and purposes of fasting in the history of the church and surrounding cultures.

[71] In *The Body and Society: Men, Women, and Sexual Renunciation in Early Christianity* (New York: Columbia University Press, 1988) Peter Brown argues that among the Desert Fathers it was widely believed that the first sin was the greed of eating the forbidden fruit. This sin overshadowed all others because it upset the equilibrium of the body, thus leading to other bodily and sexual sins (220).

[72] St. Basil's sermon can be found in translation in Kent D. Berghuis's *Christian Fasting: A Theological Approach* (Richardson, TX: Biblical Studies Press, 2007).

what we eat, and how much demonstrate what we think our responsibilities to each other and the world should be. People who fast learn that food is a gift and is not to be taken for granted or exploited (which is why they do not practice usury or take advantage of another's need). When we fast, we learn that too much of the time personal life is marked by an aggressive or rapacious disposition (which is why we might develop a gentler ego and a calmer gait). When we fast, we learn that in many of our actions we presume that the world's gifts exist for our own exclusive enjoyment (hence the need to tame the greed and develop the restraint that are at the basis of all just relationships). Fasting, in other words, leads us to a realization about the responsibilities of life together. When we refrain from eating, we not only demonstrate solidarity with those who do not have food to eat but we also demonstrate that food is the precious gift of a self-giving God. It is a gift not to be taken for granted or to be presumed upon. We need to refrain from eating from time to time so that we can more fully appreciate food as a gracious gift, and then also practice the self-offering that will enable others to eat when they don't have enough.

Fasting is a sacrificial movement not simply because of the food people give up. It is the practical discipline through which people come to terms with the tendency to presume that the world exists for personal consumption and satisfaction "on demand." It is a sacrificial movement that reorients desire, and then through this reorientation participates in the healing and restoration of relationships that are weak or broken due to unjust consuming habits. In a memorable passage the prophet Isaiah describes how fasting can be distorted into shows of false humility and competitive exercises in self-glorification. What makes these displays of fasting false is that they do not spring from a self-offering life that is directed to the need and well-being of others. God asks:

> Is not this the fast that I choose:
>   to loose the bonds of injustice,
>   to undo the thongs of the yoke,
> to let the oppressed go free,
>   and to break every yoke?
> Is it not to share your bread with the hungry,
>   and bring the homeless poor into your house;
> when you see the naked to cover them,
>   and not to hide yourself from your own kin?   (Isa. 58:6–7)

God's questioning reveals that just as eating is not reducible to the ingesting of food, so too fasting is not reducible to the abstention from food. Fasting, in its most fundamental aspiration, is about developing a sacrificial, self-offering life that addresses and nurtures the needs of others.

This way of speaking about fasting is in marked contrast with the so-called fasting that is being practiced by some of today's cultural elites. In Silicon Valley, for instance, self-discipline and self-denial are the new markers of aspirational success.[73] Here fasting is promoted as a form of weight loss or as a way to boost cognitive performance. As such, it is, as Rosie Spinks puts it, one more "practice of manipulating and systematizing your biology to enhance performance." Fasting is about increasing one's competitive advantage and optimizing one's position in life. There is some irony in seeing not eating as a marker of success when, in the past, not eating was clearly a marker of the reverse. Spinks observes that the goal of fasting here is not spiritual enlightenment or peace. It is rather "to perfect yourself as much as possible so that you can do more, better, faster work." Fasting is here turned into a competitive enterprise. But what is the one fasting competing for? It is hard to know, since by most measures these elites already have more than most people in the world.

We can see that the Silicon Valley version of fasting is a distortion because it works in a direction that is directly opposed to Sabbath as the goal of life. Because its focus is on increasing one's advantage, doing more and having more, it fails to ask what the point of all striving is. Self-offering is replaced by self-enhancement. The possibilities of thanksgiving and contentment are eclipsed by perpetual thirst and ingratitude. In this practice, there is little awareness that one should refrain from eating so that the good of others and of places might be enhanced. In it there is little recognition that the point of life is to participate in God's Sabbath rest, and thus delight in the love that is everywhere around us. Fasting is fundamental because in its practice we learn how to position ourselves in the world and with others in a humbler way. Fasting is about coming into the presence of others with restraint. It is about committing to learn how and when we misappropriate them as conquests and possessions rather than as gifts.

If this is true, then it is clear that food cannot be the only focus in a fast. The objects of gluttonous desire in our time are numerous, covering the

---

[73] For a description of this trend, see the story by Rosie Spinks, "The New Ascetics: Silicon Valley's Fasting Craze Is Proof That Self-Denial Is the New Indulgence for Elites" (available at https://qz.com/1098242/silicon-valleys-fasting-craze-is-proof-that-self-denial-is-the-new-indulgence-for-elites/July 12, 2018). My thanks to Kendall Vanderslice for alerting me to this essay.

whole range of consumable items. This is why it makes good sense to suggest that the development of a self-offering life will also require regular fasting from cars, computers, email, social media, cellphones, travel, and television (to name a few). Each of these can become addictions and obsessions that encourage the anxiety and arrogance that prevent people from opening their lives to each other.

6

∾

Eucharistic Table Manners: Eating toward Communion

We were created as *celebrants* of the sacrament of life, of its transformation into life in God, communion with God ... [R]eal life is "eucharist,"
a movement of love and adoration toward God, the movement in which
alone the meaning and value of all that exists can be revealed and
fulfilled ... [I]n Christ, the new Adam, the perfect man, this eucharistic
life was restored to man. For He Himself was the perfect Eucharist.[1]

The Eucharist not only envisions an ontology of participation and deification. It is also a model for discipleship, and thus it is profoundly ethical
and political ... the Eucharist is an expression of God's own body offered
to humanity for the purpose of constituting communion.[2]

God only wise, You delight to make your people out of food; and the food
out of which you make us is your body and blood. As we have become
your body in the eating of food, bless those with whom we share food this
week, and bless those with whom we share you and in whom we meet
you; that in being made your body, we may become food for your world,
and through the change they see in us, all may come to praise the glories
of your name.[3]

It is possible to be alive and not know what real life is. Owing to the multiple
manifestations of anxiety and exile we have already described, we can forget
or deny that life is a membership and thereby wreak havoc upon the very
relationships we need to live well. We can refuse to offer ourselves to others,
mostly take and rarely give, and so contribute – through our eating – to the
dissolution of creation's health. This is why it is not enough to rest content
with biological existence: it is not sufficient simply to grasp and swallow. We

[1] Schmemann, *For the Life of the World*, 34. [2] Montoya, *Theology of Food*, 112.
[3] A postcommunion prayer written by Sam Wells and offered in Duke Chapel, October
19, 2008.

must evaluate the *character* of our living and eating so that we can adopt ways of relating to others that honor the gift that life is.

Though a living body is made manifest in the functions it performs – digesting, reproducing, sensing, thinking – life itself is not exhausted in these functions. It extends in all directions into life-nurturing memberships with soil, plants, animals, people, and ultimately God. To know and appreciate these memberships, *and then to live sympathetically and compassionately into them*, is the crucial task. To do it well, people need guidance and help. We need the instruction of one who knows life "from the inside" and who understands its pain and potential. We need the "author of life" to reveal life's fullness and truth to us.

Christianity presents Jesus Christ as the archetype for what real life looks like. Christians believe him to be the focal point in terms of which all life is to be interpreted and evaluated. John's gospel, for instance, portrays Christ as the eternal and divine Logos who became flesh and dwelt among us. Jesus understands life because he is the Logos *through whom* all things came to be. He is the center through whom all creation circulates. *In* him, says John, was *life* (1:4). Not mere existence but life in its fullness and truth, eternal life, even resurrection life: "I am the resurrection and the life" (11:25). Jesus is the "light of life" (1:4–5 and 8:12) in terms of which we can see life for what it currently is (as perhaps broken or ill or violent) and as it will yet be. Jesus is "the way, the truth, and the life" (14:6). He puts "life" on a new path and a new trajectory that leads humanity more deeply into communion with others and God. As Paul would say it, insofar as persons are *in* Christ they cease to be what they once were: they become "a new creation" (2 Cor. 5:17).

Jesus is claimed to reveal life in its truth because he is the source and end of life. All things in heaven and on earth will "in the fullness of time" be "gathered up" in him (Ephesians 1:10). Being the "reflection of God's glory" and "the exact imprint of God's very being," Jesus is the one who creates and sustains all things "by his powerful word." He is the "appointed heir" of all things (Hebrews 1:2–3). Though Jesus was a person who tasted a specific range of foods and engaged a particular community of people, who he was and what he meant was not limited to a particular place, community, or time. Because his life is the full truth of living, Jesus is the standard by which life is to be measured. From the beginning his followers declared that his significance stretched throughout the whole of created reality, transforming it from within.[4] After departing from his geographical place, Jesus sends to

---

[4] For a recent development of this theme, see Colin Gunton's *Christ and Creation* (Carlisle: Paternoster Press; Grand Rapids: W. B. Eerdmans, 1992).

his followers the Spirit "that gives life" (John 6:63) and that will guide them in the ways of truthful living.[5]

To speak this way about Jesus is to communicate the intense intimacy between Christ and creation. Jesus is not a Gnostic teacher who visits earth to impart a few special, body-despising teachings to a select few. Rather, he is the eternally existent One who from the beginning has been at work ordering creation from the inside, making it an intelligible whole capable of membership and life.[6] Everything has its logos, what we can call its principle of intelligibility and its ability to live in cooperative relationship with others. But these relationships can become disordered and degraded. When we observe the suffering and pain of so much created life, we can understand why Paul would say that creatures currently exist in a state of futility and bondage (Romans 8:18–23). For a variety of reasons (many of them having to do with human destructiveness), they are not able to realize their logos or live in the ways God intended for them.

Christ is claimed by Christians to be the savior of the world, which means there is hope that all creatures will become what they are supposed to be when their forms of life (their logoi) overlap and participate in the divinely creative Logos. There is hope that the memberships of creation will be healed and creatures will experience life more fully when the fruits of the life-giving Spirit take hold in our memberships (Galatians 5:22–23). The seventh-century church father Maximus the Confessor gave powerful expression to this position when he wrote,

> the wisdom and sagacity of God the Father is the Lord Jesus Christ, who holds together the universals of beings by the power of wisdom, and

---

[5]   It is hard not to see Jesus' breathing upon the disciples in John 20:22, the moment when the disciples receive the Holy Spirit, as referencing and extending Genesis 2:7 where God's own breathing into the soil (*adamah*) creates the first human being (*adam*). John's description of creation through the Word parallels God's speaking creation into being in Genesis 1. What John is doing is recasting creation in terms of the life of Christ.

[6]   In his sermons on creation, the *Homelia Hexameron*, St. Basil the Great said, "God has united the entire world which is composed of many different parts, by the law of indissoluble friendship, in communion and harmony, so that the most distant things seem to be joined together by one and the same sympathy" (2.2) (www.ccel.org/ccel/schaff/npnf208.viii .html). For many of the early church fathers, Jesus shows us in the flesh what this "law of indissoluble friendship" looks like and what it entails practically speaking. In his *Commentary on the Our Father*, Maximus Confessor says, "the Word (Logos) is the uniting of what is distant" while "unreason (alogos) is the division of what is united" (in *Maximus Confessor: Selected Writings* [New York: Paulist Press, 1985]), 103. For a detailed description of the anthropology that follows from this cosmic Christology, see Lars Thunberg's *Microcosm and Mediator: The Theological Anthropology of Maximus Confessor*, 2nd edition (Chicago: Open Court, 1995).

embraces their complementary parts by the sagacity of understanding, since by nature he is the fashioner and provider of all, and through himself draws into one what is divided, and abolishes war between beings, and binds everything into peaceful friendship and undivided harmony.[7]

Maximus is elaborating on the Johannine idea that because all things exist through Christ, and because Christ is the divine Logos at work in everything giving it life and direction, he can also move through everything and transform it so that it can eventually become the true life God wants it to be. Creatures are currently living a deficient form of life. What they need is the healing and strengthening of memberships, a healing in which the church, understood as the continuation on earth of Christ's practices or way of being, has a vital role to play.[8] When this healing takes place, a healing that is glimpsed at the Eucharistic table in the eating that people do, relationships are transformed so that they testify to true life.

This way of speaking about Jesus suggests it is a serious distortion to confine his ministry and significance to the salvation of selected, individual postmortem souls. Christian faith is not about one's escape from creaturely membership. It is, instead, the way by which one learns to love the members and memberships of life as Christ did. As the early Christian hymn in Colossians described him, Jesus is "the image of the invisible God ... in him all things in heaven and on earth were created ... in him all things hold together ... in him the fullness of God was pleased to dwell, and through him God was pleased to reconcile to himself all things, whether on earth or in heaven, by making peace through the blood of his cross" (1:15–20). Jesus' life is here claimed to be about the transformation of *all this earthly life* and the reparation of creation's many memberships. Where life is broken,

---

[7] Maximus the Confessor, *Ambigua* 41: 1313B, in Andrew Louth's *Maximus the Confessor* (New York: Routledge, 1996), 161–162. For an excellent treatment of Christ's intimacy with and healing of creation, see Torstein Theodor Tollefsen's *The Christocentric Cosmology of St. Maximus Confessor* (Oxford: Oxford University Press, 2008). Tollefsen writes: "God is present in every natural process with His creative force. Instituting natural causality as such, He operates cooperatively to bring about what from eternity is conceived by Him in His *logoi*" (136).

[8] Think here of the arresting formulation by Anestis Keselopoulos, who writes out of the Greek Orthodox tradition: "The Church is primarily an image of the Creator, because of her role in holding together and unifying the cosmos; and then, because she is an image, she represents the whole world in a symbolic and figurative way. The presence of the Church in the world means the presence of God: it means that there is no part of intelligible or sensible creation from which the divine energy is absent, as the cohesive and productive force of the whole universe. The entire sensible and intelligible creation makes up an exquisite temple in which praise and glory are rendered to the Creator" (*Man and the Environment: A Study of St. Symeon the New Theologian* [Crestwood, NY: St. Vladimir's Seminary Press, 2001]), 153.

degraded, or hungry, Jesus repairs life, showing it to us as reconciled, protected, and fed.

The ministries of Christ demonstrate that the path to full or abundant life is not a magical path. It is a practical journey that begins with eating. The gospels frequently show Jesus eating with people because table fellowship is among the most powerful ways we know to extend and share in each other's lives.[9] Jesus eats with strangers and outcasts, demonstrating that table fellowship is for the nurture of others and not simply for self-enhancement (Luke 14:12–14). Jesus rejects the social systems of rejection and exclusion by welcoming everyone into communion with him. Table fellowship makes possible genuine encounters with others. This is why it is appropriate for Virgilio Elizondo to see Jesus' way of eating as a sign of the kingdom of God: "By freely eating with everyone, he breaks and challenges all the social taboos that keep people apart."[10]

The goal of life is to enact relationships with each other so that the life people experience here and now can share in the divine, Trinitarian life that creates, sustains, and fulfills creation. Following Graham Ward, we can describe Christ as "the archetype of all relation."[11] That means creation's memberships find their correction and perfection in Christological patterns of relationship that feed, heal, and reconcile life. Jesus reveals that the Father created the world out of love and wants the whole creation to participate in this divine love through the inspiration and agency of the Spirit. "God created the world because of his goodness in order to make other beings partakers too in his intertrinitarian love."[12] Or as Tertullian put it, "God lived with men as man that man might be taught to live the divine life: God lived on man's level that man might be able to live on God's level."[13]

---

[9]   For a synoptic overview of the many dimensions to Jesus' eating with others, see Robert J. Karris's *Eating Your Way through Luke's Gospel* (Collegeville, MN: Liturgical Press, 2006).

[10] Virgilio Elizondo, *The Future Is Mestizo: Life Where Cultures Meet* (Boulder: University Press of Colorado, 2000), 83.

[11] Graham Ward, *Christ and Culture* (Oxford: Blackwell, 2005), 1.

[12] Dumitru Staniloae, *The Experience of God: Volume 2, The World: Creation and Deification* (Brookline, MA: Holy Cross Orthodox Press, 2000), 18. Staniloae represents an Orthodox theological position in which the goal of creation is to share in the divine life. Compare the following summary from Metropolitan Emilianos of Silibria: "The triune God wants the beings created in his image to become divinized, according to his likeness. To achieve this end, he communicates properties or energies of his own ... Being true life, he is 'life-giving,' pouring out his love, enabling us to share the whole realm of the divine life in all its dimensions" ("The Triune God in the Life-Giving Process," in *Jesus Christ – The Life of the World: An Orthodox Contribution to the Vancouver Theme*, ed. Ion Bria [Geneva: World Council of Churches, 1982], 66).

[13] Quoted in Ward, *Christ and Culture*, 5.

Put more broadly, in the person of Jesus, God entered into interdependent and mortal flesh so that people might participate in God's perfect and communal life. In the mutual indwelling of earth and heaven that Christological life is, creaturely life becomes what God has wanted from the beginning. It becomes the occasion for Sabbath delight.

As we now have to see, the Eucharist plays a central role in the transformation of life, bringing it into alignment with Christ's way of being-in-the-world. The Eucharist isn't simply a spiritual or ecclesial reality. Centered as it is on the material elements of bread and wine, it also preserves and reorders the whole material world from which these elements come. Christ's presence in the elements, as David Grumett has recently argued, is a particularly intense exemplification of God's abiding presence to each and every creature all the time. "In every Eucharist, Christ is proclaimed to be the ultimate origin of material change and the final end of material consumption."[14]

Christ's presence in the material elements of the Eucharist gave to them a power to heal, restore, and reconcile the material world. At various times in the church's history, "The host was viewed as introducing a principle of order into a mutable, chaotic realm. Crucially, the order that it brought was not only spiritual but material. The host, through its materiality, was believed to change the course of real life events, protecting and renewing bodies and their wider physical environments."[15] This is why the presence of the host was so important in life's key moments: planting, marriage, and burial. The "bread of life" has the power to heal bodies, protect crops, and promote health and flourishing.

To believe this is to believe that material reality is never simply a brute, self-subsistent, self-sufficient reality. Its deepest meaning is to be found in God as the one who creates, sustains, and cherishes it as a sacred gift. Hannah Arendt observed in *The Human Condition* that if matter is just matter, devoid of all sacred significance, then "no object of the world will be safe from consumption and annihilation through consumption."[16] A Eucharistic orientation invites people to enter into economic relationships governed by sharing, celebration, and gratitude for the God whose love animates everything.

---

[14] David Grumett, *Material Eucharist* (Oxford: Oxford University Press, 2016), 4.
[15] Ibid., 111. Eucharistic bread, in other words, isn't ordinary bread. "Preserved from decomposition by divine power, it became a source of divine power that conserved or transformed the objects and spaces around it" (107).
[16] Quoted in ibid., 143.

COMING TO THE EUCHARISTIC TABLE

If Jesus Christ is life in all its truth and fullness, then the Eucharist is central because it is the place where we are fed by him to live the life he makes possible. At the Eucharist we receive the nurture and training we need to become people who participate in his healing and reconciling ways with the world. Eating Jesus is the ritual act that has the potential to transform eating in general so that it can be hospitable at its core and lead to a communion of life.

History demonstrates that the Eucharist has and continues to be under-stood and practiced in many different ways.[17] For some people the table is the place where Jesus is met in the earthy elements of bread and wine now transformed into his flesh and blood. Others see the table as a memorial in which believers recall the saving action of Jesus and give thanks for it. For others, eating Jesus' broken body is the occasion to imitate Christ by participating in his suffering for the world. It is to enter into the mystery of God's salvation of the world through a crucified body.[18] For still others, the Eucharist is the place where Christ's offering of himself invites a trans-formation of eaters so that their lives can become an offering to others too. It is the site where people, having consumed Jesus as their food and drink, are re-created by Christ and so taste a slice of heaven.[19]

The ritualized character of the Eucharist sometimes causes people to forget that the supper was a *meal*. It was not a nibbling session but the place where the disciples came together to obtain their inspiration, strength, and sustenance. The evidence of the early church suggests that the community of followers ate together regularly and often, and that in their eating they tried to bear witness to Christ's way of dwelling on earth. "The meal Jesus blessed

---

[17]   For an introduction to five contemporary denominational approaches (Roman Catholic, Lutheran, Reformed, Baptist, and Pentecostal), see the collection of essays edited by Gordon T. Smith in *The Lord's Supper: Five Views* (Downer's Grove, IL: InterVarsity Press Academic, 2008).

[18]   In her book on medieval women mystics and their understanding and use of food, Caroline Walker Bynum describes how, for some, "Hunger was unquenchable desire; it was suffering. To eat God, therefore, was finally to become suffering flesh with his suffering flesh; it was to imitate the cross" (*Holy Feast and Holy Fast: The Religious Significance of Food to Medieval Women* [Berkeley: University of California Press, 1987]), 54.

[19]   Hart, "'Thine Own of Thine Own'." Hart says, "The Eucharist is that same place of atonement (*hilasterion*), then, that Christ is: the chiasmus where eternity and time flow into one another, where eternity empties itself and time is raised into the eternal, and where we lose ourselves in the abyss of divine beauty to find ourselves restored in the utterly humble abandon of divine love" (157). The Eucharistic table is thus the place of reconcili-ation and *theosis*, while Eucharistic eating is the means of participating in the divine life.

that evening and claimed as his memorial was their *ordinary* partaking together of food for the body."[20] This means that daily, common eating was inspired and informed by Christ's continuing presence with them. To "remember Jesus" in their eating was not simply to recall a past event. It was to call on Jesus and invite him to transform what they were doing together.[21] Jesus' presence at the meal could thus be an "effective" presence that challenged and corrected their eating practices. Eating, in other words, was the occasion in which Christ's followers could witness to his ongoing presence in the world. To remember Jesus is to join in a *re-membering* of a world *dis-membered* by sin.

Paul's first letter to the church at Corinth demonstrates that Christ's followers could fail to eat Eucharistically: "I hear that there are divisions among you ... When you come together to eat it is not really the Lord's supper. For when the time comes to eat, each of you goes ahead with your own supper, and one goes hungry and another becomes drunk" (1 Cor. 11:18–21). On other occasions people ate in an inconsiderate manner, eating food (particularly meat that had been sacrificed to pagan gods) that bothered another's conscience (10:23–32) and caused them to "stumble" in the faith. Paul is clearly worried that in their eating the Corinthians are not bearing witness to the presence of Christ among them. People who claimed to be followers of Christ were failing to "discern the body" (11:29), which means that they were eating and drinking in ways that brought division and harm to the membership.

In some respects, the problem of internal division Paul faced was practical. Few homes in which early Christians met would have been large enough to accommodate many people. As a result, eating may have had to proceed in shifts. Since space was at a premium, and since the homeowner had to have been among the wealthy, it is likely that those of the same class would have been invited to dine in the triclinium (as opposed to the much less comfortable atrium) where the food was normally served and where eaters could recline. Moreover, Corinth was a town in which the Roman custom of serving different foods to different classes of people was prevalent. Higher class people enjoyed food of superior quality and in greater quantity.

---

[20] John Howard Yoder, *Body Politics: Five Practices of the Christian Community before the Watching World* (Scottsdale, PA: Herald Press, 1992), 16.

[21] Johannes Betz says Eucharistic remembering amounts to letting Jesus make alive in us his salvation work. Remembering Jesus is to hear him say, "do this (what I have done) in order to bring about my presence, to make really present the salvation wrought in me" ("Eucharist," in *Encyclopedia of Theology: The Concise Sacramentum Mundi*, ed. Karl Rahner [New York: Crossroad, 1975], 452).

When these factors are combined, it is easy to see how divisions could have taken hold as poorer Christians observed how and where their wealthy counterparts ate.[22]

According to Paul, when Christians ate in ways that encouraged factions and divisions, they ate in a manner unworthy of Christ. What would eating that "remembered" Christ look like? In Paul's view it would be eating that strengthened the community of his followers. It would be eating that bore witness to a transformed sense of persons as *nurturing participants* in the body of Christ. Paul says explicitly that Christians are to be members that form one body (1 Cor. 12:12). In this membership no one is dispensable or deserving of disrespect. Each has an indispensable role to play. If the community is truly Christ's body, there will be no dissension or segregation because each member will have the same care for each other (12:25). The body can be a healthy and vital whole only as each member is committed to serving the needs of the other members. No member is too lowly to be served and no member too high not to serve.

It is easy to miss the radical nature of Christian membership, particularly if we approach it from a modern, individualistic point of view. Membership is here reduced to one's voluntary and occasional participation in a group (as when I say I am a "member" of a club or national organization). The Pauline understanding of membership, much like the Johannine depiction of Jesus as the vine onto which his disciples are grafted, is much more organic and vital. If each person is joined to another like a limb is joined to a torso then there is nothing voluntary or occasional about the relationship. For the limb to flourish it must draw its life from the whole body. To be cut off from the larger body, even momentarily, is to precipitate the member's death. Joined together, all the members of the body share a common life. Though need and nurture establish the relationships and each member as indispensable, it is our care and responsibility for others that has the potential to turn mutual service into mutual celebration.

For Paul it is imperative that the membership be the body *of Christ* rather than some other body. Why? Because it is Christ who manifests what life really ought to be. Christ represents another order of life because unlike the life and death known through Adam, Jesus inaugurates a mode of living that joins people to heaven. Though Adam was a "living being," Christ is the "life-giving spirit" (1 Cor. 15:45) who leads humanity through death into resurrection life. Jesus overcomes the alienating power of death that sin is.

---

[22]   For a discussion of these practical housing matters and the Roman customs of eating, see Murphy-O'Connor's *Keys to First Corinthians*, 182–186.

Unless people participate organically in, rather than merely associate with, Jesus' life, they don't really know what it is to be alive. To be fully alive is to live sympathetically within the membership that the community is called to be, suffering with those who suffer and rejoicing with those who rejoice. It is to extend Christ's self-giving life in the world as the model for how life should be (Gal. 2:20).

Paul is making the point that life at its best is a Christ-inspired membership of self-offering. Though people may think themselves to exist as individuals, they do not become fully alive until they are intimately joined to others and committed to their well-being. This means that people can function but still be in a state of "death" if they are not related to others in life-giving ways. "If the human creature is 'alive' only as a member of the body of Christ, then when separated from the body he/she can only be classified as 'dead.'"[23] Paul is arguing that God from the beginning intended that people live with the mutuality and reciprocity of parts that make an organic whole. Unlike sin, which divides and degrades, Christians are supposed to live a life of love that is patient and kind rather than boastful or resentful. They are not to be rude, irritable, or insistent on having their own way (1 Cor. 13:4–7). When Christians truly love each other they will bear each other up, because they know that the health of the whole body requires a common service to each other. When they do this successfully they will *through their caring support of each other* become the place where the glory of God resides on earth. As Richard Hays has argued, for Paul it is the community formed by Christ that is the new temple of God (1 Cor. 3:16). For this body to suffer division is to dishonor God and deface God's presence on earth.[24]

Jerome Murphy-O'Connor has summarized Paul's position well:

The Christian community is an organic unity in which the members are vitally related to each other through participation in a common life. By love they are bound together in a mode of existence which is the antithesis of the individualistic mode of existence that constitutes the "world." Only in this mode do they exist as the Creator intended humanity to exist ... This community is "Christ" in that it prolongs incarnationally the power of love that was the essence of his mission. It represents the saving force of Christ because in the world it demonstrates the reality of an alternative mode of

---

[23] Ibid., 200.

[24] Richard B. Hays, *The Moral Vision of the New Testament: Community, Cross, New Creation* (San Francisco: Harper, 1996), 34.

existence in which humanity is not dominated by the egocentricity that provokes possessiveness, jealousy and strife.[25]

Koinonia, the sharing and fellowship that take place in the breaking of bread and drinking of wine together, is the result of those who have allowed themselves to be transformed from within by Christ's Logos and by his considerate and compassionate way of being in the world. For Paul, the Eucharist is a common, participatory event in which Christ's followers exhibit Christ through the kind of memberships they live. Through the daily meal Christians learn what it is to be present to and responsible for each other. In their economies of food production and consumption they are to testify to life rather than death.

This brief account of the Eucharist as it appears in Paul suggests that the Lord's table, and by extension also our own home table, is never simply an illustration of God's saving action in the past. Following Alexander Schmemann, we can see Eucharistic eating as manifesting God's heavenly kingdom because it *participates* in what it manifests. By eating at the Lord's table, people are given here and now a glimpse of heaven as the sort of life God desires for the whole creation. They are invited to turn from sinful ways that profane and fragment the world, and instead commit to a comprehensive reorientation in which all life is restored and made whole by the communion Christ's loving ways with the world make possible. The last supper is

> the manifestation of that kingdom of love, for the sake of which the world was created and in which it has its *telos*, its fulfillment. Through love God created the world ... Through love he sent his only-begotten Son ... And now, at this table, he manifests and grants this love as his kingdom, and his kingdom as "abiding" in love.[26]

When eating is Eucharistic the salvific reality of Christ is extended and made incarnate in the world. When Jesus broke bread and shared the cup as the giving of his own body and blood, and then asked his followers to "Do this in remembrance of me," he instituted a new way of eating in which followers are invited to give their lives to each other, to turn themselves into food for others, and in so doing nurture and strengthen the memberships of

---

[25] Murphy-O'Connor, *Keys to First Corinthians*, 206–207. Hays speaks similarly when he argues that Paul is asking followers of Christ to make communal edification rather than personal autonomy the mark of true discipleship. "All actions, however ostensibly spiritual, must meet the criterion of constructive impact on the church community" (*The Moral Vision of the New Testament*, 35).

[26] Alexander Schmemann, *The Eucharist: Sacrament of the Kingdom* (Crestwood, NY: St. Vladimir's Seminary Press, 2003), 200–201.

life. Coming to the Eucharistic table, eaters are encouraged to learn that they do not need to eat only to their own benefit and glory. They discover what is practically required to share in God's reconciliation with and within the world.

EATING JESUS

In a remarkable phrase, John's gospel tells us Jesus understood himself to be the "bread of life" (John 6:35).[27] Jesus is the "living bread" given for "the life of the world" (6:51). Calling him this it is likely that John intended to establish Jesus as the decisive step beyond Moses as the Prophet-King. Whereas Moses called down manna from heaven, Jesus is the true bread itself.[28] Those who ate the manna in the wilderness died but those who eat the flesh of the Son of Man and drink his blood will never hunger or thirst because they are being nurtured with "true" bread, the bread that will enable them to live "into the age" marked by God's rule (6:50–51). The "bread of life" saying can thus be interpreted to serve the larger purpose of establishing the Johannine community as distinct.[29] Jesus, rather than Moses, is the authoritative figure to be followed.[30]

---

[27] A diverse and complex set of debates has centered on how to interpret John 6. Paul Anderson sums them up this way: "In no other place does the same confluence of historical, literary, and theological debates come to the fore as they relate to the Gospel of John. From comparison/contrasts with Synoptic corollaries – to inferences of narrative and discourse sources – to redaction analysis – to christology, semeiology and sacramentology debates – to text disruption and rearrangement theories – to form-critical midrashic analysis – to reader-response approaches (just to mention some of the obvious critical issues), John 6 has time and again provided the *locus argumenti* for scholars wishing to make a definitive contribution to Johannine studies" (Paul N. Anderson, "The Sitz Im Leben of the Johannine Bread of Life Discourse and Its Evolving Context," in *Critical Readings of John 6*, ed. R. Alan Culpepper [Leiden: Brill, 1997], 1). For a detailed exploration of how Jesus as the bread of life falls within a larger Johannine discourse on eating and drinking as they relate to discipleship and salvation, see Jane S. Webster's *Ingesting Jesus: Eating and Drinking in the Gospel of John* (Atlanta: Society of Biblical Literature, 2003).

[28] The story of God's gracious gift of manna loomed large in the popular Jewish imagination. In some circles the gift was taken as a sign of the consummation of time. See Ernst Haenchen, *John I: A Commentary on the Gospel of John Chapters 1–6* (Philadelphia: Fortress Press, 1984), 290–291.

[29] This interpretation was given its most influential expression by J. Louis Martyn in *History and Theology in the Fourth Gospel*, rev. edition (Nashville: Abingdon, 1979).

[30] That Jesus says "I Am" (*ego eimi*) before "bread of life" is also part of a larger narrative sequence of "I Am" passages in John meant to convey Christ's divinity. Though Moses was great as a worker of signs, he would never have uttered "I Am." See Craig R. Koester's *Symbolism in the Fourth Gospel: Meaning, Mystery, Community* (Minneapolis: Fortress Press, 1995), 92–100.

The context for the "bread of life" saying is Jesus' miraculous feeding of the five thousand. In this story Jesus gave thanks over five barley loaves and two fish provided by a boy in the crowd. While distributing the food, this meager portion grew to provide enough for everyone to eat "as much as they wanted" (John 6:11). We are told that after this miraculous feeding the people rushed upon him, wanting to "take him by force to make him king" (6:15). For them, much like for the Israelites in the desert, what they most wanted was fuel to fill a digestive hole. What made Jesus so attractive to them was that he could provide the product on demand. Clearly, this was no small feat in a world on intimate terms with hunger. John's point, however, is that Jesus is not simply the *provider* of bread. He is the full meaning of bread, the nurture that "comes down from heaven and gives life to the world" (6:33). The bread that Jesus *is* is not simply a product like manna that can temporarily satisfy a physical hunger. It is food for the *healing, transformation,* and *fulfillment* of life rather than its mere continuation. If physical bread enables physiological life, the "bread of life" inspires and empowers communion life. The life that Jesus as the bread of life nurtures isn't simply unending life (as some people interpret "eternal life" to be), especially if life simply continues on and on in a deficient or degraded state. Rather, it is life that realizes all that God desires for it.

"Jesus said to them, 'Very truly, I tell you, unless you eat (*phagete*) the flesh of the Son of Man and drink his blood, you have no life in you. Those who eat (*trogon*) my flesh and drink my blood have eternal life . . . for my flesh is true food and my blood is true drink'" (John 6:53–55)? Is Jesus advocating cannibalism, as some critics of early Christian communities supposed? Significantly, John immediately tells us that eating has to do with *abiding*: "Those who eat my flesh and drink my blood abide in me, and I in them" (6:56). Eating is not simply the consumption of what comes from outside. Eucharistic eating has to do with learning to abide with Jesus so that our abiding with others can take on a Christological form. In other words, Eucharistic eating alters the relationships that make up our lives, gives them a self-offering character, and in doing so changes the practice of life itself. Though physiological eating continues as a biological necessity, the look and feel of life changes because the relationships that make life possible have been transformed.

It is helpful to recall that bread is not simply a material substance. As our earlier description of the multiple meanings of bread indicated, bread comes to be what it is because of multiple processes. People have to grow grain, transform it into flour, and then think about the social relations that can potentially develop around its production and sharing. All along the way decisions have to be made about how people relate to the land (agriculture) and each other (culture). These decisions reflect more or less appropriate forms of abiding: bread can be consumed in ways that respect and honor fields, farmworkers, and bakers but it can also be consumed as a product in which relations to land and others have been degraded. Food production and consumption, in other words, embody a logos. What we eat and how we eat it reflect whether or not we think we need to abide with others at all. When we thoughtlessly eat commodities alone and on the run, there is no time or place for abiding. But when we eat with a commitment to the strengthening of the ecological and social memberships that make food possible, then it becomes possible for eating to be an act of abiding with another.

Eating, like sexual life, is among the most intimate ways we know for relating to others. Here we have the chance to approach and savor another, taking in its full flavor and life.[31] From a physiological standpoint, food is absorbed into the person and becomes that person. As Leon Kass describes it, nourishing is "the activity of self-renewal as well as self-fueling, self-maintenance, self-healing, and self-maturation. Its essence: the transformation of materials, from other to selfsame, by the organism itself ... to preserve and to serve the organism as a living, performing whole."[32] The eating self retains its form or distinctness by destroying the identity of what is eaten. Eating, in other words, absorbs the other into me. Though another's materiality temporarily persists in my materiality, its "form," that which makes it distinct and different from me, no longer exists. The absorption of another's form into my being introduces us to one of the great paradoxes of eating: to preserve the form of my life, the form of another's life must end. "Eating is at once form preserving and form deforming. What was distinct and whole gets broken down and homogenized, in order to preserve the distinctness and wholeness of the feeder."[33] Viewed physiologically, we do not really abide with our food because in the eating of it we also destroy it.

By calling Jesus the bread of life, and then by instructing people to chomp and chew (trogon) on this bread, John's gospel is introducing people to a kind of eating in which abiding is possible and transformative. To eat the "bread of life" is not to absorb, and thereby abolish, this bread but to be altered by it. Thomas Merton summarizes this point when he writes: "For

[31] The thirteenth-century Flemish mystic Hadewijch wrote: "In the anguish or the repose or the madness of Love / The heart of each devours the other's heart. / As he who is Love itself showed us / When he gave himself to eat / ... love's most intimate union / Is through eating, tasting, and seeing interiorly" (quoted in Bynum, Holy Feast and Holy Fast, 3–4).

[32] Kass, The Hungry Soul, 31. [33] Ibid., 54.

the Living Bread, when we receive it, transforms us into itself and is not absorbed by our bodies as ordinary food. True, the species of bread dissolve within us, but the substance of the Logos becomes the nourishment of our souls in such a way that we live no longer by our own life but by His."[34] Ward describes this eating as a complex coabiding: "There is an 'abiding' *in* Christ, but there is also an abiding *of* Christ (in the one who eats) . . . I eat the flesh of Christ. I take his body into my own. Yet in this act I place myself *in* Christ – rather than simply placing Christ in me."[35]

Eating Jesus is thus the entrance of Christ's life into our own. When we come to the Eucharistic table we "remember Jesus" rather than obliterate him, and thus testify to a *continuation of his life*. As a result of this eating our life becomes a participation and continuation in him.

What our examination of John's gospel reveals is that there are two forms of eating. There is the kind of eating in which another is absorbed into me so that I can live. We can call this "natural" or physiological eating because it is the eating that all living creatures do to maintain their existence. It correlates with manna and bread, the material stuff that meets a nutritional need. But there is also the kind of eating in which the other is not simply absorbed by me. Rather than absorbing others I *remember* and thus *host* them, invite and welcome them to enter into my affective and moral imagination, and so am transformed from within. With this kind of eating I am inspired, corrected, and nourished by the other without the other being completely destroyed. *The other, that is, Jesus, continues to live on in me not as de-formed matter but as food that in-forms and re-forms life from the inside.* This is eating founded on mutual abiding.

It is important to describe this abiding as *participation* rather than absorption because absorption signals the end of relationship. When Augustine had Jesus say, "I am the food of the fully grown; grow and you will feed on me. And you will not change me into you like the food your flesh eats, but you will be changed into me,"[36] the change of self that is implied cannot mean the annihilation of that self. The one who eats Jesus maintains a personal identity as a member of his body, the church, living by the Holy Spirit, and contributing and witnessing to God's empowering presence on earth.[37] Similarly, Jesus abiding in us does not mean that he ceases to be.

---

[34] Thomas Merton, *The Living Bread* (New York: Farrar, Straus & Cudahy, 1956), 114.

[35] Ward, *Christ and Culture*, 105.

[36] Augustine, *Confessions*, trans. Henry Chadwick (Oxford: Oxford University Press, 1991), VII.x.16, 124.

[37] Scripture refers to life in Christ also as life in the Holy Spirit. For a detailed treatment of this theme, see Gordon Fee's *God's Empowering Presence: The Holy Spirit in the Letters of Paul* (Peabody, MA: Hendrickson, 1994).

Instead, he becomes the destabilizing presence within who can put personal desire and agency on a new path. Eating Jesus results in the mutual indwelling described by Paul: "It is no longer I who live, but it is Christ who lives in me. And the life I now live in the flesh I live by faith in the Son of God, who loved me and gave himself for me" (Gal. 2:20).

Persons who feed on Jesus are challenged to relate to others in a new way. Rather than engaging them primarily in utilitarian terms, absorbing them to suit personal need and satisfaction, eaters of Jesus are invited to extend his ministries of attention and welcome, feeding and forgiving, and healing and reconciliation. These are ministries that require us to remember others and keep them in our hearts and minds. *Remembering Jesus, in other words, inspires us to remember others.* Eaters of Jesus thus become hosts to the world who consider, respect, and serve the integrity of those who co-abide with them. In this co-abiding we honor the grace of life and witness to the power of love as the desire for another to freely be and develop.

It is important to observe that in hosting the world people are not only hosting each other. As we will see in Chapter 7, when we put food on the table and say grace over the life and labor there represented, we call to mind the gift and the sacrifice of nonhuman life that food is. When saying grace, the member of creation that is eaten resides within us as a remembered presence that ought to inform present and future desire and action. As a foodstuff, the other is physically absorbed into my body. But received as a gift of God, as a member of creation benefited by God's attention, care, and blessing, the other also continues to live in me as a remembered presence. As re-membered, I must henceforth attempt to eat in ways that better honor and protect the sanctity of its life. In other words, when people eat as those trained at the Eucharistic table, no life is simply fuel to be absorbed. All life becomes a sign and sacrament of God's love, a witness to the costliness and mystery of life and death, and so becomes the inspiration to greater attention and care.[38]

---

[38] Schmemann writes, "in the Orthodox experience a sacrament is primarily a revelation of the *sacramentality* of creation itself, for the world was created and given to man for conversion of creaturely life into participation in divine life" (*The Eucharist*, 33–34). This means that food is never merely fuel. Eating at its best elevates food by giving it a meaning in terms of God's own sacrificial and loving life. Schmemann continues: "the entire world was created as an 'altar of God,' as a temple, as a symbol of the kingdom. According to its conception, it is all *sacred*, and not 'profane,' for its essence lies in the divine 'very good' of Genesis. The sin of man consists in the fact that he has darkened the 'very good' in his very being and as such has torn the world away from God, made it an 'end in itself,' and therefore a fall and death" (61).

To remember Jesus, to have him abide in us, means that we are continually being dislocated and relocated outside of ourselves, called to a more attentive, sympathetic, and caring embrace of the world. Eucharistic eating at its best reconfigures people as fundamentally ecstatic and erotic, constantly moving beyond themselves with a desire for the other as other.[39] The opening through which another is welcomed into my mouth and life is also the opening through which my life is moved to respect and respond to what is other than me – starting with the humble word of thanks but then extending to the implementation of food economies that care for life.

Eucharistic eating inaugurates forms of life that are a direct challenge to programs of self-enrichment maintained at the expense of those that feed and sustain us. Jesus calls his followers to a deep commitment to fellowship (*koinonia*) with others. Eating Jesus ought to lead to new patterns of relationship in which exploitation – whether the exploitation of fields, animals, farmers (often women), cooks (often women), servers (often women) – is overcome with compassion for and service to the needs of others.[40] To join Christ's body is to begin a patient, affectionate, and responsible commitment to others so that the memberships of creation and community that feed us are strengthened to form a more integrated and healthy whole.

We can now see that Eucharistic eating is quite unlike today's predominantly consumerist approach to food, an approach dedicated to the consumer's comfort, convenience, and control. As William Cavanaugh has well observed, consumerism is as much about our detachment from things as it is attachment to things. This is because the point of shopping is not simply to have but to have constantly the option of purchasing something else. When consumerism becomes the defining feature of a person's life, it is inevitable that an individualistic and detached view of persons will emerge. The consumer gradually loses the ability to focus on, and thus cherish, what is consumed (consider Michel de Montaigne's maxim: "He who has his

---

[39] Eating becomes pornographic when this erotic or loving desire for the other is twisted into forms of domination or exploitation that deprive the other of its integrity or graced character. Put theologically, food ceases to register as a blessing from God because it has been reduced to an idol that serves us.

[40] A look at how medieval women enacted their compassion, often by giving their daily food to the hungry while feasting only on the Eucharist, demonstrates that the crucifixion has often been taken as the model for what true compassion looks like. Bynum summarizes: "To eat was to consume, to take in, to become God. And to eat was also to rend and tear God. Eating was a horribly audacious act. Yet it was only by bleeding, by being torn and rent, by dying, that God's body redeemed humanity. To become that body by eating was therefore to bleed and to save – to lift one's physicality into suffering and into glory" (*Holy Feast and Holy Fast*, 251).

mind on taking, no longer has it on what he has taken"[41]). The self is reduced to a shopper, a sovereign chooser (if the monetary means are available) but not a person deeply appreciative of and committed to the well-being of the ecosystem or local economy in which they shop.

But with the Eucharist, a fundamentally different view of persons emerges: "To consume the Eucharist is an act of anti-consumption, for here to consume is to be consumed, to be taken up into participation in something larger than the self, yet in a way in which the identity of the self is paradoxically secured."[42] The term "anti-consumption" may be too strong, since consumption of some kind must occur in the processes of nourishment. Nonetheless, Cavanaugh's point that the Eucharist leads to a different way of relating to each other remains. At the Eucharistic table people are welcomed to form their identities in a way that is focused on the needs, struggles, and joys of the memberships of which they are a contributing part. "In the Eucharistic economy ... the gift [of bread and wine] relativizes the boundaries between what is mine and what is yours by relativizing the boundary between me and you ... we participate in the divine life so that we are fed and simultaneously become food for others."[43]

To describe eating as a complex and dynamic *co*-abiding means that we never only consume the other. The other, in some sense, also consumes us. The point is not simply that we will be eaten when we die – this is what bodily decomposition is – or that we, as the presence of bacteria in our bodies attest, are being eaten all along.[44] The issue is rather that in the act of eating we can become more sensitive, appreciative, and helpful eaters who have an understanding for the memberships that feed us and are fed *by us*. As others nurture us, we have the unique opportunity to turn ourselves into a source of nurture for them. Inspired by Christ's own Eucharistic offering, people can make themselves an offering to the world by attending to its hungers and needs. To do this in a Eucharistic way, however, requires us in

---

[41] Michel de Montaigne, "Of Coaches," III:6 in *Essays*, trans. Donald Frame (New York: Alfred A. Knopf, Everyman Edition, 2003), 837.

[42] William T. Cavanaugh, *Being Consumed: Economics and Christian Desire* (Grand Rapids: W. B. Eerdmans, 2008), 84.

[43] Ibid., 97.

[44] "Every living organism is in a constant process of changing the world in which it lives by taking up materials and putting out others. Every act of consumption is also an act of production. And every act of production is also an act of consumption. When we consume food, we produce [and upon death will ourselves become] not only gases but solid waste products that are in turn the materials for consumption of some other organism" (Richard Lewontin, *Biology as Ideology: The Doctrine of DNA* [Toronto: House of Anansi Press, 1996], 88).

some sense to be *eaten by Jesus*. Eating Jesus and being eaten by him effects the transformation in us so that we can become the food that nurtures and celebrates the world.

To be eaten by Jesus is to come under the influence of his instruction and his way of being in the world. It is to submit to and let one's own life be guided by the concerns and priorities that define him. Entering into Jesus means being transformed (though not obliterated) into his body so that one's life takes on new characteristics. Bernard of Clairvaux spoke graphically of this process in his *Sermons on the Song of Songs*, when he argued that as Christians ruminate on scripture and allow its judgments to correct their living, it is as if Christ has "ground and pressed [them] with the teeth of hard discipline":

> My penitence, my salvation, are His food. I myself am His food ... I am chewed as I am reproved by Him; I am swallowed as I am taught; I am digested as I am changed; I am assimilated as I am transformed; I am made one as I am conformed. Do not wonder at this, for He feeds upon us and is fed by us that we may be the more closely bound to Him. Otherwise we are not perfectly united with Him. For if I eat and am not eaten, then He is in me, but I am not yet in Him ... But he eats me that He may have me in Himself, and He in turn is eaten by me that He may be in me.[45]

This is arresting language. What it communicates is that followers of Christ are in constant need of reproof, teaching, and conformation. Eating at the Eucharistic table there is the possibility that we will simply deform what is eaten – forget or refuse Jesus – and thereby block the potential of Christ to transform us from within. Bernard is suggesting that if people are simultaneously eaten by Jesus, meaning that Jesus is allowed to work on them from the outside, a process of purification and mortification takes place so that they can more fully be conformed to Christ's life.

To see what this can mean, consider how the processes of chewing and digesting have the effect of breaking down what is eaten. Pressure is applied from outside so that the food can be rendered amenable to its new environment. The analogy, of course, is not perfect, because the end result of this process is for the food to be absorbed into the eater. Nonetheless, the chewing and digesting image is helpful because it does indicate the need for breaking down of some sort to occur. For spiritual writers like Simone

---

[45] St. Bernard of Clairvaux. *On the Song of Songs IV*, Sermon 71, 2.5, 52, quoted in Ann W. Astell's *Eating Beauty: The Eucharist and the Spiritual Arts of the Middle Ages* (Ithaca: Cornell University Press, 2006), 76. The previous brief quote is from Sermon 72, 1.2, 64. I am indebted to Astell's excellent treatment of this theme throughout this section but also Bynum's *Holy Feast and Holy Fast*.

Weil,[46] the ego's desire to consume the world for itself or reduce reality to the limits of its own ambition or fear needs to be broken. The ego, in other words, needs to be corrected and chastened so that we can learn to receive and embrace the world as given by God. Being eaten by Jesus, much like being gardened or weeded by him, amounts to a kind of training in which people are disciplined by Jesus. To submit to living deeply within a Christ-inspired body means that one gives up claims to self-mastery. One gradually learns to see life from the community's point of view and discovers that Christ and the rule of fellowship take precedence over self-rule.

When Paul spoke of this process he described it as a dying with Christ. "Do you not know that all of us who have been baptized into Christ Jesus were baptized into his death? Therefore we have been buried with him by baptism into death, so that, just as Christ was raised from the dead by the glory of the Father, so we too might walk in newness of life" (Rom. 6:3–4).[47] Paul notes that the believer's natural or old "self" must be crucified and the body of sin destroyed (6:6) so that the life they live will be life "with him" rather than life on their own terms. Only then will the follower of Christ be brought from a deathly existence to real life. Real life presupposes the removal of all the layers of ego – think here of the chewing that is the perquisite for swallowing (as well as the spitting out of what should not be swallowed) and the digestion that preserves what is nutritious and good but excretes what is harmful or unnecessary – that prevent people from living fully in the memberships of the body of life. Resurrection life, the life that is true, abundant, and eternal, goes through crucifixion. When people are properly chewed by Christ, that is, when they are properly corrected, instructed, and trained by Christ, the sin that divides and harms the body is destroyed so that each member can serve the other with a spirit of sympathy and gladness. With the destruction of sin, we can become the nutritious food that will heal and strengthen the world.

---

[46]   In *Waiting for God* (New York: Harper & Row, Publisher, 1951), Weil says that God, as the source of all goodness and beauty, draws to himself and eats lovers of beauty. Eaten by God, people are changed so that they can more rightly and perfectly enjoy the beauty they love. They learn to enjoy beauty without destroying it. For discussion on this theme see Astell, *Eating Beauty*, 5–6, 227–253.

[47]   It is no accident that the theme of purification but also conformity to Christ should be cast in baptismal language since baptism is the prerequisite for Eucharistic participation. One cannot eat Jesus if one has not first been admitted into his life by joining the community of believers that is his body.

∞

The Gospel of John tells us that those who eat Jesus will live forever (6:51) and have eternal life (6:54).[48] This promise of new, eternal life has created a great deal of mischief. In part this is because people are often prone to think eternal life amounts to unending spiritual life or the denigration and leave-taking of this life, a departure from planet earth to some heavenly realm far, far away. The apocalyptic imagination that circulated through the Johannine community at the time of the gospel's writing is taken to mean that when Jesus says "I am from above ... I am not of this world" (8:23), he really means this present creation to be consigned to oblivion. The "dwelling place" (14:2) Jesus is preparing for his followers is thus interpreted to be anywhere but this created world.

This line of interpretation should be rejected. First, it raises the question of why the divine Logos would choose to become flesh and dwell among us (John 1:14) if this world is finally no good. The incarnation is not God's rejection of material creation but his most intimate identification with it, and in this identification also his elevation of it.[49] We must not forget that it was the fullness of God that dwelled bodily/materially in Jesus (Colossians 1), rather than simply a part or fraction of God. It would be odd, even contradictory, for the logos, understood *as the life within creatures* and as the one through whom life circulates, to turn against the life he has brought into being and continues to inform. It makes more sense to say that Jesus is turning against a "world" or cultural system of darkness that distorts and denies life. As the light of the world, Christ is set in opposition against all the forces of darkness that undermine creation and that deprive and destroy life. For Jesus to say he is not "of this world" means that he is not a part of a system of values and practices that produce division and death. His is a new way of being, a way of truth and of life (14:6). His way is to be trusted because it is the way of the Father. Jesus and the Father are one (10:30, 14:10). By being the incarnation of God the Father, Jesus is showing humanity how to receive and love everything in this world with a divine point of view in mind.

---

[48]   The Greek phrase in John 6:51 is better translated as "live to the age" (*eis ton aiona*).

[49]   David Bentley Hart argues that Eucharistic in-dwelling of Christ in us and us in him is part of a larger story of God's desire to be with us and live, as John's Apocalypse put it, among mortals (Revelation 21:3): "all of scripture testifies to the fact that, throughout the history of God's mighty and saving acts, in creation, the election of Israel, and the calling of the nations, God has been preparing for himself a habitation; and in the incarnation, death, resurrection, and ascension of God the Son, he has brought to completion that *qurban*, that reconciling 'drawing nigh' of and to the 'exceeding glory,' which is his plan for creation from before the foundation of the world" ("Thine Own of Thine Own," 159).

John is under no illusions about the difficulty and cost associated with a loving embrace of life. Those in the world of darkness who profiteer from life's exhaustion, degradation, and destruction will resist those who bring to light their sinful ways. They will hate the light. With the incarnation, however, evildoers no longer have an excuse for their sin (John 15:22). They cannot claim that they did not know what they were doing or that a better way of life was not presented to them. Those who become followers of Jesus should therefore expect persecution. They should expect that their efforts to live a communal life in accordance with the patterns or logoi of love, forgiveness, and reconciliation will be met with scorn and attack.

As Chapter 8 will show, it is difficult to know exactly what heaven, abundant life, eternal life, and resurrection life look like. At the very least we know that it means the follower has a deep level of intimacy with and participation in the life of God: "And this is eternal life, that they may know you, the only true God, and Jesus Christ whom you have sent" (John 17:3). Given the incarnational sensibility that runs throughout the gospel, a sensibility that heals anxiety of membership rather than exacerbates it, it is clear that this intimacy is not reserved for a realm "beyond" creation. God is with us and dwells among us always already as the life within life, what we might call the "liveliness of life." To meet and know God people must therefore begin with a deep commitment to serve life as they meet it because this is where God is, at the heart of all life's intersections. What needs to be resisted is the Gnostic tendency to devalue creaturely, material life. The moment this is done, God's creating and sustaining action in the world is denied. We should here recall Timothy's instruction to resist those demonic teachers who want to forbid the enjoyment of God's goodness as reflected in marriage and food. Timothy chooses a different path when he says, "For everything created by God is good, and nothing is to be rejected, provided it is received with thanksgiving; for it is sanctified by God's word and by prayer" (I Tim. 4:4–5).

However we understand "eternal life," it is important to underscore that eternity is not a rejection of created life or a flight from membership but their repair and fulfillment. "Eternal life begins now, in faith, and it continues beyond death through the promise of resurrection ... People are not inherently immortal, and even those who believe will die. Yet the relationship with God is not terminated by death. God does not abandon believers but gives them a future through resurrection."[50] What this future looks like in detail is impossible for us to know. What John's gospel suggests is that

---

[50] Craig R. Koester, *The Word of Life: A Theology of John's Gospel* (Grand Rapids: William B. Eerdmans, 2008), 32.

death is not final. Jesus inaugurates in his life a way of living that passes through death into richly communal life. In his death he shows that life is ultimately about giving oneself completely to others – "unless a grain of wheat falls into the earth and dies, it remains just a single grain; but if it dies, it bears much fruit" (John 12: 24). This is a giving that death cannot destroy, for even as the grain dies it does not disappear. It is taken up into new, fruit-bearing life.

When Jesus is eaten, people learn to give themselves away, trusting that in the sharing of their lives they participate in the divine, eternal life of sharing. They learn to make their movements a source of nurture, their lives and homes sites of hospitality, and their work an art of caring and celebration. When people fully participate in the Eucharist the world ceases to signify as a material possession and instead becomes a gift to be given and shared. In this giving the world is revealed as God's world:

> The Eucharist demonstrates that material reality *can* become charged with Jesus' life, and so proclaims hope for the whole world of matter. The material, habitually used as means of exclusion, of violence, can become a means of communion. Matter as hoarded or dominated or exploited speaks of the distortion and ultimate severance of relationship, and as such can only be the sign of *death* . . . The matter of the Eucharist, carrying the presence of the risen Jesus, can only be a sign of *life*, of triumph over the death of exclusion and isolation.[51]

In his treatise *On the Eucharist*, Albert the Great once said that eating Jesus is like swallowing a seed that then germinates in the garden of the soul. It sprouts and grows, producing good fruit, perhaps fruit like that described by Paul in his letter to the Galatians: love, joy, peace, patience, kindness, generosity, faithfulness, gentleness, and self-control (Gal. 5:22–23). Because it is the seed of Christ, we know that as the seed grows it will be a likeness of Christ, for all that is in the growth will find its origin in Christ.[52] In his own reflection on this process Bernard noted that the follower's growth in Christ is a source of nurture to Christ: "He is the good householder, who provides for his family, . . . feeding them with the bread of life . . . But as he feeds them, he is himself also fed, and fed with the food he takes most gladly, that is our progress."[53] Mutual indwelling facilitates mutual nurture, which leads

---

to mutual growth, which leads to the flowering of maximum life, which leads to Sabbath delight.

EUCHARISTIC HOSPITALITY

As early Christians struggled to remember Jesus in their eating and table fellowship, they discovered that to co-abide with Jesus called for a new social reality and a new form of life. In this life, the forms of oppression and division, degradation and violence that characterize customary eating and living needed to be overcome. They understood Jesus to be building on the prophetic traditions that spoke of a new way of organizing existence, announcing that in him people will discover the good news of healing, freedom, forgiveness, and reconciliation, all prerequisites to the experience of life in its fullness. Appealing to Isaiah, Jesus asserted that the will of God has always been that people be liberated to enjoy the gifts of the memberships of life (Luke 4:16–21):

> If you remove the yoke from among you,
>> the pointing of the finger, the speaking of evil,
> if you offer food to the hungry and satisfy the needs of the afflicted,
>> then your light shall rise in the darkness,
>> and your gloom be like the noonday.
> The Lord will guide you continually,
>> and satisfy your needs in parched places,
>> and make your bones strong;
> and you shall be like a watered garden,
>> like a spring of water,
>> whose waters never fail.   (Isa. 58:9–11)

This is imagery of life's fecundity and fresh potential. Once the bonds of oppression that maim and destroy life are removed, then life can flower into the diverse and beautiful forms that God planted in the first garden. To live in a world of injustice is like living in a parched and sterile land where little can grow and everything is exploited or hoarded. Here there is no co-abiding and thus no joy in mutual growth. The seed is there but it remains submerged in the ground. But when the water comes (recall that Jesus referred to himself as "living water" [John 4:7–15]), and when the villains that destroy life are defeated, then the whole world is poised to enter into Sabbath delight (Isa. 58:13–14).

When we turn to the witness of Christ's early followers we are given a dramatic and practical picture of the transformation in life that became possible for those who eat and are eaten by Jesus. The book of Acts records that upon being filled by the Holy Spirit, Christ's disciples began to prophesy and speak in foreign tongues. This activity may seem strange to us but it is the direct effect of people who have welcomed and made themselves available to others. Speaking in tongues and prophesying suggests that the disciples had become hosts to others. They no longer lived strictly in terms of and for their own point of view. Instead, the language and the vision of another had taken residence in them and had become their inspiration and focus. Modifying a Pauline phrase, in this early community the Holy Spirit so transformed the lives of these followers that they could say, "It is no longer I who live, but others – their needs, their joys, their hopes, but also their nurture – who live within and direct me." To genuinely co-abide with others is to remember them and thus adopt a prophetic form of life.

Among recent philosophers, few have seen as clearly as Emmanuel Levinas how a prophetic mode of living is not a special capacity for a select few but is instead the heart of a fully human and responsible life. Prophetic life is not only about making odd or grim predictions. It is about the intense seeing of the other, the radical welcome of another into my life so that what I see, and how I see it, is from the other's point of view. Prophetic subjectivity is "the other in the same," the inspiration of a living soul, even the extradition of the self to its neighbor.[54] In a prophetic mode of life a subject is given over to the other, finds its own life in responding to another's needs. It lives by going out of itself in response to the call of another. In this "going out" from itself, a subject bears witness to the truth that another is not an object or a possession. It is, instead, the animating impulse that nurtures and inspires personal life into the realms of responsibility and care.

Prophetic subjectivity makes genuine life together possible. Communion presupposes the integrity of each member *and* each self's ability to go outside the self to meet another in a shared life. This shared life does not obliterate the distinctness of each other in the name of a bland conformity or sameness but instead cherishes individual integrity as a gift of God. Genuine love requires the welcome of the other in their unique position, need, and

---

[54] Emmanuel Levinas, *Otherwise Than Being, or Beyond Essence*, trans. Alphonso Lingis (The Hague: Martinus Nijhoff, 1981), 149. The language of "extradition" (Levinas also speaks of being held "hostage" by the other) is perhaps extreme, and Graham Ward (in *Christ and Culture*, 108, but also in his essay "Hospitality and Justice towards 'Strangers': A Theological Reflection" [available online at the Katholische Akademie in Berlin]) is right to caution us about its use. The other in me does not destroy me. If it did, then I could not turn my life into a site of hospitality.

potential.[55] When love is truly operative the possibility exists that people can become genuine hosts who welcome, receive, and attend to each other's lives.

Acts gives a remarkable portrayal of the early Christian community in the following account:

> All who believed were together and had all things in common; they would sell their possessions and goods and distribute the proceeds to all, as any had need. Day by day, as they spent much time together in the temple, they broke bread at homes and ate their food with glad and generous hearts, praising God and having the goodwill of all the people. (Acts 2:44–47)

We are also told that the group of believers were "of one heart and soul, and no one claimed private ownership of any possessions," and that there was "not a needy person among them" (Acts 4:32–34). Even if one admits that the scenes as described may represent an idealized expansion on what only some groups did at intermittent times, it is significant that the redactor of this text understood that radical hospitality should have been the logical and the practical outcome of people who co-abide with Jesus.[56] To co-abide means that personal life becomes true and full to the extent that it is lived *through* the relations that join creatures to each other. To live prophetically means that the hosting of members – feeding the hungry, clothing the naked, and welcoming the widows and orphans – is the overriding concern.

John Howard Yoder has argued that what inspired these early followers to attempt such hospitality was the practice of eating food together around a table with Christ. Acts says that these people "devoted themselves to the apostles' teaching and fellowship, to the breaking of bread and the prayers" (Acts 2:42). Being at the table, sharing what they had already been given, and then "remembering" and interpreting what they had been given through the lens of Christ's life and ministry, was the inspiration (though not the guarantee) for whatever economic practices they tried:

---

[55] John Zizioulas notes that love is not a feeling toward another but a gift coming from them. It is an affirmation of uniqueness in relation: "Love is the assertion that one exists as 'other,' that is, particular and unique, *in relation to* some 'other' who affirms him or her as 'other.' In love, relation generates otherness; it does not threaten it" (*Communion and Otherness*, 55). Without the affirmation of otherness that genuine love presupposes and requires, love would be distorted into an imperial or violent gesture that annexes or absorbs the other.

[56] For commentary on the historical reliability of these texts and the sources governing their composition, see Ernst Haenchen's *The Acts of the Apostles: A Commentary* (Philadelphia: Westminster Press, 1971).

The "common purse" of the Jerusalem church was not a purse: It was a common table. It arose not as the fruit of speculation or discussion about ideal economic relations; it was not something added to what was already going on. The sharing was rather the normal, organic extension from table fellowship. Some of the first Jerusalem believers sold their estates voluntarily (Acts 5 indicates that it was not mandatory) and pooled their goods because in the Lord's presence they ate together, not the other way around.[57]

Here we can see how the common table around which people ate could at the same time be a Eucharistic table. Eating could become a time of transformation as people ruminated on what it means to receive the world and each other as gifts given by God. Contemplating Christ's self-offering could become the inspiration for them to offer themselves and their possessions to each other.

In this account we can see that breaking bread together is far more than a fueling event. It can be a radical, prophetic act of hospitality that is founded upon God's primordial and sustaining hospitality whereby the whole world is created, nurtured, and given the freedom to be itself. It can be the practical site in which existing economies are analyzed and challenged. It can even be the foretaste of the messianic age.[58] When people eat together in a Eucharistic way they learn that sharing with and caring for others is not an option. Helped by the evidence of another's comforting presence and nurturing touch, they discover that "Human beings are gifts to each other in an endless economy of God's grace whereby we are given in order to give."[59] At the table Christ reveals that *life is sharing* – the giving and receiving of gifts from each other. Learning to receive these gifts and learning to respond to this inexplicable generosity is the task of a lifetime. If we are humble, it can become the inspiration for our own generosity. It can also be the work and time of our greatest joy.

The history of the church shows that hospitality has never been easy. It has rarely attained in practice its ideal form.[60] The self-offering, welcome,

---

[57] Yoder, *Body Politics*, 17.

[58] Yoder writes, "In celebrating their fellowship around the table, the early Christians testified that the messianic age, often pictured as a banquet, had begun" (*Body Politics*, 18). In this age the needs of people are met. As Deuteronomy 15:4 describes, one of the signs of Sabbath fulfillment is that there be "no one in need among you."

[59] Ward, *Christ and Culture*, 81.

[60] For an excellent treatment of the challenges of Christian hospitality, see Christine Pohl's *Making Room: Recovering Hospitality as a Christian Tradition* (Grand Rapids: W. B. Eerdmans, 1999).

and sharing that are the hallmark of the "Eucharistic ethos"[61] are often forgotten or ignored as people approach the table with a mindset of personal ambition or fear. As the story of Ananias and Sapphira in Acts 5 makes clear, people are inclined to hold back in their self-giving, or make a show of their piety. Or people try to turn the hospitable act to their own advantage by inviting only those who can benefit or repay them (Luke 14:12–14). The temptation is to close the table, restrict the membership, and keep the guests out.

This temptation was at the heart of the early Christian community. It was revealed in the tension over the welcome of the Gentile believer Cornelius. As Acts described him, Cornelius was an Italian God-fearer. The crucial test for the church community was whether or not he would be welcomed into their membership. In a vision (a sign that prophetic subjectivity is potentially underway), God instructed Cornelius to send men to Peter so that he might come to meet with Cornelius. While these men were sent, God also gave a vision to Peter, a vision in which he saw

> the heaven opened and something like a large sheet coming down, being lowered to the ground by its four corners. In it were all kinds of four-footed creatures and reptiles and birds of the air. Then he heard a voice saying, "Get up, Peter; kill and eat." But Peter said, "By no means, Lord; for I have never eaten anything that is profane or unclean." The voice said to him again, a second time, "What God has made clean, you must not call profane." This happened three times, and the thing was suddenly taken up into heaven. (Acts 10:11–16)

In this vision we see how food and eating go to the core of our life together.

It is helpful to recall that eating is a language and a lens through which a culture communicates and clarifies its values, structures, and priorities.[62]

---

[61] "The essence of the Eucharistic ethos ... is the affirmation of the Other and of every Other as a gift to be appreciated and to evoke gratitude" (Zizioulas, *Communion and Otherness*, 90). Zizioulas goes on to say that this ethos accepts the Other unconditionally, practices unlimited forgiveness, and confirms all the relations that contribute to another's identity. This has ecological implications. It means that at the Eucharist a "cosmic liturgy" is performed in which the whole creation is affirmed and lifted up to God.

[62] Massimo Montanari writes: "Like spoken language, the food system contains and conveys the culture of its practitioner; it is the repository of traditions and of collective identity. It is therefore an extraordinary vehicle of self-representation and of cultural exchange – a means of establishing identity, to be sure, but also the first way of entering into contact with a different culture. Eating the food of the 'other' is easier, it would seem, than decoding the other's language. Far more than spoken language itself, food can serve as mediator between different cultures, opening methods of cooking to all manner of

What we eat, how we prepare and serve it, and who we eat it with are markers that define one group as distinct from another. On the one hand, food systems and traditions encode and enforce gender roles, class divisions, and other power relations. On the other hand, food traditions also reflect the regional and ethnic differences that constitute the world's many cuisines and eating traditions. Our palates and taste buds would be severely impoverished if we did not have (among many others) Mexican, Ethiopian, Chinese, or Italian cooking to enjoy. To witness food variety and distinctiveness is also to witness and celebrate the diversity of the world's people and places.

Peter's vision suggests that food *difference* becomes a problem when it is the basis for *division*. The issue is not whether cultures should be distinct but whether cultural differences are allowed to divide and alienate people from each other. As is well-known, Jewish dietary laws strictly forbid the eating of certain kinds of food. Why these laws were put in place makes for a fascinating but also very complex story.[63] What is clear, however, is that Jewish dietary law served, among other ends, to preserve Jewish holiness. Israel must be distinct from other nations, and one way to do that is to refrain from eating their diet. Another is to desist from eating with foreigners, since eating together is but the beginning of more extensive forms of comingling like intermarriage.[64] For Peter to protest that he has never eaten anything that is profane or unclean is another way of maintaining that he is a good Jew.

---

invention, cross-pollination, and contamination" (*Food Is Culture* [New York: Columbia University Press, 2006], 133). Montanari also notes that the identification between a culture and its food takes place within changing historical, geographic, and economic contexts. In a time when globalizing markets homogenize food systems, local food cultures receive more attention. In a time of food abundance, particular foods tend to play a smaller role distinguishing between classes. The more food serves to distinguish regional variation, the less it can distinguish between classes.

[63] Numerous authors, ranging from Jacob Milgrom to Mary Douglas, have given explanations for the precise character and shape of Jewish dietary laws. For an exposition that focuses on the maintenance of a distinct national identity, see David Kraemer's *Jewish Eating and Identity through the Ages* (New York: Routledge, 2007). Foods like pork may have been forbidden in part because they represented a food most readily eaten by Gentiles. Pork thus served as a symbol of what others ate, and as a reminder of Hellenistic cultural hegemony. "As a marker of cultural identity, standing at the boundary between 'Hellenist' and 'pious Jew,' pork will have been a uniquely effective tool for fighting the battle between 'us' and 'them'" (33). It is also likely that observance of dietary laws was most strict when national identity was thought most under threat.

[64] Montanari writes that in some cultures to share food signifies that "one belongs to the same family" and that sharing a table "is the first sign of membership in a group" (*Food Is Culture*, 94).

God's vision challenges Peter to reconsider his dietary practices because these are being used as the basis for exclusion. God instructs Peter to eat what he traditionally considered to be unclean because in God's view it is clean. The designations clean and unclean are here shown to be an excuse to deny fellowship and limit hospitality to others. By saying that the food associated with Gentiles is clean, God is also instructing Peter to be hospitable to Cornelius and welcome him in. If all foods are permissible then *hospitality extends to everyone.* This is an exceedingly difficult message for Peter to appreciate, suggesting how deeply eating practices are tied to personal and ethnic identity. God needs to address him multiple times on this point. Peter is puzzled, not knowing what to say or do.[65]

Under the guidance of the Holy Spirit, Peter gets up from his vision and goes to the door where he welcomes the men sent by Cornelius. Peter's openness to the Spirit, a mark of prophetic subjectivity, is the enabling factor in his hospitable act. Peter goes to Cornelius knowing that "it is unlawful for a Jew to associate with or to visit a Gentile" (Acts 10:28). Instructed by God that both Gentile food and Gentile people are clean, Peter then witnesses the Spirit descend upon the Gentiles he is with. They too speak in tongues and praise God, indicating that they are ready to participate in Christ's body. Peter's Jewish friends first criticized him for his acceptance of the Gentiles. But upon hearing his story of the visions and of their prophetic life, they repented and acknowledged that God has given even to the Gentiles "the repentance that leads to life" (Acts 11:18).

What Peter and the early Christian community needed to learn was that the peace of Christ does not allow people to show partiality. All must be received into the body and membership of Christ. Letty Russell called this the practice of "just hospitality." By this she meant practical forms of welcome that do not exclude on the basis of difference but instead promote solidarity among strangers. For communion to be "in Christ," Christians must learn to partner with (since hospitality is not something we do *to* others) people of different racial, ethnic, gender, sexual, and religious backgrounds. In this partnership members previously marginalized are brought to the center, thereby, in effect, eliminating the idea of a centralized power structure controlled by this or that group. They must be brought to the

---

[65] Haenchen suggests Peter's puzzlement is an important part of the narrative because it communicates that Peter is not acting under his own initiative and power. He is moving into a prophetic form of life in which he must "abandon himself unreservedly to the guidance of God" (*The Acts of the Apostles*, 358).

center because everyone has unique gifts to give to others, just as everyone has specific needs that can only be met if a diverse membership is aware of them. "Hospitality is an expression of unity without uniformity. Through hospitality community is built out of difference, not sameness . . . Hospitality in community is a sharing in the openness of Christ to all as he welcomed them into God's kin-dom."[66]

FROM HOSPITALITY TO RECONCILIATION

Jesus' ministries of welcome and hospitality do not end with the gathering of diverse people into a group. This is because a "group" is not yet a place of communion. It is not yet a healthy *body* of members so intimately and beneficially bound together that each individual finds in the presence of another their source of inspiration, nurture, and joy. To participate in the body of Christ is not only to have Christ in me as the one who corrects and transforms me. It is also to have others in me in such a way that what I know of life – what I need, desire, and enjoy in life – makes no sense apart from the fellowship of life together.

A life of genuine fellowship is not easy. The problem is not simply that as individuals we refuse to offer ourselves completely to others. It is also that we live in social, ecological, and theological contexts that have been thoroughly degraded by histories of sin. Many of us find it difficult even to imagine the intimacy of communion that God desires because so much of our experience is shaped by traditions and habits of fear, suspicion, arrogance, and hatred.[67] When we stand before each other in honest communication – no easy matter because we are predisposed to flee from our wrongdoing and shield ourselves from the pain of others – we discover much we need to be ashamed of. Too much of our striving and consuming is based (whether knowingly or not) on the disregard and exploitation of others, rather than their welcome and embrace.

---

[66] Letty M. Russell, *Just Hospitality: God's Welcome in a World of Difference*, ed. J. Shannon Clarkson and Kate M. Ott (Louisville: Westminster John Knox Press, 2009), 65.

[67] In *The Christian Imagination: Theology and the Origins of Race* (New Haven: Yale University Press, 2010), Willie Jennings argues persuasively that modern traditions of theology have been profoundly deformed by the histories of colonialism and racism. Christianity not only reflects but has contributed to a "diseased social imagination" that degrades people and the places that nurture life. The "body of Christ," in other words, is not a true *body* because creaturely difference has not yet been captured by the Christ who turns our strife into a loving desire for the good of the other.

According to Paul, the life, death, and resurrection of Jesus make possible an entirely new way to conceive and live out our relationships with others.

> So if anyone is in Christ, there is a new creation: everything old has passed away; see, everything has become new! All this is from God, who reconciled us to himself through Christ, and has given us the ministry of reconciliation; that is, in Christ God was reconciling the world to himself, not counting their trespasses against them, and entrusting the message of reconciliation to us. (2 Corinthians 5:17–19)

When we co-abide with Christ we learn to see with his eyes, feel with his heart, and understand with his mind. All the old patterns of seeing, touching, hearing, smelling, and tasting pass away so that everything in creation can become new. In this transformation, it is not simply we ourselves who become new. Every creature is remade because it can now be understood in terms of the creating and sustaining Logos that Christ is.[68] All relations are new because they are marked by reconciliation rather than estrangement. This means that the new community called into being by Christ is marked by a new economics and a new politics defined by the work of reconciliation. In a Christ-shaped economy and polity people can stand before each other and before all the members of creation *without shame* because they have devoted themselves to the care of each other.[69] Reconciliation describes the peaceful ordering of relationships so that our life together can bear witness to the fruit of sympathy, nurture, and celebration.

The term "reconciliation" (*katallagē*) is not used much in the New Testament. This does not mean, however, that its reality and significance are absent from Jesus' ministry. In the Sermon on the Mount (Matt. 5:24), for instance, Jesus tells his followers not to bring a gift to the sacrificial altar if relations with a brother are not right. Such an offering would be a

---

[68] Richard Hays has argued in *The Moral Vision of the New Testament* that Paul's meaning is often distorted by restricting the scope of "new creation" to humanity. The Greek text for 2 Corinthians 5:17 lacks both subject and verb, and should be translated "If anyone is in Christ – new creation!" Paul is drawing here on Isaiah 65:17–19 that speaks of God creating new heavens and a new earth, worlds in which weeping will be replaced by rejoicing and delight (20).

[69] We should recall that in the Garden of Eden, Adam and Eve were naked and without shame because they had nothing to hide – no exploitative or self-serving agenda – from each other, from God, and from the diverse members of the garden. Relationships at this early stage were convivial. But with the "fall" from creatureliness, and the anxiety of membership it reflects, relationships on all levels are broken, calling forth the need for lament and reconciliation as the healing of relationship.

sham because it is made without the self-giving that is at the heart of sacrificial living. The desire to sacrifice, when understood theologically, simply is the desire for right and reconciled relationship. It is the commitment to order one's desire and one's work around the good and the well-being of each other.

The hymn to Christ in the letter to the Colossians (1:15–20) reinforces the idea that reconciled life is what the ministry of Christ is all about. After describing Christ as the image/icon of God and as the one through whom and for whom all things in heaven and on earth are created, Christ is described as the one in whom "the fullness of God was pleased to dwell." Through Christ "God was pleased to reconcile to himself all things, whether on earth or in heaven, by making peace through the blood of his cross." This is arresting language because it indicates that life in the most ultimate sense ("the fullness of God") is a reconciled life, a life of intimacy and communion. Christ's blood saves and makes peace because his blood is the true life of self-offering that nurtures without end. Drinking this blood at the Eucharistic table we are empowered to participate in the divine self-giving that heals, feeds, and reconciles the whole creation.

It is important to underscore that the scope of God's reconciling work extends beyond humanity to include "all things, whether on earth or in heaven." For much of its history the church has suffered from a reconciliation deficit disorder. This disorder is reflected in two misguided beliefs: (1) that God cares only for human beings and (2) that people can flourish while the memberships of creation languish. The falsity of the first belief is readily shown in the varied witness of scripture attesting to God's love for the whole creation. In Genesis 1, God proclaims creation to be very good. As the physical manifestation of God's love, how could it not be? Job learns that God delights in creatures that can do him harm, indicating that creation is not reducible to its usefulness to us. Paul proclaims that God's plan from before the foundation of the world has been to gather up all things in heaven and on earth in Christ (Eph. 1:3–10), suggesting that everything God has made has a place in God's eternal life. The Christ hymn in Colossians continues this line of thinking by insisting that all things were created in him and for him. Even if one grants a unique place and role for humanity in God's creative and redemptive dramas with the world, these brief references indicate that from the beginning God's care and desire have been for all creatures. Full fellowship with God is not the fellowship of a few disembodied, placeless minds. God's eternal hope is for a new heaven and a new earth that can be the *home* of God (Rev. 21:1–4). God's eternal desire is not to be freed from but to be *with* and *dwell among* a reconciled creation.

The falsity of the second belief reflects an ecological and a theological error. Ecology teaches us that no individual lives alone. To live we must eat, which means we must attend to the bodies and the geo-bio-chemical processes that keep all of us on the move. If we fail to attend to ecological memberships and processes, we will end up with an impoverished vision of reconciliation: people who may get along with each other but are condemned to starvation, toxic habitats, and sickly bodies. Moreover, the incarnation of God in Jesus Christ teaches us that embodiment and the ways we relate to other bodies are of the greatest theological significance. Jesus was not a Gnostic teacher but (among other things) a healer and feeder of bodies. Jesus' ministry was a ministry of touch carried out by a "fleshly body" (Col. 1:22), and an invitation to his followers that we learn to be reconciled to each other in the ways we touch each other. From an ecological and theological standpoint, we can see that flourishing requires the well-being of bodies together. To live is to be in a body in a place joined to all the bodies of creation. It is our life but it is also the life God chose for himself in the body of Jesus. Embodiment is not alien to God, nor is it a reality only temporarily (and thus begrudgingly) assumed. Bodies are the places and the means of God's creating and sustaining love.

If the scope of God's reconciling work extends to the whole creation, then it becomes evident that eating, understood as our most intimate joining with the bodies of creation, must be a primary site and means through which this reconciliation becomes visible. In our eating we are not simply to be reconciled to fellow human eaters. We must also be reconciled to what we eat. How we prepare to eat, as well as the character of the eating itself, demonstrates whether or not we appreciate the wide scope of God's reconciling ways with the world.

To see how this is so, consider the shame that circulates through much industrial food production and consumption. In *Eating Animals*, Jonathan Safran Foer describes the many ways in which chickens, pigs, and cattle are made to live miserable lives and endure cruel deaths all so that we can have low-priced meat. Factory farms and large confinement feeding operations regularly crowd and restrict animals so that they cannot live their God-given potential but are made – in some cases genetically engineered – to grow to slaughter weight as quickly as possible. "Life" for these animals is so stressful and damaging that they could not survive without a steady diet of steroids and antibiotics. Of the billions that do survive this industrial ordeal, even death becomes a shame. Describing the slaughter of cattle, Foer observes that a typical steer enters a chute in which a "knocker" shoots a steel bolt into its skull, rendering the steer unconscious or dead. The steer is then hoisted up by a leg and sent down a disassembly line so it can be skinned, gutted, and carved up. In many instances "animals are bled, skinned, and dismembered while conscious."[70] Industry and government know this happens but the practice carries on. In fact, some slaughterhouse managers admit that an animal can be "too dead" and thus slow the heart rate down too quickly. The ideal, it seems, is to have a heart pump for a little while so that the blood can drain quickly and speed up the line, thereby making the overall slaughter process more efficient and profitable.

Food shame is not confined to meat production. When we consider the degradation and erosion of soils, the polluting and wasting of our watersheds, the poisoning and genetic manipulation of plants, and the abuse and exploitation of farmworkers, it is clear that our industrial farming and food systems are premised on the violation rather than the care of each other. While many would call the vast fields of corn, rice, wheat, or soybean monocultures a technological success story, they are in certain respects a reflection of creation betrayed. Why? Because these fields do not sufficiently reflect respect for the ecological relationships and the biodiversity that make for a healthy world. In industrial farming, ecological processes are bypassed, frustrated, and subverted. Ecological relationships are manipulated to serve a narrow human aim.

Sometimes our aim will appear in altruistic guise. To see this, consider the fanfare that surrounded the development of golden rice. Golden rice is golden because it has been engineered to have beta-carotene within the kernel's endosperm. Beta-carotene is a precursor to vitamin A, a crucial vitamin that can help prevent blindness in millions of children (especially in Asia). While there are many scientific and cultural issues surrounding this genetic intervention, a primary one to consider is the fact that among the many forms of rice that have developed over thousands of years not one form contains carotene in the endosperm. Craig Holdrege and Steve Talbott suggest that the plant's own longstanding resistance to what looks like a minor genetic variation ought to give us pause. "Might the excess carotene in the seed affect in some way the nourishment and growth of a germinating rice plant? . . . Can we claim to be acting responsibly when we overpower the plant, coercing a performance from it before we understand the reasons for

---

70   Foer, *Eating Animals*, 230. Foer's book is joined by several others documenting the abuses of industrial meat production. For an examination of nonindustrial meat production, see Nicolette Hahn Niman's *Righteous Porkchop: Finding a Life and Good Food beyond Factory Farms* (New York: HarperCollins, 2009).

its natural reticence?"[71] What the example of golden rice shows is our refusal to attend to and respect what is there. Both the food itself and the contexts for its production are not received as gifts but are instead manipulated to serve an alien aim. Our intervention suggests an unwillingness to abide with and learn from these gifts. The integrity, even sanctity, of the other is denied.

Reconciliation presupposes the welcome of the other as other. It entails that we enter into relationships that honor and nurture rather than degrade and deplete others. It requires attention and listening so that we can sense the damage and participate in the work of healing broken relationships. No doubt, this listening has become especially difficult in a global food economy where the people growing our food (often in the developing countries of the Global South) are far away. Many of these people live under the burdens of trade agreements and lending policies of the World Bank and International Monetary Fund that require them to grow commodities for export to the developed North rather than feed themselves. Christians who are serious about reconciliation, especially those living in countries of power and privilege, need to learn to listen to their brothers and sisters as they speak of the harsh, often life-threatening, demands that trade agreements impose upon them.[72] We need to be exposed to how our desire for "cheap food" impoverishes the lives of others and degrades the land, water, and animals these people depend upon.

The listening I have in mind is not confined to people. We need to open ourselves to the communication of animals, plants, fields, forests, and waterways that continually bear witness to our mistreatment of them.[73] Abused animals, polluted waterways, degraded soils, languishing plants, farmworker trailer parks (described by some as the new ghettos of the rural

---

[71] Craig Holdrege and Steve Talbott, *Beyond Biotechnology: The Barren Promise of Genetic Engineering* (Lexington: University Press of Kentucky, 2008), 25.

[72] See *Voices from the South: The Effects of Globalization and the WTO on Third World Countries*, ed. Sarah Anderson (Milford, CT: Food First Books and The International Forum on Globalization, 2000); Walden Bello's *Deglobalization: Ideas for a New World Economy*, rev. edition (London: ZED Books, 2005); and Vandana Shiva's *Earth Democracy: Justice, Sustainability, and Peace* (Boston: South End Press, 2005).

[73] Scripture speaks often of nonhuman creation's praise of God and its testimony to our destructiveness (Genesis 4:10–12, Deuteronomy 11:13–17 and 30:19, Micah 6:1–2, Hosea 4:1–3, Jeremiah 4:23–26). Subsequent traditions of thought have silenced their communication by classifying creatures as nonhuman and therefore as bereft of speech and intelligent action. These classificatory schemes need to be challenged. For an examination of recent philosophical reflection on the boundaries between humans and animals, and the anthropocentrism and conceptual and empirical problems these boundaries represent, see Matthew Calarco's *Zoographies: The Question of the Animal from Heidegger to Derrida* (New York: Columbia University Press, 2008).

poor) – all of these speak to us of a reconciliation that needs to happen. Sensing this need for reconciliation is very difficult to do because our "diseased social imaginations" so readily divide and then manipulate the world to our own glory rather than God's. We often lack the attention and the desire to listen or see. If reconciliation is to become a reality it must therefore begin with confession and an earnest desire to repent of our sinful, relationship-breaking ways. We need to be taught to see how our eating implicates us in processes that violate rather than serve. We need to be inspired to eat in ways that cherish food as a gift and a blessing to be shared. For the sake of our learning and our reconciliation work, Christians should begin by becoming the supporters and champions of "local economies" in which our distance, blindness, and ignorance can be overcome and replaced with knowledgeable participation and honest celebration.[74]

The Colossian Christ hymn states that the path of reconciliation and peace goes through the blood of Christ's cross. This means that there can be no reconciliation without self-offering sacrifice. Our histories of food production and consumption show that we often twist sacrifice into sacrilege. Our desire for inexpensive and convenient food demonstrates that we think we can eat without sacrifice. Ellen Davis has rightly pointed out that "Christ's sacrifice does not make our sacrifice unnecessary. Rather, his sacrifice makes ours possible."[75] Eating at the Eucharistic table we are asking to be transformed – given a life-enabling, blood infusion of sorts – so that whenever we eat, those we eat and those we eat with will have been welcomed and cherished as manifestations of God's love. This is no mere theoretical act. It is an economic and political act because it entails that all our relationships be inspired by attention and care. Jesus shows us that the best and most appropriate response to the gifts of God, the way we become worthy of the nurture of another, is for us to turn ourselves into a source of nurture for the world.

Insofar as we are caught in the grip of a reconciliation deficit disorder we will not appreciate that animal husbandry, patient gardening, advocacy for farmworkers, and sharing food at table are vital and practical expressions of God's reconciling ways with the world. But they are, insofar as they manifest Christ's self-giving love for others. To be reconciled is to be able to gather

---

[74] Few have described this economic, ecological, and cultural shift as clearly as Wendell Berry. See especially his collection of essays *What Matters? Economics for a Renewed Commonwealth* (Berkeley: Counterpoint, 2010).

[75] Ellen F. Davis. "In Him All Things Hold Together," in *Earth and Word: Classic Sermons on Saving the Planet*, ed. David Rhoads (New York: Continuum, 2007), 133.

around a table with each other without shame, celebrating the gifts to each other that we are. It is to commit to an economy and a politics in which the care of each other is our all-consuming desire.

WHAT IT (POTENTIALLY) LOOKS LIKE

In recent years, as faith communities have given more attention to the theological significance of food, remarkable new ministries have been developed in which food's production, preparation, and sharing are understood to witness to, and be the medium of, God's presence in the world. Churches are growing community gardens in which the food that is harvested is shared with the neighborhood and those in need. Often, members of the community are invited in to share in the work of planting and nurturing seed into fruit. They are hosting meals that honor the land, its creatures, and the people who eat, by serving food that is poison-free and nutritious. In this work, they are discovering that faith formation happens in the attention and care that growing and sharing food with each other requires. They are beginning to appreciate how gardens, and the work they entail, situate and orient faith communities in the neighborhoods in which they exist. Church community gardens, and church-supported agriculture more generally, are not trivial, tangential, or boutique pursuits. They go to the heart of an embodied faith that seeks the care and the healing of bodies, and that strives to make the hospitable love of God incarnate in the mundane, unglamorous places of daily life.

When the life of faith is transformed from being a preparation for the individual soul's flight to an otherworldly, heavenly realm, and instead becomes a community's extension of Jesus' ministries of feeding, healing, and reconciliation, then all manner of practical, economic, and political possibilities come into view.[76] The reclamation of abandoned lots, the repair of neighborhoods, the making fertile of wasted land, the reconciliation of broken relationships, the building of community identity and spirit through

---

[76] Nurya Love Parish has documented many of these efforts in her publication entitled "Christian Food Movement." It, along with a wealth of additional material, can be found at http://christianfoodmovement.org/. See also Jennifer R. Ayres's book *Good Food: A Grounded Practical Theology* (Waco: Baylor University Press, 2013), Fred Bahnson's *Soil and Sacrament: A Spiritual Memoir of Food and Faith* (New York: Simon & Schuster, 2013), Fred Bahnson and Norman Wirzba's *Making Peace With the Land: God's Call to Reconcile with Creation* (Downer's Grove, IL: InterVarsity Press, 2012), and Lisa Graham McMinn's *To the Table: A Spirituality of Food, Farming, and Community* (Grand Rapids: Brazos Press, 2016) for further details on creative faith-inspired food ministries that are developing in diverse contexts.

the creation of local economies (and the new economic priorities and diverse participation of peoples they require) – all these efforts now become central to the work of faith because they are the basic ways through which love is made real, made practical, made nutritious. Seminaries and theological schools, meanwhile, are discerning how gardens and farms are vital sites through which the gospel can be better understood and pastoral ministry reimagined.[77] People of faith are coming together in fields and around tables, growing food and sharing meals, and discovering how food's production and consumption can be fresh and fundamental expressions of their worship.

When people understand that eating – what they eat, how they grow it, who they eat it with – is the great connector (or divider) in life, and when they appreciate the significance of food in all the diverse dimensions of land, plant, animal, and human health then it is but a short step to a radical re-visioning of what church ministries should be. A food ministry, rather than being simply an optional program through which a church exercises a portion of its work, becomes instead a lens that refocuses ministries across the board.

To see what I mean, and what the ministry I am talking about looks like, consider the work being done by Otis and Monica Moss at Trinity United Church in Chicago's South Side. Theirs is a remarkable ministry because they are showing how attention to food and health integrates the wide, diverse expressions of church life. By making the health and reconciliation of created bodies their focus, the Mosses are making God's love for and in the world fresh and deeply meaningful.[78]

Trinity is today a large (roughly 8,500 members), predominantly African-American church. When Dr. Otis Moss III became its senior pastor in 2008, Trinity had been put in the national spotlight as the home church of soon-to-be President Barack Obama. In its relatively short history (it was founded in the Civil Rights era of the 1960s), Trinity had become a church that took its black, Christian identity seriously. How do the histories of slavery and racism, and the experiences of black people as abused and shamed, make a difference for the way church is performed? It was clear that the values and expressive forms of mainline, white, middle-class America were not up to the task, since these values, and the economic/political frameworks they put

---

77 Kendall Vanderslice describes some of these developments in "Farminaries," in *Christianity Today*, January 25, 2018 (www.christianitytoday.com/ct/2018/january-february/farminaries .html).
78 I am grateful to Monica and Otis Moss for sharing with me the stories of their life and ministry. My account is derived from personal conversation and communication.

in place, were, in large part, responsible for black poverty, marginalization, and incarceration.

It isn't obvious that Otis should make food ministry, and all it entails, central to his work as pastor. Though his grandfather was a sharecropper in Georgia, Otis is not a farmer, nor did he grow up on a farm.[79] Moreover, it is a well-known fact that the American environmental movement, and its more recent food emphases, are mostly white affairs.[80] His father, Otis Moss, Jr., however, was a well-known Cleveland pastor who had made health care a vital part of his ministry. And he married Monica, who did have a rural upbringing. Monica spent considerable time on a farm in Virginia where she helped things grow and came to appreciate the importance of nutritious and wholesome food. When Otis and Monica began their married life together, they ate a mostly vegan diet. They believed a plant diet was healthiest, and they were concerned about the abuse of animals in today's industrial agriculture. Monica knew what it was like to raise animals humanely, which is why she is not legalistic about meat consumption. But she also knew that they felt better when they ate mostly plants. And the food tasted really good.

A person visiting Trinity United Church will encounter a farmer's market within the church building and a green roof on top. The farmer's market is important because it connects parishioners (right after a worship service) with (mostly) African-American farmers, thereby providing parishioners with good food and farmers with financial support. Otis and Monica view the market as an education center where people can learn how to prepare and cook the fresh food they buy. They make smoothies because "smoothies make smiles!" The money earned at the farmer's market pays for other

---

[79] The story of Will Allen, founder of Growing Power and MacArthur Genius Award recipient, is instructive. The son of a sharecropper, the last thing Allen wanted was to do the hard work of growing food, that is, the work of former slaves and sharecroppers. What Allen discovered, however, is that growing food together in community is a powerful way to empower black youth, revitalize communities, and promote personal health. What Allen has shown is that growing and eating food together fosters healing and justice in our world. See Allen's book (with Charles Wilson) *The Good Food Revolution: Growing Healthy Food, People, and Communities* (New York: Penguin Books, 2012). For a description of how racism has affected agriculture in America, and how it is being addressed by farmers of color, see Natasha Bowens's *The Color of Food: Stories of Race, Resilience, and Farming* (Gabriola Island, BC: New Society Publishers, 2015).

[80] See Amanda J. Baugh's *God and the Green Divide: Religious Environmentalism in Black and White* (Berkeley: University of California Press, 2017) for a discussion of the white/black environmental divide as it has been worked out in Chicago's faith communities. For a broader look at race as it relates to food justice concerns, see *Cultivating Food Justice: Race, Class, and Sustainability*, ed. Alison Hope Alkon and Julian Agyeman (Cambridge, MA: The MIT Press, 2011).

ventures, like Big Mama's House, a ministry in which young and old people, along with folks from the community and area churches, come together to share basic skills like canning, sewing, and repair work and construction. Children are asked to invite adults to dinner at church so that intergenerational understanding can grow. The point is to engage people in ministries of touch so they can feel in a much more profound and practical manner what the creation and maintenance of connections require. The point is to help people become citizens who take responsibility for and pride in their neighborhood.

If you ask Monica, she will tell you that fresh, healthy food is a civil rights issue. Why? Because access to clean, nutritious food is the key to good health. Everyone deserves good and wholesome food, just as everyone deserves access to tables that foster connection and togetherness. And it is central to Christian life because the gospel is all about God's embodiment in the world for the purposes of the world's healing and nutrition, what in traditional theological language is described as the way of salvation. Scripture teaches Christians to take care of each other's bodies because that is precisely what Jesus did in his ministries. The hard work is to teach people to think about their faith in a more embodied way in which a farmer's market and community kitchen are simply obvious.

As Monica sees it, an exploration of Jesus and food naturally go together, because so many of Jesus' teachings and lessons took place during the sharing of food. Eating food together isn't simply *illustrative* of ministry but is instead its *enactment*. It is important that when Jesus (in Matthew 26:26) took bread, gave thanks, and then gave it to his disciples to eat, this happened while they were already eating. Communion happens in the very action of food fellowship. It isn't a spectator sideshow that is otherwise unconnected with daily life.

The work is ongoing, and it is difficult. Like Christians in other congregations, so-called "green initiatives" are often met with considerable suspicion (at Trinity some members thought initially that the green roof was to put in place a putting green). This is why Otis and Monica see themselves to be in this work for the long haul. With members of the congregation, they now have ambitious plans to expand and transform Trinity's physical plant to make their church a place where the health and flourishing of Chicago's South Side, a place where food insecurity and inadequate housing are still major concerns, can be the priority.

One way Trinity plans to do this is through the construction of Imani Village.[81] In this ambitious project, the church is moving well past the stage

---

[81] For a description of this project's scope and its many dimensions, see www.imanivillage.com/ July 12, 2018.

of recycling paper and cups, and adopting eco-cleaning supplies, to the design and construction of spaces that will facilitate healthy bodies through preventative health care, good eating, and shared work. The village includes multiple components, including: an education and youth development center, an organic community garden, an urban farming and agricultural center, a National Collegiate Athletic Association (NCAA) certified sports center, sustainable housing, a retail center, and a community health center. This is a striking vision that demonstrates what is possible when people of faith understand that the many dimensions of eating can be a witness to the kingdom of God. To eat well together, and in ways that reflect the love of God, requires a different way of being in the world, a way of being in which physical spaces need to be created that facilitate love and health rather than division and sickness.

It is tempting to see a project like Imani Village as a fringe ministry, and as something that only a few talented, courageous people like the Mosses can pull off. This is a mistake. Imani Village, when properly understood, goes to the core of what a church essentially is: a community of people inspired and nurtured by the Eucharist and committed to being a source of nurture to the neighborhoods in which they live. Imani Village is one creative response to what has always been the call of the church, namely "to demonstrate love by seeking justice for the poor." In this response, they are following the creative lead of the early church as reflected in the book of Acts.

We should not be surprised that our inspiration, and much of our necessary instruction, for the work of food justice will come from African-American leaders and churches. Along with migrant farmworkers and refugees from around the world, these are people who have experienced how a global economy, and food policies in particular, often works to degrade people and land alike. Those seeking a more just, merciful, celebratory food system, and a more honest theology of eating, need to taste the world from their position in society. As the parable of the Great Dinner in Luke 14 reminds us, it is not the elites who choose to dine with God. It is the poor and those at the margins who have the sense to accept and appreciate the significance of God's hospitality. It is from them that dominant cultures have much to learn.

7

ॐ

Saying Grace

Nothing before God belongs to us as our own, if not our ability to say *thank you*. What may appear as the most tenuous, the most slender of all possibilities is in truth the highest and most extensive: the praise that *responds* to the divine giving is the essence of human speech. It is in speech that the gift is received, and that we can give something of our own, in other words ourselves.[1]

Thanksgiving is the power that transforms desire and satisfaction, love and possession, into life, that fulfills everything in the world, given to us by God, into knowledge of God and communion with him.[2]

The world will be lifted, as it was always meant to be lifted, by the priestly love of man. What Christ has done is to take our broken priesthood into His and make it strong again ... It will be precisely because we loved Jerusalem enough to bear it in our bones that its textures will ascend when we rise; it will be because our eyes have relished the earth that the color of its countries will compel our hearts forever. The bread and the pastry, the cheeses, the wine, and the songs go into the Supper of the Lamb because we do: It is our love that brings the City home.[3]

To say grace or offer a benediction of thanksgiving over a meal is among the highest and most honest expressions of our humanity. In this act we show that we are committed to taking a humble place within the world among each other and before God, and demonstrate that we do not take our place and sustenance for granted. Here, around a table and before witnesses, we testify to the experience of life as a precious gift to be received and given again. We acknowledge that we do not and cannot live alone but are the beneficiaries of the kindnesses and mysteries of grace upon grace. In grateful

[1] Jean-Louis Chrétien, *The Ark of Speech* (London: Routledge, 2004), 123.
[2] Schmemann, *The Eucharist*, 188–189.   [3] Capon, *The Supper of the Lamb*, 190.

speech and action, we seek to be worthy of and faithful to gifts of life that exceed our imagining and comprehension.

The practice of thanksgiving defines people as creatures who not only ingest and digest their food but relish it as the medium of life and love. When eating is enfolded within the language and grammar of grace, and when food itself is experienced as the delectable manifestation of God's abounding and incomprehensible love, then the opportunity exists for people to dine with God as "the fountain of true delight." To eat is to see, smell, touch, and taste God's provisioning care. When people commune with God the very sensation of life is transformed, so that they are equipped "to see what is most beautiful, to hear what is most harmonious, to smell what is most fragrant, to taste what is most sweet, and to embrace what is most delightful."[4] People's perceptive and receptive faculties are renewed so that the world and its creatures are met as the place of God's communion with creation.[5] When people say grace with their entire being, express it honestly and with considered appreciation for its deep theological and practical significance, they participate, however imperfectly, in the paradise of God.[6]

To claim that people are made in the image of God is to believe that we are created to commune and converse with God as the creating and sustaining Word of life. Recall Nicholas Lash's formulation: "God's utterance

[4] Saint Bonaventure, *The Journey of the Mind to God*, trans. Philotheus Boehner (Indianapolis: Hackett, 1956), 24. Bonaventure refers to God as "the fountain of true delight" on p. 14.

[5] The extent and intimacy of creation's communion with God was most powerfully and daringly (since it verged on pantheism) expressed in the writing of the ninth-century Irish theologian John Scotus Eriugena, who said in *Periphyseon* III, 678D: "We ought not to understand God and the creature as two things distinct from one another, but as one and the same. For the creature is subsisting in God: and God, manifesting Himself, in a marvelous and ineffable manner is created in the creature, the invisible making Himself visible and the incomprehensible comprehensible, and the hidden revealed ... and creating all things He is created in all things and making all things is made in all things ... and He becomes all things in all things" (quoted in John Manoussakis's *God after Metaphysics* [Bloomington: Indiana University Press, 2007], 33). Eriugena's claim was made more precise by the fourteenth-century Byzantine Father Gregory Palamas, who insisted that God remains unexhausted and fundamentally unknown while being revealed in creation. What creatures see revealed in creation is not God's eternal essence but God's "energies" or effective and sustaining power. The eternal, Triune God is present in these energies but is not limited to them. See his exposition in *The Triads, III* in *Gregory Palamas*, ed. John Meyendorff (Mahwah: Paulist Press, 1983), 93–111.

[6] Schmemann writes: "thanksgiving is the experience of paradise ... paradise is the primordial state of man and all creation, our state before the fall ... and our state upon our salvation by Christ ... Paradise is, in other words, the *beginning* and the *end*, to which is oriented and through which is defined and determined the entire life of man and in him of all creation" (*The Eucharist*, 174).

lovingly gives life; gives all life, all unfailing freshness; gives only life, and peace, and love, and beauty, harmony and joy. And the life God gives is nothing other, nothing less, than God's own self. Life is God, given."[7] What Lash is describing here is the ancient understanding that God has always already been present to the whole creation, communicating with it from within and from without as the form of each creature's life-giving principle or logos. Writing in the fourth century, St. Athanasius argued that no part of creation is ever without Jesus as the eternal Word of God. "The Self-revealing of the Word is in every dimension – above, in creation; below, in the Incarnation; in the depth, in Hades; in the breadth, throughout the world. All things have been filled with the knowledge of God."[8] Far from being a deistic god who creates the world and then exits, the God revealed in the incarnation of Christ has always been the God of relationship, the God who desires to be known and be in communion. As members of creation, created and sustained by this communing God, and carrying within us a divine, animating logos, we are made to know and be in relationship with God as the source of our life.

To meet and receive life deeply, to be open to its mysterious and fresh vitality, is also to greet God as the incomprehensible Life within life (recall John's description of the Word as the life and light of the world in 1:4). Genuine and deep communion, what we might also call an intimate taste for life, is humanity's deepest need and hunger. We want to know how our individual lives matter, and connect to what is real and of eternal value. Nothing in creation, however, can fully or truly satisfy this hunger because whatever food item we eat is not the source of its own life but always points beyond itself to gifts of nurture that have first fed it. Creation is mortal and marked by need. Though expressing God's power, it is not itself divine or worthy of our worship and praise.

If we want to know and experience the *liveliness* of life and the *loveliness* of the love that sustains it, we must move *through* (not around) creation to its Creator. Eating is among the most intimate, practical, and regular ways we know for moving through creation. This makes eating, especially the

---

[7]   Lash, *Believing Three Ways in the One God*, 104.

[8]   Athanasius, *On the Incarnation*, §16 (Crestwood, NY: St. Vladimir's Seminary Press, 1977), 44. Athanasius describes the incarnate Word as present everywhere, ordering, directing, and giving life to all things, yet being contained by none, because in Himself the Word is Uncontained, "existing solely in His Father" (§17, 45). We should not be surprised by this, he says, because the principle of the incarnation itself, the idea that the eternal Word could enter into a specific body (Jesus of Nazareth), entails its entrance into the body of the universe (§41, 76).

eating we do together, a profoundly theological matter. Gathered at a table and prepared with an appropriate focus and sensitivity, we have the opportunity to approach and participate in the life of God. We have the opportunity to voice our thanksgiving for relationships with each other – earth, plants, animals, and ultimately God – that give us life. Scripture teaches that God meets humanity here and now as "divine love made food, made life for man. God *blesses* everything He creates, and, in biblical language, this means that He makes all creation the sign and means of His presence and wisdom, love and revelation: 'O taste and see that the Lord is good.'"[9] When we return our blessings upon the world, we acknowledge with our mouths that our senses have tasted, smelled, heard, seen, and touched this love. We bear witness as transformed creatures that are now prepared to join hands with God's work of nurture and reconciliation in the world. We commit ourselves to the protection and celebration of gift upon gift.

THE PRACTICE OF DELIGHT

A desire to express gratitude for the world requires that we first sense it as worthy of gratitude. This is no small matter, particularly in a culture prone to ignorance and tempted by atheistic materialism and conspicuous consumption. Why bother saying grace over what we do not know, or over random matter in motion, or products that might make us sick or fat?

In a brief whimsical tale, Robert Farrar Capon described how Satan once enlisted his chief tempters to deepen humanity's fall. A junior tempter rose to the occasion, suggesting that a focus on offenses against God and neighbor was a misguided approach. A more successful strategy would be to corrupt humanity's relationship with things. The key was to lead people into the stupors of boredom and into the degradations of utilitarian calculation so they would find the creatures and gifts of this world as uninteresting and uncherished things, as objects of no special significance or worth. In other words, people would gradually learn to forget about God entirely if they could be trained to think that the world is a collection of random, pointless facts rather than the site of God's creation, and that every created thing is only an object and not also an expression of God's sustaining Word. "As long as man dealt with real substances, he would himself tend to remain substantial. What was needed, therefore, was a program to deprive man of *things* . . . Above all, the door of delight must remain firmly closed."[10]

---

[9] Schmemann, *For the Life of the World*, 14.   [10] Capon, *The Supper of the Lamb*, 111.

Capon's tale captures a crucial insight: what the world *is*, what it means and how it will be received, is susceptible to manipulation and corruption. Living creatures as well as nonliving things can cease to be expressions of God's love and instead become commodified bits that serve a narrow, perhaps exclusively utilitarian, meaning. People can become exiles in the world in which they live when fellow creatures cease to evoke in them the marvel and delight that marks God's own Sabbath encounter with the world. The experience of delight is indispensable because it opens our minds and hearts so that we can sense creatures in their relationship to God.[11] Participation in God's own delight gives us the framework we need to understand the meaning and significance of the world. It provides the lens through which others appear and come into focus. How we "see" the world determines how it will signify in our speech and how it will be treated: a boor will not name or appreciate a fine meal no matter how lavish or sumptuous it is, just as a lover will pronounce and receive a dish as a feast no matter how scant or plain it is. The practice of delight teaches us to receive and engage the world as the medium of love.

Industrial, fast-food culture often has the effect of turning eaters into boors. Owing to our ignorance about food's ecological and social contexts, food is readily reduced to a fuel or a commodity. A theologically sensitive understanding of food yields a different picture:

> [T]he uniquenesses of creation are the result of continuous creative support, of effective regard by no mean lover. He *likes* onions, therefore they are. The fit, the colors, the smell, the tensions, the tastes, the textures, the lines, the shapes are a response, not to some forgotten decree that there may as well be onions as turnips, but to His present delight – His intimate and immediate joy in all you have seen, and in the thousand wonders you do not even suspect.[12]

What Capon is describing is the first Sabbath sunrise when God looked out onto the freshly made creation and saw reflected back in sensual form the full display of his own love, joy, creativity, playfulness, and curiosity. Nothing in creation had to be. For much of it we can identify no purpose. But all of it remains precious, the expression of divine poetry and the exhibition of a passionate Word. When theologians speak of creation *ex nihilo* they are

---

[11]   David Bentley Hart has argued that the beauty of the triune *perichoresis* is a movement of delight. To know anything of the Trinity will therefore require an epistemology steeped in delight: "it is delight that constitutes creation, and so only delight can comprehend it, see it aright, understand its grammar" (*The Beauty of the Infinite*, 253).

[12]   Capon, *The Supper of the Lamb*, 17.

saying creatures could just as well cease to be at any moment and return to the nothingness from which they came. That creation does not return to nothingness means that it is continually being loved into existence. Speaking of wine, Capon observes, "Wine *is* . . . because it is His very present pleasure to have it so. The creative act is contemporary, intimate, and immediate to each part, parcel and period of the world."[13] For creation to cease to exist God would have to desist from loving, because it is only God's joyful, creative speech and warm, sustaining breath (see Psalm 104) that daily enlivens and maintains each and every creature.

The experience of delight begins when love joins perception. In his commentary on Peter Lombard's *Sentences*, Aquinas wrote "Where love is, there is the eye."[14] What Aquinas is pointing to is the fact that lovers perceive what others cannot. People without love, though having physical eyes, lack the "eye" for deep seeing. Whether out of haste or anxiety, boredom or impatience, they lack the attentiveness and the fidelity to linger and remain with others long enough to be amazed with their presence and astounded by their particularity. This is why nonlovers are rarely true gardeners or good cooks. Love creates the curiosity and intimacy that leads people to experience more fully the integrity and sanctity of life. Love inspires the commitment to remain with the beloved when frustration and impatience come in. Lovers relish and revel in the presence of what is there to be loved. Rather than resting content with an assumption, stereotype or idea they have of something, lovers remain open to the mystery that each creature is.

It is important to underscore that love does not simply lead to familiarity, since familiarity often remains at a surface level of perception. Those that are familiar are also more likely to be taken for granted as already understood. What love accomplishes, particularly the dispossessive love learned in Christian discipleship, is the steadfast devotion that enables the freshness and vitality of their God-given being to surprise and overwhelm expectation. By opening up perception and by leading the perceiver beyond their self – this outward movement being the heart of genuine *eros* and *agape* – perception is

---

[13] Ibid., 85. This is another way of saying that there is nothing necessary about the existence of the world. It is pure gift, the effect of God's unimaginable delight. "Things are precious before they are contributory. It is a false piety that walks through creation looking only for lessons which can be applied somewhere else. To be sure, God remains the greatest good, but, for all that, the world is still good in itself. Indeed, since He does not need it, its whole reason for being must lie in its own goodness; He has no use for it; only delight . . . The world is no disposable ladder to heaven. Earth is not convenient, it is good; it is, by God's design, our lawful love" (86).

[14] Quoted by Josef Pieper in *Happiness and Contemplation* (South Bend, IN: St. Augustine's Press, 1998), 71.

transformed into a hospitable act in which others appear on their own terms. Besides seeking the good of others, lovers are available to what they love. They are, as Paul famously said in his first letter to the Corinthians (13:4–6), patient and kind. They are not resentful, boastful, or irritable. Nor do they insist on their own way. To love another is to let oneself be transformed by what one loves, to become fully open to the world and ourselves as revealed by the beloved. In loving what one sees, or, more precisely, by letting love be the form through which perception happens, the grace of the world begins to appear.[15] Things cease to be merely what we take them or want them to be. They begin to stand in the light of God as the graced and gifted beings that they are. As Josef Pieper puts it, contemplation is the highest form of human happiness because it affords "a direct perception of the presence of God" as "the acting basis of everything that exists."[16]

The love that opens perception also enlarges and deepens our experience of the world. Those who truly love wine, for instance, are not simply those who become drunk by its consumption. They are rather those who are open to the miracle of sunlight, water, plant, and soil transformed into grapes, open to the gift of fermentation and taste, and open to the conviviality of a shared bottle.[17]

> With wine at hand, the good man concerns himself, not with getting drunk, but with *drinking in* all the natural delectabilities of wine: taste, color, bouquet; its manifold graces; the way it complements food and enhances conversation; and its sovereign power to turn evenings into occasions, to lift eating beyond nourishment to conviviality, and to bring the race, for a few hours at least, to that happy state where men are wise and women beautiful, and even one's children begin to look promising.[18]

Given the manifold graces of wine and its ability to elevate life, we should not be surprised that Jesus, fully aware of its potential for abuse, chose it for the meal and the fellowship that testified to his resurrection life.[19]

---

[15] Hans Urs von Balthasar describes faith as "the willingness to let love have its way." See *The Glory of the Lord: A Theological Aesthetics: Volume VII, Theology: The New Covenant*, trans. Brian McNeil (San Francisco: Ignatius Press, 1989), 401.

[16] Pieper, *Happiness and Contemplation*, 78–80.

[17] See Gisela H. Kreglinger's *The Spirituality of Wine* (Grand Rapids: William B. Eerdmans Publishing, Co., 2016) for a wide-ranging exploration of the theological significance of wine production and consumption.

[18] Capon, *The Supper of the Lamb*, 91.

[19] Though water and wine were the most widely consumed beverages in the ancient world, wine was especially significant in religious observance. Among early Christians who did not want their eating together to be linked to pagan religious practices, this was a cause for

In several respects, a culture of delight moves in ways directly contrary to "fast-food" culture. Fast food does not facilitate or encourage contemplation, nor does it promote an affectionate regard for what is eaten. Fast food is an industrial product in which ingredients are chosen because they can be efficiently and profitably grown, readily manipulated and recombined, easily transported and stored, and then mindlessly prepared. It is food that has been cheapened and made as uniform and ubiquitous as possible. In it there is little respect shown for eaters, food providers, cooks, or the animals and plants eaten.[20]

It is the denial of respect and delight or, more commonly, the denial of pleasure that informs the development of "Slow Food" as an international movement. The idea behind Slow Food is that people will learn to care about food (and the ecosystems, animals, and farming/cooking cultures that make it possible) and its eaters when they take the time to be intentional and knowledgeable about its growth, production, preparation, and consumption. Its central complaint and worry is that people are not taking the time or devoting the proper amount of attention necessary to make sure that fields, waters, plants, animals, and people are appropriately understood, cared for, and celebrated. Though Slow Food is often caricatured as a highbrow, high-income movement that relishes exotic cuisine, rare breeds, heirloom plants, and leisurely meals, what defenders of the movement say they are really after is the preservation of communal habits that elevate care and conviviality over the destruction and alienation that fast-food culture promotes, habits that have long been central to indigenous cultures and peasant populations around the world. Slow Food eaters believe that the way to save the rare species of plants and animals is to care for them, and then eat them in a spirit that celebrates their unique life. The way to rescue dining from mere fuel consumption is to gather people in gardens, in kitchens, and around a table so that their perceptive awareness of food can open more fully to its delectable character.

Carlo Petrini, widely acknowledged as the founder of Slow Food, argues that what is at stake in this movement is the quality of all life. Industrial food systems and fast-food eating practices degrade life, first by gradually compromising or destroying the ecosystems all creatures need to live, and second by turning eaters into filling stations who no longer have a sense of food as a

---

concern. In some cases it resulted in a Eucharistic meal that served water or milk, or no cup at all. See McGowan, *Ascetic Eucharists*.

[20] For a treatment of the many ecological and cultural dimensions of fast food, see Schlosser, *Fast Food Nation*.

precious and delectable gift. What is needed, he says, is a new agriculture, a new culture of the land, and a new culture of eaters prepared to take responsibility for the health of animals, plants, and natural processes. What is needed is a new gastronomy that combines in one synoptic vision the pleasures of eating together, the right of healthy food and clean water for everyone, the right of farmers to grow the food that is suitable and locally adapted to specific geographical regions, the requirement to protect and maintain ecosystem processes, and the values of hospitality.[21]

Slow Food merits theological consideration because it can give expression to God's desire that people share in his delight in creation. When we remember that God's act of creating the world is also God's commitment to be in relationship with it, and remember that the food we eat bears the imprint of a divine Logos who loves and cherishes all creatures, then our careful and attentive eating can be the occasion to share in God's peaceful and joyful Triune life. Insofar as people grow food with specific attention to the health and contentment of plants and animals, and then eat with the intention of honoring food and common life as a gift to be received, nurtured, and shared, food will look, smell, touch, and taste different. It will cease to be merely fuel. It will become a sacrament, a sign of food's origin and end in God.[22]

When church members eat Eucharistically and become the "Slow Church" that is committed to cherishing God's gifts, each bite will register as a unique taste and a specific creation that bears the marks of God's particular joy in its being.[23] To be a refined and discipled eater, one who takes delight in what is eaten, is not simply to have exquisite or expensive tastes. It is rather to know and appreciate what Duns Scotus called the *haecceitas* or remarkable "thisness" of every created being.[24] It is to savor

---

[21] Carlo Petrini has authored several books. *Slow Food Nation* is particularly helpful in drawing out the cultural and agricultural commitments of the Slow Food movement.

[22] In *Living in God's Creation: Orthodox Perspectives on Ecology* (Crestwood, NY: St. Vladimir's Seminary Press, 2009), Elizabeth Theokritoff summarizes the meaning of the sacramental quality of things as the referring of them to their ultimate significance in God: "Matter used in a sacrament is not a separate category of matter, sacred as opposed to profane; it could better be described as matter unveiled, revealing to us the true Godwardness – the *sacramental quality* – of things we use and handle every day" (186).

[23] C. Christopher Smith and John Pattison have developed the idea in fruitful ways in *Slow Church: Cultivating Community in the Patient Way of Jesus* (Downer's Grove, IL: Inter-Varsity Press, 2014).

[24] For an excellent discussion of Scotus's teaching and its development in the poet Gerard Manley Hopkins, see Hans Urs von Balthasar, *The Glory of the Lord: A Theological Aesthetics: Volume. III, Lay Styles* (San Francisco: Ignatius Press, 1986), 353–399.

the life-giving logos in each thing, and then bear witness to God's continuous working in the world.

Appreciation of this sort takes time to develop. The taste that savors the world cannot be rushed. It requires a Sabbath sensibility that Eucharistic communities are uniquely positioned to promote and advance. Perceived, received, and understood as the unique creation of God, food, even an unassuming egg can be the source of unending delight.[25]

UNDERMINING DELIGHT

If the experience of delight presupposes a sustained, patient, sympathetic, and affectionate embrace of the world, then the decline of delight will be preceded by the erosion of the practical conditions that make such an embrace possible. What trends and practices in culture work to undermine a loving regard for creatures and things, and how have these trends and practices contributed to a situation in which relatively few people bow their heads before raising their forks? To answer these questions, we can begin by observing how modern cultures tend to reduce the world to a spectacle.

The age of the spectacle is particularly significant in this context because it transforms both the perceiver and how the world is perceived. Because so few people have direct and regular involvement with the sources of their livelihood, it is inevitable that the world will be experienced in superficial and ephemeral ways. In the age of the spectacle, things are lifted out of their ecological and cultural contexts so they can be re-presented in fairly stylized ways. Video screens and marketing campaigns mediate our understanding of the world. Cash or credit cards broker the transactions.

Writing about the culture of the spectacle, Guy Debord observed that what people are purchasing and consuming are images and fantasies of

[25] Capon asks us to consider an egg in the following way: "Forget for the moment the fantastic intricacy of the mechanism from which all higher forms of life spring. Disregard, too, the wonder of its parts, its divisions, and its tremendous *complications*. Omit, finally, all other eggs but one: no frogs' eggs, ducks' eggs, robins' eggs, or goose eggs; no snake eggs, no dinosaur eggs, no platypus eggs, no roe; no *ova* of any sort or kind but the eggs of the common hen. And what have you done? You have renounced a whole world only to gain a dozen in its place ... [I]n our priestly attention to the fruit of the barnyard ... we have discovered what no other animal will ever know. What will the egg not do? It will scramble, boil, bake, or fry – or go down raw if you have the stomach for it – and sustain and delight you in the bargain. And that is only the start of the prologue of the introduction. It will thicken sauces, raise dough, explode into a soufflé, or garnish your soup. It can be taken with sugar and whisky, or with salt and red pepper; and still you have hardly begun. Omelets are more numerous than the generations of the human race" (*An Offering of Uncles* [1967] in *The Romance of the Word* [Grand Rapids: Eerdmans, 1995], 97).

things. Because images are the products of (mostly) unknown corporate interests – how many people really know where food products come from or how they are processed? – both things and the people who purchase them are increasingly alienated from the life contexts that make them possible. Rather than identifying with the animal or field, one identifies with a brand.[26] In the separation of consumption from production, and in the erosion of an individual's creative participation in the means of life, people invariably become passive and bored, and thus also the pawns of competing economic and power interests.[27] "Rather than venting anger against exploitation and injustice, the working class is distracted and mollified by new cultural production, social services, and wage increases. In consumer capitalism, the working classes abandon the union hall for the shopping mall and celebrate the system that fuels the desires that it ultimately cannot satisfy."[28]

Technological devices and media of varying kinds – televisions, smartphones, computer screens, iPads, and digital recorders – have greatly facilitated the alienation of people from the sources of life. This separation has prompted postmodern theorists like Jean Baudrillard to proclaim the death of the real and the ubiquity of the hyperreal. Once things are rendered abstract and reduced to their image or sign value, a process Baudrillard termed "simulation," something like an objective world disappears. Virtual or simulated events take the place of real life or, more accurately, the category "real life" disappears behind layer after layer of simulacra:

---

[26] Food companies spend billions of dollars each year in product design, packaging, and promotion. They lobby regulatory bodies and educational institutions to make sure their beverage or snack is the one chosen. The books detailing how the food industry shapes consumer desire and determines food policies grow daily. A landmark work is Marion Nestle's *Food Politics: How the Food Industry Influences Nutrition and Health*, rev. edition (Berkeley: University of California Press, 2007). See also Michele Simon's *Appetite for Profit: How the Food Industry Undermines Our Health and How to Fight Back* (New York: Nation Books, 2006).

[27] In "Society of the Spectacle," Debord writes: "The spectacle presents itself as something enormously positive, indisputable and inaccessible. It says nothing more than 'whatever appears is good, and whatever is good appears.' The attitude it requires in principle is this passive acceptance, which in fact it has already obtained by its method of appearing without reply, by its monopoly of appearance ... The spectacle subjugates living men to itself to the extent that the economy has subjugated them. It is no more than the economy developing itself for itself" (Guy Debord, *Society of the Spectacle and Other Films* [London: Rebel Press, 1992], 65). The fact that so many people ask so few questions about the food they eat suggests a profound, though clearly unreflective, trust that whatever product is marketed as food must be good: "whatever appears is good, and whatever good appears."

[28] Steven Best and Douglas Kellner, *The Postmodern Turn* (New York: Guilford Press, 1997), 85.

Freed from any stable relationship with a signified, where the sign structure points to a distinct referent in the world, the signifier becomes its own referent, and this autonomization becomes the basis for semiological domination. The commodity form is eclipsed by the "sign form" and subsequently "bears no relation to any reality whatever: it is its own pure simulacrum." Signification is now radically relativized, and anything can pass as "meaning" or "reality."[29]

In a world of simulacra, creatures and things lose their depth. Reality is depleted by industrial processing, digital manipulation, the proliferation of images and fantasies, and the endless variations on style. The danger is that people will learn to seek out and eat the image, mostly oblivious to the food they are in fact consuming.[30]

The simulation so far described is not confined to the appearance and the purchase of food. It can also be seen in the domain of cooking. In his essay "Out of the Kitchen, onto the Couch," Michael Pollan describes how the average American spends less than thirty minutes per day on food preparation (a reduction by half in the last forty years), while at the same time showing considerable interest in the great variety of cooking shows now available on cable TV's Food Network. People who spend an hour watching programs like *Top Chef* also profess they do not have time to cook.

This is a noteworthy development, particularly when we recognize that cooking is one of the fundamental activities that situate and define people as human beings. Through cooking people learn to understand their relation to the material world. They discover what is edible, where and how it is grown, what is susceptible to particular cooking techniques, and what food goes well with another. They learn how flavor and taste are often secrets hidden within raw foods, secrets that can only be coaxed out with the proper inducement. They participate in the age-old activity that separates humans who can cook and dine from beasts who can only grasp and chew. To cook, as the anthropologist Claude Lévi-Strauss once famously put it, is to transform nature into culture and wildness into forms of domesticity. It is to take raw, plain ingredients and transform them into something nutritious, tasty, and

---

[29]   Ibid., 99.

[30]   In "The Work of Art in the Age of Mechanical Reproduction" (in *Illuminations: Essays and Reflections* [New York: Schocken Books, 1968]) Walter Benjamin famously described the loss of a thing's "aura," the quality that makes a thing unique and resonant with meaning and value, when it is lifted out of its time and place context. Benjamin was referring to art objects that are mass-produced, but one could also speak similarly with respect to food. A cake made uniformly and in multiple copies by a machine is different than a cake crafted by hand by a chef.

delectable. Through cooking, and in a manner much like gardening, we move deeply and knowledgably into the world. If our cooking is done with locally grown ingredients and follows local customs (think here, for instance, of Cajun culture and cuisine), we move from an experience of land in general (*terre*) to *terroir*, an experience in which the unique flavors of a region, climate, and production technique make their way into our eating, speaking, sharing, and imagining a world.

When cooking is transformed into a spectator sport, a person's relationship to food and the world undergoes a profound transformation. To see how this might be so, Pollan reminds us that 100 years ago if a person wanted to eat chicken they would have likely raised it, killed it, plucked and gutted it, and then decided how it would be cooked. Each act along the way would have involved multiple intelligences and sensitivities. To watch a chicken being cooked on a TV show, however, means that one can enjoy the display of cooking prowess and technique without having to touch chicken flesh or even taste it (it is enough, for some, simply to know that it is tasty to someone else!). TV cooking shows, for the most part, are not about teaching people how to cook or to think deeply about the gardening/farming realities that sustain a kitchen pantry. Their target audience is people who love to eat rather than people who love to cook. Their aim is to entertain – hence the high-octane, competitive character of many of them, and the absence of recipes or explanation of practical techniques – rather than to educate.

> These shows move so fast, in such a blur of flashing knives, frantic pantry raids and more sheer fire than you can ever want to see in your own kitchen ... The skills celebrated on the Food Network in prime time are precisely the skills necessary to succeed on the Food Network in prime time. They will come in handy nowhere else on God's green earth.[31]

This is to say that they will also be skills that further separate people from a kitchen and instead send them to a microwave or restaurant.

Studies have shown that obesity rates are inversely correlated to the amount of cooking people do at home. People would be healthier if they cooked more, ate out less, and purchased fewer packaged, prepared foods. But this is precisely what the Food Network does not want to see happen. It

---

[31]   Michael Pollan, "Out of the Kitchen, onto the Couch: How American Cooking Became a Spectator Sport, and What We Lost along the Way," *New York Times Magazine*, August 2, 2009, 31. Pollan has elaborated on many of these themes in *Cooked: A Natural History of Transformation* (New York: Penguin Books, 2013).

would be a financial disaster for TV shows if people were inspired to get up and cook. This is why the advertisements accompanying cooking shows promote prepared, convenience foods that can be purchased and prepared with the push of a microwave button. "Buying, not making, is what cooking shows are mostly now about – that and, increasingly, cooking shows themselves: the whole self-perpetuating spectacle of competition, success, and celebrity."[32]

The transformation of food and cooking into a spectacle means that it is much more difficult to experience food as a precious gift and as God's delight. Though food may appear tasty, what is savored is not the food itself or the divine care embedded in it but a commodity made possible by image and taste producers.[33] Rather than being drawn into the world and unto God as the source of its life, eaters are continually bounced between competing brands and images of food. Because so few people are directly involved in the growth of food and its preparation, much of our food experience is highly mediated by food industry professionals. As the consumers of images, eaters are hardly in the position to see or understand the destruction and distortion that happen to the sources of life on their way to becoming stylized products.

MOVING INTO GRATITUDE

It has never been easy to say grace. Though people may be familiar with traditional or stock phrases, the reality is that these formulas often become merely formulaic. Saying grace, if it is authentic and not simply ornamental, is the expression of an inspired, faithful life and a reoriented desire, and so is something that must be worked out and practiced in the diverse dimensions of daily life. Said properly, it has the potential to redefine humanity by refocusing our imaginations and redirecting practices according to the graced character of the world. Saying grace turns people's attention and hearts to a world appreciated as gift and blessing. When we daily offer a benediction on the costly miracle of life, we bear witness to a wide-ranging set of intellectual, emotional, and practical dispositions that aim to receive the members of creation in a distinct, life-honoring way. What does this way look like, presuppose, and entail?

---

[32] Ibid., 35.
[33] It bears noting that many of the flavors in food today are artificial, coming not from the foods themselves but from flavor factories that process chemical compounds into highly enticing aromas and tastes. Artificial flavoring has become necessary because the industrial processing and storage techniques associated with many foods render them nutritionally bankrupt and devoid of taste.

At the heart of a grace-saying act there is the expression of thanksgiving. Though easily reducible to the quick word "thanks," thanksgiving is a deep and expansive gesture that has the effect of taking people beyond themselves, leading them into the rich mystery of the world. To be genuinely thankful presupposes that we have made some effort to appreciate and know what we are thankful for, having devoted considerable effort to recognizing the great diversity of gifts that intersect and feed into our living. At root, when we offer thanks for fellow creatures we acknowledge that without them we could not be, let alone thrive. We confess that our health and happiness are entirely dependent on their well-being and integrity, and that we have not always served them well. We demonstrate the basic knowledge that we belong to the soil, to animals, and to each other, and then see in our belonging a need for humility, responsibility, and celebration. Grateful people understand that they cannot be thankful for others if they are at the same time knowingly engaged in their destruction. The thankful, hospitable word that *carries* the world within it – "Thank you God for these tortillas and this salsa, these friends and this guest!" – also *cares* for what it carries.

To say grace, to speak our gratitude to God before others, means that speaking is one of our primary means for bearing witness to the world as the gift of God. Through speech we are invited to take up a hospitable relation to the world, a relation in which we respond to the sanctity of God's world by carrying that world in our mouths not only as food consumed but as a praise expressed. When we speak well and with a desire for precision and honesty, what we say clarifies and honors the world that inspires us to speak in the first place. Speech opens a space in which the world can be received, carried, and offered to others and to God. When we appreciate that God's speaking of the world into existence was a hospitable act that made room for creatures to be, then it follows that human speech reaches its pinnacle when it participates in this hospitality by giving thanks for the gifts of others and by giving praise to the One who calls forth life and speech.[34]

To carry the world responsibly within one's speech is a difficult and exacting task because it presupposes that one has been faithful and just to the world one attempts to carry. It would be unfaithful, for instance, to

---

[34] Jean-Louis Chrétien summarizes these themes elegantly when he writes: "In its essence, the speech of praise is a hospitable speech, since it first had a hospitable gaze: it gives voice within itself to the polyphony of the world. Far from surveying what it sings from a remote height, it allows itself to be moved, affected by it. Human speech alone forms the link in which the praise of God for his creatures and the praise of God by his creatures meld together into one single hymn" (*The Ark of Speech*, 139).

misrepresent others in one's speech, or to give voice to them in such a way that they or others would not recognize themselves there. The key is to work so we do not deflect or get in the way of hearers catching a glimpse of the integrity of those we present in our speaking. The problem with a consumerist relation to things is that the world, insofar as it is reduced to the level of a commodity, is made to fit a marketing plan or advertising slogan.

The point is not to stop consuming, since people need to eat and use the world, but to resist the culture that would have us see the point of things as residing in their being sold and then consumed by us. It is to resist market-driven enticements that train people to be ungrateful because they do not have the latest, improved product or do not fit the current, always changing, style.

One way to move into gratitude would be to follow the practice of the Shakers who, before commencing to eat, paused in silence to reflect on what they were about to eat and what they were about to do by eating it. This mindful practice is valuable because it calms and focuses the minds of people who are normally preoccupied with matters other than food. One of the great obstacles to knowing the world with depth and insight is the anxiety or arrogance within the mind that clouds and distorts whatever it comes into contact with. By becoming silent, minds can be opened up and made attentive to the world. In this silence the possibility exists that food and eating will emerge as utterly fundamental and as worthy of our consideration and blessing. Before the world can enter in and be carried by speech, we must first be stilled so that the presence and voices of others (their need, potential, and integrity) can be felt and heard.

This Shaker practice, however, presupposes a world quite unlike our own. Living on intimate and practical terms with the sources of life (food, fiber, and energy), Shakers had a much clearer sense of the gifted character of life. Their motto "hands to work, hearts to God" inspired a practical form of life in which the patterns of daily work, when done at their best, moved fairly seamlessly into acts of gratitude and praise. Praise can be work's accompaniment if it is inspired by God's own work in the world, and if it is attentive to the divine Logos in things that leads them to life. To witness the miracles of animal birth and fresh fruit, to know that one's toil assisted this miracle, and then to taste it in one's own cooking and eating, made the expressions of gratitude and praise more natural. Much of what Shakers made and how they made it reflected the sense that life is about learning to receive from each other and from God gifts of food, energy, ingenuity, time, music, and art.

One way to think about what the Shakers were doing is to see their work as a response to the biblical command to "till and keep" God's garden world.

As several of the early church fathers understood this, tilling was never simply about growing things. Tilling has a double meaning: by working the garden people also learn to work on themselves so that through their work they can be brought more closely to an awareness of God in their midst, and then make the commitment to participate in God's beauty- and goodness-building ways in the world.[35] In other words, work is ultimately to be about a finer attunement to the world as the place of God's sustaining presence. With an awareness of God and with an appreciation for God's intention that creatures be whole and at peace, people's *use* of the world can be transformed so that the gifts of life are better cherished, nurtured, and shared.

Work of this sort stands in marked contrast to much of the work that characterizes today's industrial and global economy. For many people work is either of a menial or highly specialized sort, making it very difficult for them to see how what they do fits within a larger, life-giving and meaningful whole. It is often temporary, vulnerable, and highly movable, subject to the vicissitudes and risk-taking of corporations that are global in their reach and ambition.[36] What is done is often done for an unknown boss, serving aims that are not clearly understood or visibly realized so that workers can appreciate the effects (whether for good or ill) of those aims.

Thinking more specifically of the work connected to agricultural and food production, we need to acknowledge how much of it is despised by today's eaters. Its performance has thus fallen upon an underclass or upon (legal and illegal) immigrants and migrants. These workers, many of whom are "recruited" from around the globe, are regularly underpaid and routinely abused, scorned, ignored, or simply forgotten.[37] Agricultural and gardening work, the Godly work that nurtures the world and nourishes its eaters, has come to be viewed by us as menial and trivial, and so unworthy of respect or honor. This is a deeply troubling development because it indicates that we

[35]   John of Damascus claimed that God's invitation to Adam and Eve to eat from every tree meant that God could be tasted as the One who is "all in all." John imagines God to be saying, "Through all things, ascend to me the Creator; from every tree harvest one fruit, namely me who am the life. Let all things bear the fruit of life for you: make participation in me the stuff of your existence" (quoted in Theokritoff, *Living in God's Creation*, 84).

[36]   For a very helpful analysis of this development, see Zygmunt Bauman's *Globalization: The Human Consequences* (New York: Columbia University Press, 1998) and *Liquid Modernity* (Cambridge: Polity, 2000), especially chapter 4.

[37]   See Daniel Rothenberg's *With These Hands: The Hidden World of Migrant Farmworkers Today* (Berkeley: University of California Press, 2000); *The Human Cost of Food: Farmworkers' Lives, Labor, and Advocacy*, ed. Charles D. Thompson, Jr., and Melinda F. Wiggins (Austin: University of Texas Press, 2002); John Bowe's *Nobodies: Modern American Slave Labor and the Dark Side of the New Global Economy* (New York: Random, 2007); and David K. Shipler's *The Working Poor: Invisible in America* (New York: Viking, 2004).

will not put our energy and attention toward healthy ecosystems or convivial food production work. It is also an indication of spiritual malfunction because thanksgiving for food cannot be genuine or honest if we despise the work that brings it to the table.

It is important to understand the changing contexts of work because how one works either opens or closes the possibility for genuine gratitude. In his essay "Going to Work," Wendell Berry describes how much of the work performed today insulates people from the living contexts upon which their work depends.[38] Work happens in enclosures that prevent workers from appreciating the sources and the effects of their living. Eventually they begin to think they are working nowhere or anywhere, working in the "non-places" Augé described. Berry's point, however, is that work always does happen in a place, even if people are not aware of it. Work draws its inspiration and its resources from a particular place – a specific forest, watershed, field, community – just as it has effects and influence on particular neighborhoods and regions. Though often performed in offices and cubicles, or on assembly lines or airplanes, work has a context that invariably draws from and has effects upon a wider world. Though scripted and practiced in terms of specialties, the products and effects of work have a range that exceeds professional or market compartmentalization.

In Berry's view, it is essential that workers think deeply about *who* and *where* they are as they work. Work is a form of catechesis that trains us to see and relate to the world in particular sorts of ways. We need to question what we have been taught about the ends and goals of work and be clear about the affections and sympathies we bring to our work. We need to consider how the work we perform either nurtures or violates the integrity of the places in which our work has effects, and carefully note if what we do contributes to the overall health of communities and regions. To do all of this will require levels of attention and formation that are difficult to find or cultivate in today's fast-paced, far-flung, often unseen work environment. Attention and formation are fundamental because without them we will not be able to *see* or appreciate work as a more or less faithful response to the gifts of life. We will not be able to *carry* the world in grateful speech because the world we work in has been overlooked, degraded, or destroyed.

Another way to put this is to say that good work presupposes a mind and habits of thought and action that are at once open to the depth and wonder

[38] Wendell Berry, "Going to Work," in *The Essential Agrarian Reader: The Future of Culture, Community, and the Land*, ed. Norman Wirzba (Lexington: University Press of Kentucky, 2003), 259–266.

of the world and committed to its care and celebration.[39] The "mind" Berry thinks we need is not a pragmatic or economic mind, one dedicated to reducing consideration to cost-benefit analysis. Nor is it a mind devoted first and foremost to the growth of money, that most slippery of simulacra. In a manner reminiscent of Aquinas, Berry calls for the cultivation of a sympathetic or affectionate mind. Such a mind is difficult to define precisely or *a priori* because it is deeply responsive to the particular needs and potential in a place. Unlike the ahistorical and universalizing character of the modern, economic mind, a sympathetic mind violates the widely held economic principle that it is inefficient and unwise to leave ninety-nine sheep to look for the one that is lost.

A sympathetic mind differs from a strictly pragmatic or economic mind in the following ways: it refuses to reduce reality to the scope of what we think we know; it fears the mistake of carelessness more than it fears error; it seeks to understand things in terms of interdependent wholeness rather than isolated parts; it appreciates that a cultural landscape must grow up in faithful alignment with the natural landscape that sustains and inspires it; it acknowledges and learns from past traditions of people who have worked, succeeded, and failed; aware of humanity's great ignorance and presumption, it moves cautiously; and it accepts the view that people are creatures living in a world of creatures, all of which are mortal, fallible, and related in complex, interdependent ways. At root, says Berry, a sympathetic mind "lives within an abounding and unbounded reality, always partly mysterious, in which everything matters, in which we humans are therefore returned to our ancient need for thanksgiving, prayer, and propitiation, in which we meet again and again the ancient question: How does one become worthy to use what must be used?"[40] Put in terms of the specific concern of this book, how do we become worthy of the food we must eat, worthy of the life and death our eating requires?

Just as the cultivation of a sympathetic mind leads eaters to attend to the gardening places of food's production, so too does it lead to work that intentionally and habitually draws our attention to the places and

---

[39]   Ellen Davis, following Karl Barth, describes sloth as the converse of good work. Sloth is not simply inactivity but "stupid action" because it presumes we know in an authoritative way the truth and goodness of others. The result is that sloth undoes God's good work in creation. Good work follows from wisdom, which follows from a patient, kind, and humble relation to the world. See Ellen F. Davis *Scripture, Culture, and Agriculture: An Agrarian Reading of the Bible* (New York: Cambridge University Press, 2009), 140–147.

[40]   Wendell Berry, "Two Minds" in *Citizenship Papers* (Washington, DC: Shoemaker and Hoard, 2003), 91.

communities of work. Good work nurtures and honors the good that places and communities embody. It expands our knowledge, sympathy, devotion, and skill so that we work with less waste and to greater personal and communal benefit. It registers as a patient, long-term commitment to the places and communities in which we work. Staying put and being attentive, workers will have the opportunity to see, and where necessary correct, the harmful effects of what has been done. Staying put they will also be in the position to see and celebrate the gifts that feed into and flow out of the work that they do. Work, in short, will begin to resemble a form of prayer because it is shaped by the sensitivity and the desire to give thanks and offer appropriate worship for the grace of life together.

Martin Heidegger was aware of this need for a deeper sympathy when he called for a new form of thinking after the end of philosophy, a form, it turns out, that is exceedingly old but has been eclipsed by modernity. To think is to give thanks. In Heidegger's view, modernity reached its "end" or climax in forms of reasoning that have been realized in technological and industrial societies that reduce things to a "standing reserve" or stockpile of inputs that serve a utilitarian end.[41] What he sought and tried to inaugurate was a form of thinking closely tied to thanking, a form of thinking that did not end in utilitarian and pragmatic considerations.

In developing his account of thinking as thanking and thanking as thinking, Heidegger first observed common etymological roots that involve a close cluster of relationships between *denken* (thinking), *danken* (thanking), *Andenken* (remembrance), and *gedenken* (recollection). The Old English noun for "thought," he tells us, is *thanc*, which refers to the innermost core of a person's heart that is always reaching out to connect with the outer world. True thought is always inspired by this *thanc*, the heartfelt connection that joins us to others. As we investigate this *thanc* we move not only into a personal feeling but embark upon a whole set of practical dispositions that cultivate a "steadfast intimate concentration upon the things that essentially speak to us in every thoughtful meditation."[42] Memory is crucial here, not simply as the ability to recall previous thoughts but more importantly as the practice of patient devotion that abides with and carries others, and as the habit of attention that remains fixed on "the gathering of all that concerns us, all that we care for, all that touches us

---

[41] For a lucid treatment of Heidegger's (sometimes problematic) engagement with modernity, see Michael Zimmerman's *Heidegger's Confrontation with Modernity: Technology, Politics, and Art* (Bloomington: Indiana University Press, 1990).

[42] Martin Heidegger, *What Is Called Thinking* (New York: Harper & Row, 1968), 140

insofar as we are, as human beings."[43] Memory fixes our concentration upon all that is contiguous with us, all that intersects and nurtures our being. Thinking abides within and is inspired by these intersections of what we can call our mutual interdependence: "in giving thanks, the heart in thought recalls where it remains gathered and concentrated, because that is where it belongs. This thinking that recalls in memory is the original thanks."[44]

Heidegger shows the propensity of thinkers to forget the nurturing and inspiring context out of which they come and to which they should respond. When they return to this context, becoming hospitable to what they are attentive to, they give thanks for the gifts through which they live. But when thinkers forget, they readily turn to instrumental, utilitarian, calculating forms of reason that bend and distort the world to an alien end. Thinking that is true to the world is thankful because it maximally sees all that feeds and flows into the life of a thinking being. It is maximally open to the wonder of the world, is properly amazed by it, and so slips, from time to time, into forms of praise.[45]

Though Heidegger wrote as a philosopher, his insight that thinking and thanking go together can be extended in a distinctly theological direction. Alexander Schmemann, for instance, described thanksgiving as the knowledge of God. By this knowledge he did not mean an assortment of propositions about God assented to by a believer. Rather, he meant the intimacy of meeting and communion that can happen between God and humanity when people are deeply attentive to God's presence in the world. Though one might claim and articulate some things "about" God and not give thanks, it is impossible to know God properly and remain ungrateful because in genuine thoughtfulness one is at the same time present to and transformed by God's care and generosity. True knowledge of the world is apprehension of it as the delectable expression of God's self-giving. The point is not simply to see that everything has its cause in God, "but also that everything in the world and the world itself is a gift of God's love, a revelation by God of his very self, summoning us in everything to know God, through everything to be in communion with him, to possess everything as life in him."[46]

Like Heidegger, Schmemann called for a reorientation of mind, a conversion, that moves thought and action more deeply into God's world. Without

---

[43]   Ibid., 144.   [44]   Ibid., 145.
[45]   Chrétien writes that "the task of praise is nothing other than the patience of truth. To think is to thank, but for this to be true, to thank must be to think really and truly, in other words to see" (*The Ark of Speech*, 119). Philosophy, as the testimony of Plato, Plotinus, and Descartes (among others) shows, knows its own nontheological forms of praise.
[46]   Schmemann, *The Eucharist*, 177.

this reorientation it is difficult to appreciate what or who to be thankful for. For Schmemann it is the church's liturgical life that provides the context through which the conversion of mind and work can occur. At the heart of this liturgical life is the Eucharist as the place of remembrance, the place where life finds its true meaning. Here, around the table, Christ reveals that self-offering love is the form of God's work and the "end" or goal of our work in the world. It is for the sake of love that the world was created. It is in the realization of communion that it finds its fulfillment.

Christian remembrance is not reducible to the recollection of information or facts about the world. It is, rather, patterned on God's remembrance, which is revealed in scripture to be God's attentiveness to creation, his carrying of the world within himself, and his providential love and power that gives life to the world. Life *is* insofar as it abides in God's remembrance. This is why it is so important to be remembered by God. To be forgotten by God is, as the Psalmist (13) knew, to languish and be in a perishing state. When Christians remember properly they respond to God's remembrance of creation and take the knowledge of God's life-giving love into themselves, thereby making it effective in the way they live. "If God's remembrance of man is the gift of life, then man's remembrance of God is the reception of this life-creating gift, the constant *acquisition* of and increase in life." In this view, sin is the forgetting of God and the forfeiture of the life God makes possible. When people forget God, memory, vision, and desire turn away from the gift of creation and turn inward. Rather than perceiving and engaging each other as gifts of God, others are reduced to means or possessions that serve a narrow, self-preoccupied end. "If it is God, the giver of life and life itself whom I have forgotten, if he has ceased to be *my* memory and *my* life, my life becomes dying, and then memory, which is the knowledge and power of life, becomes knowledge of death and the constant tasting of mortality."[47] To fail to remember God is death because in this failure the world of things can register only as fleeting, finite, mortal, and ultimately valueless objects. The meaning and significance of things is reduced to the puny and arbitrary scope of personal ambition or concern. Given that ambitions conflict, the world is reduced to fodder that fuels the battles for power and success.

In his book *Great Lent*, Schmemann makes explicit how forgetting God leads not to the proper enjoyment of food but to humanity's slavery before it:

---

[47] Ibid., 126.

> The world was given to man by God as "food" – as means of life; yet life was meant to be communion with God; it had not only its end but its full content in Him ... the world and food were thus created as means of communion with God, and only if accepted for God's sake were to give life ... Thus to eat, to be alive, to know God and be in communion with Him were one and the same thing. The unfathomable tragedy of Adam was that he ate for his own sake. More than that, he ate "apart" from God in order to be independent of Him. And if he did it, it is because he believed that food had life in itself and that he, by partaking of that food, would be like God, i.e. have life in himself. To put it simply, he *believed in food* ... World, food, became his gods, the sources and principles of his life. He became their slave.[48]

People can become slaves to the idol of food. When they do they believe that life depends on their exertion and control to bring it about. Relying entirely upon themselves, and being suspicious of others and unable to trust in God, they cannot rest in the knowledge that life is a gift and that God provides.

Eating Eucharistically restores human memory to its rightful orientation. Remembering Christ we also remember Christ's giving of himself as the definitive expression of the Triune God's primordial self-giving. Receiving his offering of himself as our food and drink, we are invited to turn our lives into gifts of nurture that by sharing extend rather than deplete our common life. When we eat at this table we learn to receive and cherish the world and each other as gifts. We learn to carry the world and each other in a hospitable way, making faithful and grateful speech possible.

Practically speaking, a Christologically formed remembering of food will lead us to a careful examination of the food eaten at table. Questions of the following sort will be given serious consideration: Does the food we are about to eat reflect production practices in alignment with Christ's desire that creatures be whole and well? Were food providers honored for their work? Were they able to work in creative ways that encouraged participation in God's creative ways with the world? With respect to the food itself, we will ask if the soil and water from which our plants grow are healthy and clean. Are biological rhythms and ecological integrity observed? Were the animals respected and treated with care? And with regard to the eating practices, we will ask if the food eaten is distributed in an equitable manner. Does the eating we enjoy deprive others of the ability to eat well? Is food being grown and distributed in a way reflective of God's desire that all be fed?

---

[48]   Alexander Schmemann, *Great Lent: Journey to Pascha* (New York: St. Vladimir's Seminary Press, 1969), 94–95.

These sorts of questions presuppose that we know whom we are eating with and what we are eating. We cannot be expected to attend to the needs of our table companions if we do not understand the specific contexts in which we live together. We cannot be witnesses to God's generous hospitality and appropriately carry fellow creatures in our speech, hearts, and hands if we do not also appreciate their particular potential and commit to their realization. Admittedly, remembering of this sort is an enormously complex and time-consuming task (this is why congregations may want to start by making sure that the wine and the bread shared in Eucharistic celebrations are grown, harvested, and produced in ways that bring delight to God). There is so much to attend to and learn. But this is the most fundamental vocation God calls us to, a vocation that began in the Garden of Eden (Gen. 2:15) and finds its consummation in the watering, feeding, and healing of all nations in the new Jerusalem (Rev. 21:5–22:5). This is God's daily work. It would be an affront to God to think it work that is beneath our time and effort.

Our descriptions of a contemplative and sympathetic mind, as well as our accounts of good work and remembrance, enable us now to see that when we say grace we do not merely say a few words over our food. Rather, we demonstrate a willingness to be transformed so that our eating of life is also a sympathetic participation in the ways of life. The thoughtful, thankful eating gesture constantly takes eaters beyond themselves and into the memberships of creation so they can find there the rich, nutritious, God-given mystery of life. Thanksgiving becomes the means through which we elevate and hold before each other the sanctity and grace of the world. Saying grace, we carry God's sustaining love for the world within our speech.

When we offer thanks for food we remember as best we can the many memberships that constitute and fortify our lives, and note that these memberships have their life as a grace received. We remember so we can pledge ourselves to the celebration, maintenance, and nurture of the creatures and processes that nourish us. Put differently, when we remember truly we commit ourselves to the re-membering of organisms and communities that have been dis-membered by our greed and carelessness. We seek the health of wholeness and interdependence that comes from diverse creatures living in dynamic and vital relationships with each other. Thanksgiving thus becomes a political and economic act that unites us in solidarity with creation. It confirms our status as creatures among others, always dependent and, given our unique capacities, answerable to others concerning how well or justly we fit in.

OFFERING CREATION TO GOD

To say grace is to understand eating as a sacramental act. Sacramentality is not about "adding" a religiously defined quality to things but rather is more like an unveiling of the divine *liveliness* and *loveliness* that are always already at work within them. Far from being a denigration of materiality, a sacramental sense is open to the fecund grace at work *in* things, is open to the Logos made flesh in the world.

The eating of food becomes a sacramental experience when we acknowledge that the nourishment in our eating, its life-giving quality, is not exhausted by the stuff we eat. Though we may munch on an apple, the life of the apple itself, as well as all the lives and processes that fed it, are not extinguished or exhausted by any particular bite. This means that life itself is not a material thing. It is the demonstration of divine power at work *in* the material. Life from the beginning is the presence of God as Spirit sweeping like a wind over the waters of creation (Gen. 1: 2), bringing order, fecundity, growth, contentment, and joy to the world. From a Christian point of view, life is given its definitive expression in the incarnate Son who, precisely *through* his body, shows what life means and looks like at its best. The incarnate Christ makes sacramentality possible. He shows that spirit is not opposed to materiality. He shows that life is the glory of God revealed in materiality, a glory made manifest in bodies that grow, reproduce, delight, and ultimately offer praise back to God as the one who gives life abundantly.[49] When we eat sacramentally we refer what we eat, as well as the life-giving power in our eating, to God.

What does it mean to refer the world to God? We have already seen that in one sense it means perceiving each other as gifts of God and as the concrete expression of divine love and delight. In its practical meaning, however, to refer the world to God is to bear witness in one's daily work

---

[49] Having stated that God creates through the Son and Spirit, the early church father Irenaeus goes on to say, "For the glory of God is the living man, and the life of man is the vision of God. If the revelation of God by the creation already gives life to all the beings living on earth, how much more does the manifestation of the Father by the Word give life to those who see God!" (*Against Heresies* IV.20.7 in Robert M. Grant, *Irenaeus of Lyons* [New York: Routledge, 1997], 153). Irenaeus holds that life is a function of God's activity, and that the character of this life finds its definitive expression in the ministry of Jesus the Son. The Spirit, in turn, is the continuing, sustaining divine power at work in the world testifying to what real and abundant life is, inspiring people to become followers of and participants in Christ's life-building ways. Those who are led by the Spirit come to exhibit the fruit of the Spirit named by Paul as love, joy, peace, patience, kindness, generosity, faithfulness, gentleness, and self-control (Gal. 5:22–23), all qualities that enhance life and give glory to God.

to the life-giving Spirit of God in the world. To see God as the effective, delighting presence in things, and to understand that there is no life or joy without this presence, should lead to a desire to participate in the ways and contribute to the goals of divine power. "To confess God as Spirit is to acknowledge that the world is not in our control, nor in that of any other creature, system, force, or thing, for everything is breathed by God. To pledge ourselves pliable to God the Spirit may breed anarchy ... but it undoubtedly sets our face against all forms of fatalism."[50] The anarchy Lash has in mind is not the confusion of individual egos each seeking their own way. It is rather the unpredictability of those who have given themselves to the life-giving wind that blows where it wills. To refer the world to God is to engage creatures in such a way that God is glorified in their living.

Self-giving is crucial in any Spirit-filled life because the giving away of ourselves demonstrates that self-glorification is not our goal. The way of God is the way of sacrificial self-offering. Without sacrifice, there is no life. As theologians like Augustine and Aquinas reflected on what it means to affirm God as Holy Spirit they often focused on the character of God as love and as gift. God gives the world out of an incomprehensible love and sustains it by the continuing gift of comprehensive care. To call the Spirit "gift" (*donum*) is to suggest that God is known as the one who gives. From the beginning God *offers* Godself, and in this offering makes room and equips creatures to be themselves. "'Gift,' then, may be taken as the nearest we have to a name distinctive of the Spirit of God's love, the gift that is the very 'being-given,' or givenness, of God: God as 'donation.'"[51]

To say grace, and in doing so be brought nearer to the Spirit of God as the life-giving presence of things, is therefore to commit to turning oneself into an offering to the world and to God. What inspires the commitment is the realization that the world before us is never simply a material fact. Food is a *given* reality that depends on the sacrifices of others, all grounded in and maintained by the self-offering love of God. To withhold our own offering would be to frustrate and divert the very movement of life. To reduce creation to a stockpile of commodities that exist to serve us would be to try to contain the divine winds of Life, not realizing that all efforts toward outright possession precipitate death. The moment food ceases to register as a gift it becomes something other than itself. It becomes an entity that can then be used to distort, profiteer from, and destroy life.[52]

---

[50] Lash, *Believing Three Ways in the One God*, 85.   [51] Ibid., 92.

[52] This means that questions about the genetic modification and patenting of food needs to happen in a context informed by an understanding of the world as a gift, a world that in its

My grandfather, Wilhelm Roepke, understood better than anyone I have known the connections I have been making between gift, work, self-offering, gratitude and delight. The way he treated his chickens makes this clear. For him, chickens were first and foremost God's creatures. They were never to be tormented or abused but cared for in ways that facilitated the fulfillment of their natures. As the farmer charged with their care, he did not think it was enough to make sure they were well fed and housed. It also mattered to him that they experienced forms of delight suitable for a chicken. On summer days he would therefore take his scythe and a bucket and cut fresh grass for them. As he approached the chickens they came running, clearly excited about the grass offering they were about to receive. As they ate, my grand-father grinned and chuckled, clearly delighted that he had contributed to their pleasure.

This treatment of chickens is so noteworthy (and uncommon) because it shows that my grandfather understood his work to be a form of respect and an expression of hospitality to the creatures under his care. Chickens were never treated as economic units. They were precious gifts of God given for the nurture of our family (both in the forms of eggs and meat). To be worthy of these chickens, however, required that we offer ourselves to their well-being and happiness. From an economic standpoint, the work my grand-father did made little sense because our chickens were free to get whatever grass they wanted whenever they wanted it. The fact that my grandfather daily took the time to make the offering shows an understanding and a desire shaped by the fundamental awareness that we live by the gifts and sacrifices of others. When he sat down to eat these chickens he could be thankful in ways that few of us can because he knew that he had first given himself to them. His daily work was a form of worship because it was a lifting up of God's gifts so that they might be properly received and cared for. The taste of his chickens, in turn, was deep because it included the memory of good work, the experience of mutual delight, the knowledge of a hospitable and gracious God, and the pain and joy of sharing in the lives of others.

To receive food as God's gift is an extraordinarily difficult thing to do. Our perennial temptation is to want to possess and control. For the Israelite

givenness glorifies God and promotes life. Far from signaling an end to genetic research, appropriate research will respect the integrity of creatureliness and honor the divine Logos (the principles of life and intelligibility) in things. Research that serves the narrow purposes of profitability and power (the glorification of a corporation) rather than the nurture and health of the world, is a desecration.

nation, it took forty years of testing and wandering in the wilderness to begin to learn that life's nurture and sustenance come in the form of manna from heaven, a surprising, unknown, unmanufactured, and uncontrollable gift. It took a steady stream of prophets who cried out against the attempts of people to secure their position in life through force and violence or through the establishment of an economic order that exploited the poor, the widows, and the orphans. For Christians, it took the teaching of Christ who said, "If any want to become my followers, let them deny themselves and take up their cross and follow me. For those who want to save their life will lose it, and those who lose their life for my sake will find it" (Matt. 16:24–25; cf. Mark 8:34–35, Luke 9:23–24). It took the example of Jesus as one who laid down his own life (Phil. 2:7), and in doing so showed the world that true life is the way of kenotic self-offering.

An understanding of Christ's and the Spirit's self-giving life is the background for the Orthodox view that all our vocations have a "priestly" essence. Paul Evdokimov writes: "In the immense cathedral which is the universe of God, each person, whether scholar or manual laborer, is called to act as the priest of his whole life – to take all that is human, and to turn it into an offering, a hymn of glory."[53] Schmemann thinks similarly, stating that "to offer food, this world, this life to God is the initial 'eucharistic' function of man, his very fulfillment as man."[54] At the most fundamental level, to be a priest of the world means that one is committed to receiving the world as a gift from God, and then seeing in the sharing of these gifts their most proper use. To be a priest is to place oneself at the intersection of God's sacrificial love and the sacrifices of creation's many members as food and nurture.

If saying grace begins by learning to carry faithfully and gratefully the world within one's speech, it is fulfilled by finding generous ways to present creation to each other and to God. In this practice of offering, new ways of understanding and relating to the world as creation become possible. As John Zizioulas, one of today's key defenders of this concept of priesthood, puts it, when people recover their priestly role, the interdependence of humanity and creation is affirmed but also the participatory role of humanity in the "summing up" or recapitulation of all things in Christ (Eph. 1:10).[55]

---

[53] Quoted in Theokritoff, *Living in God's Creation*, 215.
[54] Schmemann, *For the Life of the World*, 34.
[55] John Zizioulas, "Priest of Creation," in *Environmental Stewardship: Critical Perspectives – Past and Present*, ed. R. J. Berry (London: T & T Clark International, 2006), 274.

Central to ancient Greek liturgies, says Zizioulas, is the *Anaphora*, the "lifting up" of the gifts of bread and wine to God. This lifting begins around a table understood as an altar, the heavenly place where God's self-offering, the offering by God of creatures to each other, and our self-offering meet. Reflecting on the table, Schmemann argues that "the entire world was created as an 'altar of God,' as a temple, as a symbol of the kingdom."[56] What this means is that no creature in this world exists by itself but is always already maintained by the living and the dying of others. Each member of creation and the memberships of which they are a part depends on the ways of sacrifice. As John Muir once put it, "When we try to pick out anything by itself, we find that it is bound fast by a thousand invisible cords that cannot be broken."[57] These cords are the cords of nurture given and received. When people at the altar are taken up into the self-offering ways of God, they carry with them the many members and memberships of creation and commit to the care and reconciliation of all creatures so that together we might enjoy God's eternal feast.

In ancient Israelite tradition the priest was associated with the temple, understood as the place where heaven and earth meet. By drawing the people's attention to the altar, and then encouraging them in the work of self-offering sacrifice, relationships that had been defiled by sin could be repaired and made whole. To live in the context of the temple is thus to commit to relationships governed by justice, peace, and thanksgiving. According to the Orthodox view, what a priestly role does today is "lift our hearts" to the place of heaven so that heavenly life can transform life on earth here and now. Heaven is not a faraway place but rather the transformation of every place so that the glory and grace of God are fully evident. When in priestly motion we lift our hearts to God, what we are really doing is giving ourselves and the whole world to the new creation, the "new heaven and earth" (Rev. 21:1), so that our interdependent need can be appreciated as a blessing. As priests, we begin to see creation as an altar of God's offering. This altar becomes the inspiration for our offering of the world and ourselves.

Besides helping us honor interdependent life together, a priestly role also invites humanity to participate in Christ's summing up and recapitulation of all things. Zizioulas insists that if we are to understand this idea of

---

[56]   Schmemann, *The Eucharist*, 61.
[57]   Quoted by Roderick Nash in "Aldo Leopold's Intellectual Heritage," in *Companion to a "A Sand County Almanac": Interpretive and Critical Essays*, ed. J. Baird Callicott (Madison: University of Wisconsin Press, 1987), 85.

anakephalaiosis we must first see that creation has never simply been a fact of nature, a physical realm operating according to natural laws. From the beginning, but also to its end, all creation is the expression of a divine intent that all creatures be whole and at peace, enjoying the Sabbath delight that marks God's attachment to the world.

The present state of the world, however, is frustrated and corrupted. Relationships that are to be a testimony to righteousness and peace are daily distorted, broken, or denied. The world we attempt to lift up in priestly offering is often wounded and broken. In Zizioulas's view, a view shared by many in the Orthodox tradition, much of this corruption has to do with humanity making itself rather than God the center of desire and action. People have used their freedom to manipulate the world to serve their own ends rather than glorify God. To offer the world appropriately and in a way that sums up creation in Christ will therefore require a reorientation in the ways of personal freedom.

People subvert creation when they turn it into a commodity and when they simply take and do not offer.[58] To learn to offer the world appropriately requires, then, that we learn to come to terms with our propensity to want to take rather than give. This is why Zizioulas insists that if we are to become priests of creation we must learn the art of an ascetic life. Asceticism is not contempt for bodily, material life. Rather, it is the inner detachment that uses and enjoys creation's gifts without needing to possess them. Priests teach us to offer the world to each other and to God by showing us how to make the gifts of life "pass through" our hands rather than "make them our own."[59] When we engage fellow creatures with the aim of letting them pass through our hands we acknowledge that creation is not ours, nor does it exist primarily for us. Creatures have their beginning and end in God. God's glory is revealed when they are fully alive and free to be themselves.

Another way to think about the priestly offering of the world is to see in our handling of creation an occasion to praise God or, more exactly, see in our praise a continuation of creation's own worship.[60] Scripture records that

---

[58] For an excellent treatment on the priestly role of humanity, see Theokritoff's account in *Living in God's Creation*, 211–238.

[59] Zizioulas, "Priest of Creation," 286–287.

[60] For a response to critics of the priesthood tradition like Richard Bauckham (*The Bible and Ecology: Rediscovering the Community of Creation* [Waco: Baylor University Press, 2010, 83–86) who think a priesthood approach too anthropocentric and too hierarchical, see Elizabeth Theokritoff's essay "Creation and Priesthood in Modern Orthodox Thinking," in *Ecotheology* 10:3 (2005), 344–363.

creatures themselves are united in praising God. All the earth, as the Psalm-ist says (98:4), can make a joyful noise unto the Lord:

> Praise the LORD!
> Praise the LORD from the Heavens:
>   praise him in the heights!
> Praise him, all his angels;
>   praise him, all his host!
> Praise him, sun and moon;
>   praise him, all you shining stars!
> Praise him, you highest heavens,
>   and you waters above the heavens! . . .
> Praise the LORD from the earth
>   you sea monsters and all deeps,
> fire and hail, snow and frost,
>   stormy wind fulfilling his command!
> Mountains and all hills,
>   fruit trees and all cedars!
> Wild animals and all cattle,
>   creeping things and flying birds!   (Psalm 148:1–4, 7–10)

Reflecting on this Psalm, Augustine observed that creatures do not verbally or audibly praise God with the conscious intent that people are capable of. Simply by living out their lives in a way that shows God's plan and provision, they bear witness to the fact that God made them. In contributing to the beauty and good of all creation they praise God. Their very existence amounts to their confession, "You founded me, I did not establish myself." When we as people study creation, and in our study are drawn to God as the Creator of them, creatures praise God through the appreciation, praise, and thanksgiving we offer.[61] But when creatures are commodified or exploited, as when we cease to find in them the life-giving presence of God, their praise is cut short because they are no longer living out their divinely given and ordered potential. They are now made to live for us rather than God. In Augustine's view, our attention to creatures ought always to draw our minds upward to their maker. When our minds are not drawn up, as when we consider things in terms only or primarily of their benefit to us, we no longer allow heaven to inform life on earth. We profane the world by manipulating

---

[61]   Augustine says, "But anyone who has eyes will study many of this world's creatures, and in studying them find delight in them. When these things delight us we praise them, but not for themselves. We praise God who made them, and thus all creatures praise God" ("Exposition of Psalm 148," in *Expositions of the Psalms*, trans. Maria Boulding, ed. Boniface Ramsey [Hyde Park, NY: New City Press, 2004], 486).

creatures to reflect a human rather than a divine intention. Their praise is twisted, we might say, so that it now registers as the groaning and moaning described by Paul in Romans 8:22. For creation to sing again as a gift from God, and in order for our offering to be the sort of praise that aligns itself harmoniously with creation's eternal song, we must learn to become priests who freely receive and give again the gifts of life, priests who let creation pass through us, and in this passing vibrate our being into chords of song.

As exiles from paradise, living in a fragmented and degraded world, our priestly song will often take the form of lament. This is because many of the creatures we receive come to us in a diminished and deformed state, unable to realize their God-given potential. Too much of the food we eat, when we fully see and deeply understand, lodges in our throats as a cry of offense to its dignity. Oftentimes we cannot fix the damage we have done. And so we must weep. We must learn the songs of confession and repentance. By bringing our laments and tears to God we ask God to transform cries into a resurrection song and tears into life-giving waters. We ask God to transform our eating and living so that they communicate the glory of God.

These remarks on the priestly function of humanity indicate that it is not easy to offer the world to each other and to God. We prefer to take the world, possess it, and consume it. What we do not realize is that this hoarding gesture, a gesture often founded upon a deep insecurity and anxiety within us, compromises and degrades the giving of God that is the life of the world. To receive food properly is to know it first and foremost as a gift. Our consumption of it does not ever mean that it is a possession we can hold to privately or forever. As our bodies indicate, food must continually pass through us if we are to remain healthy. In its passing, in its nurture of us and in our nurture of others, it can become a sign of God's presence in the world. Our eating, in other words, can be a witness to the offering of creatures and of God that makes life possible. "God gives all life, is intimate to every movement, animates all action, fuels freedom, breaks down barriers, breathes dead bones dancing, irrigates the desert making flowers bloom."[62]

Human life most becomes its own when we say grace over the sacrament of life, and when we transform mundane eating into an act of solidarity with creation and communion with God. As we pledge ourselves to the nurture, restoration, and celebration of life, we will invariably encounter those who maim and destroy life because of their desire to hoard or profiteer from it. They will not look kindly on efforts to serve and conserve life. But it is not

---

[62] Lash, *Believing Three Ways in the One God*, 92.

only others we need to worry about. We must also confront and tame the many desires within ourselves that seek to seize upon life and treat it as a possession rather than as a gift. In a consumerist world, a world driven by the profitability (to some) of simulated signs, it will be difficult to resist the temptation to take the world by force. This is why we will need the help of each other as we learn the art of saying grace. We need together to develop the sympathies and affections that will enable us to see and smell and touch and taste the goodness of God made manifest in our daily bread.

Life is a miraculous, inexplicable gift. It exceeds all economies of exchange. We stand within it, beggar-like, unable to receive it fully or properly because whatever we would claim or take already exceeds our longing and comprehension. The best that we can do is make our lives into an offering to others, not for purposes of repayment (how could we ever know what sufficient payment would be?) but as the effort to overcome the sinful pride and aggression that otherwise bring life to a halt. In this self-offering we do not often know what we are doing. Nor can we predict or control what the offering will accomplish. What we can do is open ourselves, commit our talents and wallets, to the many dramas of life going on around us, trusting that our offerings can enrich the multiple memberships of which we are only one part. We cannot know definitively and beforehand if our gestures, perhaps unwittingly, contribute to creation's dis-memberment. But in the act of thanksgiving we at least express our commitment to remember as best we can, and through this re-membering bring healing to creation and praise to God as the life of our life.

ca

Eating in Heaven? Consummating Communion

Everything that is loved in a fragmentary and incomplete way on earth
has always had its ultimate ground in heaven. No earthly moment can be
fully exhausted ... [I]n heaven we shall live the full and eternal content of
what on earth was present only as a transcendent, unsatisfiable
longing ... In heaven, therefore, our earthly existence – and we have
only *one* existence – will be present in an unimaginable and unimaginably
true manner.[1]

Heaven is the state of being in which all are united in love with one
another and with God. It is an *agapē*, a love feast. Whenever less than the
whole world is loved, with all the creatures in it, whenever anyone or
anything is excluded from love, the result is isolation and retreat from
heaven. Heaven is the community of those whom God loves and who love
God.[2]

On this mountain the Lord of hosts will make for all peoples a feast of
rich food, a feast of well-aged wines, of rich food filled with marrow, of
well-aged wines strained clear. And he will destroy on this mountain the
shroud that is cast over all peoples, the sheet that is spread over all
nations; he will swallow up death forever ... For the hand of the Lord
will rest on this mountain. (Isaiah 25:6–8, 10)

[I]n the spirit he carried me away to a great high mountain and showed
me the holy city Jerusalem coming down out of heaven from God ...
Then the angel showed me the river of the water of life, bright as crystal,
flowing from the throne of God and of the Lamb through the middle of
the street of the city. On either side of the river is the tree of life with its
twelve kinds of fruit, producing its fruit each month; and the leaves of the

---

[1] Balthasar, *Theo-Drama – Theological Dramatic Theory: Volume V*, 413.
[2] Jeffrey Burton Russell, *A History of Heaven: The Singing Silence* (Princeton: Princeton
University Press, 1997), 5.

tree are for the healing of the nations. Nothing accursed will be found
there any more. (Revelation 21:10, 22:1–3)

The idea of heaven is at once an indispensable and an ineffable thought. It is
indispensable because in our thinking of *the life to come* we have the
opportunity to evaluate carefully life *as it now is*. If heaven is the fulfillment
of life and the complete realization of all that life can and forever was meant
to be, then it is not only for the future: sensing and imagining heaven,
glimpsing its contours and features, we are invited to adjust the living we do
now so that our life together might more fully realize the eternal Sabbath
banquet planted within creation at its beginning. The Lord's Prayer asks that
God's kingdom and God's will for life be realized here, "on earth *as it is in
heaven*" (Matt. 6:10 – emphasis added), indicating that heaven is not simply
reserved for some future life but is to be tasted and savored now.

But heaven is also ineffable because every attempt by finite and fallible
creatures to articulate life's inexhaustible fullness is bound to distort and fall
short. We know too little and fear too much. Our love is not wide or deep
enough. When we appreciate how difficult it is to be honest about and
faithful to the short, particular life we have been given, we will also acknowledge that attempts to speak about the final goal and significance of *all* life, as
well as life in its heavenly *newness*, must proceed with caution and humility.
The counsel of Nicholas Lash is appropriate: "Because we seek to speak of
that which 'transcends' and heals all time and circumstance, we can only do
so tentatively, indirectly, metaphorically, in language drawn from our present experience, which is that of a history that has *not* yet ended, not yet
been given its final 'resolution,' 'shape' and identity."[3]

Recognizing that our imagination of heaven is invariably shaped and
colored by the experiences of earthly life, it is crucial that we pay attention
to how this life is characterized lest heaven become little more than a
projection of personal anxieties and dreams. Though life is given, a truthful
description of its significance is not given alongside it. Because of personal
pride, desperation, or sloth we can distort and degrade what life is, and in
this distortion misconstrue heaven. Heaven then becomes the opposite of all
that we fear and resent in this life, or it becomes the embellishment and
fulfillment of a private desire or longing: for those who are hungry or crave
food, heaven is a perpetual feast; for those who are weak and oppressed,

---

[3] Nicholas Lash, "Easter Meaning," in *Theology on the Way to Emmaus* (London: SCM Press,
     1986), 184.

heaven is the place where they are made strong and victorious over their oppressors; for those who are poor, heaven is the place of unimaginable riches. Heaven, in short, becomes indistinguishable from a fairy tale, the fanciful fulfillment of an often desperate wish.[4]

Various forms of this wish have prompted people to locate heaven in a faraway place. Heaven's location, though not appearing on any precise map, must be anywhere but here on earth because the world we see and presently occupy is so often a place of desolation, pain, and tragedy. People look "up" to heaven because to look "down" would bring us face to face with so much carnage. The end result is forms of spirituality that are world-denying, even world-despising. Humanity's primary mission, in this view, is to endure an earthly veil of tears as best we can so that at death our souls can take flight to heaven as the place of comfort and escape. Creation is not our home. We are only passing through on our way to treasures "laid up somewhere beyond the blue."[5]

This way of characterizing heaven is problematic because it misunderstands what it means for us to be in a place. It mistakenly identifies "space" and "place" as being pretty much the same thing, and presupposes that what makes a place significant is its location. On this view, we enter heaven once we get to the "right" location.

When we reflect more carefully, however, we discover that what makes a place really a *place* is not its location but the quality of relationships that happen there. That a place exists in some identifiable *space* (a quantifiable measurement locatable in terms of grids and size) is secondary to the more important matter that memorable experiences and distinct forms of life occur there. Though my "house" is a space that can be located on a map, my "home" is a place that is defined not by numbers, streets, latitude, or

---

[4] Friedrich Nietzsche, Karl Marx, and Sigmund Freud – commonly known as "the masters of suspicion" – developed this insight in a variety of ways. In their view, heaven is a dangerous notion because it becomes the excuse for people to postpone life's happiness and well-being to another life. Rather than challenging and correcting this life with its vision of what life is supposed to be, heaven becomes a future, fictional reward used by powerful elites to keep people mired in oppressive and unjust social structures that benefit those elites. For a balanced account of this position, and a Christian response, see Merold Westphal, *Suspicion and Faith: The Religious Uses of Modern Atheism* (Grand Rapids: Eerdmans, 1993).

[5] This line is taken from the well-known spiritual "This World Is not My Home." The stanza runs, "This world is not my home, I'm just a-passing through / My treasures are laid up somewhere beyond the blue / The angels beckon me from heaven's open door / And I can't feel at home in this world anymore." I discuss it in light of a history of philosophical and religious disdain for the earth in "Placing the Soul: An Agrarian Philosophical Principle," in *The Essential Agrarian Reader: The Future of Culture, Community, and the Land*, ed. Norman Wirzba (Lexington: University Press of Kentucky, 2003), 80–97.

longitude but by the affections and responsibilities that are always being worked out there. Houses matter. But what people crave is a home, a place of welcome, nurture, and support. Homes are precious because they hold the memories of all the life-giving relationships that have circulated through them. What we love about a house is the fact that it has become a home for us.

Heaven is better understood as a place rather than as a separable space that exists far away.[6] It is not primarily the location that makes heaven what it is but the character of the memberships that are happening in it. It is the place we most want to be because the relationships that transpire there are life-giving, joyous, and peaceful.[7] What makes the relationships heavenly is that God is present and known in them (John 17:3). As such, heaven is the ultimate and complete realization of home, the place of perfect nurture and celebration. This is not to say that heaven is without space, since every place presupposes a location of some sort. But it is to suggest that a focus on place rather than space enables us to evaluate the ways we relate to whatever location we are in.

With place as our focus we can begin to think about why so many of our locations have become places of desolation and pain rather than joy and peace. We can reflect on the reality that so many people are unhappy or dissatisfied with their place, and then perhaps realize that the problem may not be with a location but with the ways we have devised to occupy it. We need to ask the following questions: How did the world created by God as paradise, as a place that is good and beautiful and full of God's delight, become a place of hell, a place many people desire to flee? Is the problem with creation or with us? Asking these sorts of questions will compel us to come to terms with our propensity to refuse and degrade membership

---

[6] What I say here about the "place" of heaven has its parallel in the "time" of heaven. When people speak about "eternal life" in terms of its unending duration they confine it to quantitative measurement and thereby lose its qualitative dimension. The position of Jürgen Moltmann is a valuable corrective to quantitative approaches: "Eternity in time is a category, not of the extensive life, but of *intensive* life. *The presence of eternity* comes about in the wholly and entirely lived moment through undivided presence in the present. If I am wholly there – if I give myself wholly – if I expose myself wholly – if I am able to linger wholly – then I experience eternity. It is the experience of 'the fullness of time' in the wholeness of the lived life: all time becomes present ... The whole, simultaneous and complete possession and enjoyment of life is the fullness of time in the fullness of the loved life" (*The Coming of God: Christian Eschatology* [Minneapolis: Fortress Press, 1996], 291).

[7] Robert Farrar Capon observes, "Heaven is Someplace, not because it is localizable in terms of space but because it is full of persons, each of whom finally is Somebody worth taking a walk with through the Wood of Life on the way to the Wedding Feast, where a place has been prepared for us by the Lamb and his Bride" (*Food for Thought*, 64).

wherever it might be. Escaping to a new location will not solve the problem as long as the problem is us. How do we know that upon entering a faraway, future heaven – imagined as the most beautiful, luxurious, and comfortable place possible – we will not wreak the same havoc and devastation we have already let loose here in God's first paradise?[8]

  If heaven is to be rescued from false piety, and if it is to heal the anxiety of membership that currently disfigures creation, it will need to be understood from the perspective of the Creator of life. It is the Author of life who can best reveal the significance and goal of life's story. More specifically, our point of departure must be the witness of Jesus Christ who, as the eternal

---

[8] Wendell Berry's 2006 "Sabbath VI" poem (in *Leavings* [Berkeley: Counterpoint, 2010], 72–73) captures well the sense of love and pain that should accompany our thoughts of heaven:

> I know how you longed, here where you lived
> as exiles, for the presence of the essential
> Being and Maker and Knower of all things.
> But because of my unruliness, or some erring
> virtue in me never rightly schooled,
> some error clear and dear, my life
> has not taught me your desire for flight:
> dismattered, pure, and free. I long
> instead for the Heaven of creatures, of seasons,
> of day and night. Heaven enough for me
> would be this world as I know it, but redeemed
> of our abuse of it and one another. It would be
> the Heaven of knowing again. There is no marrying
> in Heaven, and I submit; even so, I would like
> to know my wife again, both of us young again,
> and I remembering always how I loved her
> when she was old. I would like to know
> my children again, all my family, all my dear ones,
> to see, to hear, to hold, more carefully
> than before, to study them lingeringly as one
> studies old verses, committing them to heart
> forever. I would like again to know my friends,
> my old companions, men and women, horses
> and dogs, in all the ages of our lives, here
> in this place that I have watched over all my life
> in all its moods and seasons, never enough.
> I will be leaving how many beauties overlooked?
> A painful Heaven this would be, for I would know
> by it how far I have fallen short. I have not
> paid enough attention, I have not been grateful
> enough. And yet this pain would be the measure
> of my love. In eternity's once and now, pain would
> place me surely in the Heaven of my earthly love.

and incarnate Word, is the sustaining life and revealing light of the world (John 1:4). Christians turn to Christ to picture heaven because his ministry, death, and resurrection are the definitive, concrete expression of life in its fullness and truth. In his life we discover what it means to live in the memberships of our life together so that these memberships are places of healing, nurture, and hope. In the flesh of Jesus, heaven and earth meet. In the action of his body we begin to see what God's kingdom looks like, and thus also what God's desire for all creation is. In the resurrection of his body all the powers that would threaten or degrade life are revealed and defeated, and all the possibilities of embodiment are realized. Insofar as we participate in Christ, as we do in baptism by sharing in his death, we also "walk in newness of life" and are united in his resurrection (Rom. 6:3–11). We become "a new creation" (2 Cor. 5:7) that is aligned with the "new heaven and new earth" envisioned by prophets like Isaiah (43:19, 65:17) and John (Rev. 21:1).[9]

Eating is not incidental to the expression of life as Christ reveals it. Indeed, eating can serve as a witness to the heavenly kingdom. Why? Because eating is the action whereby we share and strengthen life, celebrate blessings received, and enact fellowship. When we eat well with each other we perform an essential meaning of home. As Robert Karris puts it, "In Luke's Gospel Jesus is either going to a meal, at a meal, or coming from a meal."[10] Following Jesus we learn to eat like he does so that we can move into the fullness of life he makes possible. Throughout his ministry Jesus broke down the barriers that keep people apart by eating with them. In the hospitality realized at a common, inclusive table Jesus testified to God's reign on earth, inviting others to welcome and live out God's rule (it is no accident that scripture often describes the fulfillment of life as a banquet of rich food, well-aged wine, and healing fruit).[11] Jesus fed people when they were hungry, provided miraculously for thousands, demonstrating that the source of life is the God who is merciful and generous. When we eat together in Christ's name, letting Eucharistic remembrance and practice guide our table fellowship, we bear witness to God's heavenly kingdom on earth. As Matthew's gospel portrays it (26:26–29), Eucharistic eating frames and directs the eating we should do now and the eating we will do with Christ in heaven. In the

---

[9]   In *Way of Love* I develop what can be described as heaven's logic of relations. Pain and violence are defeated and banished in heaven, with the result that all relationships are inspired and empowered only by God's love.

[10] Karris, *Eating Your Way through Luke's Gospel*, 14.

[11] For passages referring to eating in the kingdom to come, see Isaiah 25:6, Amos 9:11–15, Jeremiah 31:10–14, Matthew 8:11, Luke 6:21, 12:35–48, 13:29, 28:28–30, and Revelation 19:9

sharing of the bread of life together we taste what Ignatius of Antioch called "the medicine of immortality."[12]

Will there be eating in heaven? Though no definitive or precise answer can be given, this chapter will argue that eating of some form will occur. Why? Because eating is one of the most fundamental and pleasurable ways we know for enacting communion. Because eating affirms the resurrection of a body that is what it is because of its relationships with other bodies. Because eating is so deeply intertwined with life's movements that to remove it would be to render living unintelligible to us. And because eating is a sharing in the primordial, eternal hospitality that is a mark of God's Triune life. This is not to suggest that the eating characteristic of heavenly life is a direct continuation of the eating we do now. If our eating is to witness to heaven, it will need to be transformed by Christ. Insofar as we learn to co-abide with him, eating can become a sacrament, the daily sign that the world we call our garden, kitchen, and home is also the home of God.

THE RESURRECTION OF BODIES

Throughout their history Christians have struggled with the confession of the Apostle's Creed: "We believe in the resurrection of the body." Compared to its philosophical rival – the immortality of the soul – resurrection of the body presents unique difficulties for understanding.[13] How can bodies be

[12]   Ignatius of Antioch, "The Epistle to the Ephesians, 20," in *Early Christian Writings: The Apostolic Fathers* (London: Penguin Books, 1968), 82.

[13]   Among the philosophical problems to consider, one of the most significant was the problem of identity through change. Caroline Walker Bynum, in her magisterial treatment of the history of bodily resurrection, writes: "if there is change, how can there be continuity and hence identity? If there is continuity, how will there be change and hence glory? Or to rephrase the issue in the image second century apologists used far more frequently than technical philosophical argument: if we rise as a sheaf of wheat sprouts up from a seed buried in the earth, in what sense is the sheaf (new in its matter and in its structure) the same as and therefore a redemption of the seed?" (*Resurrection of the Body in Western Christianity, 200–1336* [New York: Columbia University Press, 1995], 59–60). The issue of creation's continuity and discontinuity has also been at the center of contemporary discussions. See, for instance, John Polkinghorne's position that "a credible eschatological hope must involve both *continuity and discontinuity*. Without an element of continuity there is no real hope being expressed for creation beyond its death; without an element of discontinuity, the prospect would be that of the non-hope of mere unending repetition" (*The God of Hope and the End of the World* [New Haven: Yale University Press, 2002], 12). The difficulty lies in how the continuity and discontinuity are described. Moltmann argues, "the eschatological transformation of the world means a *fundamental transformation*, that is to say a transformation in the transcendental conditions of the world itself, and therefore of its very foundation: God himself changes his relationship to the world. God's *faithfulness* to his once created world cannot therefore limit his *freedom* to complete and perfect his

resurrected when we observe that they go into the ground and decay? Should we even want bodies to be resurrected when we can plainly see, as Socrates famously noted, that, besides being a place of suffering, imperfection, transience, decay, weakness, and death, "the body fills us with loves and desires and fears and all sorts of fancies and a great deal of nonsense, with the result that we literally never get an opportunity to think at all about anything. Wars and revolutions and battles are due simply and solely to the body and its desires" (*Phaedo*, 66c)? Though bodies may afford us some pleasures in this life, they are fleeting and often destructive. Not surprisingly, many Christians have found, and continue to find, it much simpler to hold that when they die their bodies go into the ground and their souls ascend to an immaterial heaven. As a "place" of immateriality, it is hard to see how matters of food and eating would ever come up. Bodies eat food, souls do not. End of the gustatory story.

The teaching of the immortality of the soul, particularly when presented in Pythagorean, Socratic, and Gnostic forms, is a profoundly anti-Christian teaching. Early on Tertullian understood this, prompting him to say that "one cannot be a Christian who denies that resurrection which Christians confess."[14] Immortality of the soul presupposes a negative view about materiality and embodiment, and the value and destiny of each, that goes directly against the teachings of creation, incarnation, and the "end" (*eschaton*) of all things. Moltmann is correct to say that "the idea of 'the resurrection of the body' is lost completely if salvation is supposed to consist only of the blissful beatific vision of the disembodied soul. But once this hope is lost in eschatology, the idea of the incarnation cannot be maintained in

---

temporal creation, making it a creation that is eternal – and thus changing creation's fundamental conditions" (*The Coming of God*, 272). Moltmann is clear that the "fundamental conditions" he has in mind speak not only to the "form" or arrangement of the world, but its "substance" or being "as a temporal creation capable of sin and death. If the new creation is to be an imperishable and eternal creation, it must be now not only over against the world of sin and death, but over against the first, temporal creation too. The substantial conditions of creaturely existence itself must be changed" (ibid.). This way of speaking emphasizes discontinuity to such an extent that one is left to wonder what of God's original creation is left. Owing to the complexities of this discussion, and recalling the severe limits in our understanding on these matters – are we in a position to understand what the "substantial conditions of creaturely existence" are, let alone comprehend them? – I leave it for another time.

[14] *Tertullian's Treatise on the Resurrection*, ed. Ernest Evans (London: SPCK, 1960), 13. Tertullian is here giving reinforcement to Paul's pronouncement, "if Christ has not been raised, then our proclamation has been in vain and your faith has been in vain" (1 Cor. 15:14).

Christology either. And if that is surrendered, the Christian faith becomes a world-denying, world-despising Gnosticism."[15]

Resurrection of the body entails a dramatically different estimation and affirmation of life's embodiment than does the immortality of the soul. Unlike dualist theories that despise the body and elevate the soul, Tertullian argues that the soul cannot obtain salvation unless it is in a fleshly body, making flesh "the pivot of salvation." Flesh is the thing God loves. Flesh is what God constructed "in his own image" and "with his own hands."[16] If the flesh of our bodies, indeed the flesh of the whole creation, is what God loves, then its end cannot be destruction or annihilation but rather reconciliation and peace (Col. 1:20). However Christians conceive salvation or the life of heaven, it must include bodies in relation with other bodies, because an isolated body knows no life.

As leaders in the early church worked to explain Christianity's meaning to outsiders and to each other they discovered that their worship of a risen Christ compelled them to think about life, death, and the whole of creation in fundamentally new ways. Bodies and materiality could not be despised because, most basically, their God "became flesh" and lived among them (John 1:14). In what has to be one of the most profound affirmations of embodiment, early Christians argued that it wasn't just a part or fraction of God that entered a body. Rather, "the fullness (*pleroma*) of God" resided in the body of Jesus (Col. 1:19), thereby signaling that God's eternal way of being is not in conflict with creation's material nature. The home of God was a body of blood and bone, of stomach and intestine. In the embodiment of Jesus of Nazareth, God could be touched, fed, kicked, and killed. In the resurrection of his body the deathly forces that sought to distort and deny created life were defeated. Moreover, the ministry of Jesus demonstrated again and again that bodies mattered, which is why he spent so much time touching them, feeding them, and healing them. Bodies were of singular importance to Jesus because they are God's creation, physical manifestations of God's primordial hospitality and care. Bodies are the practical medium *through which* the faith is worked out. Nothing that God has created, therefore, is worthless or to be despised.[17] Nothing is to be forgotten or abandoned, which is why, in the end, all things on heaven and earth must be

[15] Moltmann, *The Coming of God*, 270.
[16] *Tertullian's Treatise on the Resurrection*, 25, 27.
[17] We should here recall Timothy's instruction to resist those "demonic teachers" who want to forbid enjoyment of God's goodness. Timothy says: "For everything created by God is good, and nothing is to be rejected, provided it is received with thanksgiving; for it is sanctified by God's word and by prayer" (I Tim. 4:4).

gathered up and reconciled so that God can be "all in all" (Eph. 1:23, 4:6). Heaven is not ever closed to material bodies. It is only closed to the power of sin that distorts and disorients bodies so that they cannot live into their God-intended fullness.

As Christians began to tell this very different story about bodies and the goal of all life, the temptation was to accommodate and employ the terminology (and therefore also the matter-denying, body-despising presuppositions) of the immortality of the soul. Perhaps owing to a perennial frustration or impatience with bodily life – bodies so readily and commonly fall short of the power and perfection we desire – Christians have often succumbed to the Gnostic heresy that says we would be better off if bodies could simply be left behind.[18] If we turn to the example of Saint Augustine, we can see how one of Christianity's most influential teachers grappled with a body-despising urge.

Before becoming a Christian, Augustine was a member of the Manichaean sect and was thus taught to consider persons in a dualistic fashion. The struggle of life was a struggle to free the soul from the evils of the body. The promptings of sensuality, presumably even the sensual delight of good food, were to be shunned as inimical to the purification, and therefore also the release, of the soul. The soul is the divine place of perfection, while the body is a despicable lump that should be defeated, wrapped up, and then placed in an eternal prison.[19] Though Augustine would abandon the Manichees, the moral severity with respect to embodiment would continue to be attractive to him. It would also find reinforcement as he later devoted himself to the study of neo-Platonic philosophy.

Augustine's struggle with his dualist heritage returned again and again to the incarnation of God in the body of Jesus Christ. In *Confessions* he recalls that even though he found many truths in the Platonists, what he did not find there was the teaching that the Word became flesh (VII, ix, 14). Because he believed the scriptures to be true, he had to find ways to affirm that Jesus was a fully human, fully embodied person. Owing to the resurrection of Christ, he also had to find ways to affirm the resurrection of the body in place of the immortality of the soul. In his last great work, *The City of God*, Augustine gave a sustained treatment of what a resurrected body is.

---

[18]   The story of Christianity's understanding of the human body is diverse and complex. Peter Brown illuminates some of its plots in *The Body and Society*.

[19]   My treatment of this phase in Augustine's life draws on Peter Brown's magisterial biography *Augustine of Hippo* (Berkeley: University of California Press, 1967). Brown writes that "For Augustine, the need to save an untarnished oasis of perfection within himself formed, perhaps, the deepest strain of his adherence to the Manichees" (51).

Augustine is clear that the resurrection of the body is not to be mistaken for a resurrection of the soul or something spiritual within us. Christ's resurrection was a resurrection of flesh, just as his ascension to heaven was an ascension "in that same flesh" (XXII, 5).[20] But in affirming resurrection Augustine had to find a way to respond to critics who asked about the resurrection of aborted fetuses or bodies that were of varying sizes and often in less than optimum health. Surely the defects and imperfections of current bodies, and the fact that many bodies are disfigured and their parts destroyed while living, make them unworthy of heaven. Must they not first be transformed into a more perfect state to enter into heaven? Or consider the human body that has been cannibalized by another person. Is the flesh of the human body that is eaten resurrected in the cannibal's body or in its original body?

In response Augustine argued that it is presumptuous to claim to know the marvelous character or the surprising outcomes of God's resurrecting action. As many church fathers reasoned, if God can create the world from nothing, God can also create something new and whole from what already, if imperfectly, exists. Augustine believed that bodies would be resurrected into forms that realize a particular body's potential. A body that died in infancy, and thus in an undeveloped state, would rise into a body in which its potential was realized. The model, though not necessarily the rule, for the resurrected body is a body in its prime (it turns out that such a body corresponds roughly to the age of Jesus when he was raised from the dead [XXII, 15–16]). A cardinal position for Augustine is that while the defects of bodies will be removed in their resurrection, their essential nature will be preserved. This allowed him to say that women will be resurrected as women rather than as men.[21] It also allowed him to affirm that resurrected bodies will be attractive and harmonious in their proportions.

Thus far in Augustine's deliberations there is a clear affirmation of the goodness of bodies. God resurrects them whole and beautiful, having realized their full potential. Augustine insists, however, that life in the body must also be described as a sinful life. Being the descendants of Adam, our bodies

---

[20] Quotations from *The City of God* are from the translation by Henry Bettenson (London: Penguin, 1984). My thinking on these matters has been assisted by John Casey's *After Lives: A Guide to Heaven, Hell, and Purgatory* (New York: Oxford University Press, 2009), especially the chapter "Bodies Fleshly and Spiritual" (269–280).

[21] Both sexes will be in heaven though the phenomena of lust, intercourse, and childbirth will be no more. This position was in contrast to others who, perhaps influenced by Aristotle or by the Genesis 2 account that portrayed Eve as made from Adam's rib, saw the male form as the perfection of humanity, and thus reasoned that women must be resurrected as men.

are mired and engulfed in filth (quarrels, treachery, pride, cruelty, lust, promiscuity, etc.). Augustine calls this misery "a kind of hell on earth," a hell from which there is no liberation except through the grace of Christ (XXII, 22). Referring to the apostle Paul, he describes the life of the person, even the life of the believer, as a war between the ways of the flesh and the ways of the spirit. Heaven is the place where the battle is won. It is the place where bodies are made incorruptible, freed from the miseries that have shaped and dominated this life.

It would be a mistake to read Augustine as endorsing the disdain of bodies in a way reminiscent of Socrates. In part this is because Augustine is aware that Paul's distinction between flesh and spirit is not equivalent to Socrates' distinction between body and soul. Flesh and spirit refer to embodied ways of life that have differing allegiances and goals. If one lives according to the flesh, one makes self-satisfaction and self-glorification the first priority (this is revealed in "works" of the flesh like idolatry, jealousy, fornication, anger, etc.). But if one lives by the Spirit, service to others and the glorification of God are paramount (as revealed in love, joy, peace patience, kindness, generosity, faithfulness, gentleness, and self-control as "fruit" of the Spirit). These two ways of life are clearly opposed: "what the flesh desires is opposed to the Spirit, and what the Spirit desires is opposed to the flesh" (Gal. 5:17). But this opposition is not a dualism of body and soul. Both patterns of living require the effort of a whole person.

Earlier in the *City of God* Augustine testifies to this Pauline view when he says explicitly that sin and moral failing are not caused by our bodies: "those who imagine that all the ills of the soul derive from the body are mistaken" (XIV, 3). Though our bodies may be "weighed down" by corruptibility, the source and cause of this corruption is not the body itself. Referring to Paul's description in 2 Corinthians 5:1–4 of the longing that human bodies be clothed with a heavenly covering, Augustine argues that our desire is not to be without a body but to have a body that is "absorbed" or "swallowed up" by life as it really ought to be, life as God wants it. Turning the tables on his dualist teachers, he asserts "it was not the corruptible flesh that made the soul sinful; it was the sinful soul that made the flesh corruptible" (ibid.).

It is the affirmation of the body that stands behind Augustine's lengthy list of the "innumerable blessings" of created life despite the misery of "hell on earth." To appreciate the human body as good and beautiful because made by God requires a similar appreciation with respect to the nonhuman bodies of creation as well: the fruitfulness of seed, the reproductive capacities of animal bodies, the skill and art and wit of the human brain, the beauty and complexity and design of the human body, the diverse beauty of sky and earth and sea. No one can comprehend even one of these natural blessings, let alone fully appreciate them as a whole. The fact that we can *begin* to recognize created life as a blessing *while being in a corrupted and sinful state* suggests that when the defects of sin are removed, our delight in the goodness of the Creator and the splendor of the creator's works will exceed all imagining. In heaven, people will

> drink of God's Wisdom at its very source, with supreme felicity and without any difficulty. How wonderful will be that body which will be completely subdued to the spirit, will receive from the spirit all that it needs for its life, and will need no other nourishment! It will not be animal; it will be a spiritual body, possessing the substance of flesh, but untainted by any carnal corruption. (XXII, 24)

Augustine's reference to the resurrected body as a "spiritual body" seems confusing, even a contradiction in terms. To understand him we need to return to Paul. In his first letter to the Corinthians Paul uses the horticultural image of the sower laying down seed. The seed does not germinate into new life unless it first "dies" into the ground. The new life that emerges from the ground is continuous with but also different from the seed that was initially sown. Importantly, the new life is not the sower's doing but God's (1 Cor. 15:38): because germination is preceded by the death of the seed, the new life that emerges must be the result of God's life-giving Spirit. In a similar manner, our current bodies are "sown" and die (perhaps Paul has in mind here the baptismal logic of dying and rising with Christ he makes explicit in Rom. 6:3–11) so that they can be raised *by God* a "spiritual body." Paul is here presupposing a distinction between what is often translated as a physical body (*soma psychikon*) and a spiritual body (*soma pneumatikon*). What is the difference?

Augustine thinks it would be a big mistake to think the spiritual body is an "immaterial" body. Flesh is not converted into spirit in the act of resurrection. What does happen is that the physical body we now know, a body that is needy, mortal, and susceptible to the influence of a sinful soul, in death submits and becomes totally obedient to God's life-giving Spirit (XIII, 20). Being wholly subsumed by the Spirit of Life, the physical body becomes a different body, continuous but also discontinuous with its former reality. Being so subsumed it cannot any longer die, nor need it seek to provide for its needs, because God's Spirit is of life rather than death: "For the body which will be incapable of death is that which will be spiritual and immortal in virtue of the presence of a life-giving spirit" (XIII, 24). The physical body does not cease to be a physical body. Rather, it comes under a new inspiration and a new animating Spirit that provides all that it needs. The defining feature of a resurrected body is that all of its movements are the effect of God's life-giving, life-promoting love. In this body, there is no life-degrading power to be found.

N. T. Wright is in basic agreement with this Augustinian interpretation of Paul. He notes, first of all, that it is misleading to translate Paul's Greek to describe a physical versus a spiritual body. This is because the word *psychikon* should not be translated as "physical" but as "soul." The adjectives *psychikon* and *pneumatikon* are not referring to the materiality or immateriality of the bodies described (their materiality is simply assumed) but to *the power or energy that animates them* – soul/*psychikon* energy (what Paul calls the energy of Adam, the "first man") versus Spirit/*pneumatikon* energy (what Paul calls the energy of Jesus the man from heaven, the "second man" [15:45–49]). "Paul is talking about the present body, which is animated by the normal human *psychē* (the life force we all possess here and now, which gets us through the present life but is ultimately powerless against illness, injury, decay, and death), and the future body, which is animated by God's *pneuma*, God's breath of new life, the energizing power of God's new creation."[22]

Neither Paul nor Augustine claims to understand the mechanics of the resurrection of the body into an imperishable, heavenly, Spirit-infused and Spirit-directed body. Paul simply says we will be changed "in a moment, in the twinkling of an eye" (1 Cor. 15:52). Augustine admits that the resurrection of the body is incredible, but who are we to doubt what the Almighty can do? To be alive is to be a witness to unimaginable marvels all around. If we can affirm that God has created a beautiful and ordered world from nothing, why should we not also be able to affirm that God can transform an existing body into something beautiful and imperishable?[23] Augustine wisely concludes:

[22] N. T. Wright, *Surprised by Hope: Rethinking Heaven, the Resurrection, and the Mission of the Church* (New York: HarperOne, 2008), 155–156.

[23] In *Resurrection: The Power of God for Christians and Jews*, Kevin Madigan and Jon Levenson give a summary statement of the core assumption behind resurrection thinking: "The possibility of resurrection – the raising of the body by God – is thus once again rooted in the power of God at creation. If God could raise Adam out of dust, then he can surely raise a dead body at the general resurrection. The victory of God over death at the end again mirrors the primordial victory of the God of life at the beginning and reminds us that we owe our lives, before death and after, to the God who created all. We do not live, and will not live again, by nature alone" (41).

And yet we do not know what new qualities the spiritual body will have, for we are speaking of something beyond our experience. And so, when there are some things which are beyond our understanding, and on which the authority of holy Scripture offers no assistance, then we must needs be in the state described in the Book of Wisdom, in these words: "The thoughts of men are timorous and our foresight is uncertain." (XXII, 29)

WILL RESURRECTED BODIES EAT?

Our examination of the resurrection of the body has argued that the Christian heaven is not populated by disembodied souls but by fleshy bodies. This is important to underscore because it demonstrates Christianity's unfailing commitment to bodies. Bodies matter and are to be cherished because they are the physical expression of God's love. They are not temporary cages or cargo boxes to be endured for a while on the soul's way to heaven. Rather than being a valueless and damnable lump, they bear the imprint of the eternal and incarnate Logos as the One who gives and directs them into life. God's desire for these bodies always is that they know and experience life in its fullness. The question now is whether or not eating is part of this fullness.

A quick answer would be to say that eating will be a part of heaven because we have the evidence of Jesus eating in his resurrection body. Appearing to his disciples, showing them his wounds (so as to prove to them that he is a body of flesh and bone and not a ghost), Luke records: "While in their joy they were disbelieving and still wondering, he said to them, 'Have you anything here to eat?' They gave him a piece of broiled fish, and he took it and ate in their presence" (Luke 24:41–43). We need to ask, however, if the resurrected Christ's eating, like the invitation to touch his physical wounds, is simply part of a larger concern to show his disciples that he is a body and not a ghost. On this view, eating is not a demonstration of the character of resurrected, heavenly life. It is an ad hoc exhibition, serving the practical (and temporary) purpose to convince Jesus' disciples that his body is real and not a phantom.[24]

---

[24]   Saying Christ's body is "real" is not to say that it was a resuscitated corpse. Though physical it also had the unique character of entering a locked room (John 20:19). In short, scripture is clear in its assertion that Jesus' resurrected body was a real, physical body. But it was also a transformed body, having properties that we do not understand.

This interpretation is problematic because if the point of the postresurrection stories is to demonstrate and affirm that Christ's body is really a body, would not the denial of eating in heaven signal a negation of that affirmation? It is hard to imagine anything more fundamental and necessary to embodiment than eating. There are several optional functions regarding bodily life but eating is not one of them. Rather than denying eating altogether, what we need are new ways to imagine eating, fresh ways to conceive what a renewed and reconciled creation productive of food looks like. Irenaeus, for example, described heaven (drawing on the testimony of Jesus' disciple John) as a place of miraculous fertility, productive of food and wine in quantity and quality beyond our wildest imagining:

> When the just rise from the dead and reign; when also the creation renovated and freed will abundantly produce a multitude of all foods out of the rain from the heaven and the fertility of the earth: as the presbyters who had seen John the Lord's disciple remembered hearing from him how the Lord used to teach about times and say, "The days will come when vines come up each with ten thousand branches and on each branch ten thousand twigs and on each twig ten thousand shoots and on each shoot ten thousand grapes, and each grape when pressed will give twenty-five measures of wine. And when one of the saints picks a cluster, another will shout, 'I am a better cluster; pick me, bless the Lord through me.' Similarly a grain of wheat will produce ten thousand ears, and each ear will have ten thousand grains, and each grain ten pounds of pure flour; and the other fruits and seeds and herb in like proportions; and all the animals, using those foods which are taken from the ground, will become peaceful and harmonious, subject to me with all subjection."[25]

What Irenaeus is doing is trying to imagine the reality of heaven so that it takes seriously and affirms the embodied character of creaturely life. He grounds that affirmation in the incarnation of God in the body of Christ, a body that was resurrected from the dead and ascended into heaven (Luke 24:51).

Nonetheless, and for a variety of reasons, Christians have maintained that eating will not be part of heavenly life. Tertullian, for instance, contributes an early voice in this tradition that, in several respects, is representative. Near the end of his work *On the Resurrection* he responds to those who argue that if bodily functions like eating do not continue in heaven, then the heavenly body is not really a body. Bodies are what they are because of what

---

[25] Irenaeus, *Against Heresies*, V.33.3, in Robert M. Grant, *Irenaeus of Lyons* (New York: Routledge, 1997), 178–179.

they do. Bodily parts exist and are arranged precisely so that their functions can be carried out. If they cease to perform their function, they become something else. Why have a mouth and teeth if they will not be used for chewing, or a belly and intestines if they will not facilitate eating and drinking? Tertullian's answer is that so long as bodies are animated and directed by the soul, which is to say so long as we are talking about bodies known to us in this life, these bodily parts serve the vital role of providing for life's necessities. But when bodies are animated by God's life-giving Spirit, these necessities, by definition, are immediately and constantly met. Because necessities are met, the body's parts are "delivered from their functions."[26]

Being delivered from their functions, Tertullian nonetheless believes that all bodily parts should be in heaven. "God's judgment-seat demands a man in full being: in full being however he cannot be without the members, for of their substances, though not their functions, he consists."[27] Tertullian means several things here. First, the life we have lived will be judged by God. Judgment of what we have done, and therefore also an examination of the bodily functions we have performed, will be an important part of this judgment. If God's judgment about our functions is to be at all meaningful to us, then we must have full awareness of the bodily parts that made these functions possible. To understand the sin of gluttony, for instance, we need to know and have a memory of our stomachs (among other parts). To appreciate the sin of lust we need to be aware of the eyes that gave us the vision of what we wanted to possess. Second, Tertullian rejects the view of those who insist that a body and its parts are defined by function. For a ship to be a ship it must have all the appropriate parts – a keel, stem, and stern, for instance – but it is not necessary that the ship be put to work in water for it still to be a ship. Much like a shipowner who cares that the ship be whole, so too God desires that in heaven a human body be whole.

If bodily parts will not be used to fulfill their original function, will they simply become irrelevant? Tertullian does not believe so. On his view, a body part like the mouth will find its function directed to speaking the praises of God. Teeth formerly used for tearing and chewing will now become tools that modify the tongue, or they will become an adorning crown of the mouth. In other words, all bodily parts and their functions will be transformed in the resurrection to serve a worshipful, heavenly life. Because all the necessities of life are being met directly by the Spirit of God, it is no longer necessary that bodies fulfill their former roles. Heavenly bodies will

---

[26]   *Tertullian's Treatise on the Resurrection*, 179.   [27]   Ibid.

have no need to eat because God has become all the nourishment they need or could ever want. "For when death has been taken away, neither the supports of livelihood for the preservation of life, nor the replenishment of the race, will be a burden to the members."[28] Referring to the story of God's deliverance of manna to the Israelites in the wilderness (Deut. 8:3) and to Christ fasting forty days and nights in the desert (Matt. 4:4), Tertullian affirms, "One does not live by bread alone, but by every word that comes from the mouth of God."

Tertullian's position that there will be no eating in heaven follows from the basic assumption that eating is a response to need. In this respect, his position is representative of others like Augustine.[29] If heaven is the place where we experience God as the fullness of life and as the satisfaction of every true desire, then the whole category of need – and thus also food as one of our primary needs – simply disappears. But should we think that eating is *only* about the satisfaction of need?

To ask this question is to rethink the meaning of food and the purposes of eating. To be sure, food can be reduced to the physical fuel that maintains a bodylike machine, and eating to a utilitarian act that facilitates ingestion. But such a view, as this book has shown, is an impoverished one. The Wisdom writer Qoheleth, fully aware of the futility and self-deception in much of what we do, nonetheless affirmed, "feasts are made for laughter; wine gladdens life" (Eccles. 10:19). In the gospel of Matthew, Jesus gave a parable of the kingdom of heaven comparing it to a wedding banquet. A dinner is prepared, oxen and calves have been slaughtered, and everything is ready. Surprisingly, however, the people invited do not want to come. "But they made light of it [the invitation] and went away, one to his farm, another to his business, while the rest seized his [the king who issued the invitation] slaves, mistreated them, and killed them" (Matt. 22:5–6). Feasts and wedding banquets are not about need. They are about celebration and merriment,

---

[28] Ibid., 181.

[29] Commenting on the gospel account (Luke 24:43) that has Jesus eating in his resurrection body, Augustine says, "it is not the ability, it is the need to eat and drink that will be taken away from bodies like this. They will be spiritual, not by ceasing to be bodies, but by being supported in their existence by the life-giving spirit" (*The City of God*, XIII, 22). Unlike Tertullian, however, Augustine holds open the possibility that eating may take place in heaven. If it does, it will occur not because of need but for some other reason. "The bodies of the righteous, after the resurrection, will not need any tree to preserve them against death from disease or from extreme old age, nor any material nourishment to prevent any kind of distress from hunger or thirst. This is because they will be endowed with the gift of assured and inviolable immortality, and so they will eat only if they wish to eat; eating will be for them a possibility, not a necessity" (ibid.).

both of which, from a utility point of view, are unnecessary. It would be sad, though clearly not impossible, to imagine a world in which eating occurred regularly – strictly to satisfy the physiological need of hunger – but never feasting.[30]

Eating is not simply about the filling of a gustatory hole. It is also how we develop into particular kinds of people capable of Godly sensitivities, affections, responsibilities, and delights. The Eucharist teaches that when we eat together we share in God's hospitable life. More exactly, we recognize, receive, and then extend to others the gifts of life that God so graciously gives. We discover that life is not a possession but a deep and profoundly mysterious reality we participate in. Table manners developed while eating together play a crucial role in equipping us to participate in the lives of each other with understanding, appreciation, and care. Jesus spent so much time at table with others precisely because it is around food that we come to a clearer self-understanding and a more honest estimation of the world as God's creation and our place in it. He ate regularly with others so he could teach others heavenly "table manners," and through his own eating bear witness to God's rule on earth and testify to God's way of being in the world. As Sam Wells puts it, God communes with humanity in the person of Jesus who eats with us and offers himself to us as food. Eating is central because in our eating with Jesus, indeed in our eating of him in the Eucharist, we learn what worship of and friendship with God looks like and means. Eating with Jesus, becoming companions with God, people enjoy a taste of heaven.[31]

---

[30] One might argue at this point that even though feasting does not address a physiological need, it does satisfy psychological or social needs. If heaven is the place where *all* need is automatically met by the Spirit of Life, then feasting would have no place in heaven either. First, however, it is debatable whether or not feasting is about need. After all, one could imagine a social life that is forever on the level of a gathering (what the Germans call *Gesellschaft*) but never attains a strong sense of community (*Gemeinschaft*) where feasting could find its spontaneous and natural home. Nor is it necessary to see feasting as a psychological *necessity* since, again, a life can function in which feasting does not occur. Second, there is the complex philosophical question about what the elimination of all need would do to our ability to imagine any kind of life at all. Clearly, life as we know it is defined by need. To be a creature is *constantly* to be in need of what the Creator provides (either directly or through other creatures). To be without need altogether would therefore call into question our creaturely status. It would be to move in the direction of the stasis and impassibility of a Parmenides-like, self-contained god who simply *is* but never moves or develops (according to Parmenides all movement suggests becoming which presupposes lack which suggests need). Not surprisingly, a Parmenidean approach ends in a strict monism in which no sociality at all, and thus also no Trinity, is possible.

[31] Samuel Wells, *God's Companions: Reimagining Christian Ethics* (Oxford: Blackwell, 2006), 28.

In Luke's gospel, eating is the place and the time of recognition. Following the crucifixion, Jesus' disciples were in a state of shock. The women and the disciples had found an empty tomb, were told that Jesus had risen from the dead, and were alternately terrified and amazed. On the way to the village of Emmaus the risen Jesus caught up with two disciples and engaged them in conversation. He reminded them that his suffering was declared long ago by the prophets and chastised them for not believing what had been foretold in the scriptures. The conversation produced no recognition in the disciples that the man they were walking with was indeed their risen Lord. Upon nearing Emmaus the two disciples extended hospitality to the unknown man. They strongly urged him to eat with them. Jesus agreed and went into the home to be with them. "When he was at table with them, he took bread, blessed and broke it, and gave it to them. Then their eyes were opened, and they recognized him" (Luke 24:30–31).

It is tempting to read this story and assume that what enabled the recognition was not the breaking of the bread itself, a common mealtime occurrence, but rather the bread's breaking understood as a Eucharistic, ritual act, an act recalling the last Passover supper recorded in Luke 22. Perhaps a rigid distinction of this sort is not necessary, particularly if we recall that a formalized ritual called the "Lord's Supper" did not yet exist. Would it not make sense to think that the history of eating with Jesus, a history in which people learned to attend to each other and address each other's needs, had so transformed their table manners that being around the Emmaus table gave them the space and the occasion they needed to recognize the unknown man and then see who was there? Eating together is so important because it gives us the opportunity to open ourselves more completely to the wonders of life and the world, wonders that often pass by unnoticed. In other words, Jesus' ministries of hospitality (if properly learned) had the effect of transforming people so that the confusion and terror they ordinarily felt could be converted into a welcoming and loving embrace that enabled them to see and know their guests and each other for who they more truly are. Eating was the place of recognition for the disciples because eating that is inspired and formed by Christ is about learning to commune with each other. It is about discovering the truth of the world, and then together developing the skills and habits people need in order to live with each other in modes of care, generosity, and peace.

Viewed this way we can now appreciate why "eating alone" or "eating on the run" are not to be our preferred modes of eating. Luke's story enables us to see that eating serves the very important role of helping us discover the meaning and the requirements of our life together. Put in terms that we have been using throughout this book, eating is the occasion through which we discover that we are creatures nestled within multiple memberships of creation altogether dependent on our creator God. It is the time when we honor, nurture, and celebrate membership. When we eat well, with Christ in mind, heart, and stomach, we recognize the grace and the blessing and the mercy of these memberships, thereby (hopefully) becoming more graceful, grateful, and merciful ourselves.[32] Around the table, people learn to live in God's eternal self-offering life by offering themselves to each other and to the world. Eating Eucharistically can thus rightly be understood as a "rehearsal of heaven on earth."[33]

If the life of heaven is to share in the eternal life of God, then the living that occurs there must somehow be a participation in the perichoretic movement of the Triune God.[34] Divine *perichoresis*, the mutual indwelling of the three persons of the Trinity, is so difficult to understand because whenever we imagine or think about life together we think numerically; that is, we think of distinct persons who then come together in a relationship. Creaturely dwelling, even when we describe it as a unified dwelling, always seems to entail a multiplicity. The Triune God, however, is not a multiplicity. The Father, Son, and Spirit are one, which means that the relationships of

---

[32] In *Saving Paradise: How Christianity Traded Love of This World for Crucifixion and Empire* (Boston: Beacon Press, 2008), Rita Nakashima Brock and Rebecca Ann Parker argue that the church's early Eucharistic celebration was centered on the joyous reception of heaven coming to earth. Citing Cyril of Jerusalem, they argue that the Eucharist was the training ground that equipped Christians to see the divine presence in each other and in the world. As such it was the gateway to the recovery of the created world as paradise. "The beautiful feast of life returned the senses to an open, joyous experience of the world; it was an encounter with divine presence infusing physical life. The Eucharist thus bound humanity to the glory of the divine life in 'this present paradise,' and through its Eucharists, the church cultivated responsiveness to the power of holy presence in the world. Its beauty opened the heart" (145).

[33] *God's Companions*, 197. Wells continues: "All God's purposes are fulfilled – his people worship him, are his friends, and are about to eat with him. And all that God's people need to be able to be God's friends and eat with him has been provided. They have become one body, with sins forgiven, reconciliation made, peace restored, God's word proclaimed and discerned, faith affirmed, and needs heard. God's purpose has been fully communicated to his people and it has been fully embodied in their life. The veil between earth and heaven is being drawn aside, and the simple actions of sharing food anticipate the beautiful simplicity of life with God forever. This is a moment of revelation, for the true life of the saints is 'hidden with Christ in God' (Col. 3:3), and now it is made plain. Christ is being revealed through the taking, breaking and sharing of bread and wine, and 'When Christ who is your life is revealed, then you also will be revealed with him in glory' (Col. 3:4)" (ibid.).

[34] My thinking on the Trinity has been most shaped by Rowan Williams, *On Christian Theology* (Oxford: Blackwell, 2000); David Cunningham, *These Three Are One: The Practice of Trinitarian Theology* (Oxford: Blackwell, 1998); Lash, *Believing Three Ways in the One God*; Zizioulas, *Being as Communion*; and Hart, *The Beauty of the Infinite*.

the three persons do not amount to their coming together. They are always already one, sharing the one eternal *ousia* or essence in three ways. As David Bentley Hart (following Pavel Florensky) describes it, the persons of the Trinity are the eternal movement of self-offering "according to which each 'I' in God is also 'not I' but rather Thou; for the divine circumincession is always a relationality of 'self'-renunciation in favor of – an opening out to – the other."[35] In other words, the persons of the Trinity are the constant movement of offering and receiving, a movement in which there is no holding back and no one is ever alone. The divine persons *are* as gift and as love. "In the Trinity the gift is entire, and entirely 'exposed': the Father gives himself to the Son, and again to the Spirit, and the Son offers everything up to the Father in the Spirit, and the Spirit returns all to the Father through the Son, eternally. Love of, the gift to, and delight in the other is one infinite dynamism of giving and receiving, in which desire at once beholds and donates the other."[36]

Trinitarian theology asserts that all true reality, as created by God, *is* communion, *is* the giving and the receiving of gifts.[37] This means that no living thing is alone or exists by itself, in terms of itself, or for itself. Our experience with creaturely life, however, shows a perennial anxiety in the face of communion. We choose exile over fellowship. We refuse membership, thinking we can make it alone, or we attempt to manipulate the memberships of which we are a part to our own end. We find it difficult to serve and celebrate the members that continually intersect and nurture our living. Out of a desire to possess and control, we deflect or short-circuit the flow of gifts received and given again.

From a Christian point of view, understanding the Triune character of God is an existential necessity rather than an esoteric teaching reserved for the theologically sophisticated. We need to appreciate God's life in a Trinitarian way so that we can learn what it means to live in the communion of life with love and delight. Recognizing, though certainly not comprehending,

---

[35] Hart, *The Beauty of the Infinite*, 171–172.

[36] Ibid., 268. Importantly, Hart continues by saying that creation is caught up in this giving and receiving: "And creation is always already implicated in this giving of the gift because it is – in being inaugurated by the Father, effected by the Son, and perfected by the Spirit – already a gift shared among the persons of the Trinity, in transit, a word spoken by God in his Word and articulated in endless sequences of difference by the Spirit and offered back to the Father" (ibid.).

[37] John Zizioulas says that the doctrine of the Trinity is not simply a dogma about God. It is the "primordial ontological concept" making communion an ontological concept for all of creation: "It is communion that makes beings 'be': nothing exists without it, not even God" (*Being as Communion*, 17).

the eternal self-offering, self-giving life of God – this is what the person of Jesus Christ reveals to us in dramatic and sensual form – Christians are invited to participate in this life of giving, and so "donate themselves entirely to the economy of agape."[38]

Would it go too far to suggest that in our eating we have the invitation and the opportunity to learn the art of Trinitarian donation? Though the eating characteristic of creaturely life is hardly a perfect realization of Triune giving and receiving, eating may nonetheless be one of our most practical entry points into what the full measure of life is all about. Given its ability to introduce us to the nature of life together and its ability to evoke delight in that life, it may not be such a stretch to think that eating, though in a different form, will also be an integral part of the communion of heaven.

As I have already suggested, it is impossible for us to know with clarity or certainty what heavenly eating might be. Scripture does give us a hint as to its possibility, however. In a remarkable scene, God appears to Moses in the form of a burning bush. We are told that in the region of Horeb, at the mountain of God, "the angel of the Lord appeared to him in a flame of fire out of a bush; he looked, and the bush was blazing, yet it was not consumed" (Exod. 3:2). In this theophanous encounter Moses learns God's name and discovers something of the character of God as One who is present to, cares for, and liberates his people. The "life" of God, God's way of "being," is here revealed as the source of creation's light and life. Interestingly, it is a way of being that, when made visible, burns the bush but does not consume it. Moreover, the bush that is burned shines with brilliant intensity, an intensity that while bringing the bush to a new level of visibility also points beyond itself to God as its occasion for being.

When we recognize that cooking, eating, and digesting can readily be understood in terms of fire, does this passage hold out the possibility of eating that no longer consumes or destroys what is eaten? If so, this would be a form of eating radically unlike our own, yet still in continuity with it as the occasion for the enactment of communion and the sharing and celebration of life together. In this form of eating others are not deformed or destroyed. Instead, there life shines all the more brightly. Received as the visible and delectable manifestation of God's love, we taste food as the "life" that always has its origin and end in God.

Eating is about hospitality and intimacy. When we appreciate that the whole of creation manifests God's primordial hospitality, God making room

---

[38]   Hart, *The Beauty of the Infinite*, 268.

for the world and then nurturing it into life, then we can also see that the many dimensions of our eating can be a daily testimony to the love of God.

Eating is about accepting the reality of another – its life and death, its history of struggle and success, its dignity and grace – into our lives, into our mouths, into our bodies, and into our stories and hopes. When we carefully nurture and then eat apples, peas, cucumbers, tomatoes, chicken, and cattle we show that our relationships with each other are determined by responsibility and affection. When we invite other people to join us around a table we demonstrate that our life is first and foremost a shared life, a life that is possible and can only be made complete when all the members of creation are whole and are received and given again as precious gifts of God.

The brokenness of creation and the degradation of its food webs demonstrate that we have hardly begun to understand what real intimacy is and what it requires. The disrespect and the violence with which we treat the world's human and nonhuman eaters shows that for many of us the grace of intimacy is hardly yet a taste. In the context of this suffering and death, the hope of heaven, understood as the knowledge of and participation in the life of God, registers as a witness to what life is yet to be.

Though its full realization is something to be waited for, scripture is clear that the life of heaven begins at the moment of baptism.[39] To be baptized is to be buried with Jesus in death *and* to be raised with him into newness of life (Rom. 6:3–11). In this death, understood as the crucifixion of the "old self" and all its pride, anxiety, and fear, people are freed from sin so that they can live in their membership with God and each other with joy. Relationships formerly governed by suspicion, envy, hatred, and violence, are henceforth to manifest reconciliation, justice, and peace.[40]

---

[39]   Madigan and Levenson make the point that in the early church, baptism was at once the entrance, anticipation, and experience of resurrection even before death: "the change wrought by God at baptism was not only a cleansing and forgiveness of sin but a restoration of the graced candidate to the state of perfection, plenitude, and purity enjoyed by Adam and Eve in Eden" (*Resurrection*, 241).

[40]   Robert Jenson argues in "The Great Transformation" (in *The Last Things: Biblical and Theological Perspectives on Eschatology*, ed. Carl E. Braaten and Robert W. Jenson [Grand Rapids: Eerdmans, 2002]) that heaven is the place and time of the "Last Judgment" because there is no longer any need to make the relationships of creaturely membership right. The function of judgment is not to accuse but to repair and heal. It follows, therefore, that in heaven "each person takes his or her such location as an opportunity of loving service to all the rest" (38). "The primary reality of what we may await is the establishing of universal and perfect justice, which on the biblical understanding of justice is the same as the establishing of universal and perfect love" (39). Here reconciliation reigns because reconciliation "is the life of the kingdom itself" (ibid.).

It is also clear that Eucharistic formation and table fellowship are the place and time where the "new creation" characteristic of baptismal life is clarified and deepened. Gathered around a table, inspired by and abiding with Christ, people live out the movements of sacrificial self-offering, grateful reception, and reconciled relationships. If this is true, then it is also the case that people do not ever merely taste bread and wine. Properly transformed and directed, they also *taste* heaven. They gain a glimpse of life in its grace, fullness, and truth.

Heaven is the place of communion and genuine intimacy. It is the place where all the bodies and memberships of creation achieve their fulfillment and joy, because the power moving through them is only the power of God's love. If there will be eating in heaven, what its precise character will be is impossible for us to know. But insofar as just, reconciled, Eucharistic eating is possible in this life, we surely have a foretaste of what heaven is and will be. It is a taste, one can think, that will steadily deepen and expand into that full and perfect communion life where God is "all in all."

Epilogue

Faithful Eating in an Anthropocene World

> To be healed we must come with all the other creatures to the feast of Creation.[1]
>
> Life in God's Holy Spirit is . . . all things' existence purified into peace and friendliness, reconciled relationship, sharing – in delight and harmony – in the very life of God.[2]

There are politicians, economists, and engineers who welcome the Anthropocene as an unparalleled opportunity to intensify the production practices that, especially since World War II, have yielded so many calories and consumable goods. Often referred to as "ecomodernists," these people believe that economic growth, when joined with an ever more sophisticated set of technologies and computational power, will enable people to engineer themselves out of the agricultural and ecological problems we now face. In the face of looming food shortages, technicians will genetically engineer higher yielding crops and faster growing animals, or they will simply design synthetic equivalents to meat and other food products in the lab. In the face of a warming planet, they will spray the atmosphere with aerosols that will reflect the sun's light and heat away from the earth. The key to a good, even great, Anthropocene, depends on the development of new energy systems, like next-generation solar and new nuclear (fission and fusion), that will fuel the manufacture of food and consumer products. The ultimate goal is to decrease direct human dependence on nature, because insofar as the daily lives of people are decoupled from natural processes, the greater is the likelihood that wild nature will be protected and preserved.

---

[1] Berry, *The Unsettling of America*, 103–104.
[2] Lash, *Believing Three Ways in the One God*, 88.

Ecomodernists believe that people are poised to rise to a new level of planetary significance, and, when final assessments are made, we will all be proud of the new planet we create.[3] They want us to resist the doomsday predictions and the naysayers who want to stop progress and cast doubt on the powers of reason. The problem with naysayers, besides being ungrateful for all the benefits of rational pursuits, is that they have lost their faith in the human ability to solve whatever problems come their way.[4] We are not fated to a starving and dying planet. What we most need to do is develop the technologies and economies that will promote human prosperity and an ecologically vibrant planet.

Given a still-growing human population and continuing, systemic ecological degradation, it isn't obvious that we should subscribe to the ecomodernist faith. How have proponents come to it, and what does it involve? In "An Ecomodernist Manifesto," prepared by several of this movement's thought leaders, there is a clear acknowledgement that human beings have been a destructive presence.[5] Forests have been cleared, water has been wasted, species have gone extinct, and the climate has warmed, because people have relied directly on soil, timber, and fossil fuels to grow their economies. But people have also been steadily developing the technologies that lessen their reliance on, and render more efficient their use of, nature: better agriculture, cleaner energy, more streamlined production techniques, and increased urbanization have resulted in improved quality of life and a cleaner environment. These technologies need intensification. The manifesto simply assumes that people are better off when they are liberated from the burdens of growing food and providing for their energy needs.

To continue the expansion and growth of human prosperity, people must learn to separate themselves from nature. Rather than turning to nature to provide for their needs, they should turn to themselves and their powers of invention and technique. "Ecosystems around the world are threatened today because people over-rely on them ... it is the continued dependence of humans on natural environments that is the problem for the conservation

---

[3] For a critical account of this manner of thinking, see Clive Hamilton's *Earthmasters: The Dawn of the Age of Climate Engineering* (London: Yale University Press, 2013).

[4] In *Enlightenment Now: The Case for Reason, Science, Humanism, and Progress* (New York: Viking, 2018), Steven Pinker, the well-known Harvard public intellectual, argues that widespread human flourishing is well within our grasp, provided that we do not try to limit humanity's innate drive to experiment, design, and improve. Pinker's book suffers from a misreading of Enlightenment thinkers and a rather cheery interpretation of its subsequent history. Pinker seems oblivious to the horrors committed in the name of reason.

[5] "An Ecomodernist Manifesto" is available at www.ecomodernism.org/manifesto-english/.

of nature." As ecomodernists understand it, the preservation of the world and the flourishing of human life depend on the decoupling of the two. "Humans should seek to liberate the environment from the economy." Put another way, "Nature unused is nature spared." The decoupling of humanity from nature depends on the development of new technologies that will produce clean energy. Solar and nuclear energy will lessen our reliance on forests and fossil fuels, just as it will provide the fuel to make fertilizers and desalinate ocean waters (thus lessening our reliance on freshwater streams, rivers, and lakes).

Ecomodernists affirm a "deep love and emotional connection to the natural world." But the connection is mostly aesthetic, emotive, and optional.[6] It isn't embodied and economic, and thereby also practical, as when people work their bodies to provide for their needs. The curious result is a desire for "connection" with nature that is based upon a "radical decoupling" from it. "Decoupling of human welfare from environmental impacts will require a sustained commitment to technological progress and the continuing evolution of social, economic, and political institutions alongside these changes." Faith in technology and in the ability of humans to predict and avert whatever problems might come their way are crucial to this project. So is the world's desacralization. Though nature may have an affective pull on some, it is hard to know how the desire to protect and conserve nature can go hand in hand with the resolute commitment to redesign and engineer places and creatures to fulfill society's needs. Can anything be sacred if everything is susceptible to human power and control?

How does the manifesto describe humanity's place in the world? "Humans will always materially depend on nature to some degree. Even if a fully synthetic world were possible, many of us might still choose to continue to live more coupled with nature than human sustenance and technologies require. What decoupling offers is the possibility that humanity's material dependence upon nature might be less destructive." The ecomodernist world is a dense, urban world (by century's end it is expected that 80 percent of the population will reside in cities). A small number may elect to live close to nature but their decision will be a choice rather than a

---

[6] "Accelerated decoupling alone will not be enough to ensure more wild nature. There must still be a conservation politics and a wilderness movement to demand more wild nature for aesthetic and spiritual reasons. Along with decoupling humankind's material needs from nature, establishing an enduring commitment to preserve wilderness, biodiversity, and a mosaic of beautiful landscapes will require a deeper emotional connection to them."

necessity. This is a world in which people are not bound to nature. They have been emancipated from the need to know it, or practically care for it.

∾

Can we speak practically and meaningfully about human *fidelity* to creatures and places when the primary aim, as presented by ecomodernists, is to *decouple* people from nature? Can we learn to respect and nurture communities of life if we do not fully know our need of them, and believe that they are precious, even sacred, gifts that are not to be violated?

An ecomodernist way of thinking rests upon two fundamental mistakes. First, it assumes a world that will continue to function more or less as it always has, and thereby fails to appreciate that in an Anthropocene world, ecosystem stability is a thing of the past. Human power has so influenced ecosystem functioning that we cannot know the effects or predict the outcomes of large-scale human action or small-scale cellular manipulation. It is simply foolish, even reckless, to presume to manipulate earth systems or life processes when we cannot reliably know the outcome. For example, owing to the alteration of our atmosphere through global warming, it is now almost impossible to know what weather patterns will be like in any particular region. The implications for agriculture are immense, as farmers are caught between early and late frosts, or catastrophic rain and hail or prolonged drought. The thought that we might engineer our way out of climate disruption by tinkering with an atmosphere that we have hardly begun to understand is a reflection of stupendous hubris.

Second, ecomodernists falsely assume humans in their essence to be non-ecological beings, and therefore only minimally or tangentially related to earth. If necessary, we could live elsewhere.[7] This assumption, increasingly

---

[7]   It should not surprise us that there is a growing chorus of people, notable scientists among them (like Stephen Hawking), who believe that human destruction of the earth is inexorable, and that we must, therefore, make preparations to colonize other planets. This is a foolish and utterly naïve hope, because it forgets that human life is embodied life, and that our embodied life stitches us necessarily in this world and no other. There is no other world that we know that duplicates the evolutionary history, and therefore also the precise eco-life-systems in which our bodies came to be and among which they daily develop. A realistic move elsewhere would also require the relocation of the entire planetary system, ranging from soil and water, to microbes and plants, because without the system there is no us. For a description of the efforts to relocate humanity beyond earth, see Michio Kaku's *The Future of Humanity: Terraforming Mars, Interstellar Travel, Immortality, and Our Destiny beyond Earth* (New York: Doubleday, 2018). Kaku argues that for people to survive on another planet, a new science and technology, much of it yet unknown but surely to be developed through Artificial Intelligence, will have to invent a new, synthetic humanity along with the synthetic environments that will enable their flourishing. He argues that "our destiny is to

well-funded and the focus of intense research, rests on the peculiar, and utterly false, idea that the power of life is internal to us, and that we do not need others to live. If the power of life is within each one of us, a private and singular possession, we can, theoretically, live anywhere, fed by the "foods" that we have designed and manufactured for ourselves.

The anthropologist Tim Ingold has argued that this way of thinking is trapped within a "logic of inversion." According to this well-established logic, the life and identity of things is internal to them. Upon observing a human body, it is not the body that is alive but rather some invisible (soul/ mind) force acting within and through it. If life is "inside" things, a singular possession contained within a body, then it is apparent that the relationships "outside" that join bodies to each other are not constitutive. What a living thing "is" can be thought apart from whatever relationships it finds itself within. Persons committed to this logic, rather than thinking themselves to be open to and drawing their life from others, turn inward, invert the flow of life that comes from outside, and enclose life within themselves. According to Ingold, this is all a massive mistake because the logic of inversion mischaracterizes what life is.

> Bringing things to life, then, is a matter not of adding to them a sprinkling of agency but of restoring them to the generative fluxes of the world of materials in which they come into being and continue to subsist ... things are in life rather than life in things ... Things are alive and active not because they are possessed of spirit – whether *in* or *of* matter – but because the substance of which they are comprised continue to be swept up in circulations of the surrounding media that alternatively portend their dissolution or – characteristically with animate beings – ensure their regeneration. Spirit is the regenerative power of these circulatory flows which, in living organisms, are bound into tightly woven bundles or tissues of extraordinary complexity.[8]

If people are their bodies, it is impossible for a person to live except insofar as an unfathomably vast assortment of bodies – ranging from microorganisms to chickens – circulate and interweave throughout. Of all the things people do, nothing more clearly communicates the complexity

---

become the gods that we once feared and worshipped. Science will give us the means by which we can shape the universe in our image" (14).

[8] Ingold, *Being Alive*, 29. Speaking this way, Ingold endorses the phenomenologist of the body Maurice Merleau-Ponty, who argued that if the world was not sentient, we could not be sentient either. To be a living body is to be stitched into a living world. A person is not in their body. A person is its body in the world.

and the tightly woven character of our living than the act of eating. *Eating roots* us into a world with others. As was described in the introductory chapter, every living body is a complex site of hospitality that eats, hosts, and is eaten by others. Eating is the daily action that, along with breathing and drinking, *stitches* us into a world that is itself alive, ever changing, ever on the move. To unravel the threads or to refuse to be intimately woven into the lives of others – a weaving that is made evident most viscerally by our chewing and digestion – is to precipitate death. The proof? Stop eating.

The fundamental lesson of (micro)biology is that human beings are not individual or isolated beings. We do not and cannot possibly live alone. The processes of life are symbiotic, meaning that we are always already with others, inhabited by others, implicated bodily in the lives of each other, and able to grow only because of the myriad ways each of us are intertwined with others. As Donna Haraway put it, "Critters interpenetrate one another, loop around and through one another, eat each another, get indigestion, and partially digest and partially assimilate one another, and thereby establish sympoietic arrangements that are otherwise known as cells, organisms, and ecological assemblages." Critters are what they are related to. "Critters do not precede their relatings."[9]

People do not live in the world as upon a stage or as within a store. This is a mistaken picture because it presumes that the relationships that join us to places are optional, as if we could move to another stage or store if we don't like the one we are in. Ingold argues, along with many others, that the idea of a (mostly dead) world standing entirely separate from humans is a relatively recent invention. It is also a deception, because it fails to appreciate how life happens within a dynamic field of countless creatures, a field often described by traditional and indigenous peoples as a community of kinship.

Bruno Latour has gone even further, saying that the modern invention of inanimate, self-standing objects is extraordinarily bizarre and fundamentally unscientific. Why have so many people come to believe that the earth is basically dead or inert matter in motion?

> The disappearance of agency in the so-called 'materialist world view' is a stunning invention, especially since it is contradicted every step of the way by the odd resistance of reality: every consequence adds slightly to the

---

[9] Haraway, *Staying with the Trouble*, 58, 60. For a clear and wide-ranging account of symbiosis as the basis for planetary life, see *Margulis's Symbiotic Planet*.

cause. Thus, it has to have some sort of agency ... If not, there would be no possible way of discriminating causes from consequences.[10]

The mistake of this "stunning invention" is to presuppose a mechanical world in which a cause can only ever have the exact same effect again and again. But the world itself denies this, since it constantly gives birth to new creatures. What comes after is clearly not a dull repetition of what has come before. This means that a conception of the world as a mechanism, and the idea that creatures are discrete, self-contained things existing in tangential relation with other things, are fundamentally mistaken. For us to *be* is to *become with others* in a living, animate world. The emergent character of life demonstrates that a mechanical logic, though useful in some domains, is simply wrong when applied to living beings.

To be alive is to be swept up and carried along dense, dynamic flows of life that join us to countless fellow creatures. There is no life without others. Our connections to others are not optional. Eating is the daily confirmation of that fact.

FAITHFUL BECOMING

The crucial question going forward is, how are we going to "become-with-others" in this animated world? Will our becoming be a faithful becoming in which the sanctity of others is affirmed and respected, and their lives nurtured and protected? In other words, will we be content with being creatures dedicated to the healing and flourishing of the memberships of creation?

To begin, I will argue that the fundamental work ahead requires of us that we learn to appreciate, accept, and then embrace our creaturely, earthy condition as stitched into a shared fate with places and all their diverse creatures. This will not be easy to do since so many (philosophical and religious) spiritual quests have as their ultimate aim the person's flight or escape from embodiment and the materiality of this world. Various forms of dualism, both ancient and postmodern, are alive and well, and will need to be resisted, since they presume the earth and its bodily life finally to be worthless.[11] This sensibility can hardly be a source of inspiration or empowerment for people who believe every place and every living thing to

---

[10] Bruno Latour, "An Attempt at a 'Compositionist Manifesto'," *New Literary History* 41 (2010), 482.
[11] We should not forget that there is a techno-scientific version of escapist flight from embodiment and earth. Artificial Intelligence, in some of its (already realized) forms, seeks

be of sacred worth and significance, and thus worthy of our care and cherishing. Our search, says Latour, should not be for a different world but this same world engaged in "a radically new spirit."[12]

What this radically new spirit looks like, and what it practically entails, will differ depending on the religious or philosophical tradition one adheres to. For Christians, it will depend on a much more intensive embrace of what I call the "incarnation principle," the idea that bodies and materiality are not ever closed to the life of God.[13] Heaven and earth are not opposed to each other. The movement of God is not ever away from earth. As the Lord's Prayer communicates, the desire of God is, instead, for the divine will to become incarnate in bodies and operative "on earth as it is in heaven."

Some readers might object that Jesus' "ascent" into heaven is a confirmation that embodiment and the material creation are closed to heaven, and therefore also eternal life with God. Besides forgetting the Christian affirmation of the resurrection of the body (as compared to the Socratic teaching of the immortality of the soul), this reading forgets that for Jesus to ascend, he did not have to leave his body behind. There is no burial plot or tomb that holds Jesus' body. It also mistakes the character of heaven's "gates." Heaven is not closed to material bodies. It is closed to sin (understood as a disordered way of being that depends on violence and results in death), because the life of God in heaven is a life that moves only through love and peace. This does not mean that bodies are barred from heaven. Instead, it means that bodies must first be purified and then animated only by love. When they are so purified and animated, they will be living the life of heaven, and thus forever participating in the life of God (what Eastern Orthodox theologians

to liberate bodies from manual effort as much as possible, and make the world as easily available as possible. The ultimate dream, for some, is to liberate people from their bodies altogether by achieving a techno-immortality in which the information pattern that you are can live on forever and be replicated endlessly in whatever hardware is invented. For a description of some of these efforts, see Mark O'Connell's *To Be a Machine: Adventures among Cyborgs, Utopians, Hackers, and the Futurists Solving the Modest Problem of Death* (New York: Random House, 2017).

12   Latour, *Facing Gaia*, 286. Latour argues that the origins of our ecological crises are not to be found, as Lynn White, Jr. famously maintained, in the human desire to dominate the earth. Rather, the central problem is the various forms of Gnosticism that have compelled people to devalue, even forget, the earth. A humanity appropriate for an Anthropocene world will go by the name "Earthbound," because rather than taking the earth, they are taken by it. In other words, "they accept being ordinary and of this world" (253). The central task of the Earthbound is to develop the sensitivities and sympathies that will make them capable of responding to places and all their beings.

13   For a development of this theme see my *Way of Love: Recovering the Heart of Christianity* (New York: HarperOne, 2016).

call "theosis").[14] This life, as the Colossians hymn puts it, is a reconciled life
that has been prepared by the self-offering love of Christ's cross. Entrance
into heaven is not accomplished through one's transport to a new location,
as if by arriving there, everything about one's life will have changed.
Entrance to heaven is achieved in the transformation of one's life, such that
wherever one is, one finds only the power of God's love at work. Absent this
personal and social transformation, whatever paradisiacal or "heavenly"
location one arrives at will surely become damaged like the first paradise
called the Garden of Eden.

Jesus of Nazareth helps us understand these themes in his fully sensual
engagement with all the bodies of this world. Jesus does not ever despise or
devalue bodies. Instead he attends to them by feeding them when they are
hungry, healing them when they are sick, exorcising them when they are
possessed by an evil spirit, and befriending them when they are lonely. For
Jesus, it is clear that bodies are to be cherished, because, as created by God,
they are of inestimable, sacred worth. They were created out of love, are daily
sustained through love, and are desired by God to live by love alone. God's
eternal desire is not for bodies to be destroyed or left behind, because such
destruction and abandonment would reflect the rejection of God's
creating love.

As early Christians worked to give a succinct formulation of Jesus'
significance, they affirmed the sacred worth of embodiment by saying that
"in him the fullness of God was pleased to dwell" (Colossians 1:19). Not a
"shadow" of God, or merely some "part" of God, but God's "fullness" resided
in Jesus' body. It is hard to imagine a more profound affirmation of material
embodiment than this. The temptation of theologians throughout the years,
however, has been to deny this teaching – thereby witnessing to a failure of
incarnational nerve – most often because they are captivated by a dualist
metaphysic that trains them to distrust, even despise, embodiment and
materiality.[15] The crucial question to ask of any theologian is whether or

---

[14]   For a helpful summary and introduction to theosis as a theological theme, see Norman
       Russell's *Fellow Workers with God: Orthodox Thinking on Theosis* (Crestwood, NY: St.
       Vladimir's Seminary Press, 2009). This tradition of salvation as theosis was well-developed
       already in early Christian writers, especially Maximus the Confessor, who argued that "the
       Word of God and God wills always and in all things to accomplish the mystery of his
       embodiment" ("Ambiguum 7, 1084d, in *On the Cosmic Mystery of Jesus Christ: Selected
       Writings from St. Maximus the Confessor*, trans. Paul M. Blowers and Robert Louis Wilken
       [Crestwood, NY: St. Vladimir's Seminary Press, 2003], 60).

[15]   *Rerum Novarum*, a much-celebrated papal encyclical (published in 1891) devoted to
       affirming the dignity of work and the importance of private property (and thus, seemingly,
       affirming embodiment and the places of life), is typical in its expression of this otherworldly

not they believe that, in the end, bodies will ultimately be left behind. If their answer is yes, then they have denied the radical implications of the incarnation.

Dualist denial of embodiment is a theological catastrophe not only because it denies the (divinely founded) goodness of creaturely life, but also because it encourages Christians to think the created world will ultimately be destroyed rather than healed and reconciled (Colossians 1:20 & Revelation 21–22).[16] The mistake of every escapist, otherworldly spirituality is that it forgets that God's movement has never been *away* from creation and creatures but only ever *toward* creatures and places. The desire of God, as reflected in this inward-coming movement, is to bless life with the divine love that creates abundant life. It is not to destroy earth but to reconcile and redeem it. The desire of Christians should not be to flee this world but to receive God's love and then extend it throughout the world. How would the ministries of the church, and the life of faith more generally, need to change if salvation was rooted in the transformation of *this* world rather than an escape to some other? This book has argued that the sharing of food is central to this effort. Jesus' love of bodies must include a love of good agricultural practices and the ecosystem processes on which they depend, because it is impossible to have healthy bodies (for long) if the world that nurtures and sustains them is not healthy at the same time.

Second, Christians will need to embrace the far-reaching scope of reconciliation, which, according to Colossians 1:20, extends to "all things, whether on earth or in heaven." They are called to the work for reconciliation because, as disciples, they are to extend the work that Jesus has done and modeled in his life. To accomplish this work, they have the promise of the Holy Spirit to empower them. It is important to recall that for Christians, the God who creates is Triune.[17] This means, to use the ancient formula, that creation is "from" the Father, "through" the Son, and "by" the Holy Spirit. God is not ever absent from the world or from any creature. Instead, God is intimately present as the power of the Holy Spirit working to heal, reconcile,

---

sentiment: "The great truth which we learn from nature herself is also the grand Christian dogma on which religion rests as on its foundation – that, when we have given up this present life, then shall we really begin to live. God has not created us for the perishable and transitory things of earth, but for things heavenly and everlasting; He has given us this world as a place of exile, and not as our abiding place" (§21).

[16]   I develop this position in *From Nature to Creation: A Christian Vision for Understanding and Loving Our World.*

[17]   For a magisterial treatment of these themes, see Paul Blowers's *Drama of the Divine Economy: Creator and Creation in Early Christian Theology and Piety* (Oxford: Oxford University Press, 2012).

beautify, and perfect creaturely life. The fundamental task of Christians is to open themselves to God's Spirit, have it inspire and energize them, so that in their own bodily movements they can bear witness to and extend God's loving ways with the world.

In Christian teaching the power of the Holy Spirit is often characterized as the power that enables people to be "with" others in fundamentally new and life-giving ways. Rather than being in relation with others such that strife, suspicion, jealousy, division, or anger rule, those who live under the inspiration of the Holy Spirit produce relationships marked by love, joy, peace, kindness, generosity, faithfulness, gentleness, and self-control, what the apostle Paul called the "fruit of the Spirit" (Galatians 5:22–23). This is an astounding list that communicates God's profound desire that creaturely life be affirmed and realized to its fullest potential. It is also a profound indictment of all the priorities and powers that have put us in an Anthropocene world, a world marked too much by depletion, degradation, and death. Life should not be reduced to the movement of bodies in a world. Insofar as it is animated by the Holy Spirit, it should be a joyful and generous life, a life marked by kindness and fidelity. Put another way, it should be a hospitable life that extends God's eternal hospitable ways with the world.

If Christians are to eat faithfully in the Anthropocene, the Holy Spirit will need to play a central role as the power animating their bodies and teaching them to be "with others" in ways that promote mutual nurture and mutual flourishing. But what, practically speaking, might this Spirit-inspired, Spirit-empowered life look like? I believe that the teaching of the Trinity, in which the three persons of the Father, Son, and Holy Spirit are perfectly with one another, can be of some help. We should look to the Trinity not because we can copy it exactly but as the inspiration for what being-with looks like when it is empowered only by divine love and not "waterlogged by sin."[18] Attending to the Trinity, we learn that being-with involves several dimensions.

To be with another one must first be *present* in ways that communicate openness to, and a willingness to be changed by, that other. The essential posture here is that of a student who desires to learn from others the characteristics that make them who they are, and the needs and possibilities they have to which we might then respond. When presence to another is inspired by love, it will necessarily entail that one also become *attentive* to

---

[18]   In the following, I have been greatly helped by Samuel Wells's account of triune being-with as developed in *A Nazareth Manifesto: Being with God* (London: John Wiley & Sons, Ltd, 2015), especially chapters 8 and 9.

that other in all its particularity. In a fast-paced, utilitarian world, where forms of instrumental reasoning and cost-benefit accounting determine our ways of being, it is difficult to be genuinely attentive and available, because our temptation is to substitute an idea of what we think or would like the other to be, for who they in fact are. Being attentive is painful because it requires of us that we give up our agendas for how we think others should be. It requires that we respect the integrity that others are, and engage them more as a *mystery* than as a problem to be solved or a unit to be utilized. Apart from an acknowledgment of the *sanctity* of others, we will invariably violate the beings we seek to be with.

Being-with-others is not a passive spectator or consumer affair. It is, instead, an activity that demands our *participation* in another's life, an economic growing together in which mutual presence and shared effort result in mutual benefit. As we have already seen when talking about marital fidelity, the participatory work here envisioned is fundamentally of a hospitable nature: by "making room" for another and committing to its nurture, one *participates* in the flowering of its life. Witnessing to a creature that has been nurtured into its fullness gives rise to the experience of *delight*, and a sharing in the Sabbath joy that marked God's own enjoyment of a creation beautifully made.[19]

The moment we reflect rigorously and practically about what it means to be with others, to eat with others, even to eat others, we find ourselves in a nest of difficulties that exceed our powers of accounting and comprehension. Our condition is made all the more painful by the Anthropocene realization that the world and its creatures that we are called to be with bear the marks of our violent assault. How does one recommit to love and nurture others that one has systematically, if not always maliciously or knowingly, abused? There is no simple answer and no direct path that will tidy this all up and tie it with a fancy bow.

To begin, we should start with an affirmation of the sacred character of life. If, as I have argued in this book, food is God's love made nutritious and delicious, then it is clear that the places and creatures that feed us are not

---

[19] Wells offers the following summary: "God bestows upon us presence, attention, mystery, delight, participation, and partnership: this is what the process of salvation looks like; this is what enjoyment looks like; this is what grace looks like. Eternal life is our enjoying God in best imitation of and response to God's perpetual and utter enjoyment of us. God does not use us ... we are not part of some grander plan: we *are* the plan. There is no beyond to which God is reaching that includes (and therefore uses) us; we are the beyond. God's life is shaped never to be except to be with us. God enjoys us, now and forever. That is the gospel" (*A Nazareth Manifesto*, 140).

reducible to commodities or units of production to be used and modified at will. Each place and every nutrient witnesses to itself and to the divine power that affirms its goodness. This means that every creature embodies a "face" that expresses the personal power of God. Each creature is an "icon" that, through its materiality, opens a window to God's desire to be in relationship, to foster relationships, and to heal relationships that have become fragmented and broken. If we believe food to be God's primordial and daily declaration, saying "I love you. I want you to be nurtured. I want your life to nurture others too," then it is imperative that the food production and the eating people do participate as much as possible in that divine love.

To love another is not easy. If we start by saying that our eating and our being with others should have mutual health and flourishing as the overriding goals, we are still compelled to face a fundamental bewilderment. In many contexts, and facing its diverse creatures, it is not immediately obvious what love requires. To love a garden, for instance, takes a tremendous amount of time as one looks carefully, listens patiently, repents of mistakes, and then works to promote fertility, fruitfulness, and beauty. It requires that we learn from those who have lived and worked there before, and so can pass on the knowledge of failure and success.

In his own deep reflection on these matters, Wendell Berry has argued that the concept of health is rooted in the concept of wholeness, and that the concept of wholeness implicates us in an inconceivably vast membership of relationships that include the whole of creation. What is at issue is the affirmation of creation's sacred and gifted character but also the conviction that our bodies stitch us into a vast fabric of memberships with fellow creatures, all of which are anchored in the land. Speaking this way, Berry notes that the idea of a healthy individual is a contradiction in terms. "Healing is impossible in loneliness; it is the opposite of loneliness. Conviviality is healing."[20] But what does conviviality with creatures entail, especially if it will require us to eat (some of) them?

In her own reflection on these matters, Haraway admits to her fear at getting her thinking about these matters wrong. She says, "Haltingly, I will try. I suggest that it is a misstep to separate the world's beings into those that may be killed and those who may not and a misstep to pretend to live outside killing . . . the same mistake of forgetting the ecologies of all mortal beings, who live in and through the use of one another's bodies."[21] This means that all our efforts to care for others happen under the shadow of killing. The desire to be

[20]   Berry, *The Unsettling of America*, 103.
[21]   Donna J. Haraway, *When Species Meet* (Minneapolis: University of Minnesota Press, 2008), 79.

exempt from this killing is to live within a gnostic fantasy. The question, therefore, is how to become responsible and worthy of another's life and death.

Haraway suggests that our responsibility is not carried out from some moral height where we can adequately or once and for all determine the legitimacy of what we do. Instead, life with companion species requires unending response-ability to those we are with, a constant repositioning of ourselves so that we can better attend to, learn from, and be available to them. The mistake is to presume that we already know who others are and what they need, and that our obligations are clearly known. The mistake is to think that we won't make many mistakes.

> We can never do without technique, without calculation, without reasons, but these practices will never take us into that kind of open where multi-species responsibility is at stake. For that open, we will not cease to require a forgiveness we cannot exact. I do not think we can nurture living until we get better at facing killing. But also get better at dying instead of killing.[22]

Haraway has little interest in endorsing a theological position. In fact, she is clear that particular theological teachings that assume human exceptionalism (because we are made in God's image) or a clearly defined teleology with God firmly in control, are inimical to multispecies flourishing. Even so, her acknowledgment of the need for forgiveness and her call for a kind of dying on our part point, whether Haraway knows it or not, to a foundational Christian position: to follow Christ one must die to self so that one can live for others. This is not about self-loathing or self-obliteration. It is instead about admitting how an improper love of self often causes people to misperceive and mishandle others, and in doing so bring needless pain to others. It is to acknowledge how a death to the ego makes possible the kind of availability to others that Jesus showed in his own ministries with others.

The wholeness of life and the prospect of genuine conviviality depend upon our being present to each other and to our places in the modes of self-offering love. For these modalities to become operative, however, people will need to reverse a longstanding aversion to physical labor.[23] Throughout much of history, the work of growing food has been characterized as

---

[22] Ibid., 81.
[23] Speaking of the longstanding hatred of bodily work, Berry writes: "We do not want to work 'like a dog' or 'like an ox' or 'like a horse' – that is, we do not want to use ourselves as beasts. This as much as anything is the cause of our disrespect for farming and our abandonment of it to businessmen and experts. We remember, as we should, that there have been agricultural economies that used people as beasts. But that cannot be remedied, as we have attempted to do, by using people as machines, or by not using them at all ... Perhaps the

drudgery, and as the domain of idiots and simpletons. What we need to appreciate is that a historic contempt for farmers does not simply reflect a contempt for a people and a way of life. It registers, ultimately, as a refusal of the vocation given to humanity in the Garden of Eden, a vocation centered on the care of the garden and the nurture of its diverse creatures (Genesis 2:15). Farming and gardening work are not optional. They go to the core of the discovery of our humanity as dependent on fertile soil and nurtured by others. Apart from this work, people will likely live ignorantly and arrogantly, and they will eat naively. In forfeiting this necessary work, they will also forfeit the opportunity to contribute to the healing of our communities and world. As Berry describes it, "Good work is not just the maintenance of connections . . . but the enactment of connections. It *is* living, and a way of living; it . . . is one of the forms and acts of love."[24] The world will not be healed or nurtured by an abstract or merely pious and sentimental love. For healing and nurture to happen, love must become incarnate in bodies tuned to the needs and potential of fellow creatures.

Takao Furuno's farm in southern Japan is an excellent place where we can see how attention, good work, and a complex intelligence come together to produce mutual flourishing. Unlike rice farmers in other parts of the world who depend on multiple chemical inputs to grow monoculture fields, Furuno has worked to understand how the life of a rice plant can be a benefit to and be benefited by the lives of other creatures. Soon after setting his rice seedlings in the flooded rice patty, Furuno releases young ducklings into the water. These ducklings eat the insects that would otherwise eat the rice plants. Furuno then adds fish to the mix, since they thrive in this environment and are a good source of food themselves, and also azolla, a plant that fixes nitrogen and is a source of food for the fish and the ducks. While the ducks make sure that the azolla doesn't overwhelm rice growth, they also release droppings that fertilize the paddy. On the periphery of the paddy Furuno grows figs for their fruit.

Furuno's philosophy, while simple, is also complex because of what it requires him to do and, importantly, not to do. His goal, he says, "is to

---

trouble began when we started using animals disrespectfully: as 'beasts' – that is, as if they had no more feeling than a machine. Perhaps the destructiveness of our use of machines was prepared in our willingness to abuse animals" (Berry, *The Unsettling of America*, 139).

[24] Ibid., 138–139. This is not an argument claiming that every person must be a farmer. It is, instead, an argument for the importance of physical, embodied labor in the service of the care of another's life. For some, this work will take the form of farming or gardening. For others, it will be the work of cooking and hosting, or fixing and building shelter. The key is to turn one's body into a practical modality that serves another's need, and thus contributes to the flourishing of our shared life.

produce a variety of products within a limited space to achieve maximum overall productivity. But this does not consist of merely assembling all the components; it consists of allowing all components to influence each other positively in a relationship of symbiotic production."[25] In an important sense, his goal is to work on his farm in such a way that each creature is free to maximally be itself, and in being itself also contribute to the flourishing of the creatures it is with.

For the work of love, we will need a temporal modality that is calibrated to the slow pace of care rather than the restless and frenetic pace of modernity's productionist ethos, a modality in which we make time for each other.[26] Modernity is the time obsessed with growth and progress, and with the maximization of property, production, and profits. It has not produced what the apostle Paul called the "fruit of the Spirit." As Maria Puig de la Bellacasa notes, a modality of "restless futurity renders the experienced present precarious: subordinated to, suspended by or crushed under the investment in uncertain future outcomes."[27] Precarity produces anxiety, and anxiety undermines patience, kindness, gentleness, joy, goodness, and fidelity. Insofar as people are singularly fixed upon the presumed glories of some hypothetical future, they cannot be present and available to where they presently are and those they are with. The work of care – call it gardening time – takes people into another temporality, one marked by return and repetition, and by lingering and listening, as they learn to adjust their expectations and schedules to the needs of soil creatures that are constantly being born, growing, becoming ill, and dying: "care time suspends the future and distends the present, thickening it with a myriad of demanding

---

[25] As quoted by Frederick Kirschenmann in "The Current State of Agriculture," 116. Kirschenmann notes that we have much to learn from Furuno not only because his system is so productive (his yields are 20 to 50 percent higher than industrial rice production practices) but also because it is profitable (his 6-acre farm has an income that equals the income of a 600-acre industrial rice farm) and healthy and kind.

[26] The destructive character of this productionist ethos is plain to see in industrial forms of agriculture that degrade soil, water, plants, animals, farmworkers, and eaters, and in agricultural practices (like steroids, fertilizers, and herbicides) that short-circuit or override natural processes. A better agriculture is possible, one that is less about control and profit maximization, and is instead focused on attending to the needs and potential of the land. The work of Wendell Berry, Wes Jackson, Fred Kirschenmann, and many others is representative of a new approach to agriculture that assumes nature as our teacher rather than as something to be controlled and mined. For a practical statement of what this new agriculture looks like on the ground, see the 50-Year Farm Bill prepared by Berry, Jackson, and Kirschenmann as available at https://landinstitute.org/media-coverage/50-year-farm-bill/.

[27] Maria Puig de la Bellacasa, "Making Time for Soil: Technoscientific Futurity and the Pace of Care," *Social Studies of Science* 45:5 (2015), 700.

attachments. Even when care is compelled by urgency, there is a needed distance from feelings of emergency, fear and future projections in order to focus on caring well."[28]

Will people commit to this slow, demanding care if they do not also believe creatures and this world to be sacred, the embodiments of a divine love that calls for our love in return? Will they endure the frustration and the bewilderment that care always entails, if they do not also feel within their bodies the presence of a power that communicates God's love for them and for the whole world?

It is tempting to think that a temporal modality of care will lead inexorably, even if slowly, to a harmonious, always happy, state. We should be wary of blueprints for harmony, since they often presume a God's-eye view of relationships that no creature possesses. Because our knowing of others always falls short, and is in constant need of adjustment as we learn more, we need to make room for forms of knowing that acknowledge our inescapable ignorance and our constant need to come alongside others so that we can better appreciate what is needed at that specific time. When we commit to being with each other, most basically in the eating we do with them and of them, we do not always know beforehand what will be required of us or what will be given to us. What we are asked to do is learn to be attentive and humble and merciful. Our task is not to fix everything, since that presumes knowledge we often do not have. It is, instead, to come into the presence of each other and our places, and then learn to make ourselves available to their need in the varying modes of attention, listening, care, and celebration. None of this is going to be easy. Apology and repentance will be regular markers of our shared life. Being around a table, however, sharing food, sharing work, and sharing life, is surely one ideal place for the learning of these habits.

Love is not always cozy. Our attachments to others will sometimes bring us face to face with others and with processes we don't like or understand. Moreover, our attachments will invariably bring us face to face with the abuse and the hurt we have caused. The temptation, in these contexts, will be to give up or walk away. Our need to eat, however, means that we can do neither. The better way is to pursue the ways of fidelity and hospitality, knowing that we will have much to learn and much to ask forgiveness for. For this work, Christians have the inspiration of Jesus Christ and the power of the Holy Spirit. Insofar as people become faithful eaters in the world, they might yet discover how to nurture the world that nurtures them.

---

[28]   Ibid., 707.

Author Index

Abram, David, 80
Ackerman, Diane, 31
Albert the Great, 216
Allen, Will, 233
Anderson, Paul, 205
Aquinas, Thomas, 48, 169, 241
Archytas of Terentum, 78
Arendt, Hannah, 2, 199
Aristotle, 4, 42, 78
Astell, Ann, 212
Athanasius, 238
Augé, Marc, 80–81
Augustine, 208, 266, 278–283

Baal, Jan van, 168
Bahnson, Fred, 103
Bailey, Lloyd, 161
Balthasar, Hans Urs von, 47–48, 157, 242, 269
Barber, Dan, 179
Barker, Graeme, 54
Barker, Margaret, 171
Barth, Karl, 88, 144, 254
Basil the Great, 48, 190, 196
Basso, Keith, 82
Bauckham, Richard, 180, 265
Baudrillard, Jean, 246
Baugh, Amanda, 233
Bellacasa, Maria Puig de la, 309
Bello, Walden, 142
Benjamin, Walter, 247
Berger, John, 179
Berkman, John, 182
Bernard of Clairvaux, 212, 216
Berry, Wendell, 24, 40, 42, 53, 97, 113, 134, 141, 143, 146, 152, 230, 253–254, 273, 294, 306, 308
Bess, Philip, 84

Best, Stephen, 251
Betz, Johannes, 201
Biklé, Anne, 1, 12
Bishop, Jeffrey, 35, 147
Biss, Eula, 10
Blowers, Paul, 303
Bonaventure, 48, 237
Bonhoeffer, Dietrich, 119–121
Borchardt, Rudolf, 75
Bourne, Joel, 14, 23, 115–116, 129
Bowens, Natasha, 233
Bradley, Ian, 173–174
Bri, Ion, 198
Brock, Brian, 144
Brock, Rita Nakashima, 289
Brodie, Thomas, 111
Brown, Lester, 125
Brown, Peter, 190, 278
Brown, Raymond, 109
Brown, William, 79, 85
Budiansky, Stephen, 179
Bulgakov, Sergei, 41, 70, 111
Burkert, Walter, 163
Bynum, Caroline Walker, 200, 210, 275

Calarco, Matthew, 229
Čapek, Karel, 98–99, 112
Capon, Robert Farrar, 50, 156, 181, 236, 239–242, 272
Carter, Jeffrey, 162
Casey, Edward, 78, 80, 82, 99
Casey, John, 279
Cassin, Barbara, 18
Cavanaugh, William T., 210
Chakrabarty, Dipesh, 32
Chapman, Stephen, 104

Childs, Brevard, 108
Chrétien, Jean-Louis, 79, 167, 236, 250
Chrysostom, John, 188
Cicero, 30
Clough, David, 182
Collingwood, R. G., 45
Counihan, Carole, 59–60
Cronon, William, 44, 56
Cross, Gary, 145

Daly, Herman, 136
Damascus, John of, 252
Davis, Ellen, xix, 132, 230, 254
Debord, Guy, 245
Descola, Philippe, 24, 37
Diamond, Jared, 77
Dostoevsky, Fyodor, 70–72
Dulles, Avery, 172

Edwards, Denis, 49
Elizondo, Virgilio, 198
Elliott, Carl, 147
Eriugena, John Scotus, 237
Evans-Pritchard, E. E., 164
Evdokimov, Paul, 263

Fairlie, Simon, 185
Fausto, Carlos, 24
Fee, Gordon, 208
Fishbane, Michael, 73
Fitzgerald, Deborah, 34
Fletcher, J.L., 35
Foer, Jonathan Safran, 64, 227
Foltz, Bruce, 72
Fretheim, Terence, 91
Freud, Sigmund, 271
Fukuoka, Masanobu, 130

Geertz, Clifford, 37
Ghosh, Amitav, 38
Giordano, Simona, 154
Gordon, Richard, 153–154
Greenblatt, Stephen, 55
Gregory Palamas, 237
Grumett, David, 179, 190, 199
Guroian, Vigen, 106
Guthman, Julie, 117, 151

Hadewijch, 207
Hadot, Pierre, 68
Haenchen, Ernst, 219

Halweil, Brian, 141
Hamilton, Clive, 295
Haraway, Donna, 7, 299, 306
Harrison, Robert Pogue, 75, 83, 94–95, 100
Hart, David Bentley, 172–173, 200, 214, 240
Hauerwas, Stanley, 159–160, 182
Hays, Richard, 203, 225
Heidegger, Martin, 84, 255–256
Hénaff, Marcel, 23
Heschel, Abraham Joshua, 87
Hillel, Daniel, 127
Hobbes, Thomas, 3
Holdrege, Craig, 64, 228
Hornbacher, Marya, 113, 153–155
Howard, Albert, 99

Ignatius of Antioch, 275
Inge, William Ralph, 157
Ingold, Tim, 4, 9–10, 298
Irenaeus, 47, 177, 284

Jackson, Wes, 54
Jacob, H. E., 52
Jenkins, Willis, 169
Jennings, Willie, 82, 224
Jenson, Robert, 292
Jonas, Hans, 2

Kaku, Michio, 297
Karris, Robert, 274
Kass, Leon, 52, 207
Kearney, Richard, 4
Kellner, Douglas, 246
Keselopoulos, Anestis, 197
Kimbrell, Andrew, 83
Kimmerer, Robin, 83
Kingsolver, Barbara, 131, 185
Kirschenmann, Fred, 131
Klawans, Jonathan, 166
Koester, Craig, 215
Kolbert, Elizabeth, 123
Kraemer, David, 222
Kreglinger, Gisela, 242

Lafont, Ghislain, 177
Lane, Beldon, 81
Lappé, Francis Moore, 139
Lash, Nicholas, 75, 88–89, 119, 121–122, 238, 261, 267, 270, 294
Latour, Bruno, 37–38, 299
Lelwica, Michelle Mary, 154

Levenson, Jon, 161, 282
Levering, Matthew, 157, 176, 187
Levinas, Emmanuel, 73, 218
Lévi-Strauss, Claude, 247
Lewis, Jack, 165
Lewontin, Richard, 211

Madigan, Kevin, 161, 282
Madsen, Katherine Hauge, 62
Manning, Richard, 55
Marglin, Stephen, 138, 141–143
Margulis, Lynn, 7–8
Marx, Karl, 17
Masure, Eugene, 169
Maximus the Confessor, 196
McCabe, Herbert, 121
McCormick, E.B., 33
McFall-Ngai, Margaret, 8
McNeill, J. R., 123
Mencius, 95
Merleau-Ponty, Maurice, 80
Merton, Thomas, 106, 207
Milgrom, Jacob, 166
Moltmann, Jürgen, 86, 272, 276
Montaigne, Michel de, 210
Montgomery, David, 1, 12, 28, 99
Montoya, Angel F. Méndez, 70, 194
Muers, Rachel, 179, 190
Muir, John, 264
Murdoch, Iris, 96
Murphy-O'Connor, Jerome, 175, 202–203
Myers, Norman, 126

Nancy, Jean-Luc, 5
Nash, Roderick, 44
Nasr, Seyyed Hossein, 71
Nealon, Jeffrey, 183
Nerburn, Kent, 18
Nestle, Marion, 246
Neusner, Jacob, 170
Nietzsche, Friedrich, 271
Northcott, Michael, 185

O'Byrne, Anne, 5
Oliver, J. Eric, 150
Olney, Raymond, 33–34
Orr, David, 84

Parish, Nurya Love, 233
Parker, Rebecca Ann, 289
Patel, Raj, 62, 115, 140

Pattison, John, 244
Paulsell, Stephanie, 148
Petersen, Alan, 147
Petrini, Carlo, 69
Petropoulou, Maria-Zoe, 170–171
Pieper, Josef, 187
Pinker, Steven, 295
Polkinghorne, John, 173
Pollan, Michael, 1, 65, 93, 116, 149, 248
Prose, Francine, 189

Roberts, Paul, 63, 113, 124, 135, 138, 150
Romm, Joseph, 125
Rowe, Stan, 101
Ruddiman, William, 125
Ruhlman, Michael, 16
Russel, Jeffrey Burton, 269
Russell, Letty, 223

Sandøe, Peter, 62
Savoy, Lauret, 56
Schlosser, Eric, 67
Schmemann, Alexander, 40, 156, 159, 194, 204, 209, 236–237, 239, 256–257, 263
Schneider, Gregory, 11
Scott, James C., 28–29, 54, 137
Sherrard, Philip, 71, 73
Shiva, Vandana, 130, 229
Silibria, Metropolitan Emilianos of, 198
Simmel, George, 81
Sira, Joshua ben, 41
Slater, Lauren, 147
Smil, Vaclav, 114
Smith, C. Christopher, 244
Smith, J. Russell, 126
Smith, J. Z., 164
Soja, Edward, 82
Spencer, Colin, 178
Speth, James Gustave, 123, 129
Speyr, Adrienne von, 158
Staniloae, Dumitru, 198
Striffler, Steve, 64
Strousma Guy, 168
Stuart, Tristram, 178
Suzman, James, 27–28, 30
Suzuki, David, 128

Talbott, Steve, 64, 229
Tanner, Kathryn, 49
Tawney, R. H., 136
Taylor, Sarah McFarland, 58

Tertullian, 198, 276–277, 284–286
Theokritoff, Elizabeth, 244, 252, 263, 265
Thomas, Elizabeth Marshall, 60
Thunberg, Lars, 196
Tilman, David, 115
Tollefsen, Torstein Theodor, 197

Ulrich, Ferdinand, 157

Vanderslice, Kendall, 232
Volf, Miroslav, 48–50

Ward, Graham, 198, 208, 220
Webb, Stephen, 163, 180
Weil, Simone, 97, 213
Weinberg, Steven, 45
Wells, Samuel, 194, 287, 289, 304–305

Williams, Raymond, 44
Williams, Rowan, 71–72, 96, 111, 177, 216
Winne, Mark, 151
Winslow, Russel, 11
Worster, Donald, 56, 136
Wright, N. T., 282
Wyschogrod, Michael, 182

Yamamoto, Dorothy, 180
Yannaras, Christos, 79
Yoder, John Howard, 201, 219
Yong, Ed, 8, 19
Young, Frances, 175, 177

Zizioulas, John, 79, 219, 221, 264–265
Zornberg, Avivah Gottlieb, 165

Subject Index

Adam, 41, 79, 89–90, 117, 119–120, 124, 160, 190, 202, 225, 258, 279, 282, 292
advertising, 58, 189, 251
agriculture/agrarian life, 16–18, 54–57, 59–61, 76, 163, 180, 252
American Society of Agricultural Engineers, 33–35
Anaphora, 264
animal husbandry, 55, 182, 184, 186, 230
anorexia, 153, 155
Anthropocene, xviii, 16, 31–32, 38, 294, 297, 301, 304–305
anxiety, 119, 144, 148
apocalyptic, 214
asceticism, 265
atmosphere, 124
attention, 96, 100, 135, 229, 241, 251, 253, 256

baptism, 175, 213, 292–293
beauty, 20, 66, 70, 83, 86–87, 154, 173, 252, 266, 280
biotechnology, 115, 132
blessing, 54, 160, 167, 209
blood, 167, 172, 176, 205, 226
bodily exile, 146–155
body of Christ, 52, 202, 224, 284
Bosa, 59–61
bread, 51–58, 204, 207–211, 219, 234, 236, 264, 274, 288
bread of life, 205–217
bulimia, 153
burning bush, 291

Cappadocian fathers, 79
catechesis, xiii, 94, 253
chickens, 64, 131, 227, 248, 262

China Study, 178
clean/unclean food, 221, 223
climate change, 17, 115, 125
coffee, 138
collectivization, 137
commodification, 62–63, 149
commodity, xiv, 56–63, 74, 89, 100, 138, 147, 240, 251
communion, 224, 238, 257, 267–268, 293
community, 57, 73, 142, 144, 202
comparative advantage, theory of, 137–138, 140
competition, economic, 143
compost, 12, 66, 98–99
consequentialism, 143
consumerism, 58, 100, 135, 145, 210, 251
consumption, 51, 113, 140–145, 168, 179–192, 204, 211, 239, 246, 267
cooking, 247
cosmic liturgy, 221
creation, 46, 72, 85–90, 92, 101, 105–111, 119, 146, 158, 165, 181, 184, 196, 204, 237–239, 260–268, 291
Creator, 70, 72, 119, 158, 187, 238, 266, 273, 281, 289
creature/creatureliness, 71–74, 79, 86, 94, 101, 118, 155, 158, 174, 184, 196, 225, 237, 240, 252, 259, 265, 284, 289
culture, 77
Cyril of Jerusalem, 289

dead zones, 113, 128
death, 40, 65, 93–94, 127, 156–162, 166–172, 175, 178, 181, 202, 214, 257, 280, 292
deforestation, 29, 126, 135
delight, 87, 153, 187, 239–249, 259
desertification, 127

Didache, 176
dietary laws, 222
dieting, 154

eating disorder, 146–155
eating disorders, 150
ecology/ecosystem, 101, 122–133, 227
ecomodernists, 295–296
economics, 133–146
economy, anonymous, 90
ecstasy, 210
eggs, 245
environmental racism, 151
eternal life, 214, 272
eucharist, 172–177, 200, 205–213, 216, 257, 287,
    289
Eucharistic Table, 177, 200–205, 220, 293
exile, 78, 108, 114, 122–155, 240, 290
extinction, 123

Farminaries, 232
fast food, 67, 189, 243
fasting, 186–193
feasting, 186–193, 287
fellowship, 224
food democracy, 116
food markets, 139
Food Network, 247–249
forbidden fruit, 118
forests, 54, 83, 125–127
fossil fuel, 114, 124, 179
four causes, 42
Furuno Takao, 308–309

Garden of Eden, 75, 79, 89, 99, 108, 111, 118, 259,
    302, 308
gardening, 76–112, 217, 230
genetic diversity, 11, 124, 133
gift, 43, 50, 72, 85, 148, 165, 168, 244, 261–262, 267,
    290
global markets, 59, 116, 134, 139, 229
gluttony, 188–189
GMOs, 62, 261
gnosticism, 184, 277–278
God the Gardener, 77, 103–112
golden rice, 228
Good Shepherd, 164, 166, 184
grain agriculture, 55
gratitude, 167, 237–243, 249–259
greed, 58, 116, 121, 142, 188, 190–191, 259
Green Revolution, 114, 129
grocery store, 62

habitat, 52, 118, 122, 126, 132–135, 227
haecceitas, 244
health, 152
heaven, 172, 214, 264, 269–275, 284–286
holobiont, 6–7, 10–11
Holy Spirit, 47–48, 208, 218, 223, 261
hospitality, 49, 57, 74, 86, 91, 165, 168, 177,
    217–235, 274, 291
Human Microbiome Project, 11
humility, 20, 25, 93, 236–238
hunter-gatherers, 26, 28–29, 37–38, 55

icon, 71, 226, 306
idolatry, 48, 51, 175, 257, 280
ignorance, 16, 61, 75, 91, 93, 116, 141, 230, 239,
    254
image of God, 74, 88, 92, 106, 237
imaginary, 77, 95
immortality of the soul, 275–278, 301
incarnation, 184, 214–215, 227, 238, 276, 278,
    301–302
incomprehension, 41, 167–168, 174
Indian agriculture, 115
industrial agriculture, 36, 38, 130, 137, 185, 233
industrial food, 67, 97, 113, 149–150, 227, 243
industrialism, 59, 62, 150, 255
injustice, 61, 107, 113, 116–117, 169, 191, 217, 246
International Assessment of Agricultural
    Knowledge, Science and Technology for
    Development, 115
International Monetary Fund, 229
Israel, 103, 107, 164, 170, 263

Jesus Christ, 48, 104–112, 171–172, 175, 184,
    195–199, 202–217, 227, 274, 278
Jewish dietary laws, 222

Kalahari, 26–28
kenosis, 111, 157, 161, 263

lament, 267
life, 110, 158–176, 185, 194, 198, 203–213,
    227, 238
local economy, 211
Logos, 72, 195, 197, 204, 207–208, 214, 225, 238,
    244–245, 251, 260, 283
love, 241
love feast, 269

Manichees, 278
manna, 104, 205–206, 208, 263, 286
market processes, 138, 140, 142–143

membership, 41, 43, 50, 57, 61, 74, 85, 92, 100–103, 114, 118, 120, 122, 134, 143, 148, 152, 155, 159, 194–199, 202–205, 259, 264, 274
microbiome, xvi, 12
migrant workers, 252
Millennium Ecosystem Assessment, 115
modernity, 58–67, 255
monoculture, 97, 130–131, 137, 185, 228
Monsanto, 115, 132–133
Moses, 205, 291
Moss, Monica, xix, 232–234
Moss, Otis, xix, 232–234
mystery, 35, 41–43, 50, 53, 68, 93–94, 183, 259, 305

natural communion, 41
natural resources, xv, 44, 134, 136, 179
nature, 44–46, 54, 75, 122, 247, 265
Navajo, 81–82
neo-liberalism, 151
new creation, 225
Noah, 163–169

obesity, 150–151
offering, 158–177, 200, 211, 225, 261, 268

Parmenides, 287
patience, 95, 98
perichoresis, xi, 49, 289
pesticides, 12, 66–67, 90, 97, 99, 114
place, 78–84, 271
plow, 54–55
polycultures, 131
Polyface Farms, 65–67
pornographic eating, 210
practices, 77, 89, 102, 116, 134, 137, 170, 177
praise, 230, 256, 266
prayer, 73, 97, 266
priestly life, 264
production, 43, 179, 184, 204, 206–207, 228, 243, 246, 258
prophetic life, 218–223
Pythagoras, 178

Qoheleth, 286

racism, 151, 232–235
reconciliation, 172, 205, 209, 214, 217, 224–235, 292
remembrance, 201, 209, 218, 256–259
rerum novarum, 302–303
resurrection, 242, 273, 275–293

Sabbath, 84–90, 112, 144, 187, 199, 217, 240, 245, 270
sacrament, 176, 194, 209, 244, 260, 267, 275
sacrifice, 88, 111, 162–177, 184, 186, 230, 261
Salatin, Joel, 65–66
Satan, 239
science, 45, 132, 148
Scotus, Duns, 244
seed, 131–132
Shakers, 251–252
shame, 94, 120, 227–228, 231
sharing, 220
simulacra, 246, 254
sin, 117–122, 159–161, 175, 257, 280–281
sloth, 91, 100, 188, 253
Slow Food, 69, 243
Socrates, 68, 276, 280
soil, 75–77, 91–99, 115, 126–128
spectacle, 245
spiritual exercise, 67–68, 72–73, 190
sustainability, 136
sympathetic mind, 253–255

table fellowship, 198, 217, 220, 274
temple, 169–173, 182, 264
terroir, 248
thanksgiving, 249, 255
trade, 139
trade agreements, xv, 61, 116, 139, 229
Trinity, 47–50, 79, 111, 157, 173, 198, 289–291
Trinity United Church of Christ, 232–233
turkey, 64, 131

UN Food and Agriculture Organization, 139
United Nations, 127
United States Department of Agriculture, 63

vegetarianism, 177–186
virtue, 22, 24, 98, 104, 142, 144, 154, 176, 281
vocation, 75, 84, 91, 184, 259, 263, 308

water and fisheries, 128–129
wilderness, 44, 55, 103, 263
wine, 104, 177, 199–200, 204, 241–242, 259, 274, 284, 293
wisdom, 42, 82, 97, 196, 239, 281
work, 252–255
World Trade Organization, 138, 140
worship, 51, 175, 238, 255, 266, 287

Scripture Citation Index

Genesis
1:2, 260
1:28, 86
1:29, 179
2:3, 87
2:4, 79
2:7, 196
2:8, xiii, 91
2:8–9, 105
2:15, xiii, 75, 89, 92, 118, 308
2–3, 40
3:19, 95
4:10, 229
6:7, 163
8:20–21, 163
9:3, 180
9:4, 167
25:8, 161

Exodus
3:2, 291

Leviticus
17:11, 171

Deuteronomy
8:3, 286
11:10–12, 104
11:13–17, 229
11:14–15, 104
15:4, 220
30:19, 229

Job
5:26, 161
38–39, 106

Psalms
13, 257
33:6, 47
34:8, xiv
65:9–11, 105
80:8–9, 108
98:4, 266
104, 106, 241
104:10–15, xii
104:29, 47
148:1–4, 7–10, 266

Ecclesiastes
10:19, 286

Isaiah
1:10–17, 169
2:4, 54
5:7, 107
11:6–7, 180
25:6, 274
25:6–8, 269
27:2–6, 107
27:6, 108
43:19, 274
58:6–7, 191
58:9–11, 217
58:13–14, 217
65:17, 225, 274

Jeremiah
4:23–26, 229
29:5–7, 119
31:10–14, 274
32:41, 109

Hosea
4:1–3, 229
6:6, 169
14:4–7, 108

Joel
3:10, 54

Amos
9:11–15, 274

Micah
4:3, 54
6:1–2, 229

Matthew
4:4, 286
5:24, 225
6:10, 270
6:25, 188
6:25–33, 105
8:11, 274
10:8, 161
16:24–25, 263
22:5–6, 286
26:26, 234
26:26–29, 274
26:36, 105

Mark
8:34–35, 263
14:25, 176
14:32, 105

Luke
4:16–21, 217
6:21, 274
9:23–24, 263
12:35–48, 274
13:29, 274
14, 235
14:12–14, 198, 221
24:30–31, 288
24:41–43, 283
24:51, 284
24:53, 171
28:28–30, 274

John
1:1–5, 72
1:4, 195, 274

1:4–5, 111
1:14, 214, 277
1:29, 171
4:7–15, 217
4:14, 109
6:11, 206
6:15, 206
6:33, 206
6:35, 109, 205
6:50–51, 205
6:51, 205, 214
6:53–55, 206
6:54, 214
6:56, 206
6:63, 196
8:12, 195
8:23, 214
10:30, 214
10:38, 49
11:25, 195
11:25–26, 162
12:24, 111, 156, 158, 216
12:25, 158, 160
14:2, 214
14:6, 195, 214
14:10, 214
15:1, 109
15:4, 109
15:6, 110
15:15, 49
15:16, 110
15:22, 215
17:3, 215
20:15, 105
20:19, 283
20:22, 196

Acts
2:42, 219
2:44–47, 219
2:46, 171
4:32–34, 219
5, 220–221
10:9–16, 180
10:11–16, 221
10:28, 223
11:18, 223

Romans
3:25, 171–172
6:3–4, 213

Romans (cont.)
6:3–11, 274, 281, 292
6:4, 175
6:6, 213
6:11, 175
6:23, 159
8:18–23, 196
8:22, 267
11:17–24, 104
12:1, 159
14, 181

1 Corinthians
3:16, 203
5:7, 171
8, 181
10:23–32, 201
11:18–21, 201
11:26, 176
11:29, 201
12:12, 202
12:25, 202
13:4–6, 242
13:4–7, 203
15:26, 159
15:38, 281
15:45, 202
15:52, 282
15:54, 160

2 Corinthians
5:1–4, 280
5:7, 274
5:15, 175
5:17–19, 195, 225

Galatians
2:20, 175, 203, 209
5:17, 280
5:22–23, 105, 196, 216, 260, 304

Ephesians
1:3–10, 226

1:10, 195, 263
1:23, 278
4:6, 278

Philippians
2:6–8, 173
2:7, 263
3:19, 188

Colossians
1:15, 47
1:15–20, 197, 226
1:19, 277, 302
1:20, 74, 303
1:22, 227
3:3–4, 289

1 Timothy
4:4–5, 215, 277

Hebrews
1:2–3, 195
2:17, 172
9:11–15, 185
9:22, 171
9:26, 171
12:2, 172

1 John
2:2, 172
3:14–16, 158, 173

Revelation
19:9, 274
21:1, 274
21:1–4, 226
21:3, 214
21:5–22:5, 259
21:10, 270
21–22, 303
22:1–3, 270